ZAVATTINI
sequences from a cinematic life

Cesare Zavattini

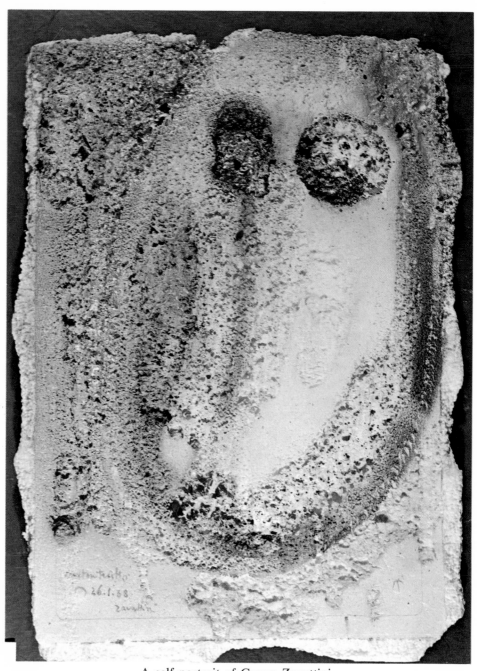

A self-portrait of Cesare Zavattini

ZAVATTINI

sequences
from a
cinematic life

Cesare Zavattini

translated and with an introduction
by *William Weaver*

Prentice-Hall, Inc., Englewood Cliffs, N.J.

ZAVATTINI: *sequences from a cinematic life*
by Cesare Zavattini, translated by William Weaver
© 1970 by William Weaver for this translation
© 1967 by Casa Editrice Valentino Bompiani
Library of Congress Catalog Card Number: 73–93102
Printed in the United States of America · *T*
13–983916–X
Prentice-Hall International, Inc., London
Prentice-Hall of Australia, Pty. Ltd., Sydney
Prentice-Hall of Canada, Ltd., Toronto
Prentice-Hall of India Private Ltd., New Delhi
Prentice-Hall of Japan, Inc., Tokyo

Publisher's note: A few, brief abridge-
ments of the original text have been made
so as to eliminate references meaningless
to the English language reader.

To *Vittorio De Sica*

The only front-rank artists that have been exclusively developed by the movie medium are, all too obviously, Garbo, Chaplin, a couple of cameramen, several directors, and the Italian screenwriter Cesare Zavattini.

An amiable hysteric with jutting chipmunk teeth, left-minded and a would-be hermit, Zavattini is the single original literary figure for which films can assume credit. . . .

—Truman Capote

A Note by the Translator

Everything about Cesare Zavattini is highly individual: the hoarse, booming, unmistakable voice; the unfailing beret which covers his bald pate; the unique collection of miniature paintings which covers the walls of his vast half-basement apartment on the outskirts of Rome, in an area where the green of the countryside has, in recent years, gradually been swallowed by the expanding city. And all this is appropriate, because the stubby, dynamic writer—now approaching seventy—has devoted his life and pen to exalting, describing, defending, and spurring on the individual, the humble, lonely man, like his memorable *Umberto D.*, who also risks being swallowed by the megalopolis that is becoming man's inescapable habitat.

Truman Capote has said that Zavattini is "the single original literary figure for which films can assume credit." From an original literary figure like Capote, this is praise; but the statement is also misleading. Though Zavattini has indeed written dozens of film scripts, including those great classics of the Italian cinema, *Shoeshine, The Bicycle Thief,* and *Umberto D.,* he has also written a great deal of other work; and before he was known in Italy as a scriptwriter, he was the much-appreciated author of a series of charming, wistful, poetic works with titles that have passed into everyday Italian speech, like folk sayings: *I poveri sono matti* (The Poor are Crazy), *Parliamo tanto di me* (Let's Talk a Lot about Me), *Io sono il diavolo* (I Am the Devil), and then an especially delightful and singular book, *Totò il buono* (Totò the Good), which later became the De Sica film *Miracle in Milan.*

The writer for the screen deals with images, and one has to read only a few pages of Zavattini's diaries (included in this volume) to see how this poet of the cinema has his eyes constantly open to catch the slightest, telling rent in the fabric of everyday life. And the cinema, as Zavattini sees it, also deals with people. Again, in his diary, we read several fascinating projects which were never carried out and which were perhaps impossible. In them, Zavattini tells how he would put Mr. Average Citizen under the microscope, making every fact about him, from his blood-type to his laundry bills, significant. Of all the famous Italian writers who live in Rome, Zavattini is the most accessible; any intruder, even the most boring, is welcomed and encouraged to talk, to furnish raw material. And in these diaries, we catch tantalizing glimpses of these encounters: a homeless young workman is mentioned and his few lines of story are the germ of *Il tetto* (The Roof), another film of Zavattini's directed by De Sica.

Famous people appear in the diaries: René Clair, the poet Ungaretti, but these pages are not about "what I said to the illustrious Mr. X and what he then confided to me alone." The celebrated, here, are on the same level as the delivery boy, the prostitute at the corner, the quarreling couple downstairs. They are simply targets who have come within Zavattini's sights.

But in addition to images and people, Zavattini is passionately concerned with language, with style, with words. And this might seem surprising in a film writer, but then Zavattini isn't a film writer. Or rather, he isn't *only* a film writer. When one mentions his fiction, his play, his other books, he says: "Ah, yes, my *real* profession," and he means it. He likes to play with words, twist them, repeat them, destroy them; and you can observe this process in his nightmare piece of fiction (he calls it a "novel," compressed into some thirty pages), the *Letter from Cuba to an Unfaithful Woman*. In the diaries, too, Zavattini often muses about words and their refractory ways.

Really to understand Zavattini the man as well as Zavattini the writer, one must know something about his birthplace: Luzzara, in the Po Valley. It crops up again and again in his writing, and it is one of the many keys to his complex personality. There are various Italies: the post-card one of Venice, Portofino, Sorrento; the classical Italy of Rome and Pompeii; the modern industrial Italy of Milan. But the valley of the Po—that broad, majestic, treacherous river—is an Italy that few outsiders know or visit. It is farmland where peasants wrest a living from lands constantly under the menace of disastrous floods, a land of taciturn men in black capes and hats, with strong feelings and hearty appetites. Not far from

Luzzara is Busseto, the birthplace of Giuseppe Verdi, who—when he had made his fortune—chose this flat, foggy region to live in.

Zavattini's love of good food and wines (and even the casual visitor to his Roman house is likely to be treated to an improvised "tasting") is a part of his birthright, along with his left-wing political fervor. In the years before Fascism and during the whole regime, the Po Valley was an area racked by factional struggles (Zavattini's visit to the Cervi family, the few survivors of a Fascist massacre, is one of the most moving episodes in his diaries); it was also a center of the Resistance. When Zavattini goes abroad—to the Holland of Van Gogh, to Franco's Spain, to the Cuba of just after Battista's downfall—he sees these countries and their people, yes, with the sophisticated eye of an internationally famous writer, but also with the eye and the heart of the humble pharmacist's son from Luzzara. And even now, whenever he can steal a few days from his work, it is to Luzzara that he flees, to walk beneath its cool arcades, to look at the bicycles propped against the walls, to eat the local dishes and drink Lambrusco, to gossip and reminisce with his friends.

He is a man of immense contradictions. Working tirelessly, he complains always about his laziness. Strangely modest about his talents as a painter, he has had one-man shows and is represented in various important collections. Exploding with good humor and hospitality, he considers himself a pessimist and a misanthrope. And even this book is a kind of contradiction, because it is really four books, four faces of the complex polyhedron named Cesare Zavattini.

William Weaver

CONTENTS

I

*diary of
cinema
and of
life*

A street in Luzzara in the province of Riggio Emilia on the River Po, where Zavattini was born. "Don't think that Luzzara has only cats and dogs. There are also elephants and camels, and some streets have passages that seem like a full-fledged circus."

Zavattini (third from left) as a soldier in Florence, 1929.

With his family a few years ago.

With his two grandchildren—daughters of his sons,
Arturo and Marco.

Scenes from

Zavattini's *Miracle at Milan.*

With Vittorio De Sica

Sophia Loren in *Yesterday, Today, and To-morrow* and *Two Women*. COURTESY PIERLUIGI

1940–1943

A FILM I'D LIKE TO MAKE—My Home Town. A cameraman, an electrician, a grip, the assistant director, and me—we'd live there for four or five months, and it would cost very little, just the film. The plot? The action? I haven't any, everything seems dust and ashes to me compared to these three or four months in my town, surrounded by about fifty children to whom I could say in dialect: *"ver la boca da peu* (open your mouth wider)."

JUST TWO ACTORS—When you're a little high, you have to take advantage of it. Othewise you'd never dare say to a producer, for instance: "I'm thinking about a film of normal length, with just two characters, in a cellar, tied to a chair." I really did think about it, and it would be enough to ruin my commercial reputation for the rest of my life if I let myself be carried away. "My good man, the expense would be nothing. The cost of the film, two actors, maybe a hundred and fifty thousand?" He would answer: "Movies mean movement." Instead I present my two characters, seated, and even tied up; I would leave their faces free, their tongues: nothing but close-ups, long ones. They're friends, they don't know who has forced them into this condition, now they're alone, a bit scared, amazed, with even a touch of gaiety. After a little while, a voice informs them about certain private matters of theirs, the one on the right is furnished proof that the one on the left has been with his wife. There they are, a few feet from each other; they spit at each other; they howl, whine, roar. Ten minutes have gone by. What happens in the other eighty minutes? Minutes of silence, close-ups of noses, of a pore, a hair. They start talking; the most disparate

1

emotions, they are about to achieve holiness, they weep together like lambs; we know their secret lives, then they start spitting again, after that they return to their platonic dialogue, tied up all the time; we see their breaths mingle in the damp cellar. The finale would be censored.

ONE MINUTE—To know an old situation in a new way: a quarrel, one minute of this furious quarrel, which becomes ninety minutes of film, without adding anything but simply accelerating, slowing down, moving backward, starting up again, stopping, enlarging, reducing, approaching, separating, placing shots before and after (on the sound-track the moans of the funeral when the dead man is still alive and functioning with a wholeness of his own, a presumption which neither he nor the others suspected, which is played out in footsteps, in actions believed original though they are void; in this way the dead man himself loses importance and a new kind of identification is asked of the spectator).

WONDER—No words we can write will ever change the age-old power of the vulgar interests that collaborate to distinguish the film from literature, creating two aesthetic systems and two moralities. We are content with the illusion that one day they will say: "from the very beginning, perhaps twenty individuals understood that the right way wasn't Hollywood's, that the spectacle which began on the boulevards with the Lumière brothers was the beginning of the sickness." The first theaters were called nickelodeons: a nickel was the price. And it was urgent to master the medium with a cost so low it could be within the reach of many individuals, like paper and ink, paints; film and lenses should have been brought into the home like sewing machines (then there would have been no producers, the apex of a bourgeois system, "applied" cinema, now defended, like a certain kind of publishing, by a wall of iron, the cliché about work being given to thousands of citizens). A return to man, to the creature who in himself is "all spectacle": this would liberate us. Set up the camera in a street, in a room, see with insatiable patience, train ourselves in the contemplation of our fellow-man in his elementary actions. We will abandon trick photography, process shots, the infinite subterfuges so dear to Méliès. The wonder must be in us, expressing itself without wonder: the best dreams are those outside the mist, which can be seen like the veins of leaves.

2

LOVE—I took shelter in a doorway, from the house opposite came the notes of a waltz, the rain stopped and on the balcony of that house a young girl appeared dressed in yellow. I couldn't see her clearly up there, I couldn't have said "her pink nostrils," but I fell in love, perhaps it was the odor of the dust raised by the downpour, perhaps the glistening of the drainpipes as the sun reappeared (we are followed on tiptoe by someone who makes the clouds, causes noises in the streets only so that they will drive us where it suits him, but in such a way that we blame the clouds and the noises). The girl on the balcony dropped a handkerchief, I ran to pick it up, then rushed through the door, up the steps. At the top of them the girl was waiting. "Thank you," she said. "What's your name?" I asked, out of breath. "Anna," she answered, and vanished. I wrote her a letter of a kind I've never written again in my life; a year later we were married. We are happy; Maria, Anna's sister, visits us often, they love each other and are very similar; even their faces are alike. One day, we talked about that summer afternoon, about how Anna and I had met. "I was on the balcony," Maria said, "and all of a sudden I dropped my handkerchief. Anna was playing the piano. I said to her: 'I dropped my handkerchief, a man is bringing it up.' She was less shy than I was, she went to the door and met you. I remember as if it were yesterday, we were both wearing yellow dresses."

COMMENDATORE—She called me Commendatore, and she was amazed at the first difficulties of the city, amazed I didn't find her short stories excellent and wouldn't publish them in the weeklies I was editing, not even the one about the dog, rightly praised by others; but it lacked a plot, and I wanted a plot for my readers of the illustrated paper.

Among other things, Giovanna Gulli was practically starving. She hadn't just arrived from Sicily, but had been here a few months. Thin, with dry red hair, her age (twenty) could be found only in her eyes and her breasts. She was looking for a second publisher, the first having refused her novel, partly for political reasons; she was always followed by a meek little sister, full of faith in Giovanna's glory. Sitting opposite them, I felt more bald, a character in one of Rovetta's mawkish plays. She delivered her manuscript pages to me one evening, insisted I read them by the next day. It took a good deal of playacting to keep from telling her I had other things in life to worry about. She understood, and dis-

3

appeared for a while. Ferrieri, perhaps kinder than I was, found her some radio work; Repaci and his wife gave her recommendations to one and all. I saw her again once in the street, from a distance, and I thought she had probably settled into a job, I devoted no more than a few seconds to her. One day I received a feverish letter from her. She said she was seriously ill but she didn't care because *Caterina Marasca* was about to appear in print. Her aim was to humiliate me since for her I represented capitalism, and other things. "You didn't have faith in me and I have found someone who does, it is a great book. Schinetti was moved, so was Garzanti, who is going to launch it and make a stir." I got up from my chair and went to see her with a bunch of flowers; since I had to walk for a bit, I felt uncomfortable, not knowing how to hide the bouquet; at her house, faced by her grieving mother, the bunch of flowers became enormous and I caught for the first time a whiff of conventionality in my actions. She wouldn't let me open my mouth, she repeated the whole letter; she became intoxicated; her arms—which had become matchsticks—conducted a triumphal march and I was at the side of her bed, forced into the image of me that she went on constructing. She might soon die, carrying behind her eyelids, along with so many other things, this disagreeable picture of me, nothing could be done, and perhaps she was right: I was that man also. She died in the summer, then her novel came out, *Caterina Marasca;* "A very powerful novel," Missiroli said to me one night.

FIVE BOYS—I invited five boys to the house, between nine and fourteen, barefoot, shaved heads, slightly delinquent faces with an occasional scar. They live near Via Angela Merici, which is one of the most beautiful spots in Rome, if I exclude that sixth floor in Piazza Acilia from which you could see the open ground below with a bowls court and tiny men following the bowls, rolling like them: I was looking for an apartment, and once I was down in the street again, I couldn't find the bowls court which from up above had been clear and findable. I played bowls in my village, going back there after a long absence, I was happy to mingle with the people of Luzzara and since I wanted more than ever to be one of them, I blasphemed the way they unfortunately do, flinging a ball which stops dead still with a bang in the place of another, and you can't figure out how it happens, your arm seems to stretch all the way there, you feel it inside, whether you'll make a hit or not,

4

hitting becomes a confirmation of something that has already happened. Well, these boys have no shyness, they earn a thousand lire a day, trafficking, or even more, and they spend it on cakes or hiring bicycles; they steal from railroad cars and sell at half the going price, they too have to rationalize, and they say: "The Americans don't give us anything to eat, so we have to look out for ourselves"; that may be, but were the Germans perhaps more generous? . . . they say, "The Americans throw stuff away, they waste things, but they don't give much"; the Americans steal gas, they say, and are afraid of the military police—the boys use the English word *police*—and if they find an Italian who is carrying off a carton of food, they beat him up, take the food and sell it themselves on the black market; the boys work Villa Borghese, "We rob them," they tell me, "when they go to the theater, we rummage in the cars where there are lots of compartments with canned goods, crackers, cigarettes." On the eighth of September these boys were at the Ostia station, one of the places where there was fighting, and when they found weapons, they shot—not at anybody in particular—they just shot; pressing the trigger was a release; from the top of the pyramid of Caius Cestius, where there was a machine gun, one of the boys, Vittorio, also did some shooting, then he threw a bomb at the Germans, not because he hated the Germans, he says: they were there and he felt like throwing a bomb; he killed four of them, then a German sees him, fires his automatic rifle and cuts a man beside him in half; the kids' shooting—there must have been a hundred of them—made the Germans believe a regiment was arriving; the Germans were hidden under the sheds in the station and when anyone appeared, they fired, wheelbarrows went by with corpses of girls, men, and boys; there were cars full of dead people in the station; the Germans had shipped them North full of *carabinieri* but they had come back, because of the air raids, and when they were opened they were full of dead bodies. "Besides us," the kids say, "other people were also taking stuff from the bodies"; they describe the death of the grenadiers, tall men who fell like nothing at all: they were brave, they were about to arrest the Germans, but some other Germans popped up behind their backs and killed them. To create confusion, the Germans had thrown open whatever there was for looting, "There are families who made millions," the boys say; at the Tiburtina station every opened car was a miracle; one car was all full of sugar, they flung themselves into it head first, feet first, "While they were carrying it off, rattattat, the

5

Germans shot at me, they flicked up stones under my feet, one foot is still wounded; there was a German who was shitting" (the boy uses the word naturally), "Seeing that ass you felt like shooting at it; I was about to, but a man stopped me so they wouldn't discover us." At the Littorio station too, again on the 8th of September, confusion and shooting, "There was a plane and we climbed into it, we fired the machine gun, we started the motor, fiddling around, and then we ran off; there was a little cannon, we pulled the cord and we hit a plane, a Macchi 202," a minute before the Germans had been running off, then they changed their minds and jumped down; when the kids saw the train standing at the Tiburtina, they hurried to Via Vasi to warn the others and they all ran there to loot.

Now they're going to steal certain inflammable material like celluloid from a train full of bombs, they handle bombs the way I handle a sandwich, all the kids in Via Merici and Via Vasi have some of this material, I see them burning it as I go off on my bicycle to visit G. in the evening when I come back they explode a lot of it and frighten the neighborhood; my parents are scared too, one man turns pale, shakes, I also jump up to my feet, the glow of the flames comes into our house like a big fire. Even when you're safe and there isn't any danger, you're still scared by the hugeness of the glow; my son, hearing these exploits, said: "Papà, let me loaf around, don't make me study."

IDEA FOR A FILM STORY—A Martian on holiday, the planets are countless, so every Saturday he goes to one or another with a machine as fast as thought, he's like us, a bit more intelligent, he happens to land on Earth, big excitement at the extraordinary arrival of this machine, and we're in the middle of a political campaign, one of the parties exploits a fake Martian; the real one barely manages to save his skin and escape into the cosmos.

THEATER—We are in the theater. The performance begins. Before the curtain rises, an actor, in street clothes, comes to the footlights. "Good evening, ladies and gentlemen. We are your servants. On this stage we will perform what you wish. If you like, a chair will be hurled across the set; and when the Count is about to kill his adulterous wife, if one of you shouts: trip him, I want the Count to trip up, then the Count will trip and fall to the floor with his legs in the air. So then, speak up. We are your servants."

6

The curtain rises, revealing some compartments so arranged that, as the actor uncovers them, we see bits of scenes: a hand with a vase of flowers, a seated man, three women in frozen attitudes, and so on to the end. "You see, you have only to choose."

But I must say that it's wrong to attach any importance to the episodes people are told in the theater, to the people waiting behind those little curtains. We can leave them there forever. We will never know anything about them. But if you question a man at random: What's your name, my good man? De Carli, he answers. Aha. De Carli seems more important to you than the others, because you know his name. If you had an orange to give somebody, to whom would you give it? As of now, to De Carli. Wait a minute: there's Pavoni. The man with the vase of flowers in his hand. You turn toward Pavoni (he laughs). Fantuzzi! Your head swings around towards Fantuzzi. You're ridiculous with that poor head of yours. Can't you understand that times have changed, and you must think of yourself, not of Fantuzzi or Pavoni. Who is more important than you? Lights. Turn on the lights in the house. (The stagehands turn on the lights in the theater.) This is what I wanted. Now we can speak to one another frankly. Don't worry: I know I must keep within certain limits, I can't press the knife home, all of you have paid your money. In your midst there's no lack of variety: there are bankrupts, adulterers, cardsharps, liars, deserters, pimps, pederasts. What more do you want? Look one another in the face for three minutes. The spectators are asked to look one another in the face, please. That's right (during these three minutes we hear little bursts of laughter, then silences, then shouts, then a revolver-shot). Lights out! Out! I'd like to take one of your number and bring him up here, illuminated by these spotlights. I'd examine him from every side, making him turn slowly, like a planet. One of you, chosen by chance. The others, from their seats, would look at him in amazement, and yet he's there, among you. You shout I, I, I, you are important, at last you assume responsibility, let the trumpets blare, you march across this stage, you break the plots that exclude you. Prevent us from coming to Act Three. But then others would come and sit in your places and all would be as before.

RETURN FROM BOVILLE, November 5, 1943—I came back last night from Boville, where my family has taken refuge for a year; I was there myself from September till now. Toward evening

7

a truck arrived with a note from De Sica, "There's a film to make and things are quieter in Rome than in Boville." We loaded the truck, passing bundles from hand to hand like buckets during a fire (the truck couldn't enter our narrow street); some Germans circle around us for a long time, they ask where we're going, meanwhile a bomb explosion is heard two or three miles away, as if it had been dropped by mistake. At midnight the night before there was a long alert, we were all on the terrace in pitch darkness, the sound of the planes was hard, tangible, we talked in whispers so as not to be heard up there, even in other villages waiting calmly under that rumbling dome the children laughed; impossible to imagine persons like ourselves inside those machines, mere sound takes on a physiognomy, and you think again of the valley, trying to stretch it, to diminish the possibility of being hit if they release the bombs; instead a perpendicular line becomes more and more precise, between the dark height and where we are, you'd like to push that line back with your hand. Yesterday smoke rose again from Ceprano, but because of the distance we couldn't see the bombers. Airplanes fly back and forth in the valley, and my children immediately identify their nationality: from the heights of Boville they seem fish weaving through transparent water. In September I was riding in a wagon when three planes passed over me, it was sunset and they seemed to be playing; with a somersault one dropped down and fired at us, it struck a fountain about twenty yards away and then it rejoined the others with a rapid semicircular sweep, we didn't even have time to be frightened. One day two automobiles appeared near the chapel of Santa Liberata, and the villagers looked down from the walls. One man with a spyglass said: "They're Germans, there's even a woman with them." We all crouched, because to stand erect, clumped together, seemed an open invitation, and we measured our words even if there was a mile between us and them. They had stopped behind the trees with a woman from Frosinone who earned her living like that; for half an hour not a leaf stirred, every now and then someone stuck his head over the wall. When they had finished their business, we saw before the cars the cloud of dust they had raised in starting their motors; they emerged from the trees already heading for Frosinone. Another time an English plane crashed a few yards from the village, a flame passed my window, wakening me; the fliers, unhurt, once out of the cockpit, kicked a boy who was staring at them. Adieu to Boville and to the Capognas: a big peasant

8

family, they all sat around the table with one huge dish in the center, and each regulated his action in taking from it, the rhythm seems casual and instead, every pause is calculated so that the oldest can choose carefully, there was the father and the mother with their little girl, and they pretended to talk with me so some time would go by between one morsel and another, the little daughter ate all she wanted but the relatives, somewhat handicapped by her voracity, were repaid by the slowness of the parents. At Ferentino in the heart of the night suddenly a sentry shouted at us to halt because the little white tail-light of the truck had remained burning: the sentry shouted, the driver couldn't hear, and I, who was huddled with the children in the midst of our household goods, couldn't reach the driver's cab with my hand, to knock, to warn him: there was a wardrobe in the way. I thought: "Now he'll shoot," that white spot was something we carried after us like a can tied to a cat's tail. We met trucks heading South with Germans sitting on the benches as in a waiting-room, their rifles in their hands, ready. We drove into the city at three o'clock, there wasn't even a night watchman about. At San Giovanni the weight broke something; we were motionless for more than an hour, afraid they would confiscate our food. At home I was amazed that I had only to press a switch to see things that reassured me.

ITALY, 1944—Lattuada, Fabbri, Monicelli, and I decide to discuss it with Ponti: It wouldn't take much money, a truck with the indispensable equipment, cameras, rolls of film, some lights. We'd leave Rome with very few pages actually written: I have the basic idea clear in my mind: the moral or rather political rough draft, I daren't say the poetical draft. The film's progress depends on the opportunities we encounter, or better, that we will make ourselves encounter in the liberated part of our country. I'll be the narrator of our adventurous itinerary, and we of the troupe will be actors or spectators, as circumstances dictate. The project came to me months ago, born from the conviction that only in this moment people have a power of sincerity that they will lose again very soon. Today a destroyed house is a destroyed house; the odor of the dead lingers; from the North we hear the echo of the last shellings; in other words, our stupor and fear are whole, it's as if we could study them in a test-tube. Our cinema must attempt this documentation, it has the means to move about like this in space and time, to collect within the spectator's pupil the multiple and the diverse, provided it abandons its usual narrative methods and adapts its language to the content (even the most modern content is still expressed in an antiquated language determined for the most part by the whims of capital). I don't know if we'll find the few millions necessary: according to Lattuada we don't need more than five, let them give us this truck and we'll go toward Naples, in Calabria, perhaps in Sicily—who knows where?—for about two months. One example: we stop in a destroyed village where the people are slowly beginning to resume life among the ruins. We talk with them in the square; I'll say I'm guilty of this and that, at first they'll consider me a monster; but this is the only way I'll be able to act also as accuser, attribute to each one his responsibilities, drag them out of their anonymity like Marsyas from the vagina of his limbs, we'll be constantly dramatizing, here and there are unhinged doors, others lie in the dust, buried under collapsed walls. I'll say: "You did nothing but shut doors behind you, all that could be heard was the sound of doors slamming after nice Italian families." Some of those present try to justify themselves and they don't realize I'm offering them a chance to get it all off their chests. Don't they say in the rest of the world that we're untrustworthy, undignified, fickle? Worse, that we lost the war on purpose, just to be able to say finally that we're worse. To tell the truth, the good villagers will be bored: then I'll have a plane appear over their heads, releasing its bombs. The bomb is about to fall: I stop it in the midst of the sky (some idiot will say it isn't possible to have evaded forever and they have forgotten their promises: "I'll be good, I'll lick the dirt provided I can still sit in front of the door of my house hearing the free sound of a bicycle passing; I ask no more than that"). Look at the bomb, motionless, a few hundred yards over your head: shall we make the bomb fall? They all start yelling "No, no," I let it drop another two hundred yards, then I stop it again. During the fall of the bomb along these two hundred yards which we follow in slow motion, I have time to pursue the men who run off, I savor their terrified faces, I force them to return in their thoughts to a year ago (and I see the scene), to ten years ago, to a point in their childhood, then move to the future, to when they'll be dead. It's extraordinary how changeable they are, and how these men standing still in the little square looking at me and the camera, who listen to me with indifference, can do so many things, become pale in a fraction of a second, jump over a hedge like hares, or give a shove as they run to an old woman

10

who—look at her there—has fallen to the ground, showing the hem of her drawers; if I make the house collapse and their children are trapped under it, they start digging in the rubble like dogs. I interrupt the digging, and now there they are, listening to my sermon, and they say they had nothing to do with it, they're innocent. We set up a primitive screen in the center of the square and we show some bits of film we've shot in other places, a field, a farmhouse, where we happened to turn our camera. The narrator (me, in other words) tries to make the people in the square understand that these other men also weep, die, kill, run off, go to bed with women; that they aren't very different from others, these men in the square, and when a glass of water goes down their throat it goes *glug glug* for those on the screen as it does for these in the square (the soundtrack must be perfect so that the *glug glug* can be heard very clearly), then I'll show the hands of a dead man emerging from a heap of stones. "Let's stop here for a moment," I'll say. They'll hold their noses, they'll be frightened, from these hands let's gradually reconstruct the rest; him, the village, the other cities, the world and, if you like, the planets (some idiots find this very hard for the cinema), then we'll go back to the hands, to their slow movements as they unfold a black shirt, one morning in the bedroom, which smells of soap, the man shaves, steps into the square, comes home, eats with his family and goes to take a little nap. This happens in '32 and in '33: we'll choose a pre-war year. From '32 we skip to '43, from '43 I go back to '32. The attention must shift constantly, from before the war to during the war and to after the war: like heads at a tennis match. But the spectators become tired, they tell the moralist to go to the devil. Then I'll suddenly make a voice come from the rubble, from that loudspeaker all dented amid the rubble, you hear the voice of Mussolini spreading through the half-destroyed village, you hear the applause, some of the applause came from that man smoking his pipe (close-up of the man smoking his pipe and applauding: it lasts five minutes). They would all like to shut up that voice from the loudspeaker, but they don't know what to do, we climb into our truck and go off: the unpredictable will be waiting for us at every turn.

THE REVOLUTION, July 31, 1945—Where I live there is often talk of revolution, it's a neighborhood surrounded by little vegetable gardens I'd almost call Japanese when the bamboo shoots that separate one from the other glisten on certain evenings. In

11

my neighborhood, if a rich man goes by, the barefoot kids shout: *re-vo-lu-tion,* pretending, as they stamp their feet, that they are ready to give chase, and the rich man starts walking faster.

Until a few months ago, if they met me, some of my neighbors—workers for the most part—asked: "When?" They were convinced, judging partly by my remarks and partly by my books and by the newspapers always sticking out of my pockets, that I was the man. But I answered evasively, I really didn't know what to answer, being half for the revolution and half against it: a sad condition.

I must tell you that mine isn't a political nature; I distrust politicians, once I thought of founding an association of young people whom I would have brought up in suspicion, or rather in incredulity; I would have scattered them about political meetings, to interrupt the orators by shouting: "That's not true!"

In the month of March, the increasing disasters of the world and the anxiety of my neighbors convinced me I was finally obliged to come out of my ambiguous political situation. I filled my eyes with pitiful images that day, and I swore a solemn oath. I set the date, without dropping the slightest hint to my family. July 31st. Today.

Today I got up earlier than usual. At six I was already walking down in my garden, I could have been supported in the air by the jet of the fountain, I was so light. I realized a carpenter was observing me over the little wall, waiting to glimpse a sign that would assure him the wheel of justice was about to be set in motion at last. I went back into my study at a quarter to seven. At seven on the dot, I had decided, operations would begin. "Against whom?," you will ask. Against myself. I, in fact, *I* was the obstacle: he had to be overturned, this individual, break his bones, as they used to say, the rest would be easy; without a blow I would raise the red flag on the public buildings, followed by the have-nots. I know it would be hard to knock down this sturdy oak, if you'll excuse the expression. During the night I studied myself from every side patiently, to discover the most vulnerable spot. The epithets that sprang to my lips most often were: "cad, hypocrite, miser, jealous, coward, liar." I laughed sardonically, pinching myself hard under the covers as I thought: tomorrow morning, tomorrow morning. Pitilessly I saw my body lying on the ground, the eyes glassy, wide, these eyes that have many times looked at their fellow-man as if he were a telegraph pole. Now you are there for eternity, eyes, with that corner of the house in your pupils, that corner of the house

12

for which—in order to buy it—you joined the party years ago. But I musn't stoop to gossip.

At one minute to seven, then, I was ready. I looked out of the window, the street was full of people; I seemed to know all of them. Their happiness depended on me. Be brave. *Dong* dong *dong* dong *dong* dong *dong*. Seven o'clock tolled. "Pig," I said, slapping myself. I also banged my head against the wall, not too hard. Before me, on a nice tray, was my breakfast: bread, milk, and butter; I took the tray and hurled it to the floor, which it struck along with the following exclamation: "You had bread and butter the day Rome was bombed!" I continued listing other sins, in confusion.

The racket summoned my wife and the maid. "Look what you've done!" my wife cried. They both fell to cleaning up the floor. I remained silent, standing still, in the midst of the room. Those fragments reminded me of old chipped dishes, apartments without heat. I should have yelled: "Long live the maid!" It would have been the second stage of the plan. Instead, I murmured: "Sorry, it slipped out of my hands." At five past seven the revolution was over, an abortive attempt, as the specialists put it. The carpenter signaled to me from the house opposite. I pretended not to see him.

IN THE CONVENT, September, 1945—At the convent of the Benedictine Camaldolese Sisters on the Clivio dei Publicii, a strong wind; they say the Pope authorized this exception to their rule of cloister, in view of the edifying aims, Elisa Cegani and the other actresses will play nuns in the film *Un giorno nella vita;* * the Mother Superior, eighty years old, is dying in her cell. Iron bars everywhere. Blasetti makes the real nuns chant a psalm so the fake nuns will learn the cadence. "You fold your hands like this," one sister says, joining her hands during the psalm, "gesticulating as little as possible"; I seem to note some smugness as she explains; perhaps tomorrow morning she will go to confession because of it. We cross a sad, jumbled little garden where a lay sister with her broom is pursuing an eddy of dust.

MATCHES, October 10, 1945—On a little truck towards Sutri, a white moon at six P.M. with the sun still over the low vineyards. Adriano Grande asks me for a match, I haven't any; the driver is without matches too; so is a cyclist who pedals by. We stop to

* A film directed by Alessandro Blasetti, script by Zavattini.

13

make water on the bank of a little gulley. What do we see there in the grass? A new box of matches.

THOUGHTS, 1946— . . . It will break out (the revolution) in about five years with looting and summary trials; during that great event we'll see men escaping from doorways, robbers not of women or of silverware but of cameras, eager to impress on film faces and objects outside the laws of cinema.

. . . The bride cries "Darling," embracing her husband returning from the war: we come out of the movie house in tears. You have to prove such conclusions true by repeating them three or four times. It's sure that the fourth time the audience will be less moved. So we must begin from the fourth time (unless you consider this a play on words) in conceiving the story.

. . . What would be the fate of painting if a tube of oil paint cost a million? The history of painting is also a deception. Few painters, few paintings—and those controlled by the censors and determined also by vast financial and political interests, to say nothing of the intervention of the capitalist's taste: "A bit more green on the right, a bit more red on the left." Industry leaves the poor only their eyes to weep with over the moral tales it commissions from writers.

*THE BEST CONDITION, 1946—*The goldfish slam their rotund mouths against the glass to find the way to the sea, and each time, during the brief journey they make with a single flick of their fin, their hopes are reborn. We are like those fish, and I myself have never been so confident in our cinema, so happy. I believe we are in the best position to prepare some message worthy of the cinema; it will have the clouds for a screen, the gigantic figures projected in Milan will be watched by millions of eyes from the gentle Vercelli plains to the estuary of the Po. We are in this position because history has rejected us for the present and in the story of a people such an unaccustomed vacation rarely occurs. Before resuming the anabasis and the catabasis which will end up in our grandchildren's textbooks, let's exploit our wonder and our solitude, the adjectives have fallen away all around us like scabs. If one bridge has remained behind our backs, let's chop it down, to prevent our retreat from what we are. I think that only the awareness of this state of grace will change a cinema which has gone on deceiving its neighbor in every part of the world.

14

We Italians have deceived him with less elegance, often wresting sighs and sobs from him. Instead we must dig out different protagonists from the very center of our character, whose knowledge we have systematically obscured with the camera. If we are not afraid of opening ourselves wide, if we don't renounce for the usual mess of pottage the primogeniture we have achieved in these years, we alone will escape the sinister words whose shadow is stretching over the world despite the events that have taken place: "nothing new." How must our new films be? They will be neither happy nor sad, and without an ending; or at least without those endings people cling to. We'll make films with any old conclusion, when—after trying and trying again—we will have found the true meaning of happiness and of sadness. Meanwhile, generous guinea pigs, we must allow the others to watch us live, as if under a glass bell. For the moment neither good nor bad, neither saints nor devils, we are only frightened by voices that are too assured and by words, since people go on calling things by names that are no longer theirs. Friends and enemies will accuse us of being unrepentant and insensitive to the cries of sorrow that are raised still from many parts of the earth. "Think of the dead," authoritative personages will say. We can't. If I weep for one dead man, how much must we weep for three dead men? A year, without a moment's respite. And for three hundred thousand dead men: my whole life tearing my hair. And for three million? We cannot be bowed and afflicted in proportion to the disasters that have befallen us.

As we wait for a sense of proportion, we cinema people are looking for a least common denominator, and we can find it in the courage to accept what we are and not what we would like to be, and to resume that examination which began during our blatant misfortunes and was interrupted by the intervention of too many who were ready to take our penitence upon themselves. Persistence in a hypocritical situation can produce only a hypocritical cinema.

NEW OVERCOAT, February, 1947—This is the first item of clothing I've bought since the war, worn for the first time one March morning, happy but not entirely, because I had a pair of shoes unworthy of this coat. In the newspaper there were no dire events that day; I could enjoy the inauguration of the new coat in peace. I realized that, walking, I struck my heels hard against the pavement, which might attract women's attention to my shoes (women have a tendency that way, and from our shoes they deduce

15

our social condition); so I slowed down. I wasn't worried about being run over, as during the war, then if I had been taken to a hospital and stripped they would have seen that the lower half of my silk shirt, its bosom and collar intact, was made of cheap cloth, or else it had no lower half. Instead, that morning, except for my shoes, I was all new and jolly. As far as neckties went, they were increasing. I had thought of urging the citizenry to go on a consumer's strike, as somebody in Milan had suggested. In the press a reduction of prices was promised; I waited, but prices were going up. I stopped in front of shop windows with neckties so that the proprietor might notice me, I cast an ambiguous glance inside the shop, to upset the lives of those merchants, making them believe I was taking notes in order to loot the shop at night or devastate it with explosives, or else that I was an agent of the tax bureau. Mentally I wrote articles against these speculators and I described them at the precise moment when at home, between one coitus and the next, they were deciding that they would raise the price of ties. All of a sudden I met Giuseppe Ungaretti.* He was walking along calmly, with his assistant, Professor Barlozzini. "Beautiful," he said. Barlozzini agreed that the overcoat was beautiful. Ungaretti added that it was soft, and in a very mild voice: "I don't have one." He said this without envy. I answered that he deprived me of the pleasure of owning it, I tried to deprecate the quality of the overcoat, saying also I had paid for it in installments. Meanwhile he kept passing his hand over the cloth as if he were patting a lamb. We said goodbye, should I perhaps send a sleeve of it to his house in true Christian spirit? How many poets have lived in poverty? Do they want glory? Let them have glory; glory plus an overcoat is too much. I went on for a while like this, clinging to a strap in the bus which was taking me home, when a cry interrupted my delirium. A passenger was shouting and beating his hands against the door of the bus, because the bus had resumed its journey before he had had time to get off. The time that lapsed between the two stops was forty seconds. He sprang to the ground, then from the sidewalk he glared at the bus and, it seemed to me, at my overcoat with contempt as he strode off to recover the two hundred yards he had lost. My overcoat? In the end I was on the protester's side through an operation even more rapid than that of Manzoni's Unnamed. These suits of ours: "a little higher, a little lower, there,

* Famous Italian poet.

16

here," in imagining people at the tailor's while they express their preferences, you want to insult them. And now the buttons, how many buttons? "Three." And why not four? The color of the cloth. "Brown." "Not gray? This in-between shade? With pinstripes?" "Yes, narrow. Don't you have any narrower ones?" A woman in front of me with a feather in her hat and a child in her arms de-maternalized herself because of that feather, she must have said at some point: "I want the feather just so long, not a fraction of an inch longer." Perhaps I wouldn't even have gone to bed with her, though she wasn't ugly, thinking of her saying "shorter, no, longer; no, shorter." She realized I was looking at her; I was looking at that thing on her head which made her feel so sure of herself. Noting my overcoat, she was a little less sure, but then my shoes, which I hadn't been quick enough to draw under the seat, authorized her to draw herself up again internally, and her bosom was influenced by this inner support. I was in a great hurry to get home and take off the coat. I was afraid someone might think I wanted Raglan sleeves, and might imagine me at the moment I was saying so. Instead they greeted me. Among the people of Via Merici, "There's the brush man." One evening I was playing ping-pong with some guests and from upstairs somebody threw a shoe-brush at us, worn out, heavy. I shouted, "Murderers"; but it was dark and nothing could be seen, everybody was apparently asleep. We never found out who threw that brush. The unknown neighbor's hand must have been driven to take arms by that precise sound of ping-pong, tick *tock tick* tock, along with our voices full of serenity.

RENE CLAIR, March 28, 1947—I looked at his black socks and gray suit, I don't remember the shirt, yet I had meant to remember everything: he was smoking, he also chewed a gumdrop, he offered me a cigarette, I said I don't smoke though in fact I do, he said he was the only one with so many bad habits. He dilates his nostrils when he smiles and bares his teeth at one side of his mouth. He has an attractive wife to whom he must have said: "I love you." The morning of March 22nd, then, I stepped into Room 19 in the Hotel Hassler and I said: "Bonjour." After a moment I began to recognize the old friends seated around Clair: D'Angelo, Fabbri, Lazzarini, la Schanzer, De Bernard, Emmer; I said in French hastily that I didn't speak French. "Tell the story," D'Angelo says. Clair crosses his legs, folds his arms, hints at a smile, and fixes his eyes on me. They all shout I'm very good at telling my stories. I

17

begin: "C'est un matin dans la grande ville. How do you say Ministry of Commerce?" All of them joyfully, enthusiastically, prompt me. And they were going down the steps? I don't dare ask how to say they were going down the steps, so I stop and look for a way to express my idea without making them go down the steps. The women's eyes are maternal, it's as if I were reciting a Christmas poem forgetting verses here and there. In the end I can't find the necessary words, I sum them up in a rotating gesture of my hand in which I hope Clair sees marvelous things. Long silence, then Clair explains the stories that don't interest him any more, stories that take place in the next world, hypothetical stories, and ones without a precise time and place. I understand half of what he says, yet enough to agree along with the others and laugh at the little joke of the distinguished French public figure: "What have *you* done?" he is asked. "I, I . . ." he answers, "I always foresaw our defeat." Somebody leans towards me: "Why don't you tell him about that man who's a kind of modern saint and works miracles?" But that's the very one I told. Maybe they're playing a big trick on me. Clair repeats that he has a horror of the surreal and the abstract; the world has to be consoled. He is one of the three or four geniuses of the cinema, but if I wanted to I could interrupt his talk by falling to the floor, or I could force him to pity me if I told him, "I have cancer of the eye, Monsieur Clair." I met him again yesterday at the Barberini Theater; four of us were waiting for him in the lobby. Fabbri says: "De Sica, Chiarini, Riccio, Zavattini, let's all hold out our hands to shake Clair's at once." Clair hesitates for a moment. Chiarini understands his infinitesimal embarrassment and withdraws his hand at the very moment when Clair is holding out his towards Chiarini. Chiarini extends his hand again; too late, Clair's is now addressed toward Riccio; but with a lightning movement Clair offers his hand again to Chiarini. Chiarini has seen Riccio's outstretched hand and doesn't move; other hands rush to the rescue. Pasinetti, arriving, adds his hand, and Clair hastens to clasp it with exaggerated effusiveness.

THE MOVIES, July 20, 1947—"I want to be in the movies": A little sailor from Apulia, twenty years old, a young Calabrese more or less the same age, a girl with a swollen cheek and another sad-eyed one less than five feet tall, from the same town as the sailor. They've come because the newspaper said I'm making a picture. Sitting on the low sofa, in a line, backs rigid, they stare at me,

18

waiting for an answer. The Calabrese is their spokesman, he says almost in dialect that they can stick it out until August, they don't eat enough; after August they'll have to go back to their home towns, they're counting on me to fix them up before then, they would be satisfied with very little pay provided the part is not too bad. His forehand, nose, and mouth are deformed by scar tissue from an old burn; his skin glistens like silk. They pay a thousand lire per month to an acting school which guarantees its pupils fame, they finished elementary school, and the sailor had two years of technical school. The girls are staying with relatives, from those sad eyes I understand that the short one sleeps with the sailor. "I'm more suited for comic roles," the Calabrese says, the girls confirm the fact that he makes people laugh, and they laugh while he blinks his reddened eyelids. I ask: "Are you sure you have the necessary qualities?" In this half-hour I've seen their awkwardness, their ignorance, their innocence, step after step from a distant point of the city they have come to me. I lead them on, making them declare themselves more confident than ever, go on, a bit more; I watch like a voyeur all this confidence with no reason behind it. Is mine different from theirs? I should make them act before me with their unbearable accent and applaud them, plumbing the depths of their common delusion.

VIA PANICO, September, 1947—De Sica said with a sweet voice and pouting lips to the woman on guard at the brothel in Via Panico who blocked the door with her little cash-box in her hand: "We want to have a look, just glance around, for a movie, I'm De Sica." The woman said, "Go ahead and look," and she preceded us, shouting: "Stand up everybody." The customers in the waiting-room stood up, not understanding what was happening. In a little parlor there was a single *carabiniere;* the *carabinieri* have a sitting room to themselves. The directress did the honors in person and said to De Sica, "We're colleagues." It's true, she was a famous entertainer in European vaudeville, ten years ago she imitated opera stars, her tawny hair pulled up like a crest, and I used to see her often. She says: "My girls are all married. I'm fair, if they want to stay at the dinner table an extra hour, I pretend not to notice. Would you like to see some of the rooms?" De Sica says: "For study purposes, the study of humanity." "First I'll take you to the infirmary, one of our girls is sick." The patient is in bed, leaning against the head of the bed is a man, her husband, the husbands come every Saturday to collect the money. "Today we gave her a purge, she'll be getting up tomorrow." She explains that all of them have children, and she's very stern about cleanliness. She knocks at another room: "Anna, open the door for a moment," voice from inside: "I'm busy." "Get up, put something around you." The door opens, a woman appears in a nightgown. De Sica has a leather bag under his arm, Biancoli's coat-collar is turned up and Guerrieri's face is hard, to make himself look older. There's a man in the bed who blinks and hastily covers himself with the blankets. De Sica looks around, says: "Good, very good." The directress knocks at another door, it opens at once, a man is buttoning his suspenders, he recognizes De Sica and smiles at him familiarly. "De Sica," he says, still smiling and shaking his head; De Sica smiles familiarly too and says, "Pleased to meet you." The girl is already dressed and asks with a glance if he wants to see more, De Sica answers, "That's fine, thank you." On the steps they encounter a girl wearing a kind of loose black net which allows you to see everything, followed by an old man, the three flatten against the wall to let the couple pass while the directress says: "Feel absolutely at home here, come when you like, you can study whatever you want."

THE MASS OF THE POOR, December 7, 1947—De Sica and Amidei walk slowly, I go on ahead with Lazzarini, who has at his side a man of about fifty with eyeglasses and raincoat, he introduces him, we tip our hats; a brief silence, as always after introductions, then we reach the church of Saints Nereo and Achilleo. The Mass of the Poor was invented in '42 by a priest who died in a Swiss tuberculosis sanitorium. In his will he said to his friends: "Continue every Sunday the Mass of the Poor, you must do this, you must do that; you, Lazzarini, will preside over the beards." We arrive, a joust of politeness between me and the man in the raincoat at the door, we enter a vestibule crowded with people talking excitedly, a hundred, perhaps two hundred, ragged beggars with faces that reveal suffering or vice, thin bodies, red eyes, many have scabs and boils. Some women carry half-naked children in their arms; one is pregnant with a pointed belly like the prow of a ship. A distinguished gentleman comes towards us rubbing his hands because of the cold. Lazzarini turns us over to him, and putting on a white apron, starts shaving, combing, de-lousing: one man's hair is so muddy that half a glass of water poured over him is absorbed as if by parched earth. Sometimes they also wash the feet, it seems

20

that special rich people come to do this, but today it's the regular five or six. Under a shed in the courtyard a great kettle is boiling, one man with two or three tin cans hanging down his back says to a woman of about forty with swollen eyelids that she is obviously in good health, and she answers that even during the war she always managed pretty well, he is trying to make the woman, who is willing (I'll follow them after the mass)—the woman has dirty hands with gnawed fingernails. A lady in a great white Persian lamb coat takes notes in the embrasure of a window; three women, one of them wearing an old army jacket, talk all together of relief payments, protesting against City Hall, the lady takes more notes, the mass is about to begin, the vestibule is empty, the last man tries to clip his moustache a bit more evenly with some scissors. The poor people are seated on benches, they are the only ones there with the priest preaching from the pulpit, since the sun suddenly enters through the big windows, he talks about the sun "which is a way the Lord comes to visit us," he says. Half are paying attention and half aren't. One man with Basedow's disease has his wife and children beside him, he is neatly combed and shaved, but without a shirt. A little boy urinates behind a column; two others are playing tag, a cadaverous woman in very short clothes is crying; two other women console her, the first woman jumps to her feet to go away, she takes five or six steps, then comes back and sits down, a few minutes later she laughs and motions to a man seated in the front row. A knock at the great door of the church; one of the directors opens the peephole and says nobody can come in, they should have come earlier. Anybody can come, but they are obliged to arrive in time for the mass: some articles of clothing are also distributed if they arrive punctually. Another two or three knocks are heard. I ask if there might be a thief or a murderer among these people. They point to the man I met outside with the raincoat and the eyeglasses, known by the name of *Cupid*, he has a nervous tic of sniffing his hands every now and then, he was arrested for attempted rape of a little girl, he's the best-dressed of all; he never sits on the benches but stands near the directors so he will be taken for a director himself.

ONCE UPON A TIME, January, 1948—Once upon a time there was a king, a wizard, a fairy godmother, a witch. But they don't exist anymore. What can we tell children about now? Once upon a time there was a man. Really once upon a time? We only have

21

to look out of the window and we see plenty of men go by. Let's catch one with a lasso. Done. Help me, we'll tie him to the chair with a bit of rope. But we must do it right, first we must make sure if he's an inhabitant of the Moon or really a man. He is. Look at his hands, the fingers, one, two, three, four, five, this one is called the index finger. Would you say it has pressed the trigger of a rifle? Bang. Somebody has fallen. Where? In some part of the world. Years ago, in wartime. Bygones, all right. Let's examine the eyes. Cover the rest of the body with tissue paper, colored paper perhaps (there's always some in the house). Let only the eyes be seen. Or only one eye. Do you think the ear is less upsetting, isolated like this? It has heard so many moans. The eye has seen a wall crumble, under it there was somebody, I could tell you the shoe size, eight and a half. The foot stuck out from the stones like a periscope. We remove the tissue paper, there he is again, all of him, in front of us. He wants to speak. "I'm not a bad man," he says. He seems to be bleating. He says he's changed. We want proof. He says: "My papers are all in order." He shows them to us. What evil can he do with all his papers in order and stamped? He says "Mama," "Daddy," "son," "friend," and "peace," he spells them correctly. If you give him a slice of cake, how gracefully he eats it, he purses his lips. Don't trust him, don't untie him, proof or no proof. And don't let yourselves be fooled if he laughs. I'm putting you on your guard, all he needs is a trumpet blast, the roll of a drum, a flag (whose?), a command in a loud voice, and he grabs a weapon. Ah, you've untied him, you're young, you've let him go, I hear his footsteps on the sidewalk, where will he go? What made you set him free once again? The same old hope?

THE WISE WOMAN, February 12, 1948—This afternoon at three we went to the Wise Woman in a little street opposite Villa Torlonia. She's about fifty, with red hair, eyes like Rasputin. We enter a crowded bedroom. The Wise Woman is seated in an armchair, one by one the visitors tell her their sufferings in loud voices, in front of everybody, she rocks a bit, invoking Jesus, then expresses her opinion as if she were in a trance. Afterwards they put a few lire on the night-table and go away.

In the script of *The Bicycle Thief* I introduced the Wise Woman, whom the protagonist visited after his bicycle was stolen; they told him the Wise Woman shuts her eyes and sees where things are. I had been there two years before to accompany a woman friend;

that's how the idea came to me. De Sica said to me: "Shall we go and see?" Some of those present recognize him despite their ulcers, their cancers, their debts; they stir, laugh, point to him. The Wise Woman doesn't recognize him. The first of my friends to confess himself says they've stolen his bicycle, we prick up our ears with the script in mind. He passes himself off as a worker, and the Wise Woman says it isn't worth his wasting time hunting for it, because the bicycle won't be found. Meanwhile an almost pretty girl appears at the door and hastily informs the Wise Woman that she has been to the lawyer and she didn't trust him. The Wise Woman doesn't allow distrust of lawyers, she says, when they're members of the bar. "Pray, my child, pray." The girl says she doesn't feel like praying any more. The Wise Woman insists: "All you have to say is 'Jesus, be near me'." The girl goes out, and the Wise Woman says the girl is leaving for the sanitorium. It's De Sica's turn. The Wise Woman: "What's your name?" She finds it a nice name. "And what does our Vittorio want?" De Sica invents something: he asks if a newspaper he is supposed to start will do well or badly. The Wise Woman says he mustn't have any uncertainties in life, everybody bends forward to hear De Sica's words; if I remember rightly he made her kiss his forehead. Suso d'Amico doesn't want to speak, but we egg her on. When the Wise Woman realizes Suso's involved in films, she exclaims: "I saw you had a strange face." Suso asks the Wise Woman if a certain film would be a success, and the Wise Woman answers that things are successful when they are done for good ends. I'm in an armchair, sleepy, with a headache, every now and then the door opens, something goes out or comes in. I try to guess the newcomer's troubles, but I'm wrong every time. A mother goes out crying because of the bad things her son does; now a fifty-year-old woman whose husband is cheating on her leaves. The Wise Woman says she wants to talk with that bald gentleman seated in her grandmother's armchair, the one who is so silent and is trying to hide. She stands up, in the silence, takes the eight or nine steps that separate her from me. She asks what my name is. She says I'm not Caesar, not that one, luckily. I remain seated and look at her from below. She touches my face and speaks in a tone that gradually becomes oracular. She says she can see a flock around me, and wants me to give her my hand, she presses it and goes on speaking with her eyes staring over my head. She says, "You must think of the trumpet, you must play the trumpet." Do I stand up or remain seated? To stand up

23

would mean solemnizing what she says, agreeing with it; remaining seated, I discredit her before her audience. She says I have a long road to go but that she will help me find it free of obstacles. I begin to be smug about her prophecies, Guerrieri bursts out laughing, so does De Sica, so does Suso, some people think they are crying because they have covered their faces with their hands, they run out of the room. How much time goes by? I don't dare raise my head, I no longer hear the Wise Woman's words, she must have gone back to her place. Slowly I raise my head, the Wise Woman is coming back toward me with a crucifix in her hand. A woman has turned on the light, a girl is sobbing, what the others are doing I don't know, I am only terrified of laughing, I don't want to laugh, I'd strangle anyone who made me laugh, rather than laugh I'm willing to cry, but the tears won't come. In a remote part of myself, which I could circumscribe with a pencil, I think that the Wise Woman might be right about me, because time and again I've said I'm a pig, and if I had the strength to be more of a pig, afterward something better would take place in me. The Wise Woman goes on talking while she walks backward with the crucifix in her hand toward her place, still staring at me, but I can't return her gaze, if they had kicked me I would have burst out laughing: kicks from those unhappy women and me there, laughing.

I'M EPILEPTIC, May 2, 1948—A man from the Veneto says: "Is there a part for me?"; he's tall, thin with a Christ-like beard. I advise him to shave it off, because it lessens his chances of being hired, he cuts off the beard, goes to Blasetti, who says: "Why did you shave off the beard?" The man telephones me to say his beard has grown back, he asks for a letter of recommendation to Freda, who isn't looking for people with beards. Another Veneto man begs me to introduce him to De Sica for the part of the thief, I warn him that there are a lot of candidates, when he hears that the thief has to fall on the ground in an epileptic fit, he lets out a scream of joy: "Me, me, I'm an epileptic."

SCIUSCIA, May 21, 1948—Applause for the kids, the protagonists of *Shoeshine* during the Oscar ceremony. They've grown up, they work. Even Francesco is a big boy. Once when De Concini scolded him for pimping, he answered calmly, "it's the men who make me do it." Another time some shoeshine boys confided to De Concini that three of them kept a girl of twelve as mistress,
24

they paid her fifty lire. "Yesterday," one of the three said, "I made her give me the money back."

SHIPWRECK, May, 1948—This is the third person in the last couple of months who's talked to me about suicide; a bricklayer's wife in Via Vasi tells me her husband stands for a long time at the window staring at one spot, he reminds me of my father when promissory notes were about to fall due. "This is Provenzano speaking," a voice says on the phone a few days ago. Who is Provenzano? Ah, the shoemaker. He used to live in Via Merici, now he has a handsome shop out towards San Giovanni. He wants to know if I still work in the movies, he has a great story to tell me about a shipwreck that took place in 1943. Ten sailors in a lifeboat off Bizerte, they threw a man in the sea, he was dying, he wouldn't have lived much longer, and they had to lighten the boat. The dying man didn't die, the sea water healed his wounds, the English picked him up, Provenzano says, and here in Rome, yesterday, the sailor met the man who threw him into the water. On June 7th, Provenzano again, he asks if he can send me his assistant, namely the protagonist. "Next week," I say, "Today I have a fever." The assistant comes to the phone, his name is Nicola d'Agostino; he can't tell me where he's from, he was born more or less everywhere, he says, laughing; he isn't the resuscitated man, he's the other: "I'm the one who threw *him* into the sea." The other's name is Foponi. He was full of wounds and didn't have a hope, then Nicola said as he abandoned him to the waves: "I'm sorry, really, but the water's turning rough. You can see for yourself, have a good trip." He says Foponi gave him a nasty look, but one dead man is better than six (there were six of them left). A little earlier they had thrown a first man who was already dead into the water; I express doubt; he insists the man was dead all right. They had found a raft with a barrel of cognac, some canned goods, they got drunk, "Then things happened I'll tell you about," he says. They had a battle with some shipwrecked Germans, they managed to keep them from climbing aboard, otherwise they'd have sunk, one of them was bald and Nicola bashed his head in with a shoe. Last May 30th Nicola was taking a walk past the Policlinico, when near a bookstall his eyes met the eyes of another man who, however, kept right on walking. He resembled Foponi. After about ten yards the man turned, he looked at Nicola, and that wasn't all. He came slowly back towards him. "You're d'Agostino," he said. Nicola nodded and went

25

pale, "You're Foponi. I killed you." "Don't be scared, shake hands. If you hadn't thrown me overboard, I would be dead."

USELESS, 1949—In the midst of the rubble we realized we had spent too few images to open the eyes of our neighbor and help him face, if not prevent, the monstrous events. To put it bluntly, the cinema had failed in choosing the way of Méliès and not the way of Lumière where the path was sown with the thorns of reality. At a lightning pace, they succeeded in thrusting the spectator as far as possible from himself and, using lots of money and talent, they made this flight definitive. One day we came out of the darkness of a movie theater and newsboys were shouting that the war was on—that is to say, a woman's arm wrenched from her body and flung on the telegraph wires, and the head of a certain Paolo Gai which landed in a flower pot at a house marked with the number 3. We could only hope that the other bombs would fall on the house opposite instead of on ours, and when the house opposite was hit and ours wasn't, we survivors hugged one another, singing. How many films had been made during the long eve? An incalculable number in fifty years between 1895 and 1944; fifty years of cinema. It sounds like a memorial plaque. Hundreds of thousands of feet of film, armies of people who worked, toiled to cover those feet of film with events, enough to wrap around the world. A statistic worthy of some cheap illustrated weekly. The report on the cinema's first half-century of life concludes with this judgment: useless. But something is appearing on the horizon. They have begun writing the history (to begin with, only technical and aesthetic) of cinema as a means of examining man and contemporary society. The cinema has resumed its destiny. This is so forcefully and naturally apparent that even the industry itself has begun to feel the consequences. An immense number of eyes can expect, with some hope at last, to see the film that will at one time express all the possible truth. The film that is to be projected against the sky, visible at the same moment in every part of the earth. It hasn't yet been made, not because we don't know the truth, but because we hide it, in fear or for expediency. We have always stopped a few feet short. Now our will is more steadfast, there is almost a contest to see who can report injustice first. This domestic Last Judgment, without trumpets, without celestial apparitions, private, begun by our films just after the war, cannot be interrupted, it would be the end of cinema, of democracy itself, if it were to be sucked back into the old life. There is a drive to study others not through the narrative synthesis of the past, but through an analysis that leads to the recognition of men's existence and suffering in their actual duration. Man is there before us, and we can watch him in slow motion to grasp the concreteness of a minute of his presence which will then show us how our own minute of absence is equally concrete. We will have to recognize that its importance is continuous, and the aforesaid presence needs no qualifying adjectives. We seem to be on the eve of rediscovering our original meaning. For that matter, the cinema *was* our original meaning; from the first lens that opened to the light, everything was equal to it, this was its most uncontaminated and promising moment, the reality buried under myths was slowly reemerging; a tree, an old man, someone eating, sleeping, weeping, but then they preferred plots, to avoid too-surprising equations: the close-up of a poor man's eye might have been taken for a rich man's, and vice versa.

POOR AND RICH, August 8, 1949—Lambrusco wine doesn't kill you: on the contrary, you believe yourself fairly immortal and you'll always find, they say, somebody to lend you a hand if you fall in a ditch (the next morning things are different, and if you stand in the center of the village, as I did in 1929, and wonder whom you can ask for a thousand lire to pay a note, many, very many people go past before you can say: he's the one. I killed myself that time, and the corpse is still on the spot, in the village square). My father died of debts more than of cirrhosis. Three days before he went, there were creditors at his bedside; he pulled the blankets over his face, and the creditors saw my father's swollen belly all shaking, then they finally realized he was crying, and they left. I've never told how, a few hours before dying, he got out of bed, we realized it when he was there at the dresser, taking from the drawer a little gold chain worth, at most, three hundred lire, his legs were sticks; he walked like a marionette. He said to my brother with gestures that he should go over the Po, to Dosolo, to a cousin of ours, to see if he could sell the chain and pay a few debts (we had a hundred and twenty thousand lire's worth of them). Before Fascism, he defended the rich; he belonged to the moderates, the *malvòn*. Alone, he faced a delegation of infuriated poor women, to defend the rich men huddled in a room at the back of our café. The women shouted, "Long live Prampolini,* with

* Famous Italian socialist 1859–1930.

27

his arms folded he confronted them, and they stepped back. He sided with the rich who said: "Charge it," instead of paying promptly, he marked it down in a big ledger and they paid months, years later because nobody had the nerve to dun them since they were rich. In my town, the poor who frequented the taverns were scorned by the rich, that's how things were then: as they went by, the rich looked inside out of the corner of their eye: those who were discovered drinking or laughing hesitated the next day to ask for work or for a raise or for the payment of a bill.

I've hated the rich since childhood, because on Sunday the women of my village filed past them under the arcades as if before a king, they became wan and let themselves be made pregnant in the woods: between me and the rich they would always have chosen the rich. I saw nothing but poor and rich, and all of life was like that. How can I hate myself, now that I am beginning to save up some money to buy a dozen acres at Luzzara (and why not fifteen)? To live there calmly without worries, I'll cover my ears, and I won't even read the newspaper; shall I have my land farmed by a sharecropper? "The peasants steal," the rich say—confiding in me, whom they now consider one of themselves.

REGINA COELI, 1950—Germi and I were recalling our arguments during the writing of *Il testimone*, he wants me to go and drink with him in a tavern, this morning while he was shooting near Regina Coeli Prison his foot was struck by a little ball of paper from above, a letter somebody else was meant to pick up, written on a sheet of copybook paper: "Dear brother, do me a favor and go to Maracchioni's mother's house and tell her when she comes to see her son on visiting day to bring you along, then you tell the son as follows. A few days ago we sent a note by Mamma for Nino which said he should be glad to help us financially, because otherwise we will report him for the robbery and for corrupting minors, and he sent word that he would use the letter to wipe his ass with, now we're waiting for Mamma's answer if we can be let out on parole, if they don't want to let us out, then we'll turn Nino over to the Royal Prosecutor saying he's responsible for the whole thing."

HER OWN STORY, May 21, 1950—Over the phone she begs me to give her half an hour of my time, no less. She came this evening at eight. She needs money to go immediately, by air, to Venezuela, and she hopes I can help her raise it. "There are plenty of people,"

28

she says, "who throw away a hundred and seventy thousand lire in a day," it seems impossible that there isn't somebody who would give up luxuries for three days. She doesn't know that the days are long even for the rich. Pale, distraught, with a burning desire to tell the whole story, no matter to whom, around ten she is still here, talking. "Can't a person sell her own story?" she asks. "With the proceeds I could join Anselmo."

Her plan is this: "Producers and directors pay a quota of ten thousand lire each, as many as are necessary to raise the required amount; they draw a name out of a hat, and for example, say Scalera comes out, Scalera becomes the owner of my story and can make a film of it, if he wants to."

I look at her, dumbfounded. Is she crazy? She's not. We can call her Maria; I'll have to change the names. She had a friend, Raissa, she's dead. They loved each other like sisters. Raissa died because of an abortion, the fruit of her sin also died, but before she died, she said to Maria: "I leave Anselmo in your care."

For a year she and Anselmo went to the cemetery regularly to take flowers to Raissa's grave, one day he lies with her in a field and gets her pregnant. Neither of the two knows how it happened, she says. Maria loves Anselmo, she's always loved him, and poor Raissa entrusted her lover to Maria for this reason. "You're the only one who can help him," she said, on her deathbed. Maria bore a fine baby girl. Maria says it's the very baby that should have been born to Raissa. But we've come to the trial. Anselmo, hidden until that moment, turns up in court. They sentence him. He's an adulterer; in fact he has a wife and two children. Raissa, moreover, was a minor. Anselmo thinks of killing himself, Maria keeps him alive. He was the manager of an automobile factory; he lost his job while evading the police, who hunted him for a year. Maria shows me the photo of Anselmo and one of the baby. She carries around with her a little album with lots of pictures of Anselmo and the baby, he's a man of about forty. "A bit irresponsible," she says, "like a child. Sometimes, when we make love, he calls out Raissa's name and not mine, but I'm not jealous, the memory I cherish of Raissa is too lofty and beautiful, still, I suffer." She stops a moment and repents; "No, no," she adds, "my love for him is so great it leaves no room for any other emotion." She explains to me the reasons why a girl like Raissa and another like herself have fallen in love with a man almost twenty years older. She talks about graying temples, and I can't help thinking that my temples are

29

gray too, but Anselmo isn't bald. By ten o'clock I'm tired, I crumple rather impolitely on the sofa making an effort to hide my yawns, my ancient yearning for sleep comes completely to the fore; in a little while I may start snoring: not even a cry from my mother could stir me, I haven't slept for three nights. "You're tired," Maria says. I explain why. "I have to go into details," she says, "There's nothing new about my story except the little things." I say, "The novelty lies in one fact: these things happened to you." "I know he's sick,"—she goes on—"He's found a job in a little garage for the present, he'll get ahead, but he has to get well, and if I'm with him, he'll get well quickly. A film troupe is leaving for Brazil, with the director Freda, make them take me with them to Brazil, from there I'll manage to reach Venezuela on my own." I feel a kind of smug satisfaction in proving to her the absurdity of this hope. "Sometimes miracles happen," she says to me at the door. I tell her to try, to write the story at once, as it is, for a newspaper and— who knows? Maybe somebody will pop up and say: "Here's your ticket for Venezuela." "It would have to be somebody," she says, "who wouldn't reproach me because Anselmo is married or blame him for Raissa's death. He's completely innocent, and only a sensitive spirit can understand that." I say she seems sincere to me, indeed she always has been, and that's enough. She owned a little piece of land near Bari, she sold it to help Anselmo when he was in prison. She waited in the vestibule four hours to see him. "You know what frightened me? The indifferent voice of the jailer who interrupted our visit: 'Time's up, get out.'" Before leaving, she asks me if I think that a great actress—she mentions the name of a great actress whom I saw this morning at the Hotel Excelsior— might make a big gesture and give her the money for the ticket. I answer, "I don't know. I believe this actress has a kind heart, but I've seen generous people refuse a hundred lire. . . ." it depends on so many things. I'd like to explain them to her, but I barely have the strength to tell her she's going the wrong way: in fact, she was about to bang her nose against the door opposite instead of climbing the steps towards the exit.

THE PEASANT, 1950—A peasant was plowing and thinking: "Shall I drink or not?" The bottle of water was there in the grass, in the shade. I'll drink when I've done the length of the field, I'll enjoy it more. "Keep moving," he said to the ox, and he didn't look at the three airplanes that were passing overhead. One darted away

30

from the others like an eel and the peasant didn't have time to notice it before rattatat it fired on him and when the peasant had flung himself on the ground the plane was already high in the sky again. The bullets made a line of smoke a few feet from him, the ox hadn't moved. They passed over several times; a few minutes later smoke was rising from Viterbo. He felt the need to sit down, but the sound of the planes grew louder instead of fading away. Then it came back. He started running toward the oak, with difficulty, over the plowed earth. The machine gun made the oak resound like a drum. He kept his eyes closed and his nose crushed against the bark of the tree, from a window in the house they shouted his name, on the road a man was speeding past on a bicycle—perhaps now he'll shoot at the cyclist—a sparrow flew from the hedge to the oak. How could he be seen from up there? They saw him, in fact the plane was arriving for the third time with a racket that tore out his guts. The peasant pretended to weep, like a baby, with the illusion of defending himself. He crawled to the other side of the oak without looking at the plane, his face next to a snail. There it was again. But it was only an acoustical effect, which disappeared as if a door had been shut. He opened his eyes. He began to look for it in the sky but didn't find it at first: it was a speck. He let a long time go by before he moved.

THE HOUSE, * *June, 1952*—I ran into the Zambons. They were married a year ago: he's a friend of my older son and she was a maid in a house near mine; now she's pregnant. They're worried; when the baby's born they would like to have a room, now they're badly fixed. Natale earns 10,000 lire a month as a bricklayer, he has to give something to his mother, so they have to find a room that doesn't cost too much. Today he's happy because tomorrow he begins a stairway, it's the first time since he's been a bricklayer that he is to work on stairs: progress. He has an idea: to build, at night, a room in a field, in the neighborhood of Val Melaina, the way others have done. Because if he can put up four walls during the night, before the police catch on, afterward they can't drive him away legally, and the baby would be born under a roof. Some friends would help him begin the minute it's dark, the house would be built by dawn; it costs about 60,000 lire. I tell him that if Rossellini's game, we'll give him the money for the house and will film the whole scene.

* This is the germ of the De Sica-Zavattini film *The Roof*.

THE PICKPOCKET, November 21, 1952—Today I talked with a pickpocket of forty. The basic methods of his trade are two: *ar core* (to the heart), namely robbing the wallet when it's in the inside pocket of the jacket, and *in culatta* (at the ass), that is when the wallet is in the rear pocket of the trousers. The object aimed at is called *er lasagno* (the *lasagna*). The difficulty lies not so much in pulling the *lasagno* from another's pocket with two *cere* (candles, i.e., fingers) as in passing it to one's friend, because there are too many people nowadays who look down at their balls instead of looking up, they look at the ground and can see the *lasagno* as it is passed. He says that in Piazzale Flaminio this summer he robbed the pay envelope of a worker, eight thousand six hundred lire, there was a little roll of paper inside, "a long one, with everything marked down, even the hours and the minutes he had worked, even his overtime, they must have American machines for that." He would have talked for hours; he's happy to talk about himself. I ask him if his wife knows anything, "She *mustn't* know a thing because she's nursing the babies, and it could harm them." Men like him are always broke because they gamble everything at cards: "We're big spenders." A friend of his left on his honeymoon with 14,000 lire and came back with 50,000; his wife, unknowing, asked him: "Does this money last forever?" He would leave his wife alone for a few minutes and then come back with the *lasagno*.

VIETNAM, February 8, 1953—One of those boys I watched grow up near my house writes me from Indochina, he's in the Foreign Legion. "I never believed the life of the Foreign Legion was so monstrous, they always send us to the most isolated countries to destroy a whole race and maybe two thousand die today, and then tomorrow in the same place you find five thousand and very often plenty of our men are taken prisoner and the next day we find them, only with their head stuck on a bamboo pole. This is something that the Legion pays back all right, and in our bunch there are some who do more horrible things than they, that's why down here you forget everything and expect only death so you will have a rest. Plenty of legionnnaires are missing in this land, wherever we march we find wooden crosses, and I've read lots of Italian names. In the Legion when they put somebody in the brig, first they throw a bucket of water on the floor where he has to lie down, the man being punished has to put his face against the wall and hold a cigarette paper against the wall with his nose for hours and hours. And if the paper falls a corporal is ready and waiting to give him a push that crushes his nose. The men are more afraid of this push than they are of death. The Vietnamese women are mostly short and thin, shapely in Laos and Cambodia. The legionnaires kill the old women to frighten the girls so they'll spread their legs without wasting time. We Italians make friends with the natives. I play cards on their houseboats, I chop wood along with them. They need medicines, with an aspirin you can buy a girl; they're grateful to anybody who does them a good turn more than anywhere else in the world, with my truck I helped them carry off the cartloads of goods when they were escaping. Look at all the teeth I've lost, legionnaires always have some teeth missing, because instead of being confined to quarters they're beaten up; for a Frenchman they pick a German to beat him, for a German vice versa, they always choose men who hate each other, but almost nobody falls down, because if you fall they hit you with their heel and it ruins your face." With my own eyes I saw where that boy lived, because one night there was a quarrel at his home and I ran up, with my brother, to see what was happening: eleven people lived in those four rooms, but there wasn't a chair, not an object; only a table in the kitchen, four beds, six children in one of them —his little brothers and sisters between two and eight, three at the head and three at the foot, looking at the quarrel with indifference because they were used to it, even if one of the brawlers had blood flowing from his nose. The emptiness seemed the greater because everything was neat and clean, and I had a feeling of the sort that came over me in a bunker near Mensola in November: I went in with Cavallaro and Renzi, it had a little antechamber and a room three yards by three, with a cement table in the middle and on this big round table I saw four little aluminum plates with soup set as if at the cardinal points of the compass. The bunker is inhabited by a married couple who're in Rovigo now in the hospital with pleurisy, here were their children all in new clothes, with shiny leggings, just received from some Committee, they live in the bunker with an uncle.

THE STREETWALKERS, February 15, 1953—At eleven, two girls who beat the pavements came, we have to question them for the documentary film I'm making with Ferreri and Ghione; also present is Lizzani, who will be the director for the part where one of these girls tells what she does from the morning up to the moment when, like a launched ship, she leaves the house and starts to ply her trade. One is married and has children. The other is unattached; she talks for an hour without stopping, and I believe she told only one lie, that she was operated on for appendicitis and afterward it slipped out that it was rhagades. She described minutely how, though she was still sick, she had to force herself out of bed one evening to make love because she needed the money; she lists her expenditures as if she were reading them from a blackboard: 45,000 per month for rent plus 1,300 tax, 22,000 in installments on her furniture, 4,500 for the mattress, 7,500 for the chandelier which is, she says, the most beautiful thing in her house, because finally she has a house like other women. With the medical examinations she has to undergo at the Central Police Station, she doesn't sleep much and this is her sorrow and her fury; they're twice a week, they could be got through in half an hour, but they take hours, then there is something she can't swallow, having all of the girls stand naked in the same room when a little screen would make all the difference.

She says: "What does a screen cost? We get up at seven when we have the exam and we lose a whole day, because we sleep until late in the evening, and in Via del Tritone after one o'clock it's all over, and if you haven't eaten by then, you don't eat."

She feels a great attraction for men in blue suits with light ties; when she sees one going by, coming out of the theater—especially if his hair is slightly tinted white (according to her, some men dye their hair white on purpose because they know women like it, "just a splash of white")—she would go with him then and there. She's in love, and when she quarrels with him and doesn't see him for a while, she asks her girl friends if they've seen him, and if one says she has, then she asks: "Was he wearing a blue suit?", because when a man wears a blue suit, according to her, it means he's going with a woman. She also went home to vote, and she gave her vote to the *flame* (MSI, the neo-fascist party), because they told her that if they won they'd change the situation for the streetwalkers, and it has to be changed because it's murder with all these debts: "As soon as I open my eyes it's 3,000 lire a day, without counting stockings, a pair is ruined every time they drag you into a car, because they're in a big hurry, it's a vicious circle of pawntickets and notes and we also have to pay the taxi when we go home late, so as not to run into the Vice Squad."

She starts talking about the screen again: "When they make us
34

climb on the sawhorse, it's no fun. Sitting there with your legs spread in front of all the other girls and if you have something, maybe even a little rash, they all see it. You come to the exam out of breath because you get up at the last minute, you also have to take a taxi so you can stay in bed an extra fifteen minutes, and then you have to strip naked in the midst of sixty others." What do they talk about among themselves while they're waiting? "I don't know," she answers, "for example, we talk about food, 'What did you eat today?' and one says 'Greens with a bit of meat,' or else she says, 'chicken,' and you answer: 'So work's going well.'" Her nerves are bad from watching out for the Vice Squad all the time: "I can't get picked up again by the Vice Squad, there're too many of us." She speaks a vulgar Roman dialect, she says that in the end she becomes attached to a certain place of work, just that stretch of street. When she thought of killing herself for love after having hunted for him in vain for three hours in the dance halls, she opened the drawers to look for cigarettes and instead she found the little tubes of permanganate, she unwrapped the silver paper and wrote "Goodbye" with the permanganate. She also wrote to the police to save trouble and to tell them "I poisoned myself on my own." "I thought it would be like the movies, where you die right away."

She explains in detail everything she felt, her tongue was thick, and the stomach pump tube at the hospital wouldn't go down, she heard a voice: "In an hour this one's in the morgue." Another man said: "Confess." "I felt the oil on my face." They slapped her to make the poison come up. "When I woke up he was there. Then I wrote on a piece of paper, because I couldn't talk: 'You've ruined my career.'" Her passions are roast lamb and bangles. To look in shopwindows she zigzags from one sidewalk to the other; she doesn't want to miss a single one. "I like opera, but I don't understand it much: I can't go because I start crying right off. I love the Royal Family like my own parents. I dream of Mussolini. I dream of Hitler too." At an *oh* of amazement from us, she rationalizes: "I dream of Hitler because he's connected with Mussolini." Of men she says: "They're dopes." Among the girls there's a lot of envy, since they're so poor. As if suddenly remembering, she shows us a long scar, she banged her head that time of the suicide: on all fours she reached the door, she managed to open it, and at that very moment a tenant arrived on the landing with a bottle of milk, the tenant was so frightened at seeing her crawling and grasp-

35

ing he fainted. The concierge below heard the thud of the milk-bottle on the floor and shouted up: "What's going on?" Nobody answered, he came up and began to yell. The others appeared, helped her and the faint man, who had a smaller bottle of milk in his pocket for his baby, with a nipple on it.

"They put the nipple in my mouth, because milk is good for you when you're poisoned, but they couldn't get my teeth open. A girl friend said: 'She did it because he left her.' I could hear her and I was thinking: 'Damn you! if you knew he wanted to leave me, you ought to have let me know!' "

We interrupt her to allow the other girl to talk. She opens her mouth from time to time to begin, but then the first one catches her breath and goes on, the other meanwhile shifts on her chair as if on a launching pad, to be ready when the moment comes, finally she is able to start: "With me, it's a different thing."

VAN GOGH, March 1, 1953—On the 30th of this month, a hundred years ago, Van Gogh was born at Groot Zundert. I visited that little village on December 3rd, 1951. I arrived in a Cadillac with the producer Graetz and his wife toward sunset. There was an avenue, with the sun at the end, which I must have seen in a painting of Van Gogh's in the Kröller-Müller collection. The proprietress of a trinket shop tells us Van Gogh's house has been destroyed, a certain Monsieur Hubert, correspondent of an Amsterdam daily paper (his daughter draws flowers while he talks about Van Gogh with us), says: "The house is standing. Also the church where his father preached, Pastor Theodorus." It's drizzling, as we walk in the darkness he explains that there are religious quarrels here, as in all Holland, and the Catholics don't love Van Gogh, there is no street named after him; the city council has been quarreling over it for roughly twenty years. Our guide lights a match: this is a little graveyard attached to the church, a dozen graves. With a second match he illuminates a stone: VINCENT VAN GOGH 1853. "Before Vincent this other Vincent was born, who died at once."

I arrived in Holland on November 28th at one P.M. by plane. At six P.M. I knocked (it was Graetz who knocked) at a little white door with an ivy leaf painted over it, in the village of Laren, twenty-five miles from Amsterdam. The door was opened by a man of about sixty, thin, white-haired, pink-faced: he was Theo's son, over whose cradle Vincent and Theo burst into tears and Vincent

36

said: "He has infinity in his eyes." We passed through two or three little wood-paneled rooms, with low ceilings, and I examined the walls, there were humble pictures not by Van Gogh. In the last room there was *Van Gogh's House in Arles* and *The Potato-eaters*. He introduced us to his family. In one corner some pictures were turned toward the wall, without frames; from one, awkwardly placed, some sunflower leaves peeped out. According to the nephew, the film should begin with a Sunday in church: "People were serious then and the pastors governed the lives of the village," he says. "The Catholics are more stern than the Protestants, because the Calvinists used to say: 'Hmph, Catholics aren't very stern.' So they try to outdo them. In Vincent's day, pastor's sons were known *comme des hommes méchants.*" The Nazis also wanted to make a film about Van Gogh, it began with the generals and the admirals going up an endless staircase at the top of which there was the Van Gogh Museum inaugurated by the Nazis.

Van Gogh's nephew hates the Germans, who killed his son, he won't buy goods made in Germany, he doesn't like the Italians, their allies at the time. He has never sold a painting, a drawing of Vincent's, he owns millions' worth. To tell the truth, he sold one, a little one, during the war, when he was forced to. He will give them all to museums. He lives by his work as an engineer, and no one must suggest buying one from him. A little girl comes in to say goodnight to us, his niece of six, in her pink pyjamas, her aunt suddenly plays the piano and the child dances, this lasts two minutes, then all say *"goede nacht,"* the child continues saying *"goede nacht"* for a long time, as she goes off. Her aunt says that the child danced before the queen with the other girls in her class at school. *"On danse beaucoup à Laren."* On the chimney piece there is a little Van Gogh: a branch of cherry or almond blossoms in a vase, with a red stripe in the background. "Types like Vincent are not rare in Holland," the nephew says, "characters who can't agree with the others. There are many individualists in our country." He shows us the originals of Vincent's letters to Theo, a neat hand, the last letter, before the suicide, two and a quarter pages, on copybook paper. There is one with some canceled-out accounts, and a penciled note in which he makes an appointment with Theo at the Louvre, on his arrival in Paris. I touched the letter to his brother which ended with the terrible "but what do you want?" There are no objects of Van Gogh's except for a bronze vase that Van Gogh painted, now filled with red flowers. He shows me a

37

little album of drawings that have never been seen, one looks like the barely-sketched head of a horse; a second is the same thing only elongated, a third still longer, in the end it's an eel.

Two days later I was going for a walk through Amsterdam with Van Gogh's nephew, and I was thinking that none of my friends would have imagined it; it was snowing slightly, the eve of the feast of Saint Nicolaas. I have never seen so many children in the streets, happy and free, as if they knew that in Holland when they're grown up they have to be more serious than in other countries, maybe this is why here they are so indulgent with children. One boy, suddenly, stopping acrobatically, put his head toward the ground, he was alone, and he stayed in that position two or three minutes, then he straightened up and went off, without looking at me.

He believes that one can speak of masochism in connection with Vincent. "However it's not true," he says, "that he cut off his ear." He says he could conceive the film also without Van Gogh, a film on Van Gogh without Van Gogh. I confide to him that so far it's the story of the two brothers that I would use as a pivot. He says: "Mmm." I haven't the courage to continue. He will publish a book on Vincent which he has been working at for many years, he will say sincerely everything he knows. Who's left who had some link with Vincent? "Cousin Kaj has a daughter," he says "and I've met her once." Cousin Kaj, the girl from Etten, so beloved. She survived Vincent for many years, she lived to see the dead man's glory take shape, but she was a happy wife. Gachet's son is alive, the son of Tersteeg, who helped Vincent though Vincent detested him. Vincent had a sister who was made pregnant but wasn't married. Vincent wrote her: "Don't be frightened, if what you did was done with love, then you were right."

It seems the daughter of this sister is alive in Marseilles.

We took a tram to go see the harbor, in order to look at him I wasn't looking at the harbor.

When it comes to his uncle's death in poverty, he says they exaggerate, and in the city museum he showed me the painting with Vincent's shoes, "They aren't such worn-out shoes," he says. Perhaps the engineer suffers at the thought that his father might be reproached for not having done all he could. But according to me, he did.

The next day we went to Nuenen, there is the house, the manse as in the drawings, and a little monument to Vincent in the square

—a stone with a sun carved in it. Vincent's house is lived in by a man from Philips who paints as a hobby. Where the dog now stays, Vincent used to work. In the restaurant they told us Vincent has a son at Nuenen. One man offered to take us to the son. Others say he isn't a son. The age however would be right, he's sixty-five; Vincent is supposed to have fathered him on a country woman who went with men easily.

We arrived in the car at a point half a mile from the village. "There he is," the young man of Nuenen said. A path from the main road led to a farmyard where peasants were digging in the mud. He was dressed in blue canvas with a pipe in his mouth, a cap with earmuffs. The young man called him, he came slowly towards us. They had told us that he doesn't know whether or not he's Van Gogh's son: his name is Nelis de Groot, thin, tall, hair still dark and one eye slightly crooked.

The young man took him aside and spoke to him. He answered with some monosyllables, looking into the distance. "He says," the young man reported, "that he doesn't want to hear any more about this business." From a little house his wife came out and confirmed that her husband didn't want to hear about any of it.

In the midst of a heath there is the cemetery. With difficulty we found the grave of Vincent's father, abandoned, and finally I saw the crows rise from a field and a wagon of black potatoes go by, but the strongest shock came a little later in the hospice of the old. There was a man of eighty-eight who had known Van Gogh, had seen him well, and he says that Vincent was good, and as for Nelis de Groot, it's true they accused Vincent of having got that woman with child, but Van Gogh went and protested to the Catholic priest. He talks in bursts, agitated, every now and then a brief belch, his name is Hensen Van der Velden, and he tells how Vincent would give 25 pennies per bird's nest; the boys climbed up in the trees to take the nests, which he copied. Graetz hands him some money but he says he'll die in a few months, and refuses it. Outside we meet another old man, who says Van Gogh made a drawing of him when he was two years old.

Then I saw Scheveningen with the sea higher than the beach, its bituminous color had sudden slashes of zinc white while my eyes sought the point of the beach where Vincent must have said to Christine: "We have to separate."

The Borinage was under snow from which the black peaks of coal emerged. The house of Denis the baker, which dripped with humidity (in Wasmes), wasn't opened at once, we shouted for a long time until a man of about forty appeared with an axe in his hand. He smiled at me. Behind his head there was a plaque that recalled that Van Gogh had lived there, at number 22. Inside, his daughter was making cut-out figures from a school exercise book. They are so poor they can't buy a newspaper, but in his wallet this Jean Richer has some very worn clippings of the time when a member of parliament unveiled the plaque.

At Auvers-sur-Oise I saw the room where Vincent died and the cemetery on the hill, in the midst of the wheat fields: the wall around the grounds was scraped by the bullets of an airplane. There was no one there, not even the watchman. I hoped not to find the graves immediately, and instead we pushed open the gate and there they were, covered with ivy, one next to the other, Vincent and Theo. I took off my beret, but the cold was so intense I had to put it back on.

The *patron* of the Café Ravoux reluctantly led us up a little stairway and we were immediately in the tiny room where Vincent died: there is a bed, a wardrobe with a dirty hanging covering it, cigarette butts on the floor, on the washbasin traces of mascara, of lipstick, and opposite the window that wall. A white Russian woman of fifty lives there, she's a waitress in the café, bleached, face swollen. Cowed by the *patron* who is in a hurry to resume his billiards, we don't stay long. Vincent heard this same sound of billiard balls as he was dying. He had gone up the steps pretending there was nothing wrong with him, and instead he had shot himself a quarter of an hour before. On the bed, in a pool of blood, Gachet's son saw him too, this little old man who has offered us a red vermouth in his house, exclaiming: *"la douce France."* He strongly resembles his father with the concentric wrinkles in his face, but he's less sad. Everything is neat, clean: the ceramics, the bronzes, the beer mugs on the mantelpiece. Without Theo, he says, there would be no Vincent. He tells the story of the hand in the pocket: that is, Vincent had the revolver for a long time with him, and when he quarreled with Doctor Gachet over the Guillaumin canvas—he reproached him for not having framed it worthily— he put his hand in his pocket to pull out the revolver. "Oh—I say—the piano." "It's the piano of Mademoiselle Gachet," he says, whom Vincent painted seated at the very same piano. I ask whose are the three pictures on the door: he painted them. He lives alone, his sister is dead, but before dying she said to Aurenche, to whom
40

she opened the door all dressed in black: "Make films about the living, not about the dead." Gachet is sorry that they write bad things about his father, like the writings of Artaud. "They were really great friends," he says, "however Vincent wasn't right in the head, from boyhood, instead of sleeping on his bed, he slept on the floor, he had a mania for harming himself."

I think this journey isn't the film on Van Gogh, but we have to hurry, before old Hannes dies and they whitewash the Ravoux's room; I would also go to look up that daughter of Vincent's sister, aged sixty-five, who is apparently in Marseilles. Vincent's sister made a mistake, she was Vincent's favorite and he wrote to her: "Love, love more and more, this is what matters."

With Aurenche I went to Arles on the 16th. We arrived there at dawn. In the lobby of the Hotel du Pin there was a vulgar painting with damask on the frame and a light illuminating it; on the register of the illustrious foreigners I saw the signatures and the thoughts of Baldwin, Mistinguette, Sessuye Hayakawa.

There wasn't the name of Van Gogh, nobody ever mentioned him. The sun came up, and we went out on the Rhone where an old boat was going by making an enormous racket. I couldn't believe my eyes: it was the *Mont Blanc,* the one Van Gogh saw. A few feet farther on, the bridge of the laundresses stood, no longer a drawbridge, but the same emerald sky. I ran to the navigation office, and they confirmed the *Mont Blanc* was Van Gogh's *Mont Blanc.*

I crossed the streets of the brothels, destroyed by the war: only bits of wall were still standing. Also the house had collapsed where Vincent put up Gauguin. I traced some things that Van Gogh painted, *les alicants,* the arena, the hospital, these olive trees that for him made an ancient murmur.

We went by car to Saint-Rhémy following the route that Vincent followed in a carriage between Roulin and the pastor. To Roulin he said, taking his leave: "We'll meet again *là haut.*" We opened the gate. Doctor Leroy allowed me to look at the registrar for 1889; on the day Van Gogh left, next to his name was written in big letters "cured." The doctor's wife offered us coffee, and the daughter was ironing, talking of Van Gogh like a member of the family. The wing where Vincent stayed is almost a ruin, now there are only a few mad women in it. The nuns called his paintings swallow-dung. There is still Van Gogh's little room, empty, with some withered flowers in tin cans, as on the poorest graves, arranged along the walls. The barred window looks out on the wheat field where he saw death reaping, not a blade of grass has been moved, in the distance the blue mountains and the little house with the red roof just after the edge of the field.

The next day I left Arles for Italy, at the station the mistral was blowing that used to shake Van Gogh's easel.

SPAIN, March 9, 1953—A baroque dome opened above us in the cathedral like an upside-down chasm; before the altar we could hear only that it was of gold, all gold, and they hold out their hands. Arriving at Toledo we met a child's funeral, a little coffin carried by four children, three of them dressed in red, followed by a dozen people who were scattered because the descent was very steep, and they looked to left and right as if they had never seen the city: along the streets there were blind men selling tickets for a lottery, there's one every day, so there's always hope, and the blind men have the number that came out the day before stuck in the buttonhole of their jackets. There is a spot from which you see the city as El Greco saw it, today it is even more dry and earthen, from the depth of the river it rises up to the spires through planes of windows and alleyways where twists of dust whirl past; for the relief of moisture the eye must come down into the Tagus again. I saw that color at Tarquinia, a long crest of wall towards the dead city, while a flock was climbing up the valley like a river of wool.

In the thirty hilly miles from Toledo to Madrid I didn't see a single bicycle, the peasants were coming back in silence from the fields on small horses that also carried spades, hoes and little plows —children's tools, one would have said. Some harmonious sparrows darted from hedge to hedge, it was sunset as when we came out of the Escurial that had a stork on its roof, and we would have carried with us the suffering of that tomb-like palace except that hundreds of children playing football with some priests filled the air with their shouts.

. . . If I had to say in a few words what the corrida is, I'd say it's that great bloodstain on the bull's flank when the animal comes from the shadow into the sun; the blood suddenly flashes and its glow is reflected in the people's faces. Carla del Poggio hid her face in her arms, then she too became used to it. Three times they stuck a stiletto into the bull's skull in vain to kill it, since the espada had been clumsy. The horses carried the bull off at a gallop amid

42

a cracking of whips, like a circus. Zampa was continually amazed that there were children among the spectators, and I was amazed that the bull's suffering was so silent, he never roared, not even when a picador widened his wound, plunging the picadilla into it as hard as he could, the bull didn't move, neither did the picador nor the horse, only the iron tip of the picadilla went deeper and deeper into the wound. Suddenly the public went "ah" and bent toward the arena; one man, who had dropped his cape, had been lifted on the bull's horn, and the others had rushed to distract the bull, the wounded man was carried out, you couldn't see the wound, only the man's pallor; half a minute went by in which he felt no pain, nothing, but he knew he had been hurt, and it was as if he were waiting for a message from heaven that his body was to begin to fail. He bent his head; the message had come. Seated in the arms of two attendants he passed along the corridor between the plank wall that surrounds the arena and the first row of spectators, you could just see his head, which bobbed up and down as if he were on a camel while the silver trumpets announced the espada's moment. As soon as the corrida is over, the six bulls are skinned and somebody says "I want the round steak, I want the tail, I want the tripe," and the experts reconstruct the story of the corrida from those holes, those emptied veins, those burst hearts.

. . . I remember in confusion a line of people stretching along avenues and narrow streets, they were lining up to go into the church to see the Jesus de Medina Coeli, who they say is one of the most miraculous and has a beard with real hair. At two in the morning I walked through the streets of Madrid with some young cinema enthusiasts, and I was delighted by the way they knew our cinema; they knew everything, they said they had learned all the good things from the Italians. The police with their three-cornered hats stand along both sides of the streets, motionless, silent, and the car passes between slowing down the word "hombra" which means the quality of being a man: around Madrid some little villages. Illianas, for example, of one-story houses which look like those places across the Po, immobile since the time of the pellagra; a pregnant peasant woman, her belly so low that she had to hold it up with her hands, walking beside her husband; nuns with coifs so wide we had to step aside for them; a journalist from New York who interviews Lattuada and bites his lip at the name Mangano with a moan of pleasure; the applause that greeted De Sica when he climbed on to the stage of the Rialto lasted so long that De Sica, who was smiling, had to stop smiling and rest a second before beginning again; the four little beds in the infirmary of the Plaza de Toros with mattresses rolled up, waiting; the Madrid of the poor, concealed from the tourist, low vast blocks of apartments (they would be the equivalent of the Roman slums; cuz *borgate,* with a more ancient color); a couple of lovers who drink their half liter of wine as we would drink an orangeade; in the newspapers Padre Lombardi's face on the front page; a man in the hotel who says the Prince de Villa Padierna is about to arrive, "A true hidalgo," he says, "one of the last, in fact the last, he's coming to pay homage to the most beautiful woman in the world, an actress I believe."

. . . "There's the *capéa,*" they said. We went with Berlanga, Ricardo and Canet into the village square, they had put carts all around and the arena was formed. The public shouted as in Madrid, and an old woman who had crawled under a cart to watch from between the wheels for nothing didn't draw back even when the raging hoofs of the bull stamped past her and threw dust in her face. The little bull was already bleeding when a boy in shirtsleeves leaped into the arena and began to *torear,* he must have been eighteen, lean and black, I found out he walked many miles from his village to go wherever there was a *capéa,* he didn't even have the money for the bus, he arrived and flung himself into the arena with a handkerchief, a little red rag, worked the bull and went off afterward without a word to anyone. The official torero hurled himself on the boy to make him leave, you could heard the chonk of fists on his face, but the little bull rushing at them forced them to separate. The alcade cheered the espada, urging him to give the bull the *coup de grâce,* the others made room, the espada clicked his heels; a great silence, the blade slipped along the neck without even scratching it; young men, in clumps, plunged into the arena and enraged the bull, waving jackets, vests, shirts in front of him, the bull went from one to the other with brief, menacing dashes, but they all managed to elude him, one didn't quite climb the fence, he was stuck on it as if on a pin, and if his friends hadn't jumped up and grabbed him, the bull would have run him through. The real torero stood to one side, insulted by the general invasion. Unexpectedly, the bull turned into an empty space that hadn't been there before, between two carts, the little streets leading into the square were also blocked by carts, but the bull put his head under the poles of a cart and raised them, opening the definitive path

44

toward the countryside. For a moment everyone was still, nothing like this had ever been seen before. Women with children in their arms took refuge under a portico, but without fear, a policeman mounted his horse, another his motorcycle, two arrested the author of the joke, many galloped off on their horses, we too climbed into the car, and the countryside filled with people running, every now and then a horse appeared on the crest of the numerous ridges, and bicycles, the bull with the banderillas on his withers like a vase of flowers crossed farmyards and hamlets, past peasants all dressed alike, with cotton smocks and berets, he fled toward his home farm, forty miles away. Passing some disheveled children with big sticks in their hands we heard a shot, at about half a mile's distance, a little group on a ridge waved their arms and a man told us the bull was dead.

THE PHOTOGRAPHER STRAND, April 13, 1953—Everywhere there were peach trees and wild jasmine that cheer even the shabbiest farmyards. At Po, Strand stopped with his camera before a wood that had been cut down, trunks stuck out of the ground a few feet high, and if you half-shut your eyes they looked like men, or rather soldiers on the march. Strand is calm, he looks at the subject then immediately at the sky; he devours images like an anteater. They remember him walking back and forth in the midst of the men in their black capes, observing everything like a revenue agent, he touched the chain on a door, a shaft, and pointed to the line of a wall.

Strand and his wife—she is from Massachusetts and he is also from New England—often consulted the map of Luzzara, the mayor gave it to him. I had never consulted it, and with them I began to know my home town, the names of the areas of the countryside, the farms: la Bruciata, le Samarote, il Cornale. Before I didn't know: what did I love then? If I saw a woodman pass by going to Po, I said summarily: he's going to Po, and instead he's going to give the woods its first cutting or its second or its third, and his interests and thoughts are different in each case.

Strand was waiting outside the saddlemaker's until there wasn't a breath of wind, otherwise the trappings would sway, and for the photograph he wants they must be still as if forever; meanwhile I prayed in my fashion that God would leave me my eyes and not embitter me toward my fellow-man, because in that case it's the same as not having eyes.

45

At Po along the embankment Number 18, a bend in the river, marked by the tallest poplars of my locality, arrives in silence (opposite Dosolo, I saw in midair the smoke that had just emerged from a musket; why a puff of smoke against the black of the woods can give such joy I don't know, first I saw the smoke, and then came the sound of the shot, and the hunter began to run). We met a line of farm-workers who were pushing barrows of wicker-shoots along the bank where they're reinforcing the dikes, they want to channel the Po so that it doesn't strike against the village: they throw down the bundles of wicker with rocks inside, and when there's a good bed of them they build the dike over it. During the last flood, another two inches and Luzzara would have been under water. In the afternoon we went to Boretto, they were dancing on the barge on the right bank, and from the left, exaggerating the trill of their bells, came hundreds of young people on bicycles bouncing over the planks of the bridge, the men at the bicycle park put tickets on each one so rapidly they seemed butterflies, after sitting so long on their bikes, the girls hastily slapped at their skirts to detach their clothes from their thighs. Strand and his wife, arm and arm, danced a few steps.

In the evening we went to see the Marghera Circus. There were no lions, but six young, plump dancing girls, the lights went on and off, "Now the fuses are going to blow," we thought, but it was done on purpose to heighten the excitement; the band meanwhile frenetically played *Cuba Cubà,* and my fellow villagers were aroused when the six girls tried to move their shoulders so their breasts would shake, cupping their hands and turning their heads to one side like Egyptian friezes. Strand laughed; his patriarch's eyes can hold anyone's stare. Afterward I strolled up and down the empty village with Antonio, who wanted to know what neorealism really is. Since tomorrow early I had to go to Vicenza I answered hurriedly: "I want, for example, to tell the story of your day, you who are a worker. I look at you, I study you, but it takes a lot to understand and describe your day, in any case I spend some time, I watch carefully how a person lives—imagine then, after all this work, I don't call you Antonio, but call you Paolo, and I put somebody else in your place; neorealism doesn't put anybody in somebody else's place." He wasn't convinced, but I had already put the key in the door.

In November I was under the arcades, in this same place. I was again putting the key in the door, the priest with his white surplice

46

and black-and-yellow stole was going along with the curate, with two altar boys in front, to collect a dead woman of eighty-five. I believed that in such cases priests saw nothing around them, they go straight on and never mistake the address, I took off my beret and assumed a grave expression; so did the others, then the priest turned toward me from the middle of the road and in his psalmist's voice shouted—since he was rather far away—in dialect: "Cesare, man dies, remember that man dies."

CATERINA, June 27, 1953—After midnight we went to shoot in Via Panama with Caterina Rigoglioso in the meadow where she spent her tearful night of remorse.* The dolly where Maselli swayed in the air was beaded with dew, and the grips' trousers as they ran in the grass were wet up to their knees. The dolly moved slowly down toward Caterina, who was lying on the ground crying, not so much to obey the director as because she was really suffering as she repeated the scene of her mistake. She's the girl who abandoned her two-year-old child at the door of a church, but the next morning ran to look for him, and found him, they tried her, and now she is reconstructing her story, herself, in person.

First the camera had framed in a long shot the bowls-players about 150 feet away: one threw his ball and trotted after it, and the game was over, they put their jackets back on, the light was turned off, and grazing past them the camera arrived at Caterina's sobs, you could hear only the sounds of the generators, the sizzle of the arc lights, which from the edge of the street illuminated the field beyond Via Panama. Maselli's assistant (Degli Espinosa) moved back and forth between the bowls-players and Maselli, and as he passed in front of the spotlights he was illuminated like a moth. Two extras were frightened because they had seen a big rat come out of a bush, so they went to the cabs of the trucks to sleep. At our bright lights the passing automobiles slowed down, and the people inside stuck their necks out like turtles to look for the actors.

A few days before I had seen hatred, when we were shooting in a house in the Trionfale quarter, where Caterina goes up some steps to see a maid—a friend of hers—and look for a job. While Caterina was talking with the maid at the door and the scene was in full progress, a man with white hair started coming up the steps.

* An episode of the film *Amore in città*.

47

Everybody motioned to him to stop, he continued to come up amid cables and electricians; he was marching. He came within a few feet of the scene, and I looked at him pursing my lips like a child pleading, the others on the landing made a barricade of gestures in front of him, without speaking because we were shooting with direct sound recording, it was like a scene among deaf-mutes, but the man didn't bat an eye, he thrust out his elbows and stamped past, pounding his feet on the steps, he had ruined everything and when they muttered after him, he shouted: "This is my house," he clung to this right, to property, since the cinema with its gleaming appearances underlined the fact that he had one foot in the grave.

Maselli dollied, the movement of the dolly was like a breath, just as each of us has his own rhythm of breath, so does everything in a film; each person knows how long he can hold his breath, or hasten it, alternate short breaths with longer ones, two people can't breathe in the identical way; the direction has to be single. "Look." If you haven't something important to say, what are these enormous spotlights they call brutes and the yards of cable that go up the stairs, enter windows, cross courtyards, halls, rooms, and the solemn moment before the sound of the clap-sticks, like the moment that always precedes a birth?

At the domestic service agency in Piazza della Maddalena: I went alone because Maselli had been there before to arrange with the owner and hire the whole works for a day, the owner included. I sat in a corner like a customer and pretended to read the newspaper. There were about ten women, between fifteen and forty years of age, the owner of the agency was on the telephone, and at the same time he talked with them. He said into the telephone that he had this girl from Perugia: "Yes, judge, she's a hard worker . . . about twenty." He turned to the girl from Perugia of about twenty and said that the heavy work was done by the butler-chauffeur, and urged her to take the job. A woman came in without looking at anybody and went straight to the owner's desk. "In Parioli," the owner said to her. She calculated the price of the trams, from where she lived she would have to take four a day, and she went off, refusing the job. A baby was whimpering, and the woman who held him in her arms pointed to me: "Look at granddad," to make him be quiet. Obviously, I thought, I'm seated like a granddad. I tried to sit differently, to assume a pose suitable to the way I felt; I had sat well, as a young man. A lady of about forty wanted a girl from northern Italy. The owner suggested one from the Abruzzi, who put on a polite manner. The lady objected that Abruzzi girls weren't clean. "But I'm really more from Lazio, from around Rieti." "Lazio girls aren't clean either." The redhead raised her voice, she *was* clean, and since the lady looked only at the owner, the girl made faces behind her back to make the others laugh, the others didn't laugh in the hope that the lady would turn to them, but she went out again, staring straight ahead.

The night before we had gone to Ferentino. A peasant woman lives there who kept Carlo, Caterina's baby, for four months. Half a mile from Ferentino there is a clump of peasant houses; the peasants get along on the seven thousand lire per month they make boarding the children of maidservants in Rome, the maids become pregnant, spend a while at the foundling hospital, then find a wet nurse or a "keeper," as the woman is called if she doesn't give her milk, in a village in Ciociaria. There are women who traffic between Rome and these villages and carry babies back and forth on buses. We got there after dark and the truck with our equipment became stuck in the mud. Our automobiles had their headlights on, the grips were quarreling; one took off his good trousers and put on his work clothes in front of everybody, meanwhile a peasant from the houses around there whom we had woken up with our racket told us, as he kept adjusting the scarf around his neck, that he never sleeps because he has an ailment that makes his sperm come out almost continuously and so he's drained dry, and the next day he can't work because he's too tired. Dawn came, and we saw a woman going by with a candle in her hand, it went out. Then another woman combing her long hair outside her door and another two or three with children in their arms, standing motionless and watching us. As the light increased so did their confidence, a young girl had some eggs in her hand, and a little later they were all drinking eggs, and the cameraman made a hole in his egg tapping it delicately against a part of the camera. Maselli had them rip the leaves off a tree in the distance so he could see clearly a girl who, at his command, was to come forward dragging a crying child after her.

OH NO, July 19, 1953—On my feet I'm wearing a pair of shoes three months old, and the heels are still unscuffed. Again today, for that matter, I watched the sunset from my study, thinking: if I could take at least a little walk before the day ends! Sometimes I manage to do it, and I reach the railroad embankment when, over the metallic towers of the Tiburtina station, the electric lights come on with a silvery timeless light of theirs. This day has lingered on the red-white-and-green flag over one of the houses under construction that will deprive me of the last piece of sky; before it came, I had the hills of the Castelli facing me with a very high sky. I've seen these houses rise from their foundations, when the trucks arrive and they noisily throw down wooden poles and iron rods, I've seen them make holes in the earth as wide as graves, and out of each one a worker's head sticks up while he digs inside. Sometimes friends have accompanied me on these brief walks, Maselli and I walked along slowly, and some children had traced out with stones the floor plan of an apartment, some were inside a rectangle, they exchanged visits, and one kept going in and out of a mud puddle, he never felt he was dirty enough, and when he had achieved a maximum dirtiness his older brother started kicking him in the behind; and we said we'd like to go around always with film in our pockets like a pencil; another time, with Franciolini, we decided to make a film in one month on this location, it was a windy day and some blue trucks were unloading dirt to raise an embankment in the midst of which a tall, simple house rose where for a long time there was no electricity so the inhabitants, like exiles, lighted lamps and candles. With Gerardo Guerrieri on the one hand, we got a bit farther, to Villa Magnani, people who dealt on the black market during the war, they lifted the mattresses, and underneath there was sheep cheese and flour; a mother and her six children were patiently transporting dirt from a field with some tin cans to behind their shack so they could plant salad, and they went back and forth for an hour in silence, as rapidly as when you're filling a break in a dike during the flood. A little while ago the workmen on the scaffoldings put down their tools; those on the highest scaffolding where the flag is, though at least two hundred yards from the house, seem huge and you're amazed at not hearing what they say. My friends don't notice, or perhaps they do, my constant glancing outside, while I speak or listen to them, like a mole in reverse, because I am clawing outside to find still a bit more daylight. Once upon a time there was an old man, on the fifth floor of the house opposite, I was walking up and down in my study as usual, and Blasetti was making notes on our conversation, and this was how my eyes met the old man's gaze. The old man was going through a period of troubles over a pension he was having a hard time collecting, and he had broken a leg. I waved

50

to him; he answered, shaking his head, then he pulled out his hands and, with them, he expressed himself clearly, as if to say to me: "I'd like to throw myself out of the window." I made a gesture to him which meant: "Oh no!" For three or four seconds we looked at each other in silence, I repeated the gesture *oh no*, then I went back to pacing up and down, it all lasted less than half a minute and Blasetti didn't even notice it.

THE HARE, August 18, 1953—At Luzzara I went hunting for hare with the gravedigger, the dogs tired before he did. He encouraged them constantly, leaping from one furrow to another with his rubber boots glistening from the damp grass. He bends down to identify the prints of the hare, three triangular dots, the mortal yapping of the dogs resounds, sudden and changed, they have scented the good trail, and he and his friends leave the edge of the field and come forward through the low mist, guns ready, preceded by the dogs' tails in the midst of the grass; the dogs' barking becomes more harmonious, and all of a sudden two rifle shots are heard, a man runs, and a minute later they are all feeling the hare, they say it's a male or a female; is it really the one that a few days ago was leaping around those fields? They blow on the fur to see more clearly where it was hit. They had set me in ambush under a grapevine. The mosquitoes lighted softly on my hands and their transparent bellies swelled with red. I asked myself what size I really saw the moon, a shield of silver, a pre-war two-lire piece, a wheel of Reggiano cheese? Magnani was waiting among the locusts, and from the distance his head looked as if a bit more wind would have made it sway like a flower, on his oilskin cap I saw the day break.

A "MAGGIO," 1953—At three in the afternoon the "maggio" began, on a clearing surrounded by twisted chestnut trees, the spectators made a wall of faces on one side. Earlier the company of actors, poor people from the hamlet of Costabona, had paraded through Cervarezza with music, the plumes of their helmets towering over the whole population. The story was that of Brunetto and Amatore, written half a century ago by Stefano Fioroni, it's his son who acts as prompter, leaping from one actor to the other, like the referee among football players, but we were so taken by the action that nobody saw this prompter.

We couldn't even see the attendant who ran around behind the heroes with the flask of wine, throats soon became dry from singing *ottava rima* with rough, but solemn and impassioned voices. The hero dueled like a youngster, despite his forty-five years, his eyes saw double, and the mirrors spattered over his costume, like those to scare larks, gave off flashes. Full of iron, of shield, of sword, when he embraced the fair, rescued maiden, he was like a stallion with a mare, he put his chin on her shoulder, and she put her chin on his shoulder; their clumsiness lent them grandeur. Every now and then the actors take their handkerchiefs from their pockets, which is a way of expressing grief; poor people here hold a handkerchief in their hand on the day of a funeral even if they don't weep. Some warriors wore sunglasses as a badge of wickedness; in fact they played the Turks. There was a moment of emotion so general that everyone turned towards his neighbor to share with him this fullness of feeling. At the climax I saw the huge head of Attilio Bertolucci, he had come from Parma with Marchi, Ferreri, and Malerba, and three hours later we ate supper with them in the plain, among the crickets, at Sacca di Colorno.

FROGS, 1953—Bartoli talked to me about the men from Dosolo, who don't go out at night with lamps to blind the frogs, they could fill their sacks easily that way, but they are purists, even if they live by this trade: they leave the house in the morning when you can just begin to see, the frog-catcher must be barefoot and hidden. Bartoli uses a spyglass; the frogs stick their eyes out of the green water, you can see only the two little eyes always alert, listening, you might say, for God knows what. With his reed pole, long or short according to the circumstances, Bartoli casts the bait, the frog sees it and cautiously comes out. The bait is made with three little wisps of cotton, you have to shake the pole so that the wisps move like insects and the frog makes up its mind, because it's greedy: the cotton sticks in its palate, the frog immediately realizes the trick and opens its mouth wide to get rid of it but, a fraction of a moment before, the frog-catcher has already given his pole a yank, so the frog is drawn through the air toward its assassin who stretches out his hand and grabs it at the moment it's suspended in midair, before the momentum of the tug is lost and the frog can fall back into the water. Then he throws it, with an automatic gesture, not even turning to look, into the opening of the wicker basket slung over his shoulder. When the frog feels itself pulled by the neck of the pole out of its regal element, it swells as much as it can against the air, to delay the end, but Bartoli's huge
52

hand is already there. They sell them for 250 lire per kilogram, alive, dirty, and 450 lire per kilogram, cleaned: to make up three kilos of clean ones Bartoli has to stay in the ditches from dawn to sunset, cleaning them is a job even if the skin comes off like a shirt, the frog's hands and feet are pathetic because they look like an infant's. They don't earn any more than the braiding-women of Villarotta, where there isn't a doorway that doesn't have a woman sitting at it braiding straw; with the braids the women make straw hats; from the motorcycle you can see against the dark hallways the white of the braids, they have to make seven hundred meters for three hundred lire, and it takes ten hours; it's the peasants who keep the market low with their competition, having nothing else to do during the winter. In addition to man, the frogs have snakes to contend with, the snake always keeps its head back a little ready to spring; it springs and it manages to grab the frog at least by one leg; both of them motionless in the mud, the snake with the leg in its mouth and the frog pulling; when you least expect it, the snake opens its mouth but only to swallow a longer bit of the frog, so that in two or three patient, lightning moves it eats the whole frog. Frogs, as the weather turns colder, go deeper and deeper into the mud; they hibernate. In May they rise again and the male lies on the female's back like a knapsack for weeks, perhaps his function is to press so the eggs will come out, but I think he must experience pleasure even if his relations with the female are different from our way.

WITH MAROTTA, September 10, 1953—Marotta took me to Mater Dei, where he lived in his early childhood. We stepped into the entrance hall; at the back an old woman was twisting her laundry, making faces as if she were strangling the clothes, however, the door was closed, the one to the room where the Marottas lived—had five of them—and where our friend began to store in his archive the sacristan's suit that flapped like a sail (I think that's what he wrote), his mother's tears and, one by one, almost all the objects of Naples.

Marotta was embarrassed when I looked into the *bassi* (the one-room, ground-floor houses of the Naples slums), because he was afraid of displeasing his fellow citizens. One says *bassi,* but each *basso* was different: in one I could see a scrap of a bed with four or five people standing around it, and finally the sheet moved since

---

* Giuseppe Marotta, Neapolitan author, cf. *Gold of Naples.*

there was a sick man under it; there wasn't a table, a chair, only that bit of bed and a lamp in front of a saint; all these dens have a little lamp, and from all these endless votive bulbs the electric company makes money. We went down by the Sanità and Marotta kept on saying: "They're looking at you." That one morning I encountered at least seven or eight people who were counting money —not much money, ten-lire pieces—and they counted it slowly, absorbed. We went through a market of fruit and fish, the mullet didn't lie soft and horizontal in the baskets, but stuck up thickly, vertical—on their feet, you might say. You could see only the circles of their mouths and the little opaque eyes. He mutters: "So the Neapolitans don't work, eh?", and points to some artisans, there was the carpenter with the curls of wood on the ground, which to Marotta as a child looked like the waves of the sea, and a mechanic making metal chairs as they did in the North, the glistening frames of the chairs, stuck one on top of another, suggested a church organ with slender pipes. "Now we'll go to the Pretura, the Magistrate's Court; Ubaldo will guide us." Ubaldo Maestri is a childhood friend of his; he says in the old days Piedigrotta * was more beautiful: "The trumpets would break your eardrums," and the black stripe on the glass panes of a funeral wagon trotting by with the coffin meant that the wagon was put in a lower category so you paid less tax, even the rich put the stripe on, the hearse is the same one, with its gaudy plumes. In the Pretura too, Marotta moved like a man afraid of pushing, with his pitying and distrustful eyes he pirouetted among the people, and I was reminded of his prose piece where he speaks of death in Naples, of bread with salt and with oil; there he seems to reach the pinnacle of sentiment beyond which lies the void, but suddenly another vision opens, like fireworks when a halo of flashes explodes from a spark that seems the last, whitening the faces of the crowd that exclaims in one voice. "You in the North are more cautious in your affection": it's a reproach. A woman was nursing her baby while waiting to be called before the judge, a lawyer was saying his client deserved a ray of sunshine because he was poor and his daughter tubercular, and therefore she was right in hanging their poor laundry on a length of wire even if the wire passed the window of his neighbor the plaintiff, besides, there was no proof of aggression, they traded blows as equals. Marotta nudged my ribs to point out an old man in the crowd: his nose was missing, his eyes were cold and his mouth nar-

* A Neapolitan song festival.

54

row. "They ate it," Marotta said with the haste of prisoners who have to communicate information secretly. In the afternoon I wandered around by myself for an hour and I bought a few walnuts, so as to be able to watch more at my ease: a person who eats in the street, even if he's a foreigner, inspires less awe: nobody ever saw an important personage eating in the street. In Via Sergente Maggiore I had my shoes shined; the shoeshine man wasn't around but like a tom-tom's sound, his name sped in a moment and I saw him arrive from the next alley, running. All of a sudden a boy put a big paper hat over my head, they call it *cantiere* which means chamber pot, and you see plenty of them around during this Piedigrotta period, you really feel as if your head, or indeed yourself, were extinguished inside it, but then you rebel and daylight returns. I asked Marotta if Vesuvius could start erupting suddenly or if it gives some warning beforehand. "It could start erupting right now." In 1908, at Avellino, his father said the same thing to him, looking out, but the ash had already darkened the sky, twenty-five miles of dark sky thanks to the sudden eruption of Vesuvius and the roofs of Avellino, soon weighed down by the ash, began to fall in, and the moans and the processions increased.

From my room I could see the Neapolitan moon, but the racket of the night robbed it of some of its spell; I had seen the universal moon a few nights before at Ansedonia from the top of the ruins, the sun declined and the moon rose, the three slender isthmuses of the Argentario also separated the realms of the red sun and the white moon; we grew smaller because the sky became larger, even the voices grew smaller, the sun disappeared, and a warm light, a pale orange, spread everywhere, it came from the sun which could no longer be seen, it looked as if it were about to turn into noon, and a lawyer started running down the slope as if he were going toward the daylight, but on Bettina's face the tawny coloring vanished, and at the same time a damp film spread over my forehead: it was evening beyond any doubt. The moon turned from transparent to solid, more and more luminous, and I heard the sound of chisels multiply, as in the marble quarries, while I couldn't take my eyes off it, walking home with slow steps.

Marotta raised his head from the sheet of paper where he was making notes for the screenplay of *The Gold of Naples* and said that when he was in Milan before the war, a truck appeared from Viale Romagna and ran over a child. They put a sheet over him, but every now and then they uncovered his face to see if somebody knew him: many schoolchildren came running up, just out

55

of school, and stopped suddenly, mute, as if on the brink of a well, until one of them began shouting and hopping, flushed with satisfaction and fright: "It's Siviero, I know him, he sits next to me, it's Siviero," and he collected greedily, like a spoon, the glances of the bystanders.

THE FAMILIAR FOOTSTEP, October, 1953—The familiar footstep along Via Vasi; for a year I've heard this footstep suddenly, precisely at five o'clock, a calm and resounding tread which vanishes towards the Via Nomentana; I didn't know who it was, and I had only to get up from my chair or my bed, give the Venetian blind a yank, peer through the slits, but my laziness kept me from doing anything until about two months ago. He was a character of about forty who, since he was walking uphill, took long and slow steps toward the leg that was ahead, and he had a face like just-washed laundry, and perhaps it seemed so serene to me because mine wasn't serene; he wore polished yellow shoes, brown socks and an open white shirt, I would have liked to know where he worked, then I forgot all about him.

What a calm night in spite of the rain! One night I saw thieves, four of them, one with an empty sack on his shoulder, and they looked at the windows the way chimneysweeps do or strolling musicians, but as soon as they saw me (I thought I was hidden in the shadow), they fled so rapidly that their crepe soles made the sound of partridges rising from the grass.

AT THE DOOR, 1953—I saw a poor man ring the bell: he asks if they will give him something, and the maid goes to the master and mistress who are eating—father, mother, and offspring—the wife says it's the same old story, "well, perhaps not," the older son says. "The maid says that the man said he has a paralyzed arm," and one of the children gets up with this napkin around his neck to go and see, he pretends to arrange the books in the shelves in the hall, he takes a look at the poor man, he can't make up his mind, more false than true, the father also goes out, last year there was one who claimed to be lame and "Since your sins will surely find you out," he says, his son happened to see the man go off no longer lame and pleased with the two hundred lire in his pocket, now the father would like to feel the man's arm, he asks him a few questions, but in the end he's no wiser than he was before; they don't come unprepared, these characters, some rub their eyes with
56

onion so they'll look as if they're crying. The wife, who has also come into the hall, goes back to the dining room by another door and again expresses suspicion. "Let's give him something." How much? She has a five-hundred note, it's too much, one of the sons has a hundred lire, and the wife says that if you ask her fifty is plenty, while the oldest boy says contemptuously, "What's fifty lire?" The father considers his son's remark stupid, raises his voice, the maid takes the hundred lire to the man who is still standing there.

A MILLION, October 20, 1953—The Po was rising four centimeters every hour. You hear constant shots because the hares, as the water gradually overruns the island, run to the middle which is a bit higher, but there, among the locust trees, the hunters have taken their stand. The surviving hares, as soon as the water has covered everything, will try to swim, but they can never hold out more than fifty yards, and the shore is much farther away. Some boatmen, bent over, with boots up to their crotches, were bailing the rain water out of the boats with huge wooden scoops, and several of my fellow townsmen were standing in silence, leaning on their bicycles, but they became excited because of a piece of wood that seemed always about to be sucked down by an eddy (over there where a big pipe discharges the water of the river, passing under the embankment, into the little valley of willows); "Go on, go on," they shouted, but when it really seemed drawn to the funnel, something helped it stay outside, a wisp of foam, a clump of leaves, something, and they couldn't understand how such a powerful force that would have defeated a strong man with worries and family couldn't master that little stick. The whirlpool was a yard in diameter, a hand's width from those three swirling feet, with a black hole in the bottom created constantly by the water's muddy spirals, there was calm as in another world and the little piece of wood swayed tranquilly. A young man said: "If they give me a million, I'll dive in. I'd be sucked into the pipe right away, and I'd pass under the embankment to the other side in four seconds." They began to argue about the million, some would have wanted twice that much to run such a risk, "You can never be sure you'll really make the pipe, maybe you'd bang your head against the pipe's edge." There were those who would have been satisfied with half a million, provided they could see it then and there, a nice pack of thousand-lire notes, stretched out on the grass like drying clothes.

"The current flows at ten miles per hour," a woodman said after having thrown a branch into the water which vanished into the distance quickly.

During the high water last year the river threatened to break the dikes in four or five places, and one of those places was at the land of a rich man who was not well liked. They were all standing with lanterns on the embankment when they heard an explosion in the darkness; it had broken through. "It's broken at X's. . ." one man shouted, it had broken at the rich man's; applause was heard along the shore.

CUBA, December 31, 1953—You come out of the hot plane as if all the world were hot, but as soon as you set foot on the steps you're struck by the icy wind, and you go forward sideways as if you were pulling a barge, with one hand on your hat and the other carrying with difficulty a suitcase, you see only scarf-ends flapping. We ran to the lavatory at the Gander airport to shave, then at 12:45 over New York I looked for the Statue of Liberty and the skyscrapers, but tied to my seat by the safety belt, I had to be content with what fitted into the square of the window: the most immense expanse of identical little houses I have ever seen, you look in vain for a grassy open space, for children's somersaults—and maybe they exist, though from here it seems there isn't room even for adults, the true inhabitants are only the automobiles glimpsed from whatever height while the human beings can be distinguished only when the plane is fifty yards above the ground. After our landing, the customs men dug their hands into the suitcases as if under a woman's skirts. I stopped less than an hour, and at two P.M. I was already on my way to Havana, sitting next to a young man who was reading a book: *breakfast in Italy is very light and is generally only a cup of coffee or milk and rolls with butter and jam.* Then I introduced myself; his name was Joaquin Garcia, he is studying second-year Italian, he says in Cuba there is very good beer and all kind of drinkables. Meanwhile Miami appears on the horizon with its abstract lights which, however, assume their functional form the lower we fly. At ten P.M. I was shaking the hands of the young people of the Havana club *Tiempo nuestro* where— finally I will say the extraordinary thing, the reason why I took a running jump at the beginning of this entry—the first thing they ask is: "What can you tell us about the Congress of Parma?" *

* A meeting of film people.

58

Lattuada was sitting next to me, all day I had pestered him with my complaints about having left Parma without replying to so many of my accusers, having read my report badly, revised and scrawled over from three in the morning to half past ten (so when I got up from my chair the chair also rose, attached to my behind), having lost a page, and Vigorelli shouting, thinking it was on purpose: "You're a great actor," and then I lost the thread of the whole thing and Sacchi said: "You got away with it," as I collected the papers with the haste of one who pulls up his pants after realizing they're falling down. And on the Atlantic I had written pages and pages to Chiarini as if guilty, but once back in Italy I would publish the first number of the bulletin on neorealism, and now, four thousand miles from Parma or six thousand, when the delegates to the Congress hadn't yet reached their homes, an olive-skinned boy standing next to a black girl asks me: "What can you tell us about the Congress of Parma?" I felt fear and happiness, a desire to applaud and even to cry at the affectionate, unrelenting smallness of the world. I answered (and I would have gladly talked for a year): "I don't know what they decided in Parma, because I left in order to be here with you this evening, but I believe the aim of the congress is to find a meeting-place for the various tendencies, not to make one poetics prevail but to reaffirm first of all the existence of neorealism and examine the possibility of its development, not only in Italy. Every cinema that seeks a close relationship with the grave problems of contemporary man is neorealistic, takes part in this movement with its own methods. Neorealism, now, is the conscience of cinema."

At this point one person wanted to know what is meant by concrete; I answer that concrete means concrete and I am about to continue, but with those eyes on me I have to be precise and I say that concrete is the opposite of that generic love of one's neighbor which some people consider sufficient scope for the film-maker; in Parma, I said, I indicated as a suitable source of inspiration the volumes of our parliamentary inquiry into poverty and unemployment, because through those statistics of suffering—fruit of real time given to the events of others—you enter a new world, a world that is in fact concrete, a world that calls for urgent and concrete solidarity, we ramify into the real life of others, *which doesn't mean talking only about poverty, the unemployed, old people living on pensions, the ill, the strikers;* respectable people will be pleased because we concern ourselves also with theaters, with palaces, with

59

Sundays, with local monuments, with songs. But they won't be pleased. Because they say the object must be changed, whereas they really want to change the moral angle from which it is observed. I said: "The neorealists in Parma have two battles to fight at the same time, a common one for the defense of neorealism and for its freedom of expression in all forms, and a second one for the defense of that specific form each believes best for him to approach reality more and more closely."

We went around Havana surrounded by a cloud of young people, they kept on saying: *una pregunta,* one question, and a student said: "Sweet on the outside, bitter on the inside" (this would be Cuba, in the verses of a Cuban poet). They were preparing for Christmas, and we were all sweating.

In one of those brothels which at first are bars like the others and afterwards you can go to a bedroom if you like, we met a woman who had taken up the profession in Italy in '45, she said it was hard in Italy because of the stairs, every time up and down the stairs, and in Cuba because of the endless nights and the drinking, you have to drink too much. Meanwhile one of her colleagues was imitating Silvana Mangano in front of a mirror.

In Cuba the man in command is Batista, in the streets there are signs that thank him for the great public works in progress which are officially the work of Batista and only of Batista, who says he has three parties with which to govern, yellow (army), blue (police), white (navy), and *pueblo* not at all; the people are in contact with the students, at the University we saw a room with the federation of students, with portraits of all the students' heroes, from Julio Antonio Mella to Ruben Batista Rubio, the first assassinated in '27, the second in '53, by the police. There were piles of refuse and inhabited shacks among these piles and the shacks also seemed refuse; you can't stand looking at them for long, it was the first time this had happened to me; I turned my face aside, as I would cover it with my hands if I were falling. Great wealth and great poverty; the upper classes feel racism and not the national problem, which is autonomy against foreign capital. We went to see Chorri, a black who plays jazz as if in ambush, his lip hangs lower and lower, he stares at the legs of a table, then he shakes himself and seems to be speaking with the Lord, all of a sudden on an off-note he starts out beating two thin drumsticks like a madman on everything: bottles, chairs, floor, cowbell, and those sticks never break, they become two resounding clubs, and you think this guy's

60

never going to stop, instead he stops abruptly, like a skater who, from a dash that engaged all the surrounding air, shifts to immobility with a little movement of his foot that barely raises a flurry of snow from the ice, and Chorri establishes a silence, even if the others go on playing, within which he lies in ambush again. We left Havana on the 9th. I flew over Yucatan with the background of emerald green sea, I had my nose pressed to the window, and I turned only to call the others to look. From below the wing sparse clouds began to appear, like the smoke from children's bonfires, with a puff you could make them vanish, but they grew and joined in groups and perhaps they were preparing a hurricane.

THE FATHER OF THE CERVI BROTHERS,* March, 1954—
You follow the embankment to Boretto, first the roofs of the houses come forward down from the bank as if the rest were submerged, and then the whole houses which still bear the signs where the water rose during the flood three years ago; at Boretto you turn off for Poviglio. "Once there was a valley here," the driver says. The roads are straight and narrow, and the frost has raised them; the gravel crackles under the car. This is the real Po plain, with elm trees to support the vines which the women are pruning, there are more women than men in the fields, with kerchiefs tied under their chins, and over the kerchief a big straw hat, they wear trousers. Some dress completely like men; the men are out at the markets. The little willow and poplar groves no longer had the foggy gray of winter but a foretaste of red, which was consoling—like something certain that has yet to be enjoyed. Twice we left squashed hens behind us; I turned and feathers were flying in the dust and a peasant came slowly to collect the victim; we just missed a family of geese which crumbled into the ditch. The hens save themselves with little flights so last-minute that they manager to graze the radiator with one wing. It is such a great joy to be in the midst of the plain that even a little hill in the distance is an annoyance, even a little rise, nothing like a car along a straight road gives the sense of penetrating into something, you want to be the husband of all the women you see, make love in dialect, pass from one to the other like a rooster, the common dialect plows the right furrow in the heart and in the body of the woman, but the truth is that you couldn't do it with more than two or three because love means a

* A whole family wiped out by the Fascists.

61

temporal quantity to give to each, to listen to them, have them listen to you, create memories together like goldsmiths. The car meanwhile races on, as I live in each of those houses under the eye of the portico, I won't see you any more bent hoeing, and you barely raise your kerchiefed head as I pass, you whose eye I have encountered, and I turn my whole body to continue the contact as long as I can but you are already talking to a child.

Via Fratelli Cervi, I can guess the house, it's ten yards from the road, a woman of about fifty is washing clothes; she answers that the Cervis live here, she must be one of the widows, she *is* one of the widows. From what direction did the black brigades come on that dawn of '43 when they burned the haystack so the besieged men would come out?

Old Cervi appears. I say, "We would like to see the house of the Cervi brothers." He says, "Come in, come in." We haven't sat down before the woman who was washing is now pulling the cork of a bottle. Cervi goes on saying, "Please look around." On one chair there is a basket of home-baked bread half-covered with a cloth, in a corner two little rolling pins which are used to make the dough for noodles roll out finer: the sound of the rolling pins on the wooden plank for the dough is heard early each morning and doesn't disturb the little boy who's sleeping, he half-dreams that today there is food to eat and for us mother and sisters have worked, covered with flour, their bare feet in clogs. There is the picture of the seven brothers, the youngest was twenty-two and the oldest forty-two; there is a picture of the old man with the four daughters-in-law and the eleven grandchildren, taken after the massacre; a credenza with dishes and glasses which can be seen through the clear panels around the frosted glass; two little ceramic dogs and a flashlight; a great diploma dated 1941 awarded to the Cervi family in the national competition for the progress of forage culti-vation, a photo with the partisan group of Campegine; a photo of Togliatti dated November 25, 1946, inscribed; the wedding photo of the Cervi parents, Alcide and his wife, a globe. The globe is cracked because it fell to the floor one day while one of the daugh-ters-in-law was cleaning up and they shouted "Fire," three or four times a fire broke out after the massacre, the blackshirts weren't satisfied and they hoped the old man would leave the farm, and since he wouldn't leave it, they resorted to fire. "But we're not go-ing away from here," the daughter-in-law said, twisting the cork-
62

screw. Were they still threatened? In silence we drank the wine, another daughter-in-law dressed in black came in and told the old man she had to go, and she went off, putting a shawl around her. "I talked with Einaudi," the old man says, "like I'm talking to you, almost three-quarters of an hour, a guard taller than that door came and said, 'The President is waiting for you.'" Antenore's widow still twists the cork and never interrupts the old man. Her son comes in for a piece of bread and she says, "It's time for you to study." In this freshly-painted room the seven Cervi brothers once ate with their wives, their father, their mother. Before coming to a famous place you try to imagine what special mark you will find there; passing her hand over his head, a woman said to a boy that first he must study, though he would like to start farming at once. "Am I right?" she says. The old man wears a long watch chain over his vest, with a heart-shaped bangle which contains the faces of his seven sons, he alternates dialect with a rough and slightly solemn Italian: "I never said, never thought that people should kill; not even when I knew who the informer was."

The old man was at Gattatico for the session in the City Hall when I came back the second time, the daughter-in-law who was preparing the feed for the chickens stood with her hands yellow with meal, hanging, suspended, all the time that we talked, with her was a little son with eyeglasses. Not even this time did I dare look really. I barely took note of tires and inner tubes hanging from a big nail and in the farmyard a little truck with farm implements that I believe belonged to a man who drove around the farms, selling them. Going to the cemetery we met many people coming back, among them a girl on a bicycle with a red flag rolled up on her shoulder. A man from the neighborhood told us that the arch under which the seven Cervis are buried is narrow, one casket, carried by hand, can barely pass through it, but when they wanted to widen it, old Cervi said: "Leave my sons in peace. Enough of this shifting them around." The doctor told the old man not to talk, not to have any visitors during a recent bronchitis, he answered that if people stopped visiting him he'd die right away, because then all of a sudden he would remember everything.

THE MOON, April, 1954—On the ocean, the moon seen from the airplane, its light makes the plane's wing placid, it's one of those moments when you think: just I and the moon in the world and

63

perhaps in the universe, but the man next to me wakes up, puts on his glasses and asserts his right to the moon, I leave it all to him and try to sleep.

FRA RAFFAELE—After Cesena, Rossellini starts driving faster, and when we pass between two automobiles I make myself as thin as possible, and it seems to me that each time we're saved because I huddle like that. Rossellini tells me that Fra Raffaele, when asked if it's true that he sees the saints, answers: "Always"; asked if he sees the Madonna, he answers: "All of her."

FRANCO AND VINCENZO—D'Orazio explains to me a short film of his on perpetual motion, at the next table two barefoot, poorly-dressed boys order half a liter and a couple of pizzas. They are from Tufello. I ask their mothers' ages. They don't know. One says his is almost old and the other that his has some white hair and some black. One says the other's father "lets his family starve to death," their names are Franco, aged nine, and Vincenzo, aged eleven. Vincenzo says that yesterday his father took four hundred lire from his pocket to go play cards and Vincenzo avenged himself by driving a hole in the tire of the old man's bicycle. The two boys come into the city. They live near each other, and on certain nights they hear the werewolf on the railroad tracks, toward the Batteria Nomentana. Vincenzo says it sounds like a train. Franco says "I come home. I give the money to my mother. I drink a glass of water, go to the can and then to bed." They don't agree about anything, "because when we go to the movies," Vincenzo says, "I like films that make you laugh, and Franco likes the ones that make you cry."

COLLABORATION—Cinema is that phenomenon of collaboration where each tries to erase all the traces of the work of the others.

I'M AFRAID, May 1, 1954—I've never been a hero. One evening at the Teatro Valle they sent me away; all citizens without the party badge were sent away. Sometimes I wore the badge and sometimes I didn't. There were plenty of sheep, because many of those who believed they weren't sheep confused the thoughts they had with the actions they performed. In '44 they killed ten boys of my village, partisans, the events of your home town allow you to touch history with your hand. I saw where they shot them, where
64

they tortured them with some others, also the daughter of Casoni who says as she gives me a vermouth: "If I pull up my skirt, you'd run away because of the state they left me in"; one of my friends, also imprisoned there, says: "You could always hear a laundress, she washed clothes all day long and this gave us hope, as if they couldn't do us too much harm while life outside was so normal." I looked to see if anything was still written on the walls, but the lady of the house explained that they had made them whitewash everything, especially the room with the blood where they cut people up, and all of a sudden, beyond the door that opened on the farmyard, I heard a slopping sound, a slamming; we opened the door and saw the laundress. "They used to shoot under my feet to frighten me, what could I do? I made as much noise as I could with the washing so I wouldn't hear the moans of the victims." To a foreign journalist I said: "If I had died before '44 I would never have known freedom," but a man said to me yesterday: "I had to make a certain declaration because otherwise I couldn't work." And besides they don't grant visas for America. I saw a bit of America by stealth going to Mexico. You arrive in one airport and you leave from another; they made me and Marisa Belli climb into a bus. They couldn't blindfold me and in front of me there was a man sitting who never turned around, he must have been a policeman. I tried in haste to collect everything into my eyes. I could say that I saw a hundred people and fifty thousand automobiles; who knows where their owners were, perhaps in the skyscrapers on the other side of the city. I remember some signs: *72 Ave., 91 Ave., Liberty Avenue, Van Wyck,* and small villas half of wood with cardboard faces of Santa Claus at the door and many black women with little hats. Then they shut us up in a room where we had to wait to be called and they forgot to feed us. Sitting next to me was a peasant from Avezzano, about twenty-five who was wearing heavy shoes and no socks. Every now and then he put his arm on his knee in order to look at the watch on his wrist. His luggage was a little suitcase a foot square, naturally tied up with string. He was going to Toronto where some relatives had sent for him. I wanted to look out, taking advantage of the fact that the guard had opened the door for a minute, look into the corridors, look at America, but the guard shut the door angrily. Undersecretary Ermini has eleven children and reads a book a day. I watched him, when I visited him in the name of the Rome Cinema Club with some friends, and he said we have to defend our institutions (of course) and morality (of even more course), in fact we are making a procession on purpose, and there will be no more war. Instead there *can* be war, and afterward Ermini and I will read a few pages of our respective reports. I was Minister, Ermini will say, and I repeated. "Morality! and you didn't shout that it wasn't true, that discriminations are going on because those in charge don't want to be disturbed about anything, since being in charge is even better than screwing."

I'LL TAKE CARE OF IT, June 4, 1954—Suddenly you remember you were supposed to do something, a thing like help your mother, and you haven't done it; the thing you had before you, clearly, that had to be taken up within an hour, an hour later wasn't there, and on recalling, it seems impossible that it should have vanished. A boy of about twelve at the Porta Portese reformatory, 1946 (I had gone there to study the background for *Shoeshine*), was in there not for his own guilt, but because of a mistaken law, and he lived in fear among those young crooks. I talked with the director, he was weary of a hundred cases, how could he keep up with everything? "I'll take care of it," I said. I jotted down the boy's name.

THEY'RE EVERYTHING, June 15, 1954—In Via Merici the taxi-driver says: "680 lire," and while I'm paying him: "How's everything, Commendatore?" I recognize him, he's driven me home other nights. "Don't I look a little thin to you?" He's a robust man, about fifty. "It's love. You, with your line of work, can give me some advice, I've fallen for this woman, and she's fallen for me too, still I have my doubts, I'll tell you the story frankly—you must decide if she's cheating on me or not, you can talk to me like a brother. It's really like a movie story, because I was in a shop buying a pair of shoes and I heard two people talking about her, I didn't imagine that the man trying on a pair of shoes there next to me was the woman's lover, they said she was doing it with the engineer, a man I know. I went to the engineer and I said to him: 'I have to ask you something confidential. My wife is always running around with this woman—you know who she is—and they tell me this woman isn't respectable, you must tell me what you think, if it's true, I won't let my wife run around with her any more.' He says to me: 'The lady seems to me beyond any suspicion.'
66

I tried to figure out the truth, but he was calm. That evening when I saw her (because it's easy for us to meet with the taxi), she walks along and as soon as she sees I don't have anybody aboard, she opens the door and we go out past San Paolo, and if something comes out one day, she says to her husband 'I took a taxi,' because she always sits behind, not next to me. Her husband's a good man, and I'm kind of sorry for him because he rides the taxi a lot too, but she keeps saying he's a fine man and all that, but when it comes to love he's never given her the least satisfaction; he has a good job, as far as food and clothes go, he never denies her anything. If you could see her, she's the sort of woman who'd maybe live with one meal a day and only a mattress on the floor, but she wants a man, she's right. I said to her out of a clear sky: 'How long since you saw the engineer?' She said; 'I've forgotten all about him,' Commendatore, could you tell me some way to find out the truth? There must be a way, because if she's whoring around I'll drop her, and I'll be better off at home too where my son is twenty years old and catches on, I even wanted to run away with her. What's your impression?" I told him to lower his voice because my neighbors sleep lightly, and every time I talk with somebody at the door of the building the people on the ground floor or the floor above complain, with little steps I had led him from the taxi to the door, which I was holding open with one foot. Rather than disappoint him completely, I remained silent as if I were reflecting, then I said: "Think of your wife, of your twenty-year-old son." My advice was inspired by my deep sleepiness, and he said what he wanted to know from me was whether she was a whore or not, I began to close the door, leaving one arm out to shake his hand, I repeated with a confessor's expression: "Think of your son." He wouldn't let go of my hand. He changed his expression; from sad, he turned radiant. "I'll be going now, but you've got to agree with me that women are a great thing." "They're everything," I answered.

WE'RE CRAZY, June 29, 1954—In Milan two months ago I met a boy: "I want to write a script about hitch-hiking," he says. He and his mother have a hard time making ends meet, and he studies at the University, every morning he comes from Cremona to Milan, hitch-hiking. He leaves his house in the morning and stands in a certain point signaling so a car will stop and pick him up, and somebody always picks him up. What faith! He hasn't missed a ride, not one single day. He even made a trip to France hitch-hiking. He isn't embarrassed with anyone. His eyes, authoritatively, dismiss the difficulties of life.

To be sure, we're all crazy, counting blindly on our fellow-man. I saw them open a little bar toward Viale Eritrea, here in Rome, in a narrow street where almost nobody goes by; the opening day, the man was behind the counter, with a dishrag in his hand mechanically rubbing it back and forth on the polished marble, never stopping; I said to myself: "Let's see if anyone goes in, who's the first, it must be somebody who's really thirsty or who wants a coffee at this split second." A man went in. The barman started the coffee machine hastily and gaily, as the steam poured out and the machine began to puff, it seemed the whole bar was about to weigh anchor.

SCARPITTA, Rome, July 17, 1954—With the painter Scarpitta and his wife in Via Santa Maria dell'Anima, opposite the church plastered with posters about the new saints Maria Goretti and Gaspare del Bufalo. The little trattoria has three tables set out in the street, a yard from the motorscooters that pass by with girls sitting behind, their arms around the driver's waist, resting their heads gently against his back as if they were doctors listening to his heart; it's a Saturday evening, that hour between nine and ten in which you see women appear at a corner who have just come down from their house for their date, their dress still hot from the iron. They look around for the man, moving their head jerkily in all directions like hens.

"Here," says Scarpitta, "in '42 the chaplains of the Afrika Corps celebrated mass in steel helmets, it's a German church." This evening he is talking in a low voice for the first time in his life, he says the moon makes him tender as it's soon thrust away from our eyes by the sirocco. He says: "Look at that hand." There is a thin little pregnant woman, but her belly propels her forward and she keeps her left hand open to ward off the air, to cling.

Clotilde says that she traveled from New York to Naples with a group of deportees, gangsters, smugglers, drug-pushers who were coming back under guard to the places they had left to hunt for work; how can you tell who they were? They too said "I'd like my chop well done or rare," "the sea is nice or rough," one had had his teeth knocked out, and his words, half Calabrese dialect and half English, emerged as saliva, nobody could understand him. "You have to tell things without believing they're exceptional or

68

else you offend reality," Scarpitta says, "The exceptional is a vice, we say what an exceptional event, but *we're* exceptional and not that event." Clotilde blinks affirmatively and in her eyes the white is deeper than the black, like the eyes of Negroes: in the dark you can see only the white. "Talk to me about painting," I say. "Aren't we talking about painting?" He looks at his wife to receive waves from her like the waves carrier pigeons feel to give them their route. He exclaims suddenly: "Ah, television." One day he was talking with Turcato and the telephone rang in that nasty way that means long distance, he shouts "Hello," it's Los Angeles calling, he's American even if his father is Italian, his mother is over there, he hasn't seen her for nine years, can she be dead? He hangs for a few minutes on that black and infinite cable like the mole awaiting the funereal sound of the enemy, it's American television, he must take a plane and come to Los Angeles, all expenses paid round trip, he must leave tomorrow, at once, he must bring some of his paintings, as many pounds as he likes, all paid. "Operator, operator, for God's sake, the voice has disappeared. I hate you, operator! I want Los Angeles!" Scarpitta yells like a drowning man, "Operator," he has had a glimpse of glory, he shakes the receiver, chokes it, the voice comes back, it was away just long enough to swallow, they'll bring him the ticket in an hour, yes with his wife and daughter. Scarpitta's mother hasn't seen her son for nine years, and meanwhile he has married in Italy, he is to meet her again on television, "We'll pay everything." Over there they display to the masses a brother who hasn't seen his sister for forty years, God knows where she is, they put the police to work, the newspapers, and they find her, with money she can be found, and in that little square screen there is the moment when brother and sister meet and faint, the aorta might even burst from surprise because they keep the thing a secret so that the emotion will be as huge as possible and everybody cries, in fact it's called the program of tears.

The head of it all handles fifteen million dollars a year, he has long lashes; I've never seen such long lashes, he greases them with a certain oil, because he's as vain about those lashes as a woman, and he says: "You stay back there." Scarpitta's mother is a few feet away, behind those wings; on the little screen they are already showing the first chapters of her life, she is all upset, she knows her son is over there, she can hear the sound of his footsteps on the wooden floor which makes the director go "Sssh."

"Mrs. Scarpitta," the announcer says, "for nine years you haven't seen your son." The mother says she left him when her grand-daughter had just been born, what was the granddaughter like? The grandmother describes her, from time to time they've sent her snapshots: "her nose is like Salvatore's and the hair is Clotilde's and the chin is almost like mine." Then the announcer says, "a little girl something like this! Ladies and gentleman, here we are, the little girl is about to appear under this lighted arch created by the Bishop Company." They push Scarpitta's daughter forward through the arch and the grandmother recognizes her and starts crying.

A 12-CALIBER CARTRIDGE, September 29, 1954—That meadow in the country near Chianciano the first time I went hunting there: the larks flew up on all sides in the rain and the sun was shining, I shot left and right without hitting one of them, I felt very high in that meadow while the rain was soaking me all over, exciting me—I don't give a damn about the rheumatism in my right leg—I went on shooting and moving toward the water which I preferred to the brief dry spaces from shelter to shelter, to feel it dripping down my face; all of a sudden in the wagon-path there was a little bird, so convenient I could have hit it without raising my gun to my shoulder; shall I shoot or not? It was tiny. Even if it flew off with the lark's clever flight I could have hit it with the range of a 12-caliber cartridge, one of those little pellets would do, the kind that slips past your teeth when you eat game and you can swallow it with impunity. I shoot. I run to pick it up and I can't find it, I hunt with mounting anxiety in the damp grass, I search like a dog, I find it, I pick it up by the tip of one wing which unfolds like an accordion and its little head slumps down to one side.

ITALIANS' DIARIES, November, 1954—I was late in realizing that I loved or hated without knowing anything, almost nothing, about the object of my hatred and love, and I began to look and to listen cursing my ignorance of shorthand; "Learn shorthand," I commanded my sons, I would have liked to capture everything with a tape-recorder or other modern instruments created especially for this purpose. "There's no need for art," I said, "I just have to place myself next to two people talking, near a telephone, and then report"; I went to the public telephones in Santa Maria in Via, where each in his stall gesticulates, shouts, or sighs as if they were all mute for me until that time and all of a sudden they were talk-
70

ing and I was listening; before, I had always done the talking. In that postwar atmosphere, I suggested a sheet of questions and answers, everybody was full of questions after the great event, I carried out the first experiment with a character who was unloading furniture, I went up to him while he was resting on a fender and I said: "I'm a journalist, if you have any questions to ask, I'm ready, I'll put you in touch with anyone you like, even the Prime Minister, the Pope, I'll act as go-between, they'll answer at once." He gave me a suspicious look and said: "I don't know what to ask." Don't you ever ask yourself questions you can't answer on your own? There are those who can help you, who have worked hard for years for this purpose. Dozens come into my mind every day, but you get used to letting them go. "Why," he said, "doesn't a man who does my kind of work get a pension?" Regretting then the too-practical nature of his question he asked another: "No, I'd like to know if it's true that ten years from now people will go to the moon." I took his address, he put a table on his back, and I went home like a monk who has been asking alms; instead of walnuts I was carrying in my pockets the questions of truck-drivers, stevedores, mechanics. Seven or eight years have gone by, and I've thought up something kin to that: commission at so much a page the diaries of workers, maidservants, the unemployed, the pensioned-off. I have here the pages of a street cleaner who says that when he is sweeping in the middle of the street he's always afraid of being struck by a car. "I went to clean the steps," a concierge says, "and I see him getting up, dressing, crossing a given space, taking a broom in his hand, and in the silence of dawn I hear the rustle of his broom." If he doesn't breathe he dies, if he doesn't eat he dies, and there is a moment when a shout makes him turn around like everyone else, daylight makes him happy and shadows make him sad, water which pours out cool when he's thirsty also gives him pleasure, and when a woman goes by he is stirred inside like the stag is stirred outside as soon as he senses a presence in the forest, and he would like to be a better man, the wish is vague, if you prefer. "But it's simpler," they say, "it's you who complicate things, he doesn't give a damn about the dawn; he sees his job of cleaning the steps and that's that. You mustn't exaggerate." Perhaps. The people I approached didn't say yes at once; some were afraid of their wives, others of their boy friend or their boss or the tax collector, and they said, "My life is always the same," or, "I don't know how to write"; then they all said yes. In the beginning they're like a forest where you hesitate to set foot because you can't see a path, but as soon as you take one step ("Good evening, may I have a word with you?") the path becomes visible. One March afternoon I was walking with Paladini near Villa Magnani, where the trains go by. At the sight of the signalman I thought: in a collection of diaries the diary of a signalman would be a good idea. The signalman was far from supposing that in a minute's time I was going to say to him: "I am X, I would like this of you." A train went by, the man raised his flag, went into his booth, came out again at once wiping his mouth with his hand. He must have gone in for a drink. I said hello, and if I hadn't said it and had gone on my way like all the others who bent down hastily to pass under the bars after a quick glance to left and right, my faith that many more things are possible if we speak out would have been undermined, at least for that day. I was eating some pumpkin seeds I had just bought from a boy on a bicycle, he was selling them to the maids who take the children to play on the railway embankment, I offered the man some in the palm of my hand and I came straight to the point. With simplicity he answered: "I have plenty of time to do what you want, this isn't my real job, I just help out my father-in-law." "This evening I'll send you a fresh notebook and a pen," I said to him. One day Gian Passeri, whom I called to lend me a hand in this collection, brought me seven people: there was a maid, a tram conductor, a mechanic; we chatted together and the tram conductor said he thought the diaries would be useful if people wrote down absolutely everything sincerely, the mechanic said it had done him good to examine his affairs for a few days calmly for half an hour before going to bed, and the maid was afraid her employers would find out and would say she was crazy. They exchanged glances, exclamations, as if they all belonged to the same family. We agreed unanimously to suppress all names if we published them. You never know, a creditor, a superior: "But if you want," they said, "put them in, we haven't told any lies." Yesterday evening I wanted to ask for five or six days of diary from one of those men who sell gasoline in the handsome glass kiosks that have multiplied along Via Nomentana, the stretch between Via XXI Aprile and the Batteria is dotted with these little stands. When I come home on foot, after midnight, there are no longer those mysterious, ancient zones of shadows, but a modern glow, very deceptive, in the midst of which (lights, metals, forms) it's hard to rediscover the essence of things. The attendants sleep inside their

72

festive, illuminated kiosks, the space must be about three square feet and you can't sleep lying down, but standing like horses or seated; one had his legs sticking out of the little door; another was huddled up like a foetus and another was on the floor with his face at the glass, his nose flattened against it with a trickle of saliva coming from his mouth, another looked like a saint's body in a glass coffin. I didn't wake any of them, but I stopped to talk with one the next day, and he told me of his battle for sleep, he barely shuts his eyes when a car stops with a scream of brakes and he has to jump up.

Now you won't be surprised if, from these diaries, I want to make cheap booklets with twenty or thirty diaries at a time, one booklet of schoolteachers' diaries, one of farm workers'; or else one all of workers in the same factory or inhabitants of the same slum or of priests, of employees in the same ministry, policemen, soldiers, there is no end of combinations—diaries of a month and of one day and of a single event to see the intersections, the indexes, the influences. They should be read in the schools, in schools they began always on the second floor and never on the ground, you never find in a textbook one line that explains what democracy means.

THE OLD WOMAN (1955)—It is 7:30 P.M., the little old woman attracts everyone's attention, she doesn't want to stay on the plane which is going to cross the Atlantic, she shouts in a lugubrious voice: "Ohohohohohohoh," she must be over eighty, on a suitcase I can read her name, Cristina Lidtsks, Yugoslavian, skinny with veins like tubes in her big hands, she is alone, they stick her in her place; they set a big suitcase beside her which shuts her into a cage, the stewards forget her and smile left and right, a Vietnamese girl looks at the old woman with indifference, a priest with the Heart of Jesus in white on his black cassock begs the old woman with his eyes to behave herself, the old woman bangs her head against the air which means "mind your own business"; meanwhile the plane takes off, she screams, and I play the trump card: "Cristina," I say, and I motion to her at the same time to keep calm, my knowing her name stops her for a few seconds, she stretches out one leg against the suitcase, she pushes, sharpening her chin, she tries to climb under the case, there is only a few inches of room, then she resumes her dry moans, moving her head around at a faster rhythm like a weasel looking for space to flee in, she no longer has the lovely tears that bathe the cheeks and the young tongue that licks

73

them savoring the salt, the old woman is without liquid, her gaze without affection, suddenly she becomes sweet in sudden inspiration, she begs me with gestures to help her get out, I stand up, it's the most I can do. I hold out my arms and murmur, "Cristina," then shame, irritation, the priest says it's the aurora borealis; in fact outside the window I see a whitish stripe with jagged edges like the diagrams of acoustical vibrations, the Niçois steward comes and says he'd like to work in the movies, I explain the usual things, it isn't enough to be a good-looking boy, there are thousands of handsome ones who have been moldering for years, they turn out the lights, only my little light stays on, I take notes on the back of the menu with words that annoy me:—*coeur de palmier mimosa, pommes noisettes persillés,* my mother also has a dark gray topcoat like the old woman, who is almost elegant with her little hat, this elegance which means a thought about each thing you wear jars against her non-thought, her intermittent "ohohoh," now she is silent, I am already in Rome with my thoughts, all of a sudden something happens: in the midst of the aisle the old woman goes by rapidly, held by the Niçois from behind in that way which prevents anybody held like that from turning around, one hand on the collar of the coat behind the neck, another on the behind, they vanish like a vision, the old woman freed herself from the trap where they had put her, I saw her again only at Paris; for the rest of the trip she had been silent in the dark, at Orly she was in a wheelchair in the midst of the expanse of luggage, looking around suspiciously, a little later they loaded her on to another plane, a hostess arrived to sort out the passengers, the old woman got in the way where she was, the hostess gave the chair a little push and it rolled forward a few yards, for a few feet it tilted to one side, it stopped, leaving the old woman with her face to the wall and her back to the other people, somebody surely calls her granny, auntie, mama, sister-in-law, if they shipped her off there must be somebody to receive her. An airplane was leaving and two women ran to see it from the terrace, it was going to Mexico, and my mind filled with white and yellow butterflies striking the windshield, hares leaping far from the strip as we landed, as if they were jumping over so many little bridges, burros among the cactus with their slender legs, fragile compared to the huge head which seemed swollen as they had to carry it forward, and horses seen from many places, from behind at times they are only a line, but just

74

one movement and then you see horse, or you see only the four broad legs since they keep their head down looking for grass, and thousands of frogs no bigger than horseflies which dived into the puddles like a single frog as we drove by while a Totonacan peasant dressed in white was a patient walking along a green ward.

FROM BOLOGNA TO REGGIO, May 2, 1955—From Bologna to Reggio I amused myself by thinking of nothing, I only watched the traffic along the Via Emilia. A little rise, as we approach, flattens like a drawbridge being lowered, and when we pass over it it's a plain. You never see who's in the cars after dusk. You would say they proceed by themselves with their huge lights that want to blind you. Now they'll turn them off, you hope, but they don't turn them off, they come forward widening their eye further and further and they humiliate you; it's a silent transit of colossuses which grow, as the roof of your car sinks lower and lower over your head. In the intersecting of the strips of light a bicycle's wheel flashes or legs pedal like pistons. One car from the distance illuminates another that precedes us. In the rear window the form of a girl is outlined as she leans toward the driver. After a truck passes, overloaded with gleaming fragments of tin cans, we plunge again into a stretch of darkness, missing a man who is walking hastily, where does he have to go at that pace which no longer belongs to our species? These wayfarers are probably on their way to have a chat in a nearby house, they look frightened, it's an underworld far from the other, all auroras, which the automobiles announce to one another.

At Reggio I read a page written on January 14, 1953: ". . . The Government has acquired the vice—it's a vice by now—of being afraid even of what shouldn't frighten it; it's annoyed by things that in '45 nobody would have imagined could annoy a government after Fascism. A chain of censors in the body of the nation has been created, so long—the producer, too, has become a censor—that the Government can even say 'It's none of my affair' because they can cover their tracks before you get to them."

Censorship reminds me of that game whose name I don't know, played by soldiers. One, selected by lot, turns his back on the other players, usually eight or nine of them. Suddenly he is given a violent slap and he turns around at once and has to guess who gave it to him. It isn't easy, because he sees before him only angelic, innocent faces, his friends, like Chinese, standing there smiling, holding one finger in the air, and the victim would almost say: "It was a dream. . . ."

POLICEMAN AND BRICKLAYER, May 3, 1955—Last month I happened to overhear a long dialogue between a bricklayer and a policeman, near Santa Emerenziana. Michele Gandin was also there listening. I'll copy out a bit of it. Policeman: "They won't let me work more than thirty hours overtime. So how can I make a living? I have to do other jobs, on the sly." Bricklayer: "You policemen still get along better than we do." Policeman: "Do people hate bricklayers?" Bricklayer: "Not me, they don't." Policeman: "They hate us: it's a real occupational hatred. So they have to pay for it, this hatred. But don't complain; when you're sixty, you have your Social Security." Bricklayer: "My father gets thirteen thousand a month: what's he supposed to do with that? You guys, when things are tough, just lay on a few more fines." Policeman: "Can't you understand that we're not the ones who pocket the fines? It's the chiefs who get the percentage. They sit in the office and we have to go around and argue with people." Bricklayer: "What we need is a strike." Policeman: "We could do that by applying the laws. You know that if we applied the laws we could paralyze the traffic of Rome, of the world?" Bricklayer: "Get moving then." Policeman: "Don't think our job is easy. Every time we have our x-ray examination, there are seven or eight TB cases. When do we sit down? Always on our feet, like waiters. You know how much we get for an hour overtime?" Bricklayer: "How much?" Policeman: "Guess. When they let you do an hour overtime, it's like they're making you a present, and then at the end of the month they hand you eighty thousand lire." Bricklayer: "But it's a steady job. Rain or shine. You're never going to starve to death." Policeman: "What kind of talk is that?"

VANITY AND AMBITION, 1955—Vanity and ambition are sometimes mixed up, and my intelligence judges such collusions severely, but as in dreams your hand can't clutch the jacket and hold the person who is going away *to see him.* Once, looking at the moon, I said it resembled me, and in fact when it isn't full, but egg-shaped, with the two spots that look like eyes and a smaller spot that's the mouth, it recalls the caricature Al made of me. They often write that I'm good, so then I do some good deed more to be

76

true to the role given me than through any real vocation of mine. In this, I have an iron will, and I believe that other people's opinion has now achieved the value of reality. I long for solitude, but if my telephone doesn't ring for half a day I feel like an orphan; I have to be deceived continually. I don't like working, and I work all the time so as not to work the next day, and somebody to slap me on the back and encourage me is something I need all the time. I display strength, as if in everything I had to set a record: "I haven't slept for two nights, sixteen hours at my desk."

There is an athletic, not a spiritual, quality in this. I possess a kind of energy so happy to exist that often it wants *only* to exist —and in that way you become aggressive and offensive. In the midst of so much turmoil, suddenly enlightenment: I've got it all wrong. You keep still for a moment, even if this happens in the street, something decisive seems about to happen, but a tram, an itch, makes you forget everything and you start running again. "This isn't life," a woman said to me calmly, making a chill run down my back.

WE WERE ALL HUGGING ONE ANOTHER, January 29, 1956—In Cuba, during a fiesta, I don't remember for what Virgin, in a house in the Regla quarter toward midnight: in the first room men and women were dancing to modern music, in the second some children were asleep in their clothes, on a big bed, in the third a black woman writhed, surrounded by other blacks who sang a short phrase over and over again, always the same. Two black men squirmed above the others, their sturdy arms never stopped with those cylindrical instruments swollen in the middle, covered at either end by drumskins and decorated with garlands of colored grain so when they shake, the noise of pounding rain is heard. I leaned against the door for three hours; I looked. On the floor there were some ritual dishes with chicken feathers and blood; instruments hung from the ceiling, the way hams are hung in our farms, like those of the two black men, stained with dried blood. I wanted to buy one, but they wouldn't sell them because they're holy. In a narrow corridor they were stewing the chickens they were going to eat as soon as my friends and I had gone away, sated with the sight of black women between fifty and sixty falling to the floor possessed by holy spirits. One girl never took her eyes off the old woman who was trying to be possessed, she shared in the genesis with chanting and little jerks, it seemed some invisible person was

77

tickling her. The fact that I was white and stood out in their midst didn't distract anyone from waiting for the miracle. One candidate had been shaking her whole body for fifteen minutes like someone who is about to reach a sexual climax and then can't make it and therefore increases the shaking which becomes frenzied, but in vain; finally she drew back, humbly, pale, with nausea. The spirit had explored her like air, was about to enter her, but then had preferred to stay outside waiting for another woman who was more suited to his form.

Almost stealthily, one woman moved to the center of the room, her eyes half-shut, she began to move sinuously. She tried gently to stretch her body as far as possible to make room for the thing that was to come; the more the rhythm increased the more she breathed only through her nostrils—that bed-like breathing you hear from a hotel room when two are making love, revealing their presence only by their breathing. She had white hair and thick lips, she must have been a cook, a housewife, with a big bottom, low breasts that swayed from one side of her belly to the other. She passed from an obscene movement, where her body showed its real age and even more, to a graceful movement, a flick of the hips or the shoulders which made a shudder run through her body and rejuvenate it. She fainted. When she reopened her eyes, she was returning from a secret colloquy, delicate, despite the drool at the corners of her mouth. She went around hugging all present. She carried herself about like a monstrance, ugly thongs held up her stockings; she had pulled her skirts up as soon as the spirit entered her, to make male movements, since the spirit that possessed her was male, she expressed him with masculine poses including that of Oriental dancing men when they come forward with their legs bent as if they were seated and their knees pointing outwards. We were all hugging one another, even us foreigners with a show of unreflecting participation, in the other room an old crone also fell to the floor. The blacks' eyes flashed at once toward that room, the crone got up immediately, supported by somebody, wagging her head as if she were shaking off water. So there were two Chosen Women who moved about the house continuing to hug everyone in silence, and all allowed themselves to be hugged gladly because it was the spirit himself who embraced them. Meanwhile in the first room the couples glistened every time they danced past the image of the Virgin surrounded by twenty or thirty little light bulbs and silver paper as in Naples, there they dance as frequently as we sing at
78

home. At the end of a boxing match the victory of the Cuban boxer was hailed by the notes of a band, and four or five people carried into the ring the statue of the Madonna who protected the local champion, they held her up before the photographers over the head of the victor, but meanwhile they began to sketch a few dancesteps, I would say without being aware of it, like breathing.

HAPPINESS, August 25, 1956—I feel I've never touched happiness the way I did the 5th, 6th, 7th of this July. Leaning against a column of the arcades in Luzzara after midnight, talking about nothing with my fellow-townsmen, little by little I let myself slide down till my behind touched the ground, the cool pavement, and my suit was finally covered with its dust. Go slowly, I said to the hours, simply to enjoy the passing of the flotillas of bicycles in the night and the threat of a thunderstorm, toward the Po you could see some poplars beginning to move; motionless, they had seemed one object, but as the wind rose they were transformed, expanding into a multiplication of leaves, or tightening into nothing but trunk, and with the same rhythm as the wind, the cries rose half joyous and half frightened, of the little girls in the courtyard, without looking in I could see them get up and slam from one wall to the other, but so light inside that they couldn't hurt themselves.

When, in the empty streets of Luzzara after dinner, you hear the sound of a woman's clogs as she goes for an ice-cream, even the most absent ears are pricked up and through walls the eyes see the handsome sturdy legs which have emerged from homely baths in washtubs. I sit outside my house on a wicker chair and I rehearse old age: will this doing everything only with the eyes be enough? Perhaps yes, because somebody takes care of you like a servant and shifts things so that when you're fifty they have one look and when you're sixty, another.

In these three days I also went to Pomponesco, in the tavern against the embankment we all talked so much we didn't even let the song of the crickets enter. Only when we came out there was a moment of silence in the 18th century square, we all scattered in the darkness to make water, and Saturday, young Marchesi broke the awkwardness saying how Negri insists the pleasure of life lies in eating *cappelletti*, a little chicken with its bones well broken, then walking past the café with a toothpick in your mouth (from holding one in his mouth, Negri has carved a niche in his lip), staying there until a woman goes by and as she rapidly adjusts her

79

clothes makes a "click" with the elastic of her garter-belt which slaps against her thigh. Once at Guastalla there was a character, a kind of lawyer, who had working for him a humble clerk, taciturn and devout. The lawyer was stingy, but he set great store by being respected and one day he said to his clerk, who is still alive and whom we'll call Bottazzi: "Bottazzi, I'm going to offer you a coffee every day, at the café in the square." Bottazzi looked at him wide-eyed and the lawyer explained: "I'll say to you: 'Bottazzi, would you like a coffee?' And you'll say: 'No, no thank you, sir.' If I should insist, you repeat: 'No, sir, no thank you.'" Everyone admired the generosity of the one and the discretion of the other. Every time the lawyer changed the tone of his voice as he made his offer and Bottazzi also changed the tone of his refusal. At the slightest gesture, if the lawyer pointed his thumb toward the coffee machine, Bottazzi would shake his head promptly; the lawyer arrived at using the diminutive: *"Un caffettino. . . ?"* he would say. One time some joker said: "Accept it, Bottazzi!" and others joined in this encouragement, he began to ward them off, you couldn't see the lawyer any more, they all crowded around, they shook him, they raised their voices until he said: "Yes." Afterward, in the office, the lawyer looked at him in silence, shaking his head: "This isn't the way, Bottazzi, this isn't the way. . . ."

. . . Yesterday at Luzzara, while we were arguing, Flaiano and I saw a man's long arm emerging from a grille twenty yards away from my house, clutching the waist of a girl standing on the sidewalk, the girl wriggled to free herself, the arm moved like an eel, it had a life of its own and it was only after I shouted, at the moment when the girl was biting the arm ("Cut that out!" I cried), that the arm disappeared and a young man's black head appeared and I looked away because I had been stupid to intervene.

. . . I was at Po one Sunday morning in a poplar grove a few yards from the water, and over the flames of some willow twigs my friends were frying the fish that had just been caught. Some children were watching us as if we were gods. The salt dissolved at once on the gilded backs of the fish which, when served, made grease marks on the yellow paper, the bottle of white wine moving over our heads filled the glasses so quickly that we could lift them to our lips with the foam still high. We couldn't see the mosquitoes that brought sudden red stains to the cheek of one or the other of us in the midst of the rays that shone down on all sides, clear or veiled amid the foliage, perpendicular, oblique, so that my friends' faces moved

80

from unreal, flaming zones to the calmest normality. The evening before, there had been flashes of lightning for three hours without a sound, but faster and faster, so the dark moments didn't exist any more, toward Mantua a huge cloud against the immensity which was first black with edges of fire in the lightning, then white with black edges, and the release of water never came, we were in a kind of intermediary life.

VERDI, October 21, 1956—Inside the Villa Sant'Agata where Verdi worked for thirty years, the silence is broken by the malicious hieroglyphics of the mosquitoes, two visitors have gone through the exit gate on tiptoe rather than give a tip to the caretaker. I felt pleasure at seeing a grammatical error in one of Verdi's letters and in another how he says to his farm manager: "In well-run farms, straw and fodder are produced at home and money isn't spent to buy them." There is a decayed spinet and a few real hairs of his beard cling to the plaster death mask, but I feel nothing ridiculous or macabre, not even in the heavy plush and the commemorative vellum scrolls from the Italian towns that hymn the praise of the Swan of Busseto. In the midst of these old things one feels only the infinite satisfaction, typical of this plain, in praising a man. Toward evening I went off from the Parma plain leaving behind me the dust of the Fiat and Fahar tractors, and the hens like so many half-moons pecking at the smoking compost heaps. The automobile went through civilized landscapes seen perhaps by Verdi; who knows if then there were these dahlia hedges outside the peasants' houses which hold the sun even after the bicycles have turned on their headlights? With hasty hoes groups of girls broke the chunks of earth, too big, turned up by the plow, some wear gloves during this work so that afterward their dancing partner won't feel their hands are rough. When we had passed Parma, darkness arrived and an occasional gust of fog. The people in the fields work even at night, the motor of a plow made a grim sound, you couldn't see plow or driver, only the two rocking headlights. They save time because there aren't many machines and the sowing season is about to end. The rain will arrive suddenly, we hope, to knead the seeds well in the furrows. At the Reggio Emilia market last Tuesday I saw harrows displayed in a shop window like jewels. I have never stayed so long in this neighborhood, three months in a row, and each contact seems emblematic to me. I try to take my place in the habits and most common, vulgar customs, regretting

81

my delay in acquiring the local merits and defects, therefore I plunge rapidly and gladly into the abyss of songs and curses, beating time on the tables of the taverns whose walls are decorated with calendars from fertilizer companies and posters calling up boys born in 1935. The women vibrate like guitar strings at these male exclamations.

CHILDREN, November 20, 1956—Today, November 19, has been for me the children's day, or rather yesterday, if I want to be exact, since it's now three o'clock in the morning. It began with the usual new-born or almost new-born babe, he always wakes up abruptly and begins to cry—he lives under my bedroom—immediately the mother, then the father, talk to him, their voices first sleepy and cross, then distinct, jesting, you hear heels, like bangs on a drum, of somebody crossing the floor who hasn't put on slippers but doesn't want the cold of the tiles under his soles of his feet, then the clack of the blinds pulled up a few inches to see how light it is: there is still the moon with icicles. They manage to put the baby back to sleep with his bottle, and afterward, sometimes, they make love, then there follows a silence so deep it affects everything and seems another kind of time—longer, among other things—until the moment of the general rising around me, below, at either side, above, with noises that dart from here to there and I can no longer tell where they originate.

At eleven, I was dragging a garter, hanging from one sock, all around the house like a chain and I thought: I'll never want to bend over and hook it, and instead you suddenly find yourself with your foot on the arm of a chair. At noon I was in Largo Argentina, in front of walls covered with drawings by children of the village of Nasino, near Albenga, who paint suns, not the way Rouault sometimes does to create a luminous nail on which to hang a heavy picture, but whirling or dripping suns over the good and the wicked (this phrase recurs often in the simple explanations the schoolchildren give their work on the back of the drawing). Once again I feel the desire to make a film in which the oldest character is seven. . . . Yesterday for the second time in ten years I saw an immense cloud of birds in Rome. The person with me was walking ahead to reach our car, afraid of being caught later in the rush-hour, and in vain I called after him: "Look," until finally I said it to a stranger, who was grateful to me. The cloud transformed itself into the most varied things and its vastness diminished with

82

the suddenness of the changes, it had the frequent shifts of color of a leaf in gusts of wind. Transparent, in a flash it became black, from black it turned into a dot; the eye sought it hopelessly in the sky, on the Tiber which was the point of reference. But there, it was formed again and penetrated into the blue with a swirling eddy, then suddenly it came down, first like the ballast of a balloon, then gradually losing intensity until it became confused with the air itself, but it reappeared, it had much of the quality of the raincloud that swells up, it also seemed a distant parachute that cradled itself as it descended, but a flare made it cross the whole sky with the speed of a glance.

MEXICO, December 13, 1956—Mexico is about six times the size of Italy. "We are too far from God, and too close to the United States," they say.

In 1955 women voted for the first time, and I arrived there during that important summer, the women were in line, dazed by this new action, they stretched out their hands with the ballot to put it in the box in a way that recalled their gesture when they touch the holy-water stoup with the tips of their fingers.

That Sunday I rode around for a long time in a taxi. There are lots of taxis, never parked in ranks. They keep driving around to pick up a fare on the wing, like hunters. The cars are new, shiny, the colors taut, on the verge of being smashed. The foreigners, including me, along the Avenida Juarez, walked with their hands laden with shawls, blankets, baked clay objects painted by the poor people, to carry beyond the border to our comfortable houses, and it seemed to me that when we encountered one another we lowered our eyes for a fraction of a second feeling like thieves, nice ones perhaps, but still thieves, through our complicity with that vast commerce from which only a few coins end up in the artisans' pockets. The Mexican is ready, like no one else, to bend over when in the *mirada del blanco,* the white man's gaze, he senses the ancient flash of the master, but as soon as he senses that the other man considers him an equal, he expands like a fish taken from a bucket and put in a lake, and all the things I know I have learned in fact from the dozens of people I stopped in the street, with the help of Gamboa—Fernando Gamboa—my guide on the trip.

With Italians they are affectionate, they ask you to speak. It's our speech that they like; they repeated one of my words like notes. Instead they don't like the Americans, the *gringos.* I asked some children in a school who were the most beloved patriotic figures; they all shouted *"Niños heroes de Chapultepec,"* the child heroes of Chapultepec, an episode of the war against the Americans in 1847.

Compared to the Spaniards', their way of reasoning is more psychoanalytic than historical; in their hearts they are against the old Spain, against the *conquistadores;* an Indian who has none of that blood in his veins would perhaps be entitled to this, but it's surprising in the mestizo, who is half-and-half: the mestizo adores in himself only the mother and not the father; for some this would be a proof of the Mexican's natural tendency always to protect the weaker, the Indian part, represented by the mother who was raped by the father, Señor Hernando Cortez, when he arrived with his white horses. It was Sunday then, and everything was sustained by color, the Mexicans need color to get through the day. The color of colors—the most beloved one—is *tlapalli;* it is our bright red, our *solferino,* as bloody a color as the battle of the same name, they make it from the cochineals that feed on the nopal, the national plant onto which, one morning in 1312, the eagle plunged down from the sky to clutch the serpent, as you see in the Mexican coat of arms, and therefore, according to the prophecy, the Aztecs in that wondrous but inconvenient place founded a city on pilings which is today the capital, 2400 meters above sea level.

A poor peasant was wandering around the streets with a turkey to sell, thrown over his shoulder, suddenly the turkey opened its fantail and his owner proceeded like an ancient warrior with a halo of feathers; kids ride on bicycles decorated with paper flowers and ribbons like Sicilian horses, and in fact these velocipedes also have tails behind their seats, of real horsehair; the vendors of tickets for the daily lotteries pursue the automobiles waving their broad red or blue chances like flags; infants, in pots, in baskets, are everywhere, in the markets, their mouths constantly in search of the nipple which escapes them because the mother keeps moving about to arrange the scanty fruit even more harmoniously in front of her or to comb her hair, this combing and recombing is continual as if the saleswoman wanted to renew her hope that afterward the buyer will come; a procession with a little girl on a truck playing the Madonna and four children at her feet, angels, dazzling with their hands joined in an attitude of prayer, and since the procession lasts for hours, the angels' mothers secretly slip them a piece of fruit, so we watch furtive bites followed by pious re-clasping of

84

hands; a little crowd around a holy man who for a few centavos will give you packs of orations as he constantly mentions the Pope, and at every mention of the Pope they all take off their hats; the billiard-players in the long halls, the dark faces disappearing; it seems that only their hair moves in that green atmosphere (at Tehuantepec the women came forward raising the dust with their bare feet, their hair was loose over their shoulders and they wore long blue and pink satin skirts that swelled and they swayed in them; at Papantla, land of the vanilla that costs so much labor to those who harvest it, the Totonacan women wear a dress that was once of satin, today it's of nylon, it resembles priests' embroidered surplices, this vaporous and virginal whiteness is set ablaze with necklaces that are fluorescent like the ads on the superhighway when your headlights strike them).

Two Taraumaras at Chihuahua, a tiny, minute Indian bridal couple, about twenty, she wearing as many garments as a cardinal, gaudy, and they were begging; they had spent four or five days coming on foot from the mountains, they're great walkers, with the greatest endurance and speed, they hunt the stag pursuing him in relays, it's a tribe that's vanishing little by little, from time to time public opinion is moved by them, but public opinion is cautious on the Indian question, it dismisses all racial questions, asserting that *"Cuando el mestizo es pobre es un indio, cuando el indio es rico, es un blanco."*

Sitting next to them on the sidewalk we badgered them with questions, they answered reluctantly and didn't want to give any information about the place they came from. My friend got them to confide that it's best for us not to go to their native villages; nobody is welcomed there. They spoke without looking us in the face. Afterward I followed them, they walked side by side; her hand and his touched every now and then as they went along until he hooked one finger and held her hand fast.

That Sunday couldn't have been clearer, and in a clear country like Mexico this means light, the kind God found good and separated from the darkness, calling it day. In the immense Chapultepec park the middle-class citizens of the capital strolled by, an endless roundabout of cars tailing one another, filled only with girls, five or six per car, as in showcases; from the opposite direction the men came, also packed into automobiles, they smile or exchange rapid words, but are unable to stop, but then they meet a second, a third time, to conclude their conversations.

On all sides I ran into whole families that migrated from one quarter of the city to another for their Sunday amusements. The family is the pivot of Mexican civilization, even if the male is as adulterous as we Italians are, or even more so. One boy, not the least vulgar and also in love—here they marry so young—had gone off to make the rounds that very night with his friends, his wedding night, rather than stay in bed with his wife: this was to assert his authority at once.

Long lines outside the movie-houses. I was reminded of opium dens because, while they waited, some of them drank without thirst, sensually turning the neck of the Coca-Cola bottle in their mouths. After the United States, Mexico comes second in the world in its consumption of soft drinks, and Coca-Cola and Pepsi Cola, with their advertising, are a part of the landscape.

On foot I walked along the Calle San Juan de Letràn, a kind of extended Pigalle; this is where their satire is born, the so-called *chistes,* and the comedians attack anyone at all and risk jail, the criticism is based on basic straightforward feelings, the Mexican is always against *él que gana,* those who earn, in an instinctive sense of outraged justice, at every change of Viceroy they were ordered: "Be silent, you are made to be silent," informers were always active among the Indians to snatch even the rare words they uttered, then that instinctive discretion about speaking in public grew up, or about speaking of oneself; "The less they know me," the Mexican says, "the less they can harm me." During parades, of whatever kind, they throw noisy fireworks in the air like flowers, but words are spoken in a low voice. In a market I heard only whispers, murmurs, you turned and it was some girls calling your attention to their wares: polite, even melancholy summonses, with the tip of the tongue against their teeth.

Rivers of people flowed toward the bull arena or entered the *fronton,* that is to say the pelota court. There are some superb *frontones,* I saw one where the players are all women, sturdy Basque girls with black hair who roll on the floor as the game demands and display their legs, but nobody is aware of their sex any longer, they insult the girls if they make them lose their bets: *burra, desgarrada, bruja.* As in Italy, the vocabulary of insults is copious and terrible but never touches the mother. "Son of a pig," yes, "son of a sow" never, or else they open those knives that have written on them *"No me saques sin rason ni me guardas sin honor."*

Only in Mexico is there a monument to The Mother. In the
86

amusement quarter the *pulquerias,* where they get drunk on pulque, extracted from the century plant, have dreamlike names: "The Cup of Oblivion, "The Loves of Cupid," "The Future," and you go in, opening with your chest the doors that then swing back and forth behind you for a long time.

In front of the Salón México there were maids, soldiers, workers; this famous dance hall is thirty years old now; it holds fifteen hundred couples; once it was popular with the petty bourgeoisie, now only workers or poor people come to dance and then sit at the little tables with an Orange Crush, the cheapest orangeade; in the expanse of tables this uniformity of drink stands out, no glasses, just the little bottle with a straw inside. You have to stand only ten minutes at the door of the hall to see young people who, breaking off their dance, run away to go and kiss more comfortably somewhere else, or a girl crying, or rivals beating each other up. Love is open, a street affair, precocious, the solitude of couples within the crowd confirms a relationship between the distrust of public life and attachment to sexual and family life, the family can be seen and touched, the political parties' promises become less and less palapable. For the past decade and a half, the common people no longer control the revolution, properly speaking; they don't even have the floor. The middle class has taken it over, to do nothing with it.

Toward evening a red light shines on the top of Mexico's tallest skyscraper, forty-two stories, and along Calle Panama the prostitutes, mestizas for the most part, are all in a row, motionless, as if hanging from a nail outside their doors; there are no corridors to pass along or tiled steps to climb: it's all right there, inside a filthy stall.

I paid the fee, each girl has in her hand a little notebook (which she never lets go of, not even when she makes love) where she makes a cross for each customer with the precise time; the boss is far away but the supervisor could turn up any minute. Nearby there is Plaza Garibaldi with the *mariachis,* double basses as big as wardrobes, and unbelievably long trumpets; always sleepy because they start moving early in the morning, they are called also to private homes, especially on Saturdays and Sundays; the Mexican, like the Cuban, starts dancing suddenly; in the midst of his sorrows he suddenly wants music and song, in their *corridos* or folk songs they are never mediocre, and good and evil struggle in them violently.

I heard a very beautiful song at Guanajuato, which once produced a third of the world's silver and had two hundred thousand inhabitants, now there are only thirty thousand. It was hailing, the downhill road had become a river which was dragging along stones weighing a hundred pounds and little trees, the water red as fire, the lightning bolts straight and precise; at Guanajuato once there was a flood that left thousands dead. People came by car from the old abandoned mines; from above you see all Guanajuato below, huddled, it looks as if you could soak it with one bucket of water; there was the sun, the terraced houses, something Mediterranean in the midst of the mountains, an Amalfi, but in a few minutes the hurricane came. The miners have a hard time, some die of silicosis and to earn eleven pesos a day they have to handle that electric hammer that makes muscles and guts shake for too many hours, they've formed a cooperative but it only serves to collect their sufferings, the salaries are fixed far away, very far away and the silver—in drums that look like gasoline cans, a dark sand where only the expert eye sees a few scales glisten—goes to Monterey; in the factory at Monterey I held ingots of gold and silver in my hand; it fills you with a special emotion; they showed them to us all piled up, stamped under the eyes of smiling guards with big revolvers whose butts stuck out of the holsters; and in Guanajuato I had seen a miner draw his pay at a window, signing the receipt with his thumb.

Suddenly we had to take refuge inside a house, our automobile was almost swept away by the water. The water came into the house, then we climbed on the chairs, it was the house of the caretaker of a villa. A lady with us began to turn pale, the caretaker's wife, a woman of about forty from the Altos de Jalisco (where nature is so wild that when you open a window in the morning the landscape always has something new, Siquieros told me) and her two daughters kept saying: "Make yourselves at home, climb up on whatever you like, on the table, on the beds." They thought only of their guests; meanwhile the water was rooting out boxes from under the beds and dusty shoes that navigated slowly from one room to another. When the water began to recede, they wrung out their skirts which were soaked to the knee, singing a song. I noted down only seven or eight verses, which I translate badly: "My love is like the little rabbit, sensitive as a stag, it is not like grass grown too high, old, but like the first tip of the grass when it has barely sprouted under the moon. Oh, my beloved, when you go by under my window always wear your hat, otherwise I'll think you're a prisoner" (this means that the girl was generally aware of her lover's going by beneath her window only because of his high hat).

In the capital night is falling, but the churches are still open, doors flung wide. I don't know to what degree the ancient idols have been transformed into the new saints, but here they seek help in need and sorrow from anything over life-size. In Oaxaca a peasant woman had tied her chicken to the gold altar rail to be more free to pray, and the chicken flapped and she wept, imploring help, she told her story in a heartrending voice which reechoed in the church.

Seeing these examples of a race that has suffered so much, you understand their Christs that look like something on the crime page, with great broad wounds in their ribs, or twisted in pain like roots, one with a staring eye cutting through the mass of hair, another all arms, a two-yard span, thinning into a little infantile body with a huge nail through the feet. But for the Mexican nothing can equal the Virgin of Guadalupe. This Virign should be the most unifying factor in Mexico because she appeared to an Indian; and the faith had been imposed by the sword like slavery; with this miracle the colored people established their own contacts with heaven, in fact the feast of the Virgin of Guadalupe, in December, unites the Christian tenderness of Christmas with pre-Columbian explosions, fanatical, even bloody.

I believe no people has a greater desire than the Mexicans to know themselves, in books and conversations the recurrent theme is: "What it means to be Mexican"; among their complexes this is one of the noblest and most urgent, to free themselves from great humiliations. You don't have to go back to the tortures of the young hero Cuauhtemac (the conquistadors burned the soles of his feet trying in vain to find out where the treasure of Montezuma was hidden), it's enough to go back to the days of the foreign companies that controlled the petroleum, almost all of us were already born and were already buying books on the Maya ruins of Chichenitza, and meanwhile there was a white man, an Englishman, the boss of the mines, who never looked his Mexican employees in the face when he spoke to them, he always turned his back on them, twenty-five years ago, not centuries ago. And one day when there was a fire in the Tampico wells, the Mexican workmen ran to help, but the English said: "We don't need you." It was the rejection of any shadow of gratitude, of any life together.

In fact, they needed only the Mexicans' petroleum, they carried off as much as they could, even ruining the sources, They would have sucked them dry to save the petroleum of their country, and to make immense basins, reserves in view of the approaching war. National expropriation took place on March 18, 1939, and I can't understand why nobody has yet told the story in a film. Up to that day the Mexicans were used for the humblest jobs, the foreigners even hid the pipes and the machinery from them so they wouldn't learn anything. The power of the big companies was so vast that if they wanted to buy some oil-bearing land and its proprietor didn't want to sell it to them, the companies didn't worry too much—as you can understand from the expression: *the widow would sell it to them later*. One day the workers, feeling they were weak because they were broken up into too many unions, finally formed a single union and began to make a list of their basic requirements, they asked for a general increase in wages, coming to about twenty-eight million pesos. There was an arbitrated settlement which the companies didn't accept, they were sure of winning, their governments would stand fast as always and President Cardenas would retreat, leaving the strikers alone. It didn't work out that way. The Supreme Court handed down a decree that took five hours to read, and it said at the end to the companies: "You have to respect the decision. Pay up." A deadline was set, the companies went on thinking this can't be true and refused to pay. Then the Confederation of the workers asked for the support of the whole working population, also the students, the artists. The companies tried to frighten the Mexicans, warning them to be careful, not to touch a single lever, otherwise they would all blow up; "You don't know how, you aren't capable," they said, "you'll all be blown sky high," this is why the bosses had kept the serfs far from the mechanics of it all. When Cardenas decided on expropriation, the people all turned in their gold objects to pay the indemnity to the companies and make a good showing before the rest of the world, one man sold his house and his cows to help the *compañeros* hold out, if a pipe broke, a hundred volunteers came running, when ten were enough; along the golden strip of the oil deposits toward the Pacific, mestizos, Indians and creoles helped one another and nothing blew up: the Mexicans had watched during those years, out of the corners of their eyes, stealing the secrets.

From Mount Alban, we could see, as you can often see in Mexico, a limitless space. Meanwhile, a former cabinet minister was talking to me about agrarian reform with statistics behind which I glimpsed the terribly rich and the terribly poor of the country, with one eye I looked at him and with the other at the landscape, those millions of acres that, for the most part, have been parceled out on paper only. About twenty miles away it was raining and the sheets of water seemed the trains of fabulous creatures who concealed the upper part of their bodies in the clouds; we could also hear the thunder, while in another zone the mountains were blatantly blue against the azure sky, a peaceful area with two or three little Greek clouds which made it all the more remote from any thought of bad weather; farther to the right a great stormy darkness with a hole in the middle like a skylight from which the sun illuminated meadows, little lakes, and hills—another aspect of this immense coevality of images.

When you're in an automobile, you have the impression that by turning the wheel slightly you can avoid a dark zone—the outlines are so sharp—and then you can swing into the light and happiness of the fine zone; but a slight gust is enough, you can't tell where it comes from, and the drops spatter on the windshield and a minute later everything has turned to water, you come across the *campesinos* with their fragile raincoats of woven reeds and palm leaves, which repel the water. In one hour you go from wind and rain to calm and sunshine and vice versa again and again, the faster the car the more these contrasts of hope and despair stand out.

Of the four hundred and twenty million acres that make up Mexico, only thirty million could be cultivated with modern means, and no more than seventeen or eighteen are actually under cultivation: a bit over three million are irrigated artificially with dams, including some huge ones—I saw them—and with artificial rain; the other fifteen million are prey to rain and ice, the rain is always too much or too little and every four or five years there's a freeze, *la helada*, the *noche triste* of the peasant.

But it's not all woe, you only have to go to the North to find they no longer use the same plow as the ancient Egyptians which the peasant carries on his back at evening when he goes home to his hovel; I saw machines and sea-like expanses of cotton. This is the future of Mexico, those farmers will compete with ours, there isn't the magic to prevent science, whereby centuries ago the forests came forward and buried the cities.

They struggle against the *picudo,* against the golden *gusano,* the insects that burrow into the cotton and ruin it, in the city of Obregon I watched the perilous work of the fliers who generally live there from April to August and scatter insecticides over the cotton fields; the owners insist they fly lower and lower, they must actually graze the plants so that not a grain of the insecticide will be wasted. I saw the insecticides being loaded onto the planes by men with handkerchiefs over their faces like bandits; the flier is also masked for his protection, he takes off and flies over the field assigned to him, straight along the strip to be disinfested as if he had a ruler, suddenly he pulls the lever that drops the insecticide and he looks like a motorboat with his foaming wake behind him; then he has to swing around as abruptly as he can, to save time; we see him as he passes behind the smoky curtain he left earlier. They are almost all Army pilots; in the Army they earned a thousand pesos a month, and here they make up to seventy thousand a year, this year two pilots lost their lives. At Obregon the *pizcas de algodón* were about to start picking the cotton, through the whole Yaqui valley, those who do the picking are called *pizcadores,* they "fish" the cotton when they reach out to pull it from the plant and put it into the great sack-like pocket of their aprons, there were some children working in a field, their heads barely sticking up above the stalks. They had just come, en masse, from various parts of Mexico in the hope of being hired. For this domestic emigration they had spent all their savings. Little handbills said: "On July 20 the *pizca* of 220,000 acres of cotton will begin. *Campesino,* bring your family to Ciudad Obregon and you will have the *oportunidad de ganar dinero.* Suitable lodging."

They were camped by the thousands in the city stadium awaiting orders to leave for this or that zone. They were eating watermelon, redder than ours and very cheap. Their faces vanished into those half-melons, and there were rinds everywhere. When I arrived there was a sudden commotion because they had mistaken me for a man who hired people; they were tired, irritated, they had been waiting to go for several days and they were cursing the *capataz* who kept telling them all was well; since I had a notebook in my hand and wrote in it from time to time, they thought I was an authority of some kind. There were shouts and snickers around us, they yelled that with five pesos a day—the amount they were given during the time they waited for work to begin—they couldn't eat, they were joking and they were serious—they didn't themselves know which; suddenly there was a great pushing toward the interior

92

of the stadium, we were almost trampled on, and my face was grazed by a handful of mud somebody threw.

Going to Toluca we passed four Indians in a row, bent forward, marching against the wind, with short, fast steps; they had huge hats and identical clothes, white and black; we came back from Toluca six hours later and we came upon them still walking in a row, looking ahead. At the Toluca market, from behind the mothers' backs, from the folds of their dresses, a clump of hair, the eyes of a child appeared (the high infant mortality rate is caused by enteritis) and here again there were no shouts, barely a murmuring, the lined-up faces of the women selling, silent rivals; a great traffic in *tortillas*, which are their bread, in this silence they exchanged them like coins, taking them from baskets where they are kept warm under fairly white cloths (if you want to form an idea of *tortillas*, remember the scene where Chaplin counts rapidly on his fingers and shares the pancakes with Jackie Coogan; they're the same as tortillas); in the midst of those heads, Aztec, Toltec, Miztec, red flowers went by, poinsettias (which in Piazza di Spagna cost a fortune and cost nothing there), or white ones with great yellow pistils. A young man, whose nose protruded less than his mouth, gave a horse-like bite to a piece of sugar cane. Some children were transporting wares like the grownups and asked for alms without insisting. The porters carried enormous weights on their heads— it's difficult to explain how: around their heads, like a Roman *infula*, there is a ribbon of cord which falls down their back and they fix weights to it which would floor the man if, with his forehead, a towering forehead, he didn't sustain the whole thing.

We ate a fruit that you swallow like an oyster, gelatinous, except for the seeds which you crunch pleasantly, and I saw another kind of fruit being eaten by Lattuada who said: "It's nourishing, containing butter, and so in spite of everything, nobody dies of starvation." From the pastel colors of the medicinal herbs we passed to the rugs opened like suns and to the rivers of fake-silk shawls which descended in the midst of these crammed, dazed people.

The night of the Virgin of Guadalupe, in the square of Mexico City, the sky was streaked with balloons lighted from inside; the cathedral was made of little white electric bulbs with a sign of blue bulbs in the center: *"Non fecit taliter omni nationi,"* which is a

93

mark of that Mexican pride that is found also in the title of a book by Siqueiros: *There Is No Other Way but Ours.*

The church looked crooked; its foundations are rickety, like those of so many other buildings, because of certain telluric movements which, luckily, are slow and gentle, so there is no danger; I like this unevenness. We managed to enter the church, stepping over piles of people; I don't want to say anything sacrilegious, but under some of the blankets there were four or five people wound around one another. The church isn't immense, but it seemed so because from the altar you could see a very narrow path opening among the faithful, and somebody was proceeding forward painfully on his knees under a roof of eyes, two male nurses were following him, without touching him, as if he were a bicycle racer who had exhausted his strength, without even the energy to thrust out his chest to break the ribbon, but who still rejected all help: there were stretcher-bearers with their stretchers ready, because once, advancing in that way to ask a favor from God knows whom, the man reached the altar, looked at the Madonna with a suppliant expression, and collapsed. He was immediately carried off on the stretcher, while along the path another deformed penitent came into view, and in the square there were Red Cross tents where they set them one next to the other in haste, as if a battle were raging.

It's worth crossing the ocean just to see: the square was an endless dance floor; from the distance, varicolored plumes appeared, echoes of music came, as in exotic documentary films; we moved forward encountering groups of dancers from every part of Mexico, with their addresses on their banners, they had started dancing the day before and were still holding out. The Madonna mingled with the old fetishes, in fact one tribe, which had instruments of every shade of red, including the *teponatzle* which emits a sound like penpoints stuck in a school desk, displayed an idol that seemed a puzzle of Greek-key patterns, a labyrinth of vertical and horizontal planes with never a curve. They were playing a *mañatina,* a "little morning," an aubade to the Virgin because dawn had come.

I ran from one group to the other in my greed to see: one Indian's body looked as if he had rolled in a mattress of honey and then in one of feathers; they call him the Lord Eagle. Somebody shouted: "I work for *Cinema Nuovo;* my name is Persichini." I couldn't express my surprise to him because at that moment a huge flight of doves burst out from a big box on a tall pole with ribbons of multicolored silk which each dancer held by one end; and the dancers

94

moved around it like carousel horses with a sound of walnuts in a sack, in fact they had rattles of wooden bones at their ankles, and with a steady rhythm they wove among one another, first tangling all the ribbons, then untangling them, and then the box opened and the doves flew up, frightened by the noise of the firecrackers, which made them hesitate a moment before finding their route.

The first edition of the *Excelsior* had already appeared: "More than half a million souls gathered today for the Dark Virgin, Saint Mary of Guadalupe." Then: "Bloody day for the faith: *muertos* 4, *graves* 6, *leves* 682." At evening they flung me on to the stage of the Chapultepec and before twenty-five hundred spectators I said: "The neorealists think of their films as Diego Rivera thinks of his frescoes, he hopes his people, seeing its story told on walls, will become more aware of itself." As I left I was introduced to Siqueiros: "The means we painters use is ancient, and to make it modern is difficult, whereas films belong to today. Content isn't enough, a new technique is needed, a new material." For thirty years he has been painting on walls so that as many people as possible will see his work; Italian neorealism too is opposed to easel cinema; Rivera says the cinema in Mexico is in a critical state because it doesn't explain the motives of the Mexico of today, it will find the right path if it expounds, imaginatively, our most urgent problems.

"I understood certain things in Italy," he says, "in '21, there was fighting in the streets, in Milan I lived at night in a railway car, in the streets I saw what there was on the walls of the primitives, and I came to Mexico to paint, Posada too was of great use to us."

He introduces me to his driver, a colonel of the revolution, in the Tescoco murals Rivero put Zapata, there is a man who is working under the lash of the rich, then he becomes organized with his companions, but they kill him; his spirit remains alive. The wind and the rain crown these events, the little round windows through which the light enters from the park are exploited in the painting, and one of the windows is turned into a vulva, like a huge nurse, on the door is written: "A land free for men."

Another great figure is Buñuel, who says: "Three cheers for neorealism, but if I need to narrate instinct to others, I depict it, because an evil, even an obscene thought that occurs to me is just as real as a man working." As he speaks he becomes agitated, he reacts against his bourgeois background, against his Catholic origins, he is so sincere that he opens all the doors and stands in the drafts, but his final cry to free himself from all contradiction

95

is: "I will give up everything as long as I can be useful for something." He accompanied me to Tepito where they sell humble, even broken, worn objects; I thought they were refuse. Then we went to the street of the prostitutes who were glimpsed inside the doors like calves through the planks of a cattle car. On each door was a sign that meant *Forbidden:* for those few days everything had been closed down by the authorities, then the Tenampa where there are two orchestras side by side who play at the customers' bidding; each plays different songs, and nobody is bothered by the confusion, I had one play *"Siete leguas,"* a song about Pancho Villa, his white horse and the horizon, and the woman who wrote it, the madam of a brothel, sang it to me and Lattuada, with her constipated voice, she also sang a vulgar but spontaneous song whose chorus went "Go shove it . . ." and this is followed by the names of peoples and protagonists of living history who ought to have it shoved. . . . The fervid wave of sound swept us up into the chorus too. Rivera said to me: "If I were young, I'd make films, those who made the Russian films were painters. Pudovkin painted and so did Mayakovsky." Henry Moore once told me that what he saw at the Museum of Mexican Art is even greater than what he saw in Athens and in Rome.

In a *pulqueria* there was a neon sign *no se fia,* which I believe means "no credit," and there were men pissing in the same room, a few feet from the bar, while an American jukebox was playing and some men with glasses of *pulque* in their hands, some leading and some following, were dancing, removed from the others, and the one who was following danced backward, moving his behind, and as he gradually approached his partner the others shouted indiscreet cries and laughter which was transformed into that odious Tyrolean vocalizing.

Near Texcoco a polite man came up to us with a child in his arms and asked us if we wanted to see something really beautiful. We followed him for two hundred yards of dark countryside and entered a modest house where he showed us a crib and we had to say that it was very beautiful, his wife looked at him with a grim expression because he was always disturbing her by bringing people into the house. I bought two rugs, costing eight thousand lire each, at Xochimilco, a canal with other little canals and an atmosphere like the springs of Clitumnus, only larger; you climb into a flower-decked boat which you hire by the hour on that green, thick water
96

among the mimosas, another little boat came toward us with musicians, they had a Guatemalan xylophone and other instruments, soft music, true water music; our boat was grazed by others with vendors of beer, Coca-Cola and rugs, who insisted politely with their offers, standing in their boats and following us with their rugs unfurled like sails; one woman with her basket of *tortillas* didn't enter the competition, dejected, she just said *"Tortillas"* and with silent oar she hastened towards an American honeymooning couple who had just arrived and were being photographed, embracing.

OSCARS ET CETERA, February 10, 1957—My mother settles into her chair as if she were in a theater, the television news program is about to show yesterday's "Silver Ribbon" ceremony, the Italian Oscars. I'm going to appear, too. But instead I don't appear at all; somebody (snip!) cut me—of all people—right out.

A lady of the Roman bourgeoisie, last Sunday, was sitting by the fireplace with her husband, she in her nightgown, he in underwear. They had sniffed a bit of cocaine, just to try it out, she told me, they had had it in the bureau for the past month. They waited for a long time in front of the fire, in silence, but nothing happened.

I tried to console him. He's bald, and last night at the Fiamma Theater he realized that directly behind him his mistress of twenty years before was sitting. She surely did nothing but stare at his bald head and his wrinkles.

Apropos of false teeth, in 1946, one dawn, a famous director was quarreling in my little study with another director who was later to become famous. Every now and then I shushed them because the neighbors had already complained, banging on the wall. The young director shouted: "You're a grammarian." The old man sprang to his feet: "Noooooo!" His shout made his plate burst from his mouth like a projectile. He looked at us, wide-eyed, aged, flung himself to the floor, and with nervous hand found the false teeth under a table, mumbling: "Where's the bathroom?" . . .

In 1956 at the bar of a hotel in Monte Carlo a foreign actor and I were moving toward each other, smiling, to introduce ourselves. Halfway to me, he stopped, turned away, muttering and fumbling

97

as if he were trying to light a cigarette in the wind. The interpreter explained: "He has great respect for you, sir, and he says that first he has to put in his false teeth."

In '36 there was an old sailor of the ship on which Repaci was going around the world. When it seemed that the ship was going to crash on the rocks near Oporto, while everyone else was worried about life savers, the old bos'n ran to put in his teeth.

Toward midnight, Flaiano, Pinelli and I are walking up and down Via Merici, the building where the nuns live has one window alight on the top floor; the curtain swells in the breeze. A boy on a Vespa shouts: "Which way is the Circonvallazione Nomentana?" "Straight ahead," we say. He goes off with a headlight that illuminates barely five feet of the street ahead of him. We go on talking about the nuns, and ten minutes later he reappears; "I'm looking for Number 220," he says. "Try over toward the Barrier," I say. Noisily he takes the rise of Via Merici, we forget him again and look at the prostitutes at the corner of Via Asmara who have created a kind of salon, but they are safe because they lean against the bus stop when the police go by, as if they were waiting for the bus. For the third time the boy on the Vespa, his mouth emitting clouds of steam in the cold. "I can't find it," he says. Cursing, he stops. "Is it something serious?" He answers: "A summons." He's been riding around since this morning, he earns fifty lire for every summons, today's been a good day, he says, he's served several dozen. "Often I don't even make my expenses." "And you go waking people up at this hour?" "Yes, by law, I have to get there before midnight; it's a quarter to twelve." He zooms off again.

Amato is in the water—it's one P.M.—under the sun, De Sica is sitting in a deck chair in the shade. For a year the two of them haven't spoken. There was an exchange of serious insults on the subject of a film *A Dozen Red Roses*. Suddenly, nobody knows who it was, a hand was raised in greeting. Amato comes out of the water like a shot. Vittorio springs to his feet, they run toward each other with Neapolitan heartiness. But suddenly they stop, jumping about and flinging insults. From the distance they seem to be dancing. It was the sand that was burning the soles of their feet. They were reconciled later.

Villarotta, toward Tigrai, a quarter of poor people, where many

98

women were plaiting straw. One woman shouted in a loud voice: "Signora Maria." Signora Maria appeared at the window. "Would you mind," the woman shouted, "if your daughter went begging with mine?" "Why no, not at all," Signora Maria answered.

The film writer began: "Paola was a sweet young girl." In the next room the producer was giving orders, signing checks, telephoning, in the courtyard below the dollies went by and the trucks with the spotlights; the director was graciously granting an interview. The familiar machinery had been set into motion before the writer had come up with the idea of the story. Then he erased his words and wrote: "Paola was a whore."

There was a corpse, about two years ago, and the solderer was soldering the zinc coffin in the entrance hall two hours before the funeral. That noise barely broke the death-silence and the summer-silence weighing on that house in Luzzara: all of a sudden somebody was heard coming down the steps with a tinny click-clack, slamming, and sighing; it was the widow with a little kettle over her arm. Removing it she said, in a faint voice: "While you're about it, put a drop of lead over this hole."

With Francesca Bertini * at the Grand Hotel. I say that she is still a great actress and a beautiful woman; she stands up and slowly runs her hands down over her hips, starting with the ribs and coming down to the hips themselves, with her head in profile. Then she sits down and we look at each other, smiling.

I talk and Ingrid Bergman knits a stocking in the meanwhile. Maybe it's a stocking and maybe it's a sweater, but we always say stocking in our parts when a woman has those two needles in her hands and a ball of yarn in her lap. For the film *We Women* I tell her various stories including the one about the man who writes a one-act play with a betrayed husband as the protagonist, then goes to her, Bergman, and to persuade her to read the manuscript, confesses that he himself is the husband, that it's all true. She interrupts me and says: "I'd like something amusing. We mustn't force people never to laugh with us." And she starts laughing, then stops abruptly and says: "Something terribly funny occurred to me, but

* Old Italian silent film actress.

99

I can't tell." She blushes and goes back to her knitting, looking at Rossellini, who must have understood because he is laughing too.

When Bacchelli * first approached the cinema he was intimidated by the technical words, for a long time he didn't dare utter them. He never said close-up, medium shot, fade-out. After a week he tried jotting down a first scene on his own; Biancoli and Genina suddenly heard him exclaim: "My God, what have I written!" He had written: "dissolve."

ROSSELLINI, March 5, 1957—Listening to Rossellini talk about India for three hours I saw black nights with black shadows that grazed a man, a dog, a wagon like a black wing. In the daytime the colors are confused, you rarely say what a white, what a red, sounds on the contrary are always distinct, even the most remote ones if you listen carefully. The Indians are spare, thin as no one else can be, when you come back home it looks like a hospital, with the various forms of grossness and deformity to which we are accustomed; for the average Indian, the ideal still is the plump god. Rossellini browses among these memories with sudden outbursts or digressions: five hundred horses at the Tibet border with truck tires on their backs; the heads of Indians moving like fans; the hollow eyes of children in a village looking at Rossellini and as soon as they hear the foreigner's name they burst out laughing because names ending in "ini" are for women; and he, weeping affectionately, his head on the shoulder of a wise man or saint who was talking to him about life and death.

PADRE PIO, April 10, 1957—Easter Saturday we left Rome in the rain heading for the Gargano, we kept our speed about eighty, not because the situation permitted it (the roads were slippery), but within ourselves we admitted no obstacles, as if we were in the air, where the line between desire and fact is faint. However certain sudden blinding spurts of water forced us to slow down abruptly, bringing us back to our true dimension. In my corner I was trying to meditate.

But moving down toward Foggia, amid flights of white and black magpies and the transparent umbrellas of motionless shepherds,

* Riccardo Bacchelli, Italian novelist, born 1891.

we encountered a sudden opening of the horizon. It was the plateau of the Puglie, a plain like Emilia, but it seems an endless farm where only the eye is master. But on this just-washed green grass—there's a zone where the cows seem to be eating snow and instead that white is the first daisies—the struggle of man against man is harsh—you come upon handsome wrought-iron gates between stone columns, as if before villas, which perhaps do exist in the distance though they can't be seen, and opening on to the immense country-side they look like symbolic gateways to private property.

At Manfredonia three polite policemen persuaded us to stop for the night at S. Giovanni Rotondo, Padre Pio of Pietralcina lives there and the hotels are comfortable. On the hill the stars were coming out, we began to sing, a pilgrim was running up the slope among cars with out-of-town plates, announcing that Padre Pio had already begun the mass. I had only to remove my hat and I would see that monk whom my friend Angilen for years had been pressing me to visit, convinced that afterward many wonderful things would happen to me, as he says. An automobile's headlights came on and a child who had turned to pee against a wall was caught in the beam; after glancing into the light he took refuge in the darkness with a leap.

With effort we entered the overcrowded church, I was forced to stand at the door for a few minutes without seeing anything, the cold air from outside all concentrating on my bald head. "I'll be ill," I said. I tried to stand on tiptoe until I saw a broad white head emerging from a gold and silken chasuble as it bent over the altar. He'll turn around, I thought, and I didn't take my eyes from that head so as not to miss the moment when he turned. I quickly pol-ished my eyeglasses. I thought of the expression on my fellow-townsmen Angilen's face when he would read my postcard, "I have seen Padre Pio," he's the sort that would cry over it, when I meet him next summer I'll tell him the rest too, my fear of bron-chitis and other incessant thoughts like the squirrel as he turns the illusory cage (I cast however furtive glances at my neighbors as if those thoughts of mine, in their profanity, might echo in that silence). I imagined I was Number 15. Because you have to have a number in order to speak to him, put your name on a list. "Num-ber 15's turn." He is perfect inside his circle, and I would speak to him only of things outside his circle. I've been told he says: "Do you really want to confess?" Otherwise he won't listen. I would ask him: "Did you see the Foggia newspaper yesterday?" A four-column headline announces that God wants it; what does he want? He wants people in the next election to "vote in conformity." In conformity with the article which is violent in its attack on Benedetto Croce, on the young people who from the very shores of their Christianity thought they could build a bridge toward socialism, "given over to the principles of dialectical and historical materialism." Then, framed, in the same page, a black box that says Donna Rachele Mussolini was a recent visitor in the city, welcomed with flowers by the Fascists, she will come to pay a visit to Padre Pio. I have nothing against Donna Rachele, poor woman. The mass proceeded at an exceptionally slow pace, but I noticed no weariness in anyone, they were waiting from moment to moment for something from that motionless man who still wouldn't turn around, as if he were talking to the tabernacle and then with his last strength would utter a revelation. I tried to shift my position farther and farther forward with those movements of the body that are feral (as in a tram when somebody wants to reach the exit he finds hostile backs and bottoms and pushes with greater acrimony). He turned. With the host in his fingers, he displayed it, still, perhaps for a minute. I heard the expelled gasp of those who had been holding their breath. A face with a short, white beard. I couldn't see the eyes, he was too far away. Will I ever have the courage to talk with him man-to-man? It might be considered disrespectful or idle or might steal time from somebody whose soul is really suffering, whom that balm would help. Is it a sin, I thought, to feel content if I read they've killed Franco who genuflects again and again in the course of the day? I would have tried to explain to him that the older I grow, the less I can stand anyone who speaks or acts as if no one could take his place, even when he's silent, asleep. Franco says, "You millions and millions of people need me," he grows old, and the photographers go on taking his picture from special angles so you can't see he's short.

At the end of mass they all crowded around the altar, like the leaves of the sensitive plant, for communion. When he went out, ten or twenty of them rushed into a little hallway to overtake him. I rushed too and found myself in the sacristy, a step away from Padre Pio, who was taking off his vestments assisted by two Capuchins. There was the same silence as in the church. Padre Pio broke that too-tense atmosphere: "We must go now, it's late," in an ordinary tone, a truly good smile, and he added: "Happy Easter to all," without raising his voice as he headed for the little door. One man began shouting: "Padre Pio, your blessing, Padre Pio, your blessing," a Capuchin said: "Keep to your places." Padre Pio said, and I heard him distinctly, with a hint of reproach: "Go ahead and pinch, go ahead," to a man who was reaching out his hands to touch his stigmata; another had a huge package of bread which he held above the heads of all so that it would be blessed. Padre Pio disappeared through a little door, we went to buy postcards and my daughter bought a little frame with the picture of Padre Pio to give to her grandmother: it's as if he were already dead with those thousands of pictures of him on sale showing him laughing, weeping, saying mass. I too waited for him to look at me, and, since they say he senses thoughts, to shake his head in silent disapproval, but none of this happened, it was another manifestation of my vanity.

The next morning at Montesantangelo two children of about ten wanted to show us around for a few coins. "How much do you want?" They went into a huddle off to one side and murmured sums, all hugged together, then they said "Six hundred lire." Along the streets braziers shrouded our path in wisps of smoke, among hanging lambs with purple ink stamped on their skinned haunches, symbols of political parties, men in mourning. Beneath the girls' stockings you could glimpse reddened, blotchy legs, perhaps because they scald themselves standing too near the braziers at home.

We reached Rodi Garganico which was heralded from the distance by a long row of men's backs sitting on a low wall of the square, and a few minutes later we were facing these men while the loudspeaker broadcast the priest's noon sermon through the village.

We skirted the sea, mountain and sea, out of contact with Italy, slopes dense with prickly pears which, when scattered here and there, keep the traveler company, but when they are too concentrated they become overwhelming. In May it's as if everything expanded, they say, everything seems to rise: the sea glistens until it seems to be at our level, even up here; you discover longer and longer stretches of deserted golden beach which in our minds we populate with ourselves only. Mattinata is a town that changes gradually as you circle around it, you're made happy by its perfection of form from whatever point you look at it, you couldn't add a window, a wall, a color to make it more perfect, and you don't know how it has come about, certainly man had little to do with it, maybe it was the wind. Before losing sight of it we noticed

103

some new buildings which are offensive, the wrong note, you don't consider that they are homes, that they will help somebody and that in fact more are needed, the eye becomes detached from the reason, demanding order on its own.

A news item that grieved me contains the information that Padre Pio himself voted in the last elections. Because I fear he voted for the party opposing mine; with our votes he and I loaded invisible rifles, this is always what a vote is; but he must never load any rifle. That evening I came away from S. Giovanni Rotondo with something in my spirit that reminded me a little of the first time I saw Assisi, thirty-five years ago: I was eating a chocolate and I stopped; when I entered the restaurant in S. Giovanni Rotondo I expected to see the pilgrims, who had just come out of that extraordinary evening mass, thrust away the menus handed them by the waiters, saying in a still-dazed voice: "Give me the worst food you have."

OLD AGE, April 12, 1957—In the saline-iodic-bromic peace I feel like a raw recruit, finally free of civilian responsibilities. There can't be more than thirty of us taking the cure here at the beginning of the season, and we are constantly running into one another in the Assyro-Babylonian halls of the baths, bowing as if to attribute to our neighbors nonexistent values, as we all go on our way, erect and more stupid.

I am writing in the steam room which reminds me of my spiritual life, just look at it: a room beclouded by curative vapors, when you first come inside you see only shadows which little by little turn into human beings seated at tables with a tablecloth in front of them to protect their clothing from the sulphur which is good for the bronchial tubes, which irrigates them in a capillary fashion; by nature I tend always toward these uncertain realms where things assume forms desired by the imagination. On the sheet of paper which has become damp, the ink is expanding, a *t* has already gone to pieces, slowing, ramifying, better read the newspaper, I'll read books when I'm old, I'm putting many away for this purpose, but when does old age begin?

BUDAPEST, Rome, May 1957—I reached Budapest a year ago; the curfew was in effect. If anybody whistled in the street, it caused a sensation. A driver told me that Rakosi would like to come back, insisting that the members of the party now are fewer than when

104

he was here, so he is needed. Then I told the driver that if Rakosi were to come back I too would come, rheumatism and all, to lend a hand against the politician, because Dulles' misdeeds can never make us forget Rakosi's. "Happy is the man," I said to a journalist, "who can carry out socialism as water irrigates a field, penetrating everywhere, following the shape of the land; and woe to him who imposes socialism as if it came from the moon." It was very cold. Snow fell all the time, so the six days shrank, however, I saw four films, spoke with people, and one man asked me: "What do you think of socialist realism?" I walked along those streets where the wounds of 1956 have healed, but not all of them. And once again, more urgently, I was convinced that no writer is alien to what happens. He even determines it, though to varying degrees. What is socialist realism except this awareness of the artist's constant responsibility toward life, political life? I believe in something precise, practical, in something that immediately becomes action, I can't throw a stone in the water without making waves which stretch to God knows where. Artists throw their stones, but they don't want anybody to hear the noise of the stone when it strikes the water; they tend to make this operation silent and abstract. But in Hungary some artists have lost their lives and their freedom, and they believed in socialism.

Did they have the right to speak, to say what they thought? They had a duty to do it, that's why they were socialists. Is there, then, a conflict between art and politics, if both are socialist and yet find themselves on opposite sides of the barricades? In my mind, hopeless when it comes to theory and over-long argument, questions and answers sprang up and died down without stopping. I'll try to collect a few of those sparks, the way you try to make a match last as long as possible to light up a few yards along the road you have to go, and you hold your breath as if to keep it from going out. And I would like to allow these thoughts to emerge intact, unchanged, good and bad, as they were formed while I watched a citizen of Budapest climb into a tram or enter a shop or do any of those thousand daily things that are so similar to our own actions, and yet there wasn't one of those people who didn't seem to me a silent hero of what had happened, whether he had been pro or contra; they were the consequences of thought, of a way of looking at life that one morning turned into machine-gun fire, wounded, dead. What was social realism? Art is socialist, I thought; it can only be socialist, *always*. Even when the artist doesn't want it to

105

be. Even abstract art is socialist; it represents movement, change, there cannot be two arts. When a bourgeois appreciates art, he is living a socialist *moment*. His subsequent reasoning is no longer socialist: if he were coherent he should derive the consequences for his life from that aesthetic experience, instead he separates them, and this process of separation is typically reactionary. A socialist unites the phases of the spirit, as he has united all men in a common definition, and he cannot therefore consider the artist differently from the politician, just as he cannot consider the development of an artistic act different, in its human aims, from a political act. The way I look at it, the awareness of the artist, of his socialist position, enormously increases his rights and his duties, the word freedom is no longer a pretty butterfly to chase, never knowing where it will light; it means the freedom to carry his socialist argument to its conclusion *against anyone*. I can't say I'm a socialist and then forget it as an artist. Better then to say I'm not a socialist. But if I do say I'm a socialist, the division I later make between my work as an artist and my work as a citizen is a contradiction. The great new fact of the postwar period—and it was felt also in Italian neorealism—was the socialist artist's humble and enthusiastic acceptance of a fighting role, that is against the old concept of an art that isn't *co-creator* of political life, but something that always comes before or after, and not the act itself, in other words never *on a par* with the politician. But mustn't the socialist politician also have his *crisis* just as the socialist artist had his? He must have had it, breaking away from a view of art similar to the one that bourgeois politics has generally imposed. Otherwise we would notice a monstrous thing (and we did notice it): a politics that demands of art a socialist *novelty* without being, itself, structured, prepared, to receive this *novelty,* to co-create—I repeat—with it. Socialism was the first to offer art an immediately political role; if afterward it is intimidated by it, socialism is wrong. And it would betray not so much art as socialism in trying to restrain this "presence" it has unleashed.

THE EARTHQUAKE, October 16, 1957—I came back last night from a too-long vacation at Luzzara, wonderful days but fast as heartbeats. I didn't do anything, I merely allowed some thoughts to rise up suddenly like the circle of water when a fish bites. The limpid air helped me see that modicum of good and that modicum of evil I have done, precisely drawn like the boundaries of states.

A month ago I decided I wouldn't come back to Rome again, with a couple of articles a month I could live here, I thought, and not requiring the big sums of the city any more, I'll be able to tell the truth, cabinet ministers will listen to me and so will the others who by now are satisfied with mere lyrical liberty, liberty specially made for the artist, and this happens when you no longer have the strength, the patience to defend the other liberty, political liberty, which embraces everything. In the center of a steep, freshly-plowed field, I felt I was the pivot of a great scales with one dish up high on my right, the seven A.M. moon, and the other below to my left, the sun which was very slowly rising. In the farmyards the orange corn was glistening as they had just removed the tarpaulin which protects it from the dampness of the night. I was waiting for a pheasant, which had just darted by, flying from an oak to a cypress that, with three or four other cypresses, lent a Tuscan gentility to the landscape, to be flushed by a peasant with his slingshot. Meanwhile I repeated: I won't go back to Rome again. It seemed too far away, that time when the Italian cinema was able to believe in a collective vocation, as if the history of the cinema began only in '45 and was nothing less than the vocation of a whole country. Today we continue hunting for new definitions of this cinema when the juice of the old ones remains to be squeezed; and—I'm the first—we believe or pretend to believe that we can act as the moral vanguard without giving up any of the bourgeois habits the film industry cultivates. Has a film monk emerged perhaps, a person who maybe in 16 millimeters has made a really forbidden film? There are poets—that's true—and ones Italy can be proud of, perhaps nothing is abundant except poetry, however, there's a lack of that material which to be expressed requires civil courage. We held out a hand to the established order and the established order took arm, body, and soul. Now we're going to the moon and this new dimension of the spirit underlines, it seems to me, the fact that we film authors no longer launch even tins of acetylene into the sky of modern problems. Now we knock at God's door, piercing space like drills, and amongst us neoconformity is born, like an art, which from individuals extends to parties, which finds subtle and sometimes furious justifications for our own lack of spine. In fact we are not only conformists, but we fight tooth and nail not to seem so. We have sunk more and more each year, and only our eyes have remained above the surface so that we can see, but not our hands with which we could act.

Yesterday, with joy, I discovered the portulaca. I had reached my present age without ever having heard so much as its name, though it was always visible, at the base of the walls of many houses in the country where the wind is trapped with its seeds: and those little clumps of flowers that seem made of tissue paper, white, yellow, red, violet, are so compact and happy in the tough, protecting grass that not even a peasant's heavy boot succeeds in killing them. I appreciate the portulaca, therefore, and I know other things that are not vulgar, like this: that the eel can go from one stream to another crossing the woods at the early hour when the grass is damp, sliding over the dew for hundreds and hundreds of yards, but if he tries it in broad daylight he becomes heavy with dirt and his straining makes him lose the air-trail that was leading him to the river (for sparrows and swallows on the other hand both dawn and sunset are mortal because they see less and are tempted to fly along the white roads where they slam into the car radiators). I came home in the afternoon with the others, informing them that Rome would never see me again. The girls, a touch of powder on their cheeks, were beginning to come out of their houses and display themselves in the street. We kept sticking our heads out of the windows to shout "Hey, beautiful," for miles and miles our shouts alternated with the scream of the brakes, then we fell back in our seats as if we had possessed those beauties. It was amazing how, passing a group of women at the speed of the wind, the eye could still catch the good points and the defects of each one, the flavor: this one would make a good wife, this other one a good mistress, one promised a great deal with her lovely black hair that grew down her cheeks to the level of her ears then disappeared leaving her skin in its entire whiteness. We talked about them, adjusting them to our needs: a bit more bosom, a bit less hip, longer legs, like gluttons discussing food, and this would continue to the next encounter which like a wave swept away the women we had just left behind who had seemed unforgettable. I was filled with such a joy at the thought of a different life, far from the capital, that seeing a garden of dahlias coming toward me, still thick in the autumn in the Po valley where they cover all the marble in the cemeteries, I wanted the car to speed into those colors without braking and I wanted, in that blaring rain of leaves, to bash my head in for good. Instead I ended up telling the others about the earthquake in Mexico: that Saturday afternoon I had gone with friends to an old farmhouse which had been transformed into the finest
108

of hotels. We set out beneath a black sky at five in the afternoon along a row of outstretched hands with a few flowers in each, poor people offer them to you at the sides of the superhighway that goes to Acapulco. The proprietor gave us a huge key with the number of the room printed on a bangle, so we sounded like cows coming home from pasture with the clank-clank of iron against iron in that cloister-like corridor. At half past one that night the newspaper I was reading settled on my face with reassuring lightness. For fear of dispelling that wonderful drowsiness I didn't even turn out the light. I smiled like an infant when he lets go of the nipple to fall asleep. The concerns that earlier had been buzzing in my head had retired to their proper distance. I opened my eyes and everything was trembling. Fractions of seconds count in these situations as they do in world championships, they're solid entities. In a fraction of a second I dismissed the honeymoon couple hypothesis—in the hotel I had come from, a favorite with honeymooners, almost every night and even during the day walls and also floors shook a little. That sound resembled the noises of war, but the brain said not war, not truck, not storm. Not truck because there was only grass around the hotel, there wasn't the asphalt of Via Merici which makes trucks echo louder than drums. In short I jumped from the bed like a frog, and I can't reconstruct the way I put on my pants—I had no pyjamas because I had lent them to a lady who had forgotten her suitcase in the city—and a blue terry-cloth shirt. I see only the space and the time in which I dressed, the frames between my jumping out of bed and the moment when I found myself on the terrace in my slippers have been cut, and those slippers are usually hard to put on because they're the soft, flat kind. I had a pocket flashlight in my hand and the impression I had leapt out of a boat because one of my hands had reached out toward something in the room—to support me, I imagine—and had missed it, as if it were rocking in water. I had bought the flashlight eight hours earlier and it illuminated the stones of the terrace while I looked into a sky where the stars grew thicker toward the peak, giving a sense of cupola. Nothing trembled any more and the electricity had gone off, God knows when. Some shooting stars marked their trajectories with a flashing chalk. The dogs, surely, had been barking already for some time, and the cows were lowing, the horses whinnying, short rapid barks, millions of dogs because in Mexico the dogs really do run into the millions. (This is why so many babies are born, they say, because the dogs wake the peons too often in the night.) But up to that instant, beyond the steady creak like the one you hear in the belly of a ship during a storm, everything had taken place in my silence which was finally broken, allowing those animal sounds to penetrate, which someone else, my double, had nevertheless perceived earlier. I saw Cuernavaca a few miles off with its little crown of lights, which made me think the earthquake had taken place only in the hotel. My ears, which were gradually regaining their hearing as when you get off a plane, picked up human sounds, they came from a room where, through the slits of the blinds, I saw a light that came on and went out, matches surely. Shall I waken my friends? I wondered, turning the beam of the flashlight to their doors. Outside one of the doors there was a couple, clinging together, frightened, in white pyjamas; I immediately turned the light away, it was the American honeymoon couple who from ten P.M. to one A.M. had kissed in front of everybody on a bench near a waterfall which well-placed spotlights made full and glistening. Somebody called me. My name was like a weapon. I ran and a friend said to me: "Did you feel *el temblor*?" In the corridor a dozen people were moving in silence or almost, one also had a flashlight and our beams met. Afterward I saw his black shape with its white halo preceding him as he hurried toward the steps. A lady in a rather loud voice, to make conversation with somebody, said the quake had lasted half a minute. Somebody answered in a low voice that it had lasted a minute, another said that since it had been long and strong the shock wouldn't be repeated but the dogs' barking began every now and then with shrill gusts, and this meant there were still little shocks which only they could feel.

With a brusque turn of the key one man locked himself in his room, and then the separation into the rooms began, some remained open and from one came the aroma of coffee. In low voices whispered thank-you's and don't-mention-it's were exchanged, a head went by illuminated by a candle, but it was walking too fast and I would say then that the head was blown out. I went back on the terrace, meeting some hotel guards preceded by a huge dog which, exceptionally, made no impression on me even though he wasn't on a leash. I sat down on a step looking toward where I would have fallen if a shock had made the terrace collapse, Italy was really far away. Slowly daylight came with some cock-a-doodle-doos that seemed to burst from roosters as big as calves, and I went to bed, read the newspaper. The news in it seemed different, tired. At eight I went downstairs and found a number of people

110

around a portable radio which was talking about buildings destroyed in Mexico D.F. and victims. It's hard for me to explain, but I immediately felt a desire to have been there rather than here where nothing had been destroyed. I learned later that in one deluxe hotel where the bellboys wear golden jackets, a five-inch crack appeared all along the facade, and the guests, most of them foreigners, fled screaming, dressed as they were; caught at the front door by the light of the hotel's emergency lamps, while outside all was black, they calmed down. In the darkness the poor people under their broad-brimmed hats watched, as if in a theater, those distracted women (it was written in the paper), their golden slippers, their furs and vanity cases of red or white morocco leather, on the top floor there's a glass ballroom where they were dancing at the moment of the quake, from up there all of a sudden they saw the immense city swaying, the skyscrapers swaying against a sky filled with strange flashes because of the electric wires that were snapping. The Mexicans behaved well, they all helped one another, the ambulances that raced from one point to another of the metropolis with dead and wounded found the streets cleared, the people walked on the sidewalk calmly looking up to see if the building under which they were passing had cracks or other sinister signs.

ZURICH, November 3, 1957—In this moment before beginning to write, it seems everything can be said easily, you confuse the visibility of the object with its narratability, nothingness flies like a bird from one thing to another with the darts of the gulls on the lake in Zurich where a crust of bread thrown from the dock is enough to make them deviate from the point toward which they were speeding and, with flattened wings, catch the crust an inch from the water. But then I really must write, and the girl with light breath puts on annoying clogs, everything makes noise, even a faint "e," the first sentences always remind me of bakers when they are kneading; I used to watch them as a child in my grandfather's bakery when they had a hard time freeing their fingers from the dough and I would become worried for their sake. Shall I try speaking of Zurich, then? A few years ago in a hotel in that city I signed a contract for a script on Van Gogh amid clouds of white birds and celluloid swans that came alive unexpectedly with a trembling of their necks. In Zurich the girls cluster on the dock over the lake, they collect the glances of the few Swiss men who look at them in a begging bowl, you hear the "clunk" of each alms-offering. They

111

will grow old quickly; in Italy a woman of fifty can still arouse desire; there, never, because after forty they resemble men more and more, even in their way of walking.

. . . Bucharest would be a good subject but I wouldn't finish it by one o'clock, I thought, and today I would be happy to sit down to dinner with my family, however, I'll enjoy the food more if I've finished writing. I have to choose a subject that can be dealt with in a hurry, and as usual I postpone the long enterprises, but I'll go to my sister in the mountains, she has a little room with a tiny window where I ought to be able to stay at my writing table for a month without stopping; my shoulders feel they can rest well against that wall and the arrangement of those few rustic objects corresponds to my breathing, I'll write a book, at last. With me it's the way love is with some people, beforehand they tell themselves they'll spend hours with the woman they love—an hour just to kiss her nose, an hour for her ears, an hour or two for her mouth and the great moment will arrive only with the light of dawn but, with one thing and another, all of a sudden the poor bastard hears a burst of cries and of warm stars that swell, illuminating the room like broad daylight, and he realizes he has finished everything while the dress the woman has taken off is still warm on the chair; our friend is already thinking of putting his clothes back on and he wonders if that body lying at his side will ever interest him again, he imagines it won't, and not even the strongest imagination can enjoy a future pleasure in such a situation, it's really finished, for months and months he'll do without these pieces of flesh and will take advantage of this time to work. But thank God, all of a sudden, like music in a film when the sun rises and you hear first one note, which could be a cricket in the immense prairie, and then two, three crickets, a chorus of speaking bushes, streams, of authoritative persons and homely neighbors, which pushes up the sun as if with one hand until it fills the whole screen and overflows into the theater, he stretches his fingers toward the woman, who a moment before was made of cardboard, and brushes aside the leaves with the touch of the faun who is seeing her for the first time. In the literary equivalent, however, setting out for a slow, minute possession of the subject, with a single sentence I enjoy it too hastily and my mind prompts me in vain to go back to it. Impatience drives me elsewhere.

The thing that made the deepest impression on me in Bucharest,
112

as soon as I arrived one Sunday, was seeing only people modestly or even poorly dressed, as if a burst of wind had just blown away the rich class; the automobiles themselves in that atmosphere lost their appearance of idleness and wealth that they have especially in Mexico (in Mexico there are yards of used but still handsome cars, which turn slowly on high stands, violent spotlights strike them and the surrounding reality, reflected on their paint, is turned into a river of sparks: those who haven't cars dream of crimes in order to have one, the poor people have little part in political life and take refuge in things that mask their own weakness). In an antique shop window I saw, among gold-bordered plates, dusty ceramics and old medals, a French perfume bottle at an enoromus price, it was part of the residue of the bourgeois heritage, on Monday there's the market where those who used to give orders now go to sell their last silk handkerchiefs, clocks, top hats and sheets, "It's heart-rending," one Italian said to me. Even in the theater there is no longer that rustling, that splendor in the audience that, without having to go far, you can find at the Teatro Eliseo in Rome, but the people are dressed as if they had just come from work; at first I was irked, I would have protested that evening in the hotel as I opened my suitcase which from its leather to my ties expressed my delicate vices. One person said to me, "Culture has brought us up like grandmothers, we don't know how to give up the privileges our grandmothers gave us, and civilization can no longer be only the story of these privileges." The newspapers they bring me with my coffee speak on the same page of Zhukov and of planet No. 2. They have dismissed Zhukov, and they must be ready also to dismiss Khrushchev if he makes Zhukov's mistakes. If I may quote myself:

The battle against the personality cult cannot be stopped now by anyone, not even by those who would be better off; and shall we erect monuments only to those who teach us to do without themselves, to those who prepare structures which can automatically be turned against themselves when they become too fond of power? That father who killed himself because he was afraid that during his seizures he might harm his children did not have the forma mentis *of a chief of state.*

. . . In St. James's, boys and girls were lying in each other's arms on the glistening grass; one girl was stretched out on top of the

113

boy and they were kissing, but calmly, among children, sparrows and leaves that the wind made you mistake for sparrows.

To me the English seem—this is just an impression, I was there only twenty-four hours—Neapolitans *manqués*. They are about to raise their voices but they never do, to run but they don't run, they follow their impulses but always at a slight distance, like remote cousins at a funeral. I jumped to one side as I watched the red soldier with the black shako standing at attention outside Buckingham Palace, he didn't bat an eye and the pigeons could have lighted on his head; my son Marco was taking my picture next to this guardsman who was basically a big boy with a pink-and-white face; all of a sudden he snapped, stamped his foot on the ground the way you do when you want to drive somebody away, made a sharp right-face, turned inside the gate kicking his feet out like a German, stopped, did an about-face, alone in the immense courtyard, went off, came back, and arrived at a little sentry-box where the shadow left only his trousers visible. He stood at parade rest. I went away, but I believe he comes out again at regular intervals like a cuckoo.

. . . In New York four months ago I spent another dozen hours, robbed from my stern passport, it was the 4th of July, and I went to Long Island, while all around they were shooting off firecrackers for the national holiday, many Negro families were returning from their cheap celebrations dragging their feet. There were also some whites naturally, but I saw only these Negroes with children's rattles and great ice-cream cones while behind them in the amusement park parachutes with more Negroes came down from a tower about a hundred and fifty feet high, for a few cents. I said to the Puerto Rican driver, "Drive around," and he drove around for a long time in that excited but perfect air, we were prompted to go away on tiptoe for fear of causing, through our own alienness, some rent in the terrible harmony so amazing that it can be imagined even if you weren't there.

BEAUTIFUL, 1957—From '38 to '45 where were my literary idols? I worshiped them to such a degree that I felt they could have prevented the war. But not with their works. I wanted them to die already as heroes and to have the courage I lacked, to "participate" more than I did. Beautiful, I agree: but with this lofty thesis, which had become a part of my blood, it happened the other night,

114

at the end of Dassin's film, that I didn't embrace Dassin and instead spoke words of cautious praise; because it wasn't all beautiful. I sacrificed one of the most spontaneous impulses: to embrace the author of a work that was, in any case, fearless.

WHITE-HAIRED CHAPLIN, November 16, 1957—Chaplin today in his old tramp costume. Each of us imagines him in his way, as the Christians do with their saints: I, with white hair and slightly-black moustache; Charlot, the real Charlot, vanished from the world after his last film, it seems to me twenty years ago; he has taken refuge on a mountain; there he has lived among goats and birds without encountering a single human being. One day this year, a young girl gets lost during an excursion, he sees her, doesn't want to be seen, since by now he is afraid of people. In him the shyness and the vanity of the old days are born again, until finally, as evening falls, touched by the girl's heartrending appeals, he finally shows himself. He doesn't say a word because he has lost the habit of speech, with gestures he points out to her the path toward the valley. He walks with her for a few hundred yards, when he has shown her the path he wants to turn back, goodbye, goodbye, but then with various excuses he follows her for another ten yards, then another ten. The girl, in the fullness of her heart, invites him to her home but he wards off the invitation, he will never abandon his retreat, it's marvelous, with gestures he describes how he spends his day, hour by hour, from the stars to the other stars while down below in the city all is fierce, false, only betrayal exists, and uttering first some sound, a few grunts, he has started speaking without realizing it, he begins to enjoy it, he is almost incapable now of being silent. And so they go on, and they meet a shepherd, then a hut with a peasant, his wife and their son, all three plowing, little by little life comes toward him with its noises and all the rest, a large town can already be glimpsed. He says goodbye to the girl who would gladly take him with her for a few days as a mark of her gratitude, goodbye, goodbye, he must go back to his retreat. But when the girl is about to disappear on the horizon, he suddenly runs after her as if he were fifty years younger. And he comes with her into the center of the big city. I don't know whether the girl is rich or poor, but he surely spends enchanting days, he becomes fond of old objects again, discovers new ones, sings, he wants to dye his hair, "How beautiful life is and I stayed away from it—imagine!—for all this time!" They've bought him

115

a new suit—picking it out in the department store wasn't easy—and an overcoat, shoes, a new derby, a new cane; but with his walk and his eyes, we recognize him from far away, even changed as he is: how he enjoys every little thing, how he savors the pleasure of greeting others and being greeted, of being in the crowd, of looking in shop windows, reading posters. To recover lost time, greedy for everything, he takes part in everything, he runs from a funeral to a wedding, to a baptism, nothing is alien to him; at funerals he is sincerely mournful, at baptisms he suggests names for the baby, at weddings he improvises toasts: coming upon him, few ask who he is, because he is so natural and his companionship seems so spontaneous. He enjoys himself like a child, watching television, amazed that they let you see so many things without paying, wonderful women, exotic landscapes, the moon. At times he is upset because most people don't enjoy life as he does, they seem accustomed by now to all these marvels.

After he has been living in this surprising world for a few days and has renounced his remote mountain, one morning he opens the window with his most radiant smile and the war breaks out. The change is instantaneous. Have they gone mad? Air-raid shelters, deaths, horrors. Before, he seemed bound to everyone else by invisible threads, now he's alone as in the past. His hosts get rid of him. We're halfway through the film.

A CAN OF PAINT, December 1, 1957—What is this order that is mentioned in the second article of the law on censorship? Not the order of Confucius: perfecting knowledge, the sage says, consists in examining things; when things have been examined, knowledge is perfect; if knowledge is perfect, then thought is truthful; if thought is truthful, then the heart is sincere; if the heart is sincere, then the personality is developed; if the personality is developed, then at last is the house in order; then, and only then, is there order in the State. Since 1947 we haven't been examining things, above all with our films, it's as if we took them out of an archive. It may therefore seem strange now if I say I would be happy to see somebody write a script entitled *A Can of Paint.*

I can imagine already the poster on the walls, with its simple power: a boy of about eighteen who throws a can of black paint at a man who is addressing the crowd from the stage of a theater. It would be the very event that this morning blackened the snowy

116

hair of Ferruccio Parri.* Perhaps somebody has spanked the boy, and then the nasty story ended. Instead I feel as if I were his father, with this spirit I want to know the reason, to follow with him the course of his action to be aware and make others aware of the episodes that take place in my country and shift from the streets into the houses and vice versa, expressing in so many ways the conflict between the spirit of the Resistance and the conservative spirit. At first sight you want, as usual, to skip this theme, considering it too political; you imagine, in your unconscious, as you reject it, that it offers few dramatic possibilities. But here is our boy, coming into the theater on this cold Sunday morning, among the flags, huddled in his seat, waiting for his moment. Has he some highly placed accomplices who will reward him with a hearty slap on the back, or has he come here all alone, like a mole through the tunnel of ignorance? Perhaps we mustn't imagine the boy entirely from our own point of view (tomorrow we'll see his face in the newspapers) and if somebody does tackle the story, I wouldn't be surprised if he wanted first to meet the boy, question him, find out where he lives. Later invention will move with the fanciful bounds of a kite, but the string will be held in a firm hand. Nor is it credible that the boy will be composed entirely of mistakes, of wickedness, and that in the end he will burst into tears and beg forgiveness. He will have his reasons and will reflect the reasons of others; in the beginning he doesn't want to open his mouth (this could be one of the hundred plot-lines of the story); they carried him bodily into a dressing room of the theater to save him from the wrath of the public, the questioning begins at once, a police officer, three or four people, and he won't talk, perhaps he can be made to tell his name, he has an address, a father and a mother. Somebody comes in who knows him, his former teacher, he says the boy was a good student, he loved his country. What does this mean? Our country is changing before our eyes like a field with the passing of the seasons; suddenly his mother will arrive, terrified, somebody ran to call her, and friends of the boy burst in, some laughing and some serious, but all in agreement with him. The police report is written out, the mother is frightened of prison, she doesn't want them to put him in jail not even for an hour, panic-stricken she tells about their home life, describes minute by minute the food, the debts,

* Resistance leader and former Italian prime minister.

117

the conversations, she is one of those Italian women who always shout at home that the family should keep out of politics; she begs them. Meanwhile in the theater the political meeting begins and snatches of it are heard through the door as it opens and shuts. Little by little older men find themselves face to face with these boys, two, three generations, all of them with phrases in their heads, encrusted there from generations back; every now and then one of the boys says old people can't understand certain things. There will be no lack of sudden shifts of action in this trial, if we want to call it that, the poet might even run the risk of allowing himself to be too easily attracted by strong situations: an attempted escape, his friends who want to liberate him with student-like strong-headedness, the discovery of the man who sent him, or else a scene when the boy is left alone with the man struck by the can of paint, the arrival of the boy's girl friend, all with their passions, their concerns, their dead, their bills, and a key character who wants to know, wants to understand, wants to explain what freedom is. If we can't succeed in explaining our feelings, our historical choices, how can we reproach or attack this boy?

WORDS, January 1, 1958—On a piece of air-mail paper I find, marked down without order, some words which were to represent so many points of departure for my diary; they were accumulated in four or five days among exploding firecrackers and the door opening and closing with deliverymen, postmen and concièrge coming to wish us Merry Christmas. *Saquisili; poets; confidence.* I'll try to remember what I wanted to say. *Saquilisi* is a town in Equador three thousand meters above sea level, a young Italian with a Paillard took some shots of that place, and as I saw them projected on a wall of my apartment, I couldn't stop regretting that they ended too soon; Chiavarelli says his camera jammed at that moment. There was a flat windy clearing, crowded with natives, the men and the women wearing felt hats like those of the peasants of the Po valley, with short ponchos, generally red or else orange, which the Kodachrome film made blatant against a white house. At the beginning the lens was aimed more on the clothes than on the faces; a tailor, outdoors, in the midst of the crowd, was sewing the ponchos on an old Singer. The whole screen was filled by a wife pushing aside her drunken husband, he walked like a sleepwalker trying to find his way back to the tavern (what do they drink there?). The Indians sucked into the black interior of the tavern left
118

a great whiteness behind them. From the tavern an old woman burst out, rolling on the ground, and the others almost trampled on her, and as she tried to raise her stunned face, the film ended, on my wall a sudden glare buried under a snowy blanket those visual pleasures and an enormous and at the same time common world from which our farewell was made definitive by the sudden flapping of the tangled end of the film, even if down there they are still living.

Poets. I must have been inspired to write down this word by having seen Bernardo Bertolucci's * poems in *Botteghe oscure.* Not only does Attilio have a son, but a son who writes poems (he has his father's clarity). This discovery caught me at a bad moment, I would have liked to write a letter that night to Attilio and to Bernardo to ask their help in escaping from my contradiction, my confusion: I love poets and I hate them. At this moment I cover my ears and shout: "Don't listen to them." If the wind merely comes from the morning-glories and grazes my skin, if the gurgle of a stream involves us like a tree, the great facts are left behind, along the water. Intellectuals were dear in '45. Good and evil touched them. Each had a jar of alcohol, containing a hand or some piece of a dead person, each had chosen a corpse between '40 and '45 that fitted his own feelings. But as time went by they began mixing, in their poems, clouds with the dead, flowers with hunger, and in this mixture it's always hunger and the dead who lose out.

Poets mustn't be listened to this year, or we'll be late again in Calabria or the Delta, or in Via Arnone where a mother slammed her two children against the wall because, not having on their Christmas tree anything but the tree itself, they had started eating the leaves. It's a true story, but there's a bit of demagoguery in citing it. Naturally I'm ashamed of these summary rebellions against respected men, how many times have I dreamed of being light like them, to be able to soar on the breathing of a child; to confront a tulip and pay attention to it for the first time, even though I have said the word tulip hundreds of times in my life, with one finger I enter its calyx bee-like and I draw the finger out covered with a yellow dust, the pistils tremble and the eye moves to the green stem and begins to count the shades of green. However, I tire at once.

* Attilio Bertolucci is a well-known poet. Bern. is his son, now a film director.

119

Poets instead leave their hearts in the sun for long seasons until they become full of flavor like raisins. For a while now they no longer mingle with those who sign protests against events. Not signing is like signing; everything that happens is endorsed by their non-signature, so that life seems normal, you no longer know where to start biting for fear of spoiling its perfection, good editions in half-leather appear, but are we unaware that lentils, if worm-eaten, are sold at fifty percent of the price? And on the Berkel scales, no matter how thin, the slices of Negroni salami cause the net weight's trembling hand to move up; with each additional slice the cost also goes up and a housewife looks at the scale, illustrated also in *Graphis,* uncertain whether to say that's enough or to make bold and ask for another few ounces.

Confidence—There is such a network of bureaucrats, journalists, financiers, committees that even when the new law protecting Italian cinema is passed we'll feel like sitting dejected at the base of the mountain as if we had to climb it barefoot. And yet 1958 should be the year of confidence. As after a funeral, when they open the windows, beat the mattresses, and even the taste of water seems new. Everything is dead, and we begin again from the beginning, and we'll make cinema on paper, if there's no other way, we'll expound every day an idea, a plan, a story, it would be disastrous if we did nothing but complain. Authoritative persons affirm that ideas are born at the right moment spontaneously like mushrooms, but the opposite case must be considered intrinsic to our cinema, and it isn't true that sooner or later good ideas always prevail (unless by "later" you mean the Catholic measure of centuries) and therefore public meetings, congresses, assemblies, conventions shouldn't be necessary. The year 1958 might even be the year of 16 millimeter. Don't leave this humble film only to amateurs; we, the old hands in the profession, could make bold and use it, thanks to the many servitudes from which it is free and the different internal and external practice it involves. The noisy itinerary of the normal film becomes more and more weighed down by customs duties and for every film-maker who finds this his natural condition there are many who are pushed aside to the margins. At 16 millimeter, at 8 millimeter, you can't make films for the normal circuits of distribution, but for clubs, to be shown in streets, in houses, provided there's an idea. Our enemies are right, because we've slowed down the pace of our ideas until one might suspect—
120

as Martini suspected with sculpture though it turned out not to be true—that cinema is a dead language; it no longer plays a part in the dialectics of our time.

Popular songs—In '47 I confessed I had always longed to write pop songs, and Rota * said: "Let's try together." I had in mind a person who doesn't know whether he's happy or sad, strong or weak, heroic or cowardly, cynical or in love and he goes around the streets asking what he's like, "Tell me what I'm like." I would also have enjoyed asking some "questions," danceable ones, of the people who are in the news, a king, a murderer, an actress. To stand next to a man whose hands fly over the keyboard, and I at the first shower of notes roll on the floor like a trout in the coldest, most silvery foam, then with my hoarse voice I shamelessly sing everything that wells up, beating time with the palm of my hand on the hard things that are around me, walls, tables, doors, panes, and I rattle the coffee spoon on the bottles of liquor, march musically about the room as when you have such total joy that you recognize no obstacles even if you're heavy and middle-aged, you climb on a chair with a leap like a bird's when it darts from the lowest rung to the highest, you fall back on the sofa. With a single step you climb over a person and you want to smash some valuable object.

Cencio—This is the name of a restaurant in Trastevere where they sing improvised *stornelli* with words like pimp, whore, cuckold; foreigners come, drawn by the lascivious atmosphere; the general laughter seems to protect those present from any allusion to themselves, as everyone's eyes become narrow, hidden by the laughter and they coldly judge the others as whores, pimps, cuckolds. Even the waiters, as they serve the tables, address the customers singing, and at the climax the proprietor arrives with his maracas. A Scandinavian woman wants to kiss him, for no reason, to show that all is for the best in the best of all possible worlds; her husband, tall and pale, stands up to conduct the chorus with his knife, those verses that run down their chins like gravy; another foreign woman of about fifty, who has never smoked, lights a cigarette, coughs and transforms the Roman dialect into an intermittent bleating; all

* Nino Rota, serious Italian composer—also composes music for Fellini's films.

snicker, the woman blushes and to seem nonchalant, also kisses the proprietor, knocking the coins from the plate that one of the musicians is passing around.

Bread and milk—I've just finished eating bread and milk. As my tongue searches my warm mouth for the echo of those beloved tastes, perhaps because these are the first days of the year, a watershed, I slip toward the past among the crumbs of bread that I brush from the lapel of my bathrobe with my free middle finger: fifty years ago, forty years ago, thirty years ago, twenty years ago: a year later there was the war. We walked along the Via Veneto with the usual step (and yet there must have been something different) and those who preferred their orange juice with plain water and not soda said I want it with plain water, I read a book and if it was good it entered the course of nature like the stars and the winds, the newspapers the maid brought up as she did this morning, were there, not wrinkled before my hand leafed through them, and my hand still moves toward them with a certain hope. Should we be afraid for ourselves, or have pity, seeing that we lived, we scolded the children, or embraced; at a performance, "Hi, how are you?," that day when a Fascist big shot slapped a citizen who was caught shaking a friend's hand rather than giving him the Roman salute? It was as if by law we had to wear a papier-mâché nose. But we don't speak willingly of that time, so imagine if anyone says to someone else: "I remember when you had a papier-mâché nose, you came to the café with a papier-mâché nose." "You came there once, too, with a shoe on your head; it was obligatory." They said, about a film story of mine: "Change the ending." Because a boss kicked a worker. Of course, I answered. Did I dip rolls into milk even then as I do now? Suddenly I let out a cry (an inner cry, of course): I did dip them. I touch my nose.

BUONGIORNO ITALIA, 1958—These are notes for an animated cartoon written for the Gammafilm Company, it begins with a list of my collaborators: eight million Lombards, six million Veneti, seven million Emilians and so on with Sardinians, Neapolitans, Sicilians, et cetera, who make up naturally the fifty million inhabitants of our country. Little by little the screen fills with black while, at the corner of the frame, pushing it aside like paper, the face of a famous actor appears—the narrator—who suggests we speak in low voices because in Italy almost everybody is still asleep; but the

122

sun is already on its way, it's abandoned remote lands to come to us; meanwhile he lights a match: beneath him, in the darkness, you can glimpse our boot, with the white glints of the waves that rumble on its long coasts: we move closer, there, in flashes, a mountain, a road, a lake, and the Roman Forum no less, among whose columns hordes of cats chase one another, their backs shiny in the moonlight.

"Dawn is about to break, ladies and gentlemen." In the far corner of the frame a hint of grey palpitates. The flapping of the wings of birds as they migrate toward distant lands: a row of them flies over the Wain of Ursa Major, which pales. The beloved phantoms that come every night to keep us company are returning to their realms. Gusts of phantoms, almost like clouds, cross the screen going off toward infinity. But one comes forward in a mad dash, a fugitive: it's Mussolini, his eyes rolling, as other spirits armed with sticks appear at his heels, and in this group we recognize Garibaldi and Mazzini. Pursued and pursuers fade away toward the top of the frame and a crackling of bullets batters the screen as if it were tin.

One bullet has pierced the wall of night because the first faint ray of sun arrives before us and strikes a city, illuminates one of its monuments for a moment: the famous tower of Pisa, the Campo with its white wonders. But the remaining black of the frame, like an octopus waking from its torpor, tries to close that hole. A battle breaks out between blackness and light: the soldiers of light attack the monstrous black, from its wounds a glow leads out, glints that strike like swords this or that spot in Italy, a little Lucanian village, a Lombard lake, a bridge of barges over the Po, a Gothic spire of the Milan cathedral.

Finally the light, transformed into the sun, wins and the narrator can shout: "BUONGIORNO ITALIA!" One of its rays reaches a Sicilian cart revealing the Christian and pagan figures at the very moment when, because of the light's arrival, they break off their battle.

At Monfalcone, a launched ship speeds down the ways into the sea, raising dazzling waves peopled with fish which plunge into the sea where the little fish are swallowed by the big fish.

On the Apuan Alps, the reign of marble, there is a host of stonecutters banging with loud hammers along the solemn wall that little by little grows smaller as if a sole, gigantic sculptor were reducing it with his creative hands, until, of the whole mountain, only one block of marble remains, a statue which is being sketched out violently: it's the Rondanini Pietà of Michelangelo.

An impetuous noise of rubber-stamps. It looks as if the screen were being stamped, as a succession of neatly-inked words appears: *Urgent—Very Urgent—Private—Personal—Secret—Top Secret—Municipal—Province—Region—Undersecretary—Division Chief—Station Master;* first a little stamp, then a big one, a still bigger one, even an iron press that stamps the words Case Closed. We are evidently in the bureaucratic palaces of the capital. At the pension office, lines of wounded men, of disabled veterans, with the uniforms of our various wars, a Garibaldino, a *bersagliere* of Libya, a crusader, an ancient Roman, and women in widow's weeds. And at the tax office people complaining in the tone of an ancient funeral lament. Then corridors, shelves, flights of steps with clerks moving along them, bumping into one another, crossing one another's path, their hands full of papers, they are looking for a dossier; drawers are opened and shut, from each come spurts of dust and of music of the various periods, even remote times, and suddenly the notes of "Giovinezza" and some heads wearing the Fascists' black fezzes, but the filing clerk shuts it hastily again and keeps leaping from one drawer to another, following the indications that he finds in each case: "Go back to the first number." "Weep." "Tomorrow." (The sequence assumes the forms and colors of a Parchesi game, where the citizen is shifted around like a die.)

Outside in the open, clumps of children go to school playing with the patches of sunlight: some are coming along a country road with their bookbags slung over their shoulders and one of these is carrying on his back another child with crutches, as in the sentimental stories of De Amicis: it's a cover picture of the "Domenica del Corriere." And there is the school in the distance, with its imposing shape; they come toward it from all directions, children on foot, on bicycles, astride other children. All seem to be engulfed by the solemn front door except for one who plays hookey and goes skipping off toward the countryside. He actually looks like Pinocchio.

Suddenly the screen is a great curtain, struck by the sunlight as it opens: Naples. First a sky with baroque clouds, full of saints who are looking toward the earth where imploring voices are heard asking for favors, miracles, numbers to bet in the lottery: some of the saints move down, bringing numbers, television sets, handsome clothes, Vespas, luxurious clocks. There is a bustling to and fro, between heaven and earth, the saints rise up again laden with *ex*

124

votos in exchange for their miracles, silver hands, hearts, and crutches.

Teeming markets and we pan over some numbers: the prices of the merchandise, number after number, stuck on the wares, on the food. A cascade of plucked chickens, and a man's eyes looking at the price of a chicken, prohibitive for him. And the struggle begins as this man tries to reduce those enormous figures, some eights cut in two with a swoop become zeroes; with another slash some fives are turned into threes; a vain and hairy ten thousand, as the one is cut away, is reduced to a poor row of noughts which slump down like deflated bladders, a nine is attacked and turned upside down to be reduced to six, but the number manages to struggle up and be a nine once more; an eight, tired and wounded, sits down on a four. The battle rages and the adding machines come into action squeezing out myriads of numbers, arithmetic signs: plus—minus—multiplied by—come from the machine as little bells ring, there is a hailstorm and a final plus ($+$) falls on the pile, like a cross, burying the man.

At the border, armies of cameras are entering our country, crowds of foreigners who begin avidly taking pictures, scattering everywhere: in Rome they photograph the Colosseum, running away suddenly because a roaring lion has appeared among the ruins; they photograph everything, a stone, a woman's behind, a monument and, by mistake, also each other. There is an abrupt volley of machine-gun fire; a woman falls to the ground, mortally wounded.

She really does look exactly like Anna Magnani in *Open City*. But the tourists have no time to stop or comment on the many things they must see. In Florence, in the Uffizi Gallery, they pass before the famous paintings, spurred on by the explanations of the guide, so hurriedly that the Botticelli "Venus" is mixed up with a picture by Titian and the Raphaels are bundled into the Piero della Francescas.

The tourists visit a bar as if it were a monument, rolling their eyes with pleasure as they drink a coffee: the barman raises and lowers the levers of the shining espresso machine. It shakes, pops, hisses, and in mounting noise the counter starts moving and sails off like a steamship, dragging them all with it. They go to St. Peter's: black priests, red priests, black nuns, blue, brown ones; cardinals passing in their silks rustle like waterfalls, solemn Roman

125

princes, many with one eye bandaged as in a famous painting. Suddenly somebody shouts: "The Devil!" They've discovered a devil perched on a column: in a flash all lenses are turned on the devil, as an angel bursts from a fresco and hurls himself on the enemy, a chase among the columns, capitals, pulpits, altars, candelabra, while the crowd watches as if at a race and comments with loud cries, snapping pictures. Then the tourists go down in the catacombs, become lost as if in a maze, somebody opens a humble little door and immediately finds himself right in hell. Here are the circles that recall Doré's illustrations of the *Inferno:* Paolo and Francesca go by embracing in a whirlwind which blows off everyone's hat. When they come to Count Ugolino the tourists throw him food the way you do the animals at the zoo, but Count Ugolino refuses it scornfully and goes on gnawing his enemy's skull.

From the frozen Cocytus emerges the sinister apparition of the Prince of Darkness, his fearsome mouth chewing some people whose heads are inside with the legs dangling over the lips: one of the heads is seen for a fraction of a moment and we recognize Hitler: one tourist, evidently a German, also recognizes him and snaps out a salute shouting: "Heil Hitler," then goes on with the others, but a huge hand comes after him and he, too, is crammed into the terrible mouth.

The tourists, taking advantage of being underground, cross Italy, so we now see it in its geological cross section, among other wonders: caverns, ancient tombs, lakes of petroleum where the oil prospectors' drills penetrate. And so they come to Milan where they reappear in the sunlight from a manhole directly in the cathedral square. But the guide, as he is about to begin his panegyric on the Ambrosian church, all of a sudden slaps his forehead, shouting: "We forgot Sicily!"

In a split second, along the Superhighway of the Sun, a big bus is rumbling South. Like visions, the superhighway panoramas go past: the stripes, the signals, the racetrack sounds of the cars, the colors, the different shapes of the vehicles, the motorcyclists of the oddest appearance, at times ghostly as Martians, at times a swarm of blue overalls; there are even priests on motorcycles and nuns with their white coifs like albatrosses. Some couples actually make love on motorcycles, amorous acrobats, kissing each other in every position as the motorcycle proceeds on its own. The bus passes the bridge over the Po at Piacenza, passes the hills of olive trees in Tuscany, is pursued by wild colts in Maremma. The bus stops

126

with a great squeal of its brakes: a bandit with a sugarloaf hat, cloak, and blunderbuss, as in the nineteenth century, has taken his stand in the middle of the road, menacingly. The tourists, especially the women, shudder with delicious fear. But the bandit bursts out in a dazzling high note as if he were on the opera stage. The tourists' faces are full of admiration as the high note goes on and the bus resumes its speedy course. We reach Sicily, the glistening waters of the straits, where the sirens sing marvelous songs and the guide orders all his charges to stop up their ears, otherwise they won't resist the song and will dive into the water. However, though he urges the others to cover their ears, he forgets his own and so, suddenly, he is the one who plunges into the water, and the others all follow him, diving in unison. The sirens, like maidens, make the tourists chase them, and the tourists are drunk with happiness, darting fishlike through the underwater miracles. But the love scenes are interrupted because from over their heads, at the surface of the sea, they hear fierce shouts: it's the tuna fishermen who, with their cadenced cries, are harpooning dozens and dozens of tuna whose blood turns the water red. The sirens and the tourists, clinging to one another in fear, look at the red wave coming down toward them.

In Rome a blonde descends the Spanish steps and Italians and foreigners at the bottom look at her legs and the legs of the other women, the forest of legs coming down, legs of every shape, with stockings, bare, with mesh stockings, woolen stockings, colonnades of legs through which the men wander spellbound like children in a wood; a man climbs up one of those legs as if to pick a fruit, the others also rush up, it's a contest to see who'll arrive first, but the one in the lead strikes his head against the top of the frame as if against a ceiling and plunges down with a bump on his crown. Following one of these superb women, a young man wears shoes that squeak; the new shoes emit melodies like an organ. Another displays his tie. Another his curly hair. In their imagination, the contest between the men following the woman gradually becomes more bitter, and as they go on following her with apparent indifference, in their imagination they attack each other with automatic rifles.

But other women, no less fascinating, cross the street: the men's eyes pop from their sockets and stick, as if magnetized, to the women, on this one's or that one's hips, as the women with a little shake get rid of them; the number of these beautiful women grows, and each man would like to follow them all, until suddenly the men are dismembered: an arm follows the brunette, a leg goes after the redhead, the eyes pursue the blonde.

The sky is abruptly filled with the chirping of birds. There is a man raising his arms, inviting them. He's Saint Francis, no less, we recognize him by his little beard, his monk's robe and his gentle expression, a bit ostentatiously gentle to tell the truth. The birds make delicate patterns in the air, coming from the farthest point of the horizon, first dots, then swarms that swoop in the air, now gray, now black, now transparent as a veil, flying around the man, then some light on his head and on his inviting arms. All of a sudden, the man we believe to be Saint Francis turns and signals to somebody—he winks, in fact; the sound of a rifle is abruptly heard, and the little birds are shot. We are just in time to see a hunter hiding behind a tree a few paces from the false Saint Francis while in the silence the feathers descend lightly in the air.

The piercing sound of a siren announces noon, the cannon on the Janiculum fires its famous daily shot, in Venice the Moors strike their hammers on the bells, a tarantella fills the air! "I'm a poor beggar, homeless, without a roof over my head, I'd sell my pants for a dish of macaroni. . . ."

The spaghetti symphony begins; curtains of spaghetti drop before us like the beaded curtains of Italian barbershops. And through these curtains, entering and leaving in speedy pursuit, come many Pulcinellas with plates of spaghetti in their hands, they try to eat it while perhaps a gentleman with a cane is at their heels, meaning to prevent them. A tourist, unskilled in the proper use of the fork, becomes tangled in the spaghetti as in a ball of yarn and people come running up to extricate him, but they too are drawn into the tangle forming a desperate Laocoön group, then cries of alarm are heard, the firemen's sirens, the firemen with their ladders, hoses, hatchets, unravel the tangle. A voice, to the rhythm of the tarantella, sings to us meanwhile that man needs x vitamins to live; we see a human outline as in anatomy class and the spaghetti enters the outlined stomach, from which blood immediately flows through the body, ramifying everywhere. The heart turns nice and red and beats vigorously. We require x amount of fats, and we see them lined up before us schematically: butter, eggs, sugar, as they go into that body which palpitates with joy, seems to gain strength, to radiate marvelous colors. But if we take away the butter, the meat, the sugar, the body turns pale and slumps, the bones weaken, above
128

In Mexico City. In the foreground, laughing, is the producer
Manolo Barbachano.

Cesare Zavattini

With Grillo Pontecorvo, the director of *The Battle of Algiers*.

At the Gianferrari Gallery in Milan where Zavattini had the first exhibition of his work as a painter (1966).

One of the typical sandbanks along the Po.

The source of the River Po (see "Little Journey Along the Po").

In Red Square (October, 1967).

With a group of young cinema fans in Rome.

all the spinal column slowly bends—there, it's bending, further and further. We see many men in the street, actually bending, greeting in an exaggerated fashion some other people who are obviously better off and more authoritative. One of them strikes us especially; he seems an acrobat in his bending, his greeting; he greets them all, becoming more and more bent until he can't straighten up again.

The sun is now beating on the walls, the walls of Italy, of the villages, the cities, which in the noonday silence narrate with a *graffito*, with some mark, moments of history, great and small, ancient or recent. There are still snatches of slogans from the past, there is still a rather battered swastika, the German trademark; and immediately we see behind that proud emblem the Germans in flight, along the banks of the Po, terror-stricken: some enter the river with their horses, others in teetering tubs, others attempt to swim as the partisans' rifles resound at their backs. The great river, swollen and rapid, overwhelms the fugitives and the horses' eyes go mad like the Germans', we see only frightened, dilated eyes which the water extinguishes one by one.

On another wall there are bullet holes. It is a wall of the village of Marzabotto, against which men, women and children are huddled and a target's concentric circles on this or that part of their bodies as the Germans machine-gun them.

In Milan, another wall is half-crumbling, the remains of an air-raid; like a screen it fills with images; the alarm sirens start screaming; the bombs fall from the sky like black birds and explode. Outlines of Milan at night, of other Italian cities, the lights of the fire flash in the darkness, alternating with the tourists today, taking pictures.

As one bomb explodes a young man is blown to bits: his body scatters in ten, fifteen pieces, white on black; from the background a scream of grief, the face of a mother who comes forward with her arms outstretched, desperately trying to put together the destroyed form of her son, and she seems about to recompose it, we can already recognize its shape but once, twice, three times, some part is always missing to complete it and bring him alive again, like a Meccano set of which some pieces have been lost.

On another wall: *Viva Bartali, Viva Coppi, Viva la Lazio.* We're in a huge stadium as a football player is giving the ball a penalty kick. All hearts are beating, little hearts and big ones, in all shades of red, as they swell and seem about to burst or to stop beating,

129

and one makes the sound of a little piston, another the tick-tock of a watch. In the silence we can hear all this various beating of hearts, and when the player is about to kick the ball, the hearts stop for a moment. The ball, struck, flies into the net. The hearts resume beating at a mad pace, some glow, others go limp, others trill like bells, except for one: we see a stretcher in the distance carrying off a spectator, dead.

On the outskirts of Turin on a wall among old slogans and new, a boy is drawing infantile scrawls that the sun animates: flowers, dogs, children made with a circle and two dots for eyes. Suddenly the boy leaves these creatures of his to join his friends playing in the weeds of a nearby field. But what is this rusty object that sticks out of the ground? Our child picks it up, full of curiosity, and calls to the others, but even before the others can reach him, the object explodes. It's a mine that has remained buried there since the war. We see the child's white hearse and behind it come the children, the animals, and the other creatures just as he drew them a short while before.

At this point the sun must have grown a little tired, absent-minded, because some clouds approach him and fall on him like bandits trying to put a man's head in a sack. But the sun wakes up and begins, with his rays, to fight off the clouds, which multiply and as the sun's sword-rays cut some into tiny pieces myriads blossom from them as if by magic. Meanwhile on the earth the leaden shadow covers this or that spot, and the places alternate from light to darkness according to the stages of the battle in the sky, the black herds of water buffalo, the red crests of hens in a barnyard. But the clouds are about to gain the upper hand, they have become immense, menacing, and in their bosom they are already preparing the noisy hailstorm, shaking it like a cocktail.

On the ground only frightened faces can be seen watching the war in the air as the wind raises dust and slams doors. A southern peasant with his sickle emerges in the middle of his little garden which is being threatened, he tries to work magic against the clouds and waves his sickle as he pronounces the ritual words. But in vain. With a portentous din the storm bursts, the lightning flashes shear the sheep, scattering the wool in the air, and knock down trees. An occasional thunderbolt is victoriously swallowed by the lightning rods and discharged underground, where its sizzling flames spread out along many passages illuminating moles' nests, tangles of snakes, roots. One of the thunderbolts circles angrily around a

130

trullo house in Lucania, like a ravenous wolf trying to enter, while children's frightened faces, pressed against the windowpanes, follow its movements. But the exhausted thunderbolt finally releases its fury against a henhouse where it kills the poor hen; a clump of golden chicks comes peeping from beneath her.

Meanwhile torrents of water pour down from the mountains, and we see those terraces, painfully sown by the peasants, once orderly and neat, now overrun and transformed into a muddy stream that rushes to the valley.

Plains are invaded by the rising water; it reaches the roofs of the houses, and the roofs stick out of the sad immense grayness, with families taking refuge on them, while a table, a bed, an array of poor objects float by on the current.

But at last, the sun with a gigantic effort breaks the grim blanket that is stifling him and, by enchantment, everything turns calm, peace comes back, life after the storm. The cities, still damp from the rain, glisten in still more beautiful and fantastic aspects. The rainbow gleams, as bands of children slide down it as in a playground.

Now they all want to talk. They talk and gesticulate, so we see only hands and arms waving in the most varied mimic efforts. The words rise toward the sky like tiny balloons, words of varying size, form, color: short words, whole sentences, words we hear in the most banal conversations, words that become animated like persons, assuming almost the shape of persons, dark, brilliant, tender. Here is the word *independence,* which comes forward with a slightly pompous manner and suddenly encounters the feminine word *salary*. The two words look at each other for a moment; with a rapid about-face they move away, obviously not wanting to establish any sort of relationship, but then *salary* winks her eye at the other word; seduction is a rather long process but finally *independence* succumbs and takes *salary*'s arm, though she immediately seems smaller, thinner, and all the little banners that gleamed on her head go limp. Other words: *best wishes—call me up—professor—commendatore—lawyer—doctor,* come forward with exaggerated insistence, wanting to put down the other words. Noisily, trying to place itself before all the others, the sentence: *You don't realize to whom you're speaking.* Then others: *I always speak my mind. I came up the hard way. I promise. Give me a letter of recommendation. If you don't love me, I'll kill you.* Then a blast of *Me, me, me* written in every possible way, in all hands, pronounced in all

131

tones of voice, finally invades the screen, definitively and over-poweringly.

Meanwhile the sun is about to enter the water and on the shores of Naples people climb on each other's shoulders to get a better look at the grandiose sunset.

The great flaming ball of the sun descends, sinks lower, enters the water with an immense sizzling which raises clouds of steam as it disappears entirely into liquid, releasing a final green ray, while the silver moon rises from the sea, all dripping.

Headlights of cars come on, of motorcycles, bicycles, fishing boats, from the chimney pots of the Capital come wisps of smoke among the television aerials which announce the supper hour: thin smoke and thick, fast and slow, the wisps assume the form of what is being cooked on the stove, a golden-brown duck, a suckling pig, ravioli, a sausage, cutlets, rice, but also a scrawny little fish and a cat. A cat is peacefully dozing on the bed watching this culinary parade of smoke as if it were a film, but when he sees that one of his own kind is being cooked on some fire, he runs off from roof to roof until, for greater safety, with one big leap he springs onto the moon.

It's evening, the hour when the pizzas come out of the oven and if we move in to a close-up of them, the surface no longer seems a pizza's but suggests a legendary landscape, the dough swells, raising mountains which then open at the top like a crater, emitting smoke and lava, and amid the flames of the oven, the frightful disaster of Pompeii with the sky first red and then covered with ash which falls like a blanket on the luminous, gay Roman villas, on the fleeing people, arresting them in a final gesture before their death.

Little by little the pizza resumes its modest dimensions even if the leaves of oregano crumple in the heat like trees, like burned forests. But there's nothing to fear: the song of the musicians with their mandolins reassures us.

Inside the houses the people are also listening to songs. They are all clustered around the TV. Songs, songs, songs. Old songs like "Santa Lucia"; on a ship the emigrants see Napoli move away with tears in their eyes, but all of a sudden, when Naples is about to vanish from their sight, irresistibly they all dive into the water, and swim with broad strokes towards their invoked city. Songs like "Mamma": processions of Italians invoking their Mammas, waving banners and signboards on which *"Mamma"* is written. A slow,

132

solemn song is heard, the voice of a ballad-singer tells us of the death of the Sicilian Turiddu; peasants with their tools on their shoulders, on foot, on horses, on bicycles, led by Turiddu, invade a great uncultivated field and promptly fall to work joyfully, but from behind a hedge two peaked caps can be glimpsed, two rifle barrels from which a volley strikes Turiddu, who from the back of his horse was happily watching that joyous resumption of labor. From the dry trees all around, with a smile of satisfaction, some grim birds with baronial coats-of-arms rise and fly off.

In the taverns of Tuscany, Emilia, Lombardy, Genoa, Piedmont, the poor people play cards in the smoke of the pipes and cigars. The cards are hurled forcefully on the table, the volume of the voices rises, they shout in their various dialects until an argument begins. Blasts of trumpets are heard, the armies of the king of hearts confront the armies of the king of spades. The clubs forces clash with those of the diamonds, assuming positions that recall the battle pictures of the old Italian masters.

In a little Sicilian village a young man is galloping across the countryside on a fiery horse, on its back there is also a girl whom he has evidently just kidnaped, and she is trying with all her strength to writhe free. On their trail are her relatives who also gallop and shoot into the air, illuminating sheepfolds, wolves' eyes, martens' tails, shepherds motionless as statues with rifles over their shoulders. The horses' hoofs strike sparks. The young man tries to kiss the girl, who continues to rebel. Now we see on the screen only these two immense mouths, as if the moonlight illuminated nothing else, one evading, the other more and more avidly approaching, afire, until it seems about to press the girl's; but her mouth eludes his again. Finally the girl's lips succumb, join his, under the menace of the rifles, and the night is suddenly aglow with fireworks which fill the sky with grinning masks, cascades of polychrome Harlequins, of Pantaloons with red cloaks, of innocent Columbines.

But after a final flicker of light the blackest of blacks invades the countryside: there is only a little glow in the distance, as in fairy tales; we reach it, we go inside this humble peasant hut where a Mamma is singing a lullaby, a *ninna-nanna,* to her child to put him to sleep:

Ninna nanna, you're here with your Mamma.
Outside the wicked wolf is lurking,
And the deceitful fox,

133

The weasel that bites,
The owl that brings death,
And the bat that covers the moon.

And we see this nocturnal life where the wolf's eyes glisten, and the weasel enters the henhouse in the terrified cackling of the chickens, and the owl opens and shuts his eyes reflecting in his pupils an endless row of crosses, and the bat sows shadows like dust.

But it isn't only in nature that we find frightening things. Chaplin —yes Charlie Chaplin—comes along the road with his trusting smile, he is approaching us when a sudden, terrible burst of gunfire strikes him, pierces the whole screen and Chaplin himself, like a colander. Farewell Charlie.

In fact, on all sides many murderous weapons are being manufactured, in every part of the world. And at an accelerated pace they are also manufacturing medals for bravery, gold, silver, bronze, iron, which shine on the rows of chests that come forward, forward, menacingly.

Midnight strikes. The streets are deserted. Only along the Via Veneto some night people still linger, at the rows of café tables, a gentleman comes by and is greeted deferentially by all, as if he were a cabinet minister. Suddenly we realize, from the tail that sticks out behind him, he is the Devil.

Now the Italians are sleeping, dreaming. We see many real faces of women, children, old people, men, with various expressions, immersed in sleep and in dreams: this man dreams he is the wind blowing over Italy and drawing the most beautiful women after him, tearing them from their fathers, husbands, homes. This other man dreams hosts of eyes in the darkness, looking at his wife, whose beautiful body is lying asleep beside him; the jealous husband rushes around with a snuffer, like a sacristan putting out candles, extinguishing all those eyes, he snuffs out one here and another glows over there, but by running furiously he manages to put them all out, all but one, with which the struggle continues because it slips away on every side like an eel, growing narrow, dilating until it fills almost the whole screen, but finally the man can shout victory. When he turns toward his wife then, he sees her in another's arms: he is about to fling himself on the adulterers; however, he stops and expresses his grief in a song, of which we hear the beginning, only the beginning because other dreams are driving us on. A man
134

dreams of a balcony, a nice balcony, on his little house, all for himself. He looks out on the balcony, looks at nature all around, breathes the pure air, feels inspired to exclaim: "How beautiful nature is!" but as he is enjoying his balcony, leaning on the railing with his hands, he repeats the exclamation and almost without realizing it, little by little, he repeats it in a dictatorial tone and begins a speech on nature, bombastically: "Italians! How beautiful nature is!" and we seem to hear the stentorious echo of another voice familiar to all Italians: "Italians! these trees, this green . . ." A burst of applause drowns out his words, along with cadenced shouts of "Na-ture, na-ture, na-ture . . ."

A woman is dreaming of how to turn her husband's old overcoat into a new overcoat for her little son, who is standing in front of her waiting, nude and still as a dummy. She starts cutting and piecing, trying to avoid with her scissors the big hole in the coat. And, to avoid, it, she keeps cutting and cutting until finally with a slip of the scissors she manages to avoid it for good: the new overcoat is ready, the little boy puts it on, but the pockets are so low that, as he walks, he bends over until he almost touches the ground.

Another man dreams that one morning he flings open the shutters and outside his window, lined up by the hundreds, by the thousands, there are flying saucers full of Martians which have arrived during the night, Martians so similar to us that they are hanging out their washing as if they were in the narrow alleyways of Naples.

But the pace of the dreams increases, and the edges of one man's dream alternate with another man's, they overlap, are fused, creating wild compositions, as if it were a dream of our painters of yesterday and today, expressing a harmony of forms and Italian colors from which, like a hope, comes that man whom we saw earlier so bent over, as if he were groveling in front of others, but now he comes towards us smiling, straightening up little by little in his dignity, he and his wife with their children, whom they are holding by the hand.

GIRO D'ITALIA, * *1958*—The wheels crackle light on the asphalt preceded by solemn motorcycles with very high antennae. There is something priestly about them, Girardengo, with his old fox's face, drives a red car on which the spare bicycles' wheels turn slowly; one racer manages to pee, spattering it everywhere. Monks,

* Big Italian bicycle race.

135

boarding-school girls, butchers in bloody white smocks form lines along the sides of the procession. The voice of the radio begins to scatter numbers in the air and the reporters bend abruptly over their bits of paper. I see blond Camoriano and De Martino and we wave, our hands flapping outside the car windows, after twenty years in which we haven't met. The race seems almost to be taking place between us, with this shifting of the journalists' automobiles which pass one another in the beautiful empty streets with Sunday ease; a man dressed in black, carrying a black umbrella, wants to watch the Giro despite a recent death in the family. It's half-past one. It could be any other hour because the day's light is now subject to the influence of our emotions. The heat turns everything gray, but at the news that one group has gained a hundred meters, the air stirs, opens. At Vigna di Valle, Gianni Brera's round face looks back with an expert's smile; in fact, we're on the little rise, where something unexpected might happen. Some gasping girls have just arrived from the fields; they point down at the racers, actually frightened, "At Manziana the group is going by five minutes late according to the race chart," the car radio says. We speed off, raising the girls' skirts. Number 2, Baroni, vomits without slowing the cadence of his pedaling; Number 79 throws water over his head. I'm happy—I'm ashamed to say so, but I've dreamed of seeing this all my life. The photographers, as the car races on, snap pictures, the race manager with a mime's gestures moves trucks aside, makes cars slow down, until he is supplanted by a spurt of poppies. The driver says there is a stabilizer under the car, a Tem-dritt or Tem-drott, the latest model, which allows us to take curves this mad way. There is Orio Vergani with his gray hair, somebody else I haven't run into for fifteen years, "Hi, hi," it's marvelous this going forward and backward in time. We have just left behind some burnt fields with groups of sheep motionless in the middle, all of them gathered around one; a few hundred yards from Civitavecchia a breath of wind came from the sea and rustled the blue ribbons on the *bersaglieri's* fezzes, people in bathing suits, still dripping, came shamelessly to the road and yelled "Hurray for Fabbri," in their haste to become a part of the general excitement.

The Tarquinia lap is won by Poblet who comes forward, bald, not even breathing hard. "He can win the lap today," Borel says. A dispatch-rider with a medical manner wears a little blackboard on his back with the Tarquinia arrival times on it. You can see only
136

the racers' legs moving in unison, one raises his head because a helicopter is grazing the road, they are not so much faces as flashes of faces—grimaces, twisted mouths, faces that are lifted and lowered following the rhythm of their pedaling, hiding from the greedy eyes of their fans. At Montalto di Castro along the road are scattered the attendants with their colored bags of spare parts, with a bound I say hello to Bianca Ugo, I barely have time to see her through the maze of the Atala bicycle spokes, but she is a dear friend of my ten great Milanese years, she's heading toward the capital. The voice of Giubilo or of Martellini—I don't know which —informs us in spurts about the undulating formation and the dispersal of the groups, large and small, and from above it must look like cells moving, forming endless combinations and, in our case, creating and extinguishing hopes. One tried making a dash, for three quarters of a mile he felt like a winner even if in his back there is the thief's childish fear with the police at his heels, in fact, the group swallows him like a whale's mouth. Perhaps each would like to tell his private troubles, to persuade the others that only he would derive complete joy from the victory; but they are all in the same condition and so they are silent and they exchange glances in which you can read their reciprocal, intermittent request for solidarity and their hostility. Barozzi comes from Reggio like me; I cheer him on, he's among those in the lead, but looking back, we see the mass of the others arriving like the wind, with the force of reality. We are thirty-five miles from Grosseto, the TV reporters stop every now and then and look for odd angles; one rolls down a ditch to frame the arriving cyclists between the horns of a Maremma ox. Other oxen in the center of a field with their behinds toward us seem put there as punishment. At twenty-eight miles from Grosseto I shout to Mantella: "How are you?" It takes me back to 1947. On my left, silvery Ansedonia and on my right, Signora Ramperti: I wave my arm but she can't imagine this arm belongs to a friend she hasn't seen since 1940. I am more and more puzzled by these encounters—I almost suspect it's a trap, the race is only a pretext. In Grosseto, an hour from now, awaiting the racers to arrive on the track we'll hear news of the elections. The calm atmosphere is broken by a "Watch out, watch out," spoken dramatically: "Railroad crossing closed." The train goes by, the waiters in the dining car looking from the windows as if from a balcony. Our automobiles speed up to reach the stadium in time,

137

leaving behind forever the Ente Maremma * signs, the couples of lovers who watch the passing of the racers with all possible admiration but without breaking the contact between themselves, the children held up in parents' arms, pots on the stove coming to a boil, gas flames with no pots over them, a moment of general oblivion when the passing of the Giro like a needle threads us all into the same necklace with a fictitious fraternity which doesn't seem fictitious: as if this evening we were all going to eat the same meal. To reach the stadium track we go beneath narrow, dark underpasses like the corridors in the bull ring, with the addition of the smell of Sloan's liniment. On the track, an important emotion: for the first time I watch the arrival from the center of the field and not from the stands, I too am one of these unnatural lords I have envied since childhood, those who know and see, who touch things we will never touch or know. Now, between the green of the grass and the cement of the track, I try to understand what this privilege means. I haven't time to dictate any more to my young fellow-Emilian, Davoli, because the sound of a bell is heard, I see a bouquet of flowers, I hear a name I've never heard before, racers drop their bicycles into random hands and dive on cases of mineral water and you see only heads thrown back, the bottle perpendicular over their mouths, all emptied in two or three gulps.

SPEED, August 1, 1958—From Prague to Brussels in an hour, in a Russian jet; to make things even more extraordinary there were only two of us aboard, when there is room for seventy passengers. At thirty thousand feet the earth below is clear, recognizable as at twelve thousand. Perhaps the only new impression is that you take off not feeling the void beneath you. I would say it resembles climbing up a bank. Brousil and I start talking, as if in a tram; I didn't feel I was going at six hundred miles per hour because speed is measured with the eyes, while the plane covers a stretch from one river to another river and takes two minutes, the eye takes only a second, and you feel that nothing can prevent man's reaching the speed of your eye, sooner or later; it's so natural and along the same technological line. And then? With me, as with others, infinite wonder ends often in non-wonder, and when we unveil God, after a lovely ceremony, all will be as before. I play the skeptic, but an hour ago a child could make me rejoice when he confessed his fear,

* Italian bureau for developing underdeveloped Maremma region.

138

as a box climbed a wall: it was an elevator, which he was seeing for the first time; and the letter from a man in my village telling about another villager, who on these hot motionless nights stands in the center of the village until dawn to hear the rustling of the women as they get out of bed and come to the window to seek a breath of air; then the married ones waken their husbands and it's obvious why; other women go and pee, he says, and from the sound he can tell whether or not they're virgins, certain strong, straight jets would enter the neck of a bottle.

THE FUNERAL, September 28, 1958—The other day Salvioni telephoned to ask if I would go with him to see the funeral of a fifty-year-old widow, mother of four, who died of heart failure because they took away her furniture against back taxes left unpaid by her husband. I was to write for a weekly magazine what they call "my impressions." We arrived there in the sunlight and looked for the place. From a side street came a hearse, its gold cross shining brightly, and we followed it until it also stopped outside a café to ask directions: it was lost. It turned back, with us after it, and soon we came to a narrow street, almost a country road, where at a certain point there were a few more people than elsewhere and we realized this was the right place.

I was embarrassed, as if I were committing a misdeed. Everything had happened suddenly. I still couldn't figure out my motive for saying yes. If a person insists, I always end up by saying yes. They would pay me for the article and I was to be like a policeman, who doesn't overlook a single detail. I had already begun to make mental notes of the smell of burnt grass, certain cheap housing, a whole Fascist landscape (here the adjective is not pejorative): it's one of those big villages that sprang up about twenty-five years ago, and its size is saddening, that scabby grandeur, much more remote than the old songs of the time.

There must have been thirty or forty women with children in their arms; many of them were slatternly; faces red from the sun or from crying. Mostly poor people among whom, as usual, a well-dressed relative stood out, wearing a black mourning button in his lapel. There was the little head of a boy with hair so red against those mourning weeds that my eyes were often drawn to him and I was irked by my readiness to be distracted just when sighs and murmured words around me encouraged me to see everything in black and white. Without realizing it, I came to the door of the

139

little house and, moving from the shadow into the sunlight, I noticed—for the first time since I've owned it—that my blue suit was bright, and my blue tie, rather than subdue, accentuated its shade. I sparkled, profaning the ceremony. I pulled my beret over my forehead to lend a touch of disorder to my appearance, and with one finger I pushed down the tip of the handkerchief sticking out of my breast pocket.

I can't express why I was incapable of being simple, direct, why I couldn't collect information and at the same time dispense the proper amount of compassion to the weeping daughters who rested their heads on the shoulders of the men supporting them as the hearse moved off. I have always envied objective reporters who write whole columns every day: this happened, that happened. I've often asked how they manage, for me it's an unendurable task, though they say it's very easy. I read the newspaper account of the building that collapsed recently on the Via Nomentana, and since I had been there the previous evening to see for myself, I had to admit that the reporter had proved his concreteness, with names and statistics, his natural relationship with others—the thing I envy. While I wandered around among a hundred silent people who were waiting to see at last an arm or a foot appear belonging to the workers buried in the rubble that the firemen were slowly removing, my spirit never rested in one point for a moment, it became exalted in moral considerations, or it was dejected in feeling the fragility of the human lot which is also my lot, or I said to myself I don't understand anything, nothing can be understood; the firemen's tall ladder, a technical marvel, drove me to assert that perhaps I was mistaken in being such an accuser in my life, in wanting radical changes as if nothing had been done: look at that ladder, it's the fruit of constant toiling toward good. Then I thought: no, the builder who made it ten yards longer wasn't aiming at good, he was working "for himself," like a mathematician; seeing the tangled movements of the arms, legs, backs of the rescue squad, I could no longer find a motive of protest. I was frightened at feeling without motives of protest, of conflict: what will I do tomorrow? And I went to seek stimulation in another bunch of people. They were talking about too much sand in the cement, of iron rods too scarce in the columns, penny-pinching. "Let's lynch them!" I would have lynched the contractors. Mentally I slapped a fat man who I decided must be the builder. It's amazing how he took on a physiognomy of precise fury with his reactions to my slaps, though in
140

reality he was standing there calmly with some others. I found myself plunged into this fierce wrestling bout, from which I was distracted by a man talking about the bicycle of the youngest of the dead workmen; for ten minutes with other workmen he argued what make the bicycle was, one workman who had survived, having abandoned the site a few minutes before the crash in order to relieve himself, said he had hung his jacket on the bicycle once and so he was sure of its make. He broke off to run after the firemen, who were leaving; "We'll come back early tomorrow morning," the firemen said. "No, you mustn't stop for a single minute, work in shifts," he shouted. The head of the rescue squad from the car with its engine running shouted that he wouldn't risk live men for dead men, everything could collapse, and they had to wait until it was light tomorrow morning. A chorus of protests was heard, including my own "Ohhh," muted by the suspicion that technically the firemen weren't wrong. But one man said that in Naples during the war he had taken part in operations of this sort and they never quit until the bodies were found. The head fireman, who was in civilian clothes, leaned from the car window to shout: "What kind of shithead nonsense is that?" and I too would have thrown rocks at the car as it drove off. Some young men were talking about God: "Why was it those three, in particular, who got it in the neck? One of them was just married." I came at the end of the discussion, the oldest shook his head insisting they hadn't convinced him; talk always seems to make things work out. Dispersed and reassembled by those voices, I would never have been able to find a unity, to say this is how it happened; at the moment when I was about to say it was like this, a slight sound made me turn my eyes somewhere else. When I grow older, I should lose this sharpness of hearing; I would take advantage of the loss to order the things I have inside me, but when I feel I've reached a sure fact, a thought that strengthens and summarizes, I run away instinctively as from a trap.

I was among the last to follow the bier (I resume the first story). We were going past a large field where, out of the corner of my eye, I recognized the faded chalk lines of an old football field; a photographer, lifting his Leica to his eye with his elbows pointed in opposite directions, took rapid photographs of everything he could: he crouched, he stood up, he drew back with rapid little steps, he dived on somebody who was making a grimace of sorrow, he even photographed me. He was the photographer from the weekly magazine. I signaled to him with my finger to stop, and he

141

vanished among those women with handkerchiefs in their hands, waiting for tears, then he popped up again here and there as if from black waves until we came up to the church and, having seen the photographer, I understood less and less the sense of my being there. I felt a portion of weakness—I'm here only because I didn't know how to say no—a portion of honest curiosity, a portion of vanity, one of cynicism, at least that modicum that always exists in a writer throughout the passage between the emotion of the thing and his telling about it.

I had been able to cast a glance into the little house—two or three rooms—from which the dead woman had come, and in the first room, though it was perhaps twelve feet square, there were a number of people because it really was empty, the law had carried away all the furniture. I looked every now and then at my watch to calculate if I would finish in time to reach Rome and see some documentaries by Questi and Vancini which were being shown at five. To please me, the sun had stopped. They were lifting the coffin from the hearse when there was some odd commotion around it. Perhaps somebody had fainted. The coffin, borne by six people, had started toward the door of the church about seven or eight paces away, but it didn't have the usual rectilinear steadiness, it lurched up and down as if on a wave, and I finally realized there was a struggle: one arm of the photographer was holding the camera in the air as if to rescue it from the waves. The silence was broken by shouts and moans from the women, and twenty or thirty people were running around in confusion. As the coffin disappeared into the darkness of the church, the photographer slumped to the ground, his face flushed and his hands on his private parts, somebody had kicked him in the testicles. "He's been taking pictures all morning," a relative said, breathless, "We don't want him." Four or five of us carried the photographer to a bar where, by chance, we found the masseur of the local football team, the Romulea. He went off with the photographer, still in a state of shock, for a first look; he had seen the member was streaked with blood. In broken words, they argued around him, if he was entitled or not to take pictures in such cases; and I felt they were all right: the family, the photographer, the police who came to confiscate the camera, and Salvioni, who after having run up to help, to restore calm, murmured that we would never make it to Rome by five. "They're newspaper men," the people said, pointing at us, and we couldn't tell if they were against us or not. In the churchyard the hearse was
142

standing alone. I couldn't help thinking of the film I'm writing about a photographer, and I don't know if it was diabolical or divine providence that made me run into a photographer who was then crying: "No, they're not going to take away my camera, they don't have the right," and he was calculating the cost of his camera; he was a young man who had come from Bologna to seek his fortune; on the same day he came from the arrival of a cabinet minister to events like this. Tomorrow he'll have to photograph the man who wants to be turned into a woman.

At five we were at the police station and not in Rome. We telephoned our friends to warn them of our delay. Once more things became confused, at the same time I was admiring the invention of the telephone, which puts us in touch with the world in a few seconds and thus gave me a base on which to rest my confusion, but while the sergeant was questioning the photographer, I was also imagining Questi in Rome talking with the proprietors of the projection room to see if they could postpone the showing another half hour, and it was all so far from that blonde girl, the dead woman's youngest daughter whose sobs were surely being renewed by the *Dies irae dies illa* of the priest. Every now and then Salvioni came out of the sergeant's office to assure us we'd be leaving any minute. We waited in the courtyard which was as silent as in full summer; a policeman came out from a kind of garage with shaving things and a towel and looked at us without any curiosity. At the end of a little road that led to the highway the funeral procession went by—they were going to bury the poor woman in Rome—with seven or eight automobiles following her. Perhaps we'll overtake them. I would huddle in the back of the car so as not to be recognized. But we didn't overtake them, and I was amazed because they must have gone at a speed of fifty miles per hour at least, a funeral procession. In Rome then, about ten that night, I learned a member of the dead woman's family had called the magazine to say they weren't really as poor as they seemed.

PIGEONS AND A DATE, June 8, 1959—The little shuttle-train was ready, the one that goes to Guastalla, stopping at all the little stations with saints' names where the chickens peck between the wheels of the trains. You pass hedges, and if you just reach out, you can tear off a leaf or a twig while the telegraph wires seem to wave up and down when you go by the poles that support them, the grass is almost taller than the peasants whose heads you can see occasion-

143

ally and the sparks of their scythes or their pitchforks. But I didn't take the train. I took a car, spending three thousand lire in order to enjoy a quarter-hour more of daylight in Luzzara. At Reggio I should have gone to see my brother-in-law Gino, who is always up on the roof, he's spent his free time like that for forty years. Where's Gino? His wife answers: "On the roof"; which is, really, a garret; he aims his pale eyes at the horizon when there are the races, waiting, his heart pounding as if it were the first time, to see a little dot there in the distance, his pigeon arriving from a trip of four hundred miles. As soon as it arrives, he removes from its leg a little sealed roll which he sticks into a time-clock, then he ships the clock to some Commission or other which compares all the rolls from the competing zone and gives the prize to the fastest. Modest prizes, as a rule, everything is modest, simple, taking place in the air; a pigeon eats thirty grams of food a day, with a few hundred lire you can keep forty of them.

He told me they're used only for espionage nowadays. But with modern scientific progress they aren't even used for that any more, so recently the army turned its pigeons loose. They fly at forty, fifty miles an hour on the average and aren't stopped even by lightning, but when they go through certain obligatory passes, in the Marches, there is always somebody in ambush who shoots and kills some, arresting their flight toward a record and toward love. Because the secret of making them fly to the limit of their power lies in the technique called widowing; they've trained them by giving them a female the minute they come back from a long flight; it's their desire that multiplies the beating of their wings. As soon as they're in the cote, they begin to caress, kiss with their beaks, they take things slowly at first, then in the end they perform rapid movements like roosters, and they can repeat it seven or eight times a day. Gino has a son who knows almost more than he does about pigeons, even if the boy's been forbidden to enter the cote for fear he'll catch the same mania; it's wonderful, Gino says, but wives are sacrificed, and on Sundays they wait in vain to be taken out for a stroll. Gino is my age, and he says that every now and then he has to rub his hand over his eyes because staring for a long time at the great whiteness of the sky makes little spots appear from nowhere, and they can be mistaken for pigeons. My typist protests politely about pigeons because a man in her building has put his cote near her bedroom window, and not only do they begin to coo before dawn, but after making love in their happiness they fly around the building in
144

frenetic joy, passing over the flowers and destroying them like the wind, then they go back to the cote, make love again, then off once more, shaking their wings with a noise like dishcloths.

In the car I thought again of a plot. I've condensed it into one day, June 10th, 1940, in Rome, with the voice of Mussolini making the fatal announcement.* That day, in the morning, didn't seem so different, after all, from other days. I was in Rome, in a rented room, looking at my opened suitcases, ready to go back to the North. Well then, in a Roman apartment, probably downtown, a schoolteacher lives with his wife and his little daughter; he loves his wife and believes he is loved, but that very day he has found a note that arouses his suspicions about his wife's fidelity. In the evening, along the stairs you hear the footsteps of the people taking refuge in the air raid shelter in the basement, while the antiaircraft artillery shoots at the French planes which have turned up at once. At school that morning he had spoken about the Duce's speech: what would the Duce say in the afternoon? From the conversation between him and the boys we glimpse the conditions of the Italian family at that time. The papers were, of course, convincing, and the majority of the people had gladly relinquished everything to the others to manage. What about the woman? She may be a very admirable woman; she says everything that's in her heart. How can you love someone you don't love? A different taste of the skin is enough. We want to get to the bottom of these problems at this crucial moment, and for that matter on that historic day people lied, stole, did good works, children were born, others died, there were baptisms, arguments, embraces, tears, prostitutes, pimps, adulterers, deflorations, tender loves, dreams, and black shirts. It isn't easy to find the key. That day is emblematic as if a man in uniform all of a sudden, at the very moment he is saluting in the square with his usual diligence and the troops dash by, feels his pants fall down. Our protagonist was perhaps a Fascist out of laziness. His life has been one long habit. Why should his wife be unfaithful to him? The wife, after an attempt at silence, speaks, answers everything. Luckily she hasn't even modesty any more, she has entered another dimension, and calmly she tells him that after a few months of marriage she no longer loved him, and he almost goes mad: how can this be, when everything went on, so simple and clear, and his wife moaned with pleasure in bed when they made love? With a new coldness she

---

* Declaration of war against France. "Stab in the back."

explains to him how this happens, and for that matter you can't behave any differently in Italy, we're obliged to lie, to adapt ourselves, to delude ourselves. Husband and wife are like two Cartesians at certain moments, beyond passion, but he can't stand it, and the more she reasons, explains, the more he broods; all of a sudden he explodes, beats her up, there is a scene in the shelter. Then he runs outside where the air-raid wardens now and then shout to somebody to put out a light. They stop him, and they almost take him to the police station because he says exasperated things, against them, against Fascism, at random, muddled; but they feel pity and fear at his words, too. In bed, he and his wife, their eyes wide in the darkness, with a few noises that suggest history, have nothing behind them but error. They should have done this, they should have done that, they really should: but must things always be rehashed? Everything can be understood—if you want to understand it—in a moment. But it's painful, better to be a cuckold, almost all men think; they don't think, it's an act that resembles thinking, an aura, nothing precise, sketches, and God always helps them—from their point of view—to remain in that imprecision.

PORT OF NAPLES, October 15, 1959—In August we were on the dock in the port of Naples; one of Lauro's ships was leaving in an hour's time for Australia. Mario Soldati * was asking some emigrant if he had a book in his trunk, and our report on *Reading Italy* progressed among the farewells; we stumbled over the peasants' sacks tagged Sydney and were tripped by the television cables. I had already seen a similar sailing some years ago, but this time the shouts of the people separating were even more desperate, one girl acted as if she were being disemboweled, and for half an hour she held out her arms toward her sister who was already on the ship, while a group of peasants formed and broke up like a ballet, moving from passionate embraces to invocations to sudden immobility, silences, or brief words concerned with the tickets or a document, only to resume their moans immediately afterward. You couldn't make out who was leaving and who was staying behind, you couldn't calculate the degree of kinship. "Be careful," one old woman kept shouting to her daughter, who stared down at her from the deck, when she wasn't shouting her warning she repeated it to herself in a low voice, never stopping. From that swarm of black

* Mario Soldati, writer and film director.

clothes and swollen faces I ran to the odalisques who could be seen through the portholes at the prow. They belonged to the King of Yemen. The bodyguards with little short legs carried guns and ropes of cartridges over their tunics and moved around on the foredeck to defend their master, who was probably in the arms of one of the women. Every now and then an odalisque jumped up to display her face better to her admirers, and then a little group of soldiers out on a short pass shouted as when the *artiste* in a vaudeville act wiggles her hips. Those fabled women were almost within reach. One bared only her forehead and her eyes, playing with a kind of silvery shawl; quickly she covered herself again and with her hand she slowly opened a crack in the shawl through which an eye flashed or her mouth could be glimpsed. Our soldiers were making absurd gestures, inviting them to write or else: "Wait and we'll swim out" or else "We'll get married," striking their two index fingers, extended, against each other. The blackest of the women must have been the favorite, remote in her darkness, with an occasional flash of teeth, and in vain they shouted: "Make that one come closer"; she wouldn't move and she merged with the wall, in shadow. Carlo Musso and I went aboard the ship. I saw the hold where the cranes were lowering the cargo; it seemed deeper than the ship itself. The gleaming wood that smells of wax and varnish can deceive you, even the brass of the handles and the other finishings that shone everywhere, but the difference in classes is more striking than on trains: to think you couldn't go on a certain deck or down a hall that the others use when you're in the midst of the ocean is a thought that takes your breath away. We were walking in a deserted part of the ship, along the farther side from the dock where they were still crying, running, frightened by the siren's first, pitiless, terrible sound announcing that the sailing was imminent; here, instead, there was a great calm, waiting for the passengers to put their handkerchiefs back in their pockets, a mile out of the harbor. Passing a door somewhat wider than the others, I happened to glance inside. There was the King of Yemen. An elderly man, heavy, half-reclining on some carpets, with enormous eyes. I saw the eyes before I saw the turban and the silk and velvet clothes, green, white, pink. He looked at me without moving his head, just shifting his eyes. My first thought was: I could kill him easily, and not because of conflicts between me and Yemen, but as revenge against the guards who, on the other side, with hostile expressions were preventing anybody from approaching the royal area. We went

147

off immediately because it's instinctive not to continue looking at the *monstrum* you discover, but to remove it in a kind of mixture of modesty and a need to think the matter over, remember it. Then you go back, trying to savor the wonder that at times seems mortifying: so, feigning indifference, we passed the king again who, this time, didn't even condescend to glance at us, he must have taken us for Italian police, also keeping guard over him.

We went to tell Soldati that if he wanted to see the King of Yemen, this was his chance, but he was asking some dumbfounded Calabrese: "What are you reading?" I had forgotten my spyglass in the hotel. I would have liked to examine the odalisques with it, the blackest one. At times, after having caught someone greedily with my spyglass, I've lowered it in dismay: somebody who is two hundred, three hundred yards away is drawn before me, helpless; such power makes you afraid. My heart would start pounding as I turned the little wheel that brings things closer or makes them go away, the slow, silent approach of a person, first hazy, then clear. Near Punta Ala an old woman was sitting in the middle of a farmyard, and I turned the spyglass away from her because in that silence I seemed to hear her thoughts. A girl coming back from the sugar-beet harvest: I followed her with the glass up to her room: the window was open a bit and she appeared in that narrow opening with a little mirror, looking at herself and fixing her hair. The little mirror reflected a milky line along her nose in that cool, half-dark room. No curiosity seized me, only regret at not being young enough to write to that girl "I love you." She joined the others who were eating, leaning against the wall of the farmhouse. I went to rest in the early afternoon hour with distant heads that passed through the cornfield; it's disconcerting to see a person enlarged, with wrinkles you can count, two or three times life-size, and not to hear that voice, even though it's speaking. Also at Lake Averno, while Soldati was framing the sunset between the two mountains over the bay of Pozzuoli, the antiquated ships encouraged the sensation of complete stillness, and I looked with my glass at a house and all I could see was a pair of hens and poverty. A young girl appeared at the door, and became aware of me, of the spyglass; after seeming almost crushed, she tried shyly to fix herself up. Her gaze met mine, even if mine was hidden by the instrument: I stood there seeking the meaning of my arbitrary act. I understood little, very little, and I saw so much. As a poet huddles down when he
148

writes a verse, occupying as little space as possible in the air, so the eye, in order to see, must narrow, rather than open wide.

WHY?, 1960—Why do I always paint priests? Their form is easy for a poor draftsman like me, basically the art I dream of is going around with a simple frame and, if I should see something that strikes me, framing it and with a shout inviting passersby to have a look, only for a moment since something else will attract me at once, and so, leaving a wake of masterpieces in the air, I come home exhausted and sleep. Months go by and I don't pick up a brush, in the illusion that you can train mentally to become a weight lifter. "I don't want to be a priest," I used to shout, and I hoped that my too-sweet face would become hard, my aunts peeked out at me when, at six, dressed as an altar boy in the surplices they had embroidered, I went to serve funerals—the candle I carried was taller than I was—and when I came back they kissed me. I slept between my aunts with holy cards plastered to their hips with sweat, one of them settled down with a married man and when she died they wouldn't let her be buried by the priest, the hearse had no procession in front of it and when the horses stopped outside the church from habit, the driver started them up again with a tug at the reins. In Bergamo I was brought up by dear Silvia, an atheist relative, she corresponded with a priest, she writing against God and the priest in favor, as the war of '14 approached; from the diocesan seminary a road descended which at the promenade hour was full of black swaying hats, and I felt better when the lines of seminarians gradually left the street clear; there were thirty canons at Alatri, in processions; one of them wore a gold cope with two priests, left and right, holding the edges in the air; he seemed larger in the smoke from the censer, I didn't kneel down as he passed because we loved the same woman, a handsome, white-haired, poor woman who marched along spilling litanies and never looked at me; in Rome in Via del Tritone a tall, blond, bareheaded priest, after midnight, suddenly sprang from the sidewalk opposite the streetwalkers as if he were going to snatch one and take her away, unexpectedly he veered and came leaping back, his cassock belling out until he entered a little hotel in Via del Lavatore opposite the damp wall of the Quirinal and I never knew any more about him; from a balcony in Ostia I saw a priest speaking outside a cabin in the middle of hundreds of empty cabins with the winter sea behind him. A nun

149

came from the cabin, the two walked toward the road, I caught them with my spyglass, they realized it, slowed down for a fraction of a second, started gesticulating to extricate themselves from my importunity, until not they but I stepped back like a guilty man; on the steps in the Arena of Verona I insulted the gold-laden priests of Aida: move more easily, even crooked, but easily, like me; with a pin I stuck them through their heavy costumes and ran off with a leap as in an animated cartoon; meeting Don Gnocchi * I never opened my mouth, my words would have rung false after his which had the only possible syntax, established through grace in his mother's womb; those limpid eyes of his could have stared unabashed at anyone for hours and he left their corneas to others who needed them; I wouldn't do it, I couldn't give up a last, absurd hope. It's easy for me to draw a priest with many variations: the line follows its own law, and you are one of its countless promulgators; does a purely technical destiny therefore exist, outside of the human material? Let us sit down on the shore and wait for something different to go by, but it will never be so totally different that it doesn't leave room for those who will come afterward (however, in the course your hand follows to collect a stole or a tiara, the more you follow it, the more you are tiara-ed and be-stoled).

NOCTURNE, 1960—Sometimes insomnia is a punishment for having prolonged unduly the pleasure of reading, an immediate pleasure which damages sleep. Sleep instead is a savings for later that you don't enjoy at the time. I looked for a long moment at my big toe, which was sticking up at the end of the sheet, with movements of its own. I couldn't fill the space between me and the toe; there was a valley of absence. I pulled up my leg, reuniting the big toe with the rest of me, and the blanket took on the form of a mountain. It was being crossed by an insect whose name I have been trying to discover for years, or rather I want to discover it but I don't set anything decisive in motion. It's no larger than the mark made by the sharpened point of a pencil on a sheet of paper. It isn't easy to capture; to the naked eye it can be mistakened for a . . . (another word I know, that hides when I look for it). I confronted the insect with my finger to prevent it from going on, the invisible little dot stopped, turned aside, moved back, we

* Don Gnocchi, Italian priest and social worker, left his eyes to the blind.

struggled a long time, until the finger crushed it, or rather, touched it involuntarily, and I could barely find the remains on my fingertip. A little hour's doze was tormented by dreaming I was unexpectedly on a stage before an audience of eyes, enemies and friends, waiting for me to open my mouth and I didn't know my role. Why did I accept it? And I kept hoping I was somebody else.

CUBA 1960, January 11, 1960—I arrived here a month ago. As soon as I stepped out of the plane I looked around for the evidence of the famous events that had just happened and which are still happening, but the light, everything, was normal except one woman with a white dress and a face so black she seemed almost not to have one. I think my breath would be taken away—this is a fleeting impression—if I were totally black. My friends came toward me and an officer, twenty, with a huge beard; they say he's a hero. I observed him out of the corner of my eye in the car, with the rest of my eye I saw palm trees pass, rising and swelling toward the center like the neck of an ostrich that has swallowed an apple. They took me to the same hotel as in '53; in those days Batista was in charge, the automobiles flashed, as they do now, along the streets and it took genius and recklessness to realize that everything had to be changed, from the roots, at the cost of lives, while the newspapers went on publishing every day the arrivals and departures of smiling ambassadors, and while Cardinal Arteaga went on blessing. Just at that time, Fidel had attacked the Quartel Moncada with about ninety comrades. It went badly, the government troops killed many of them, they castrated one man to learn names, Fidel was caught in the mountains but the officer didn't say he was Fidel and so saved his life. In prison then Fidel wrote that speech to be delivered before the judges, which ends: "history will absolve me." On the island Lattuada and I bought records of Afro-cuban music (we stopped there two days, then went on to Mexico). No, we didn't buy only records, we talked for a long time about films with the Cubans, we answered their questions in a crowded hall with Professor Rodriguez, who teaches cinema at the University, about a concept that was dear to me: *knowing, in order to take measures* —the civil sense of neorealism—which became the emblem of that meeting of ours with the young people of Cuba. On that occasion I met many of the people who now in my hotel room were telling me the events of the revolution. Alfredo Guevara, Massip, Titon, Garcia Espinosa. Evening fell, the Atlantic beat under the windows

151

with hard waves, they always explained things from the beginning, for the same reason that Fidel Castro's speeches to the people last as long as eight hours, because nobody knew before and nobody wanted to know, the Cubans had sunk into a dire lassitude, a form of mental libertinism which corresponds to our sterile snicker or Bronx cheer. Here are the words of a chambermaid: *"Before* there was no hope, now we can begin to hope." The heart of this revolution goes beyond Cuba's material interests, it reveals the modern flagrance of ancient conflicts: weak versus strong, rich versus poor, big nation versus small nation; and on this subject the world's thinking had become stagnant. They told me about the invasion march, from the South toward the North, led by Cienfuegos and by Che. Their feet were big as elephants' and they drank horses' blood to slake their thirst. In that atmosphere my Christian doubts vanished. I convinced myself that I too was born to die with a weapon in my hand at the age of twenty (but it's too late now; girls stand up in trams to offer me a seat), and I sketched a prayer: give me the strength to kill with awareness. The war, in fact, not a painting or a statue, revealed to me the truth of Martí's words: after the sea, man is the most beautiful thing in creation. Martí died by a Spanish bullet in his forehead in 1895. He had a prescience of death, toward which he proceeded as if that were the only way of being wholly a man. His is the invocation: *versos o nos condenan juntos o nos salvamos los dos* ("Verses, either we are condemned together or we are both saved"). Against the European masters of doubt, who have a fascination also here, Martí reveals a participation in the struggle so pressing and direct that politician and artist in him hadn't time to separate.

Cuban artists, the great majority of them, are with Fidel even if they are progressives in ethics and conservatives in aesthetics. Art is long, too long for one who is hungry and thirsty. Nobody wants them to sing of the agrarian reform which is meant to be the crucial point of the revolution, but can't the agrarian reform in its less vulgar contributory causes be related to our most private ego and, if you like, to our melancholy? Can't a lyrical and philosophical object be made of it, an absolute, as love and hatred once were? Or can't it at least be vibrant in the variety of impulses and intuitions released by the end of a dictatorship, of a handicapped life? Let them annotate the loveliest and freest emotions of the soul (this applies to literature, let it apply also to cinema) provided that, beyond the sufferings of taste, they address themselves to the search

152

for values, for correlations that help people take their place in reality with a more aware and independent criterion.

Cuba is called the naturalist's paradise because of the variety of the flora. There are no ferocious animals except the alligators and the *tiburones* (sharks). From the royal palm the peasants derive amber, oil, feed for their pig, brooms, baskets and the building materials for their houses, the *bohios,* the mortal habitation of a poor people who live in a rich land, *guests on their own soil.* The *terratenientes* often are distant, beyond the sea, and in fact they have created the figure of the *no residente* proprietor. They exploited a zone in haste, rapaciously, then abandoned it for another; afterward the peasant came in with his rudimentary means trying to extract something from it still, though knowing his product had to pass through onerous middlemen, *el colono mayor,* or else *la central azucarera.* In the higher terrains they grow coffee, they dry it on the sierra, transporting it to the valley with mules, long lines of mules whose gentle bells can be heard miles away; along the roads you often smell the aroma of good cigars, this is the other big crop after sugar, but cigars are smoked best in closed rooms because even the slightest breeze can immediately change their taste. In the cigar factories the workers, whose hands are no less agile than the Mexicans', roll the leaves, put the cigars in the oriental-colored boxes in aluminum tubes, or tubes of crystal or cedar bark—there are even very crooked cigars called *culebras,* or garter snakes, woven together in threes, fascinating—there is still the reader, *el leydor,* who from a high school reads books chosen by vote, it's an ancient tradition, and this is why the tobacco workers have always been among the most educated. Both coffee and tobacco need much care, like flowers, unlike sugar cane, *la caña,* which occupies more than half the territory of Cuba and which has always brought joy and sorrow to the Cubans, since sugar counts for eighty percent of their exports. I went into an *ingenio,* one of the immense factories as tall as hangars where for four months heavy machines smash wagonload after wagonload of cane like straw. As soon as I was inside, a Negro with two or three deft whacks of his machete peeled a cane for me, making it become all white, in fact I tried to bite into it. The juice of the cane was foaming in a tub, they gave me a glass and, brushing aside the foam as you do with milk fresh from the cow, I drank it in one gulp. Meanwhile workers went by with rifles, this was the union militia, a shift that was going to the fields where they would spend the night to see that saboteurs didn't

153

set fire to the *cañaverales*. They make twenty-five hundred sacks of sugar every eight hours. They've invented a little machine which, with a delicate and precise movement, like judo, makes the sacks fall erect, as they're sewn by a huge Singer, over a rack that lifts them up. Imagine a wall, sacks piled up, a hundred yards long and twenty yards high: behind such walls you could imagine Thebes. But this industry provides work for only a third of the year, afterward the dead season begins when food is reduced to tubers and some grasses. Only a few workers continue earning, repairing the machines which, during the intense work, decay like teeth. This is the drama of one-crop cultivation, derived from a feudal agriculture, great gentlemen and bad agronomists who had no motive for seeing things in a national perspective. Now it is certain that the same amount of sugar can be produced even when the terrain is also sown with other groups. The newspaper headlines speak every day on the front page about sugar cane, which is going up in price or going down. The Americans will buy or won't buy it; everyone is holding his breath. This form of blackmail has been going on for half a century, and Fidel is trying to break it, they'll have to sweat more blood, Nicolas Guillen says: *el negro junto al cañaveral—el Yanqui sobre el cañaveral—la tierra bajo el cañaveral—sangre que se nos va* ("The black man united with the cane field—the Yankee over the cane field—the earth below the cane field—blood that we shed"). They spent forty million pesos on American rice every year, and America threatened sanctions if the Cuban rice cultivation was extended. If they didn't want to be dominated by a single market and a single product, with the fluctuations this involved, it wasn't enough to change the top men once again and leave the interests the same. Under Batista in Cuba they built only with tourism in mind, and for the capital, where the Americans can come in three quarters of an hour for the most corrupt of vacations; the spurts of prosperity, an increase in the price of sugar, coincided always with world disasters; this fortuitous economy had caused somebody—I can't remember who—to say its phases were always founded on millions of corpses; and there was an equally fortuitous psychology if you consider that the number of lotteries had risen to three a day. Cuba had achieved the technical and moral aspect of a surrogate country with a ruling class derived always from the same elements, that's why Fidel Castro thought of a revolution and not of a putsch from that morning of July 26th, and his words received much support from the very ones who today try to block his

154

actions. When the *barbudos* arrived in the capital in early January of '59, even on the doors of houses in the residential districts there were signs that said *"gracias Fidel,"* but as soon as the first law burst upon them, the one that cut rents in half overnight, those signs vanished.

. . . I was in a movie theater from four in the afternoon until four in the morning, twelve hours without ever moving from my seat. On the facade the multicolored light bulbs spelled the title of the film: *El rey y yo.* They had forgotten and left them burning from the day before, the whole advertising apparatus. Inside the hall there was quite a different show, the trial of about forty officers accused of sedition. On the stage I saw the War Tribunal, the presiding officer with two judges on either side, and to the right *el fiscal,* the district attorney, and to the left five lawyers for the defense, the chief of whom said that Batista had once had a democratic vocation. In the first four rows of the orchestra sat the accused and, behind them, a dozen soldiers with guns and white helmets. They drank, they ate ice cream, they greeted their families, seated still farther back in the orchestra and worried. Every now and then the soldiers were relieved, without ritual, you never heard heels click. Herbert Matos, the most prominent of the defendants, could be sentenced to death, he had been a good *rebelde,* then he conspired. The yellow press is making a martyr of him because he said communism is infiltrating the revolution. All of a sudden Fidel Castro arrived as a witness. A twenty-year-old soldier, who had been treating me with deference until that moment, began to shake me like a tree you're trying to shake the fruit from, and he said that in Latin America you can't find a man like Fidel. I saw him pass before me, even more impressive than in his photographs, with a halo of hands around his body. Fidel took his oath and began *in medias res;* I observed with all the ill will I could summon, I thanked my luck that having just come from Europe, I could examine him as if through the keyhole, I settled and shifted in my seat, convinced I would leave there with the truth in my pocket. He spoke for seven hours with a thirty-minute intermission. In front of me sat the girl of one of the soldiers, and every now and then she begged him to go outside for a while with her and he kept answering with a nudge to make her shut up, not moving his head from the back of the seat in front of him where he had set his chin. An hour earlier I had been in the military prison. I had spoken

155

with some men condemned to death, looked at the aviator who carried away the escaping Batista on the night of December 31, 1958; with his talcum-white hand he caressed his thin wounded leg; they arrested him when he came down from the sky at Trinidad, convinced the city would welcome him as a liberator, and instead all that waving of handkerchiefs had been a trick to make him land and to capture him. My guide urged me to ask them what I liked, but I asked only one question, which seemed affected, of a captain: if he had a family, and he answered yes, a wife and two children. In the big cell with the seventeen condemned men, one was sleeping, two were playing cards, one was preparing some shiny Christmas ornaments on his bed, another was reading. I stared at one, wanting to find in his expression the signs of a crime, but I couldn't be sure and I compared his with faces of notoriously honest people of my village, and the difference after all wasn't so great. I reasoned in this way: you believe in the revolution and then you begin to have scruples; in how many moments of your day, and even on this trip of yours from Italy to the Antilles, are you acting according to this faith, causing consequences? Which are, in the end, the only serious thing. Drop this look of condolence. I tried to be casual so they would consider my visit that of a foreigner coming to have a look, a man who can't say a word in their favor to the authorities. There was still hope of a pardon from President Dorticos. The big cell's barred door opened on to the courtyard where about a hundred prisoners, not sentenced to death, were playing volleyball: Negroes, mulattos, whites, the majority of them stripped to the waist; some slowed down the game to look at us, with indifference; others drank some Coca-Cola, taking it from a red refrigerator. From the prison they took me to the *Paredón,* the big wall—an immense wall, in fact, against which many Cubans had been shot under the various regimes. The bulletmarks could be confused with the cracks made by nature where little plants grew, so tender that one came apart in my fingers like a butterfly.

Now I was listening to Fidel Castro. He emits fierce shouts, waving his arms, his index fingers striking each other like two needles knitting something constantly; from these shouts he drops to calmer tones, as if at a café table. He says to Matos, who wanted to reconcile the peasant with the landowner, the proprietor with the tenant that the revolution has done nothing different from what it said it would do, that the revolution couldn't be made with *todos y para todos,* in a world where half the people are hungry and the
156

other half see them suffer without worrying much about it. He says Matos knew this was the revolution of the poor for the poor, and that when Fidel came, as the song goes, the unemployed were 650,000. The *campesinos* who lived in miserable huts with their animals, the children swollen with disease, numbered more than five hundred thousand; there were four hundred thousand workers whose wages went from the bosses' hands to the usurers'; a hundred thousand small farmers who couldn't love or improve their land, plant a citron or an orange because any minute a bailiff might arrive with a rural guard to drive them away; thirty thousand scandalously underpaid teachers, and twenty thousand small tradesmen at the mercy of a rotten bureaucracy. He recalls that the first Cuban they met landing from the Granma was a charcoal-burner, "the first to come with us, and the first to die, were peasants, *guajiros*" (which means peasant-peasant), "Our first food was given us by the peasants, the first houses burned were the peasants', the great battle has always been for the land." Che Guevara in his manual on guerrilla warfare also confirms this, for here as in China, in Indochina, and in Algeria, the national aspirations always have at their root the need to rescue the peasant from the so-called geophagi.

I heard Fidel again on television, at two in the morning he was still talking; as I crossed the streets his voice came from a house, I left it in the buildings around the Hotel Capri with its entrance like a royal palace, and I found it again along the half-dark Melecon, coming from the antenna of an automobile. This faith of his in words is moving, it's requited because the people believe in him, believe in the *honradez* of Fidel and his men; and you can well say their honesty, in a land of traditionally thieving rulers, occupies the place of an ideology. On certain nights Fidel can be found, without bodyguards, in any street of Havana talking with five or six people till dawn, as I do under the arcades of my hometown; and one night in a taxi toward Miramar I came upon a group with Fidel in their midst, and you could see the smoke of his cigar rise above the clump of people.

In these Cuban events you are struck by the constant reference to the human dimension, there are no great numbers, even the weapons the *rebeldes* had at their disposal were few, around one machine gun there were fifty *rebeldes* so if one died another was ready; that precious gun was not to be abandoned; and when they attacked, ten men with guns went first, another ten without guns followed them ready to pick up the rifle a wounded or slain man

157

had dropped. Once they called for reinforcements from the second front, Raul's front; Raul sent four men who crossed sixty miles of forest on foot. Opposing them there were thousands of soldiers, cannons, planes, carloads of bullets, and there was America, but not reason and love of glory. Some soldiers were fourteen, fifteen, having run away from home in their short pants to go and *pelear* against Batista. One was so little that when he fired for the first time, emptying his magazine, he found himself many yards behind the point where he had begun shooting, because of the recoil against his shoulder. Since they wouldn't accept these boys in Fidel's army unless they brought a weapon, one arrived on the sierra with a Cristobal. He had risked his life to procure it; he had climbed up through the woods in search of the *barbudos,* he was also afraid and was about to turn back, then he came upon the *barbudos* and said, "I'm here ready to fight, to shoot." They put a broom in his hand and what's more, they sent him to learn to read and write. Out of a thousand, six hundred couldn't say whether or not Cuba is an island. Up there at Mina del Frio, among the icy clouds, drizzling rain, and Batista's planes bombing, those boys learned to read and write and trained ten hours a day for battle, with big sticks instead of rifles that didn't exist. One of them told me how in the midst of a battle they buried five *rebeldes* killed by a single volley of enemy machine-gun fire: he had waited for that moment to put his hands on a rifle, a Garand, an *escopeta,* but then he remained with the dead, as if he had become adult in a moment, to brush the flies from their faces. In this Mina del Frio they slept in hammocks or on the ground, and one cigarette passed from mouth to mouth, twenty of them smoking it, but nobody took a longer drag than the others, each time the glow was the same. They took refuge in a tunnel during the constant air-raids because the explosions could break your teeth. It was so hard that seventy percent had to go back to their *pueblitos,* and those who returned to that warmth left their shoes and undershirts to the others. One boy of sixteen said: "We need an aviation too." Raul answered him that there was no money to buy planes and nobody wanted to sell them to the *barbudos.* "Then let's steal them," the boy said, the next day he stole an airplane and brought it to their lines, having learned how to fly through a correspondence course.

In the past fifty years they have built five thousand schools for the *guajiritos;* now in a few months ten thousand go up, for whites and blacks all together. *Ni negro ni blanco, cubano.* But there is
158

some racist residue, which will disappear only with real, general economic improvement. There are clubs that the Negroes can't dream of entering. The Negroes still live to themselves, I don't know whether it's a sub-life or the main life; they still distrust the whites, it will take time to erase the old evil of the whites from their memory. Fidel nevertheless can count on the Negroes; one of them told me that if Fidel were to marry a black woman, the race question would jump forward half a century. "But," the Negro says to me "going with a black woman or a white woman is a question of preference, ideas have nothing to do with it, I like white woman, my wife is white, whereas white women don't like black men much because they have soft tongues" (In Italy we would say that they ruin a woman's reputation); this man showed me a conch shell I wasn't allowed to touch because it's sacred; he says that the basis of everything is these shells, these *caracoles,* and he is never without his *caracol.* To marry a white women he had to give up the Atenas club, the most aristocratic of the Negro clubs, and she had to leave a white club. Along the Calle Aguila are ancient houses inhabited by humble people who in many ways seem Neapolitan, in the entrance halls there are mirrors in *art nouveau* frames, portraits of heroes, long, thick tangles of electric wire—for here electricity is expensive—and I saw many mulatto and black women, dressed in satin, who suddenly slipped out of one door and darted into another, as if they were going from one *basso* to another in Naples, with their broad bottoms, the most showy I've ever seen; in Cuba a woman with a scrawny behind has no success, so they tighten their waists until it hurts with girdles and other instruments comparable to bras and similar deceits, this has been going on for centuries, so after thinking and thinking about it they really do have this thing and they carry it around smiling. During the war of liberation the women wore loose skirts because they hid weapons under them. Batista found out and prohibited loose skirts.

One day we went to the Tropical, where thousands of colored people dance; the feet of the dancers, striking the empty beer bottles that everyone throws on the floor, make a sound like crickets and it recalls the other, softer sound in the Chinese quarter, in the room where they play dominos, the sound of the pieces being shaken. The Tropical is a park with a little stream nearby, and there are only colored women with beer bottles in their hands. One Negro who was missing four or five front teeth was dancing with a black woman who had a body that could inspire crimes, every part of it

159

would have justified one, and in her delight she blinked like a dove in the arms of her ugly partner.

Fidel's decree admitting Negroes to the *playa*, to the beach, since they had formerly been excluded from some beaches, has aroused diatribes. On the Varadero beaches, which for miles have a fine, white sand, the white ladies wear gloves and broad hats so that the sun won't burn their skin and cause them to be mistaken for half-breeds. The hostile phase, the phase of cruel exploitation, is past, and so is the stage the specialists call "transitory," when sensual love begins to create *la mezcla,* the mingling, and also the phase of adaptation, slow and dissembled, hiding the black wife or the black mother so their loving presence won't harm the descendants. Then has the fourth phase come when the black man is no longer ashamed of his origins? That one is still ahead, Ortiz says, the phase when the two cultures fuse, bringing into existence a third *quid,* then racial prejudice will lose its divisionary malice forever. Meanwhile Fidel has put Almeida, a Negro, in charge of the army, and Raul compares him to Maceo, the bronze titan who is a pillar of the Cuban *risorgimento,* as Garibaldi is of ours.

I worked with the young people of the Institute of Cuban Cinema for a few days on a film idea: a body discovered by chance in a manhole in the middle of a square in Havana, a month before the *rebelde* army arrived. You could see at the bottom of the narrow hole only that it was a body. Chinese, mulatto, white, black? Even before they succeeded in pulling it up, they learned that somebody, passing the *quartel* of the police that night had shouted "Shit," then had run off, but they had overtaken him and dropped him down the manhole, his body full of bullets. The police pretended to know nothing, wandering around among the comments, some shy, some bold, which gave a picture of the mood and the concerns during that period of vigil. In the end, after the body had seemed black, white, young, old; and after the shifting despair of those who thought they recognized the body of a friend or a relative, they saw he was a Negro. I don't remember why we gave up a subject that was promising both in content and in form; we were going to tell it in its real time, and the place had already been chosen—an inter-section near the port where you can constantly hear a loudspeaker calling the stevedores to work, by their full names. Nearby there's a restaurant where you eat fried frogs with drumsticks like pullets'. If you just turn the corner there are little bars with Negro prosti-tutes, their behinds so protruding that you could set a tray down

160

on them; mostly you drink rum and Coke or the good local beer. There are also little shops of the artisans of the cigar: a table, a man, and his hands spreading out tobacco leaves like silk; they earn their living by making about two hundred *puros* a day; crowded little shops of barbers in white, like doctors, who turn the customer upside down in the chair forcing him to read the magazine *Bohemia* with his head down. But these details don't count, what you want to see is life during the *clandestinaje* time, the painful blossoming of a feeling of solidarity, of unity. "What dead man's life am I living?" Ratemar asks himself. Among the film projects there was one on the last days of Batista. Batista had a silver chamber pot and a golden bed, he was one of the shrewdest men in the Caribbean. He used to practice, like firemen, to be ready for flight with his suitcases. To see him jump out of the golden bed, dress hastily, pulling on socks, underwear, shirt, pants, jacket!, in the end, forced to choose between a cabinet minister and chestful of dollars, because of the weight limit, we know he left the minister behind. Trujillo insulted him when Batista phoned that night to say he was coming to him. Batista, trying to soften Trujillo, made his wife and children talk over the phone. Batista's wife was good probably, but the unhappy woman had that disease where if she didn't have a child every year her limbs grew out of all proportion. This is the only biographical fact about Batista that doesn't lend itself to satire. He put many *s*'s in his addresses because he knew that cultivated language has more *s*'s than popular speech.

I went to Santiago de Cuba, in Oriente, where there is the Sierra Maestra. They were decorating trees with tinfoil; colored tinfoil is everywhere, houses are papered with tinfoil, light bulbs, Christmas cribs. In one revolutionary cell there is a courtyard full of broken toys, baskets of dolls, toy cars without wheels, guns without barrels. They are repairing them to distribute to the children of the *campesinos*. One woman who fought with a real gun on the Sierra Maestra directs all those eager hands that scrape, paste, paint.

Frank País was from Santiago, the police killed him on June 30th, 1957, he was twenty-three and had been a conspirator since adolescence. One woman saw everything. From behind the bars of a window she tells it to me. She says he was coming down that street toward evening. "The police had been circling around for hours, he came out of a house about thirty yards farther on, look, over there, suddenly a squad car appeared; the chief of police was in it, Canizares." "There he is," Canizares shouted, and they im-

161

mediately heard the machine gun. Frank País ran in that direction. They hit him at once, they dragged the body over to that wall, put a revolver in his hand, and left him there. We went into the Plazita, a little square with the benches and the noises of intimate squares, a few children playing, a pair of lovers laughing. Frank País and other young people used to gather here. In '56 they attempted an uprising, when Fidel was getting off the Granma; it failed. In this little square, under a plaque covered with names of young people assassinated by Batista, I thought about a film: *Revolución a Cuba*, to narrate the revolution—revisiting its principal stages, reconstructing, as I did with that woman a little while ago. I was gripped by that sincere voice and by the others around her who explained, added; one pointed to the wall, another played the part of Frank País coming down the street. A reportage-film made by a foreigner, as I am, who comes to Cuba, who leaves the capital then goes to Santiago, to the Quartel Moncada, and from there begins his journey with the help of the people. What would the stops be? I'll know the answer better in a month's time. Fidel's landing on December 2, 1956 at Niquero, that dark night; Fidel's first battle at La Plata; the attack on the Presidential Palace in Havana, a mad and sublime enterprise led by Echeverría; the death of Frank País; the assassination of Cowley in Holguin where I'll go tomorrow, and then on to January 2, 1950. Cowley was ferocious; dressed always in white, he slapped anyone who looked at him in the street. He kept the zone in a reign of terror, and while he was alive it was hard to open a second front. He was buying a tube of compressed air for his little plane, and barely had time to turn before they drove five or six bullets into his head. In Oriente I met some *rebeldes* girls, dressed like *rebeldes* soldiers in olive drab, with revolvers. The girls are employed especially for the census, they go into the mountain to bring people alive where before there were only ghosts. One was frying bananas, boiling rice, which they usually eat with black beans, similar in taste to lentils, and water. She was cooking, with a huge revolver slapped against her hip. One girl was black, there were two or three mulattos, another two or three like us. But there was something strange, because every now and then I saw one of them go back and forth hastily, almost secretly, with a woman's dress over her arm and little shoes in her hand. The others conversed with me politely, but their thoughts were elsewhere. There was a party in honor of Isabella; it was her birthday. For eight months they hadn't worn a dress; they had always worn mili-
162

tary pants and tunic. Two hours later we were at Isabella's house, a hut, a real hut, but very clean. They were roasting a little pig, an old woman turning the wooden spit. The *barbudos* were going to arrive towards evening. The girls and the *barbudos* love one another, the girls prefer them to civilians, not because they love uniforms, there's no myth of the army; they feel like the others, but the joy of having won is still fresh and it binds them all together. They shot, buried the dead, and soon they'll marry. One of Isabella's brothers was trying to make a record-player work; he had found a dynamo for electricity, and he was getting it ready for the evening. Isabella and two girl friends disappeared. Isabella's mother let out a little cry because an enormous centipede had turned up in the kitchen. Some children were sitting, watching the grownups, prepared to watch us for hours; for them the show had begun. Sugar cane and trees of every kind surrounded the *bohio*. Isabella and her friends reappeared in dresses, cheap but showy. One girl said: "I don't know if I can still walk with heels." There were exclamations, praise from everyone, then silence. They sat down and we considered whether they were better like this or before, each according to his own feelings; they too, after that apparition of five minutes earlier, had withdrawn into themselves to make comparisons.

. . . Along the Prado I saw the Cuban carnival floats go by between nine in the evening and four in the morning. There were allegorical floats as in Nice, as in Viareggio, but there the Negroes and the mulattos form the parade, and the Negroes, in their costumes that mix one historical period with another on the same person, still drag after them a kind of echo of chains covered by the Afro-cuban rhythms. With some mysterious hint of nostalgia they themselves arouse images of their not-remote slavery; one of the most sumptuous floats was called the *Cabildo Mangà del día del rey,* it symbolized the free day given to the slaves by the king in colonial times, and this group, this *comparsa,* as they call each band of singers and dancers representing in special costumes and particular music the various parts of the island, displayed Negro kings and queens with huge earrings and satins, velvets of every color. The wind flapped the pale-blue silk trousers and the *trajes de vuelo,* those huge gossamer sleeves that make the upper part of the body enormous, like carnations, and the legs slender, and, swelling like sails, the cloaks on which a great golden eagle shone. The wind threatened the *faroles,* which are like large luminous tabernacles on the top of a plank, the great weight supported with diffi-

163

culty, and the bearers, attacked by the wind, were transformed into jugglers, their eyes fixed on the top of the plank. A black woman stopped in front of the box of Fidel and Dorticos, not dancing showily, hardly moving, and they explained that she was dancing "religiously," her eyes on the ground; another Negro man was dancing with a full glass of water on his head while a little group of *diablitos,* some hooded men—frightening once perhaps, but not today thanks to their colors and the up-to-date music—came forward like the Sardinian *mamutones* but with more grace. On all the balconies over the boulevard the people danced along with those in the procession, these are the moments when the Cuban transforms his whole body into a drum. A solitary trumpet player let out some blasts in front of Fidel and they couldn't make him go away until he was swept off by the body of the crowd that closes the parade like the religious processions at home, and it is only a pullulating of black and white heads, more dark than white, with a rhythmic shuffling of feet on the asphalt.

In this zone you may happen to hear, in the heart of the night, the sharp sound of little shoes with wooden soles, you don't know immediately where it's coming from until she appears, an old prostitute, thin and blondish like a Parisienne in her sixties, with a very short and very full skirt of red velvet, she does nothing but walk around in her little gold shoes, and they say an occasional foreigner goes with her even if she never stands still and is a bit mad. You can also find a couple of men, under the arcades of the center of town, who in the dead of night are playing checkers.

A RECOMMENDATION, June 27, 1960—I hurried back to the village for a funeral of a friend who died too young. It would be easy to love God if he knew nothing of what happens, but he knows everything. Your shoes became stuck in a mush of leaves that the soles raise from the asphalt with a sucking sound; some people lining the street looked at us as if we were dead too. From time to time I discovered in the procession people I hadn't seen for twenty or thirty years, and at first they looked like their fathers or their uncles; one face was so wrinkled that I had to suppose my own cheeks were beginning to sag like a bloodhound's. Though some of the women wore veils and others were weeping or else silent and bent over, barely perceptible movements, meetings of eyes at corners between those in the lead and those at the end of the cortège were enough to let you see the secret determination to live that

164

stirred in those who followed the bier. A head emerged, of a man who had sent me a recommendation for some relative, asking me to find him a job in films, and with his head he wanted to remind me. I rehearsed the words I would be speaking a little later to convince him of the difficulties a young man comes up against trying to break into the world of actors. But when we had come out of the cemetery, we started talking, people of the town, along the road, gradually raising our voices, and hardly a day seemed to have gone by since the last, remote time when we had met, despite the different envelope of flesh which the funeral, like a scale, had just weighed for us.

AT THE DENTIST'S, 1960—I was walking peacefully along the Via Nomentana when a molar started aching. A little later the dentist's examining lamp illuminated my mouth like daylight. I complained with some ohs and ahs, a bit like a child weeping for no purpose or like a woman on her wedding night, *Oh, oh, oh oh,* I was the same man the concierge had just greeted in Via Merici, *Ah uhh,* my snail-like tongue separated its reign from the implements, *Oh ah oh ah,* I thought of Alleg, Henri Alleg, Alleg d'Algerie, they squeezed his testicles with their fingers. The drill striking the nerve burst into long, sharp lights that emerged from the eye socket, at a new *uhh* I asked for an anesthetic, my saliva trickled down with little streaks of blood toward the stainless hole of the basin, it's over. *El sereno* assures me that the world isn't getting along badly. Henri Alleg, in vain they try to get from him a name shorter than the breath to blow out a match, without raising his voice one of them says let's see if we can knock even more shit out of him. With exact jerks improved by long experience they pull out his thumbnails. The bent manicurist warms our fingers with her breath for three hundred lire, at that moment an investigation carried out by Maigret affirms that ninety percent of the French read *il n'y a pas chose si belle qu'on puisse.* A strange trade I have, a sparrow flies from a drainpipe to God knows where, it'll take me some time to turn my eyes from his course.

BICYCLES, January, 1961—You could draw a portrait of the province of Emilia, talking only about bicycles; there are bicycles all over the world, but this seems to be their natural place—the Po valley—where suddenly they arrive from a country road or a doorway or even appear on their own, standing out on the banks

165

of the river against the sky. The bicycle has the force of a local symbol like the low moon. If a railroad crossing is closed only for a few minutes, dozens and dozens of these vehicles crowd at it immediately; travelers on the little local trains and on the big expresses have time, before they're whisked far away, to see the bars rising and the swarm of cyclists with their big straw hats stained with copper sulphate and their vests with their watchchains, set off again, unhurrying, nobody speeds on a bicycle here, as if its pace—unlike the noisy new means of transport—were the only one that encourages conversation with nature and with your fellow-man, thus restoring speech to its proper dimension.

The Emilians don't use their bicycles for toilsome, tiring journeys, but for short, very short ones, or for nothing, even if poor people perpetuate the utility of every implement (for example, the peasant who takes to the cheese factory his daily bucket of milk, the woodman who reaches the distant banks of the Po every morning just after the Ave Maria without sickle and axe because he left them there the day before hidden among the hornbeams); they use the bicycle as they use a hat, which you can't get rid of, since it's a part of your person even when it's inconvenient. The bicycle around our parts is something like a dog, a constant companion you take with you perhaps even without riding it, to go from your house to the café fifty feet from your door. This is why you see dozens of them leaning against the columns of the arcades, while their owners play cards and argue monotonously about sports. They leave them to bake in the sun, to rust in the fog or the rain, and if they fall, perhaps making a racket, nobody picks them up to display their faithful sturdiness. A man can leave his bicycle outdoors even overnight, thefts are very rare because a bicycle can be recognized by its owner or by his family or friends from a distance, like a face.

Once the pride of owning a famous make was great and costly; now the less shiny a bicycle is, the less ornamented, the more it's cherished, in harmony with its primordial function; classes are no longer distinguished by a handsome bicycle or an ugly one; a rich landowner, a cheese manufacturer, satisfies his vanity with his automobile, while with his bicycle, consciously or unconsciously, he satisfies emotions like the pleasure of feeling temporarily the same as everybody else.

Like *carabinieri*, the cyclists of the Po valley are happy to go around in pairs; pairing off with another, a cyclist is naturally breaking the traffic laws, but thick groups of cyclists are formed thanks
166

to this need to talk, to communicate, our familiar sociability which transforms bicycle seats into homely armchairs for conversation. The people stand there in the center of the village with one leg on the ground and the other hanging along the frame, especially on market day, so close that the pedals of one bicycle almost become tangled with those of the other, mazes of wheels and crossbars which it would seem difficult to unravel, but they are unraveled gracefully, even if ridden by bulky men who then head off toward home with discreet trills of their bells and brief whistles to warn pedestrians. But the atmosphere isn't always idyllic: I saw one man lift a bicycle like a twig to hurl it furiously at somebody he was arguing with.

There are endless lines of bicycles at celebrations in the villages made closer neighbors by the easy flatland, or following a funeral with a flower on the handlebars; returning from the cemetery they disperse along the country paths without increasing their speed, when they are far from the village perhaps they will pedal harder to release their desire to live, building up as they followed the corpse.

At dawn the fishermen with their poles over their shoulders begin the day; the majority set out on bicycles toward the river or the irrigation ditches, the poplars behind them—dozens of fishermen, each distant from the other, announcing with brusque gestures the weight of the perch they have just caught, or perhaps one points toward the grass where a lambrusco bottle peeks out, the local wine for three quarters of the region at least, though it still conceals behind this one name a variety of colors, tastes, foam like no other wine, to confirm the fact that behind all those local faces, square and red, there are as many opinions and moods.

If dawn belongs to fishermen, twilight belongs to lovers. They move from the houses toward evening, he with his arm around her shoulder; then the sudden headlights of the truck transporting grapes or poplar trunks, later on, illuminate them, embracing, bicycles abandoned at the edge of the ditch. These are also the hours when the dance halls turn into magic places, and dancers come by the hundreds even from the Lombardy shore across the bridges of boats whose wooden floors are almost as compact as a cycling stadium, and the bicycles pile up, this time by the hundreds, with the parking lots' hanging tags, flames shooting from the wheels' spokes under the electric light. Inside the dance hall the young people cling to each other, not standing on ceremony: many chil-

167

dren are born before the wedding, here all talk of love as much as in Catania, constantly, but between their words and their satisfaction there isn't that long gap of the South: the sense of the present is so strong the young are driven to enjoy immediately what is offered.

You come across boys riding their bicycles like madmen, no hands, to display their acrobatic prowess to little girls of their age, and this is their very first love. Old people try to use their bicycles to the end, and even when their legs are weak they manage to hoist themselves onto the seat and ride off, they go to buy the bread for their daughters-in-law, with the illusion of a speed of their own.

THE SUPERHIGHWAY OF THE SUN, July 7, 1961—Taking the superhighway at Florence around midnight, at two A.M. I was in Luzzara. In a year, when they've finished the other stretch I'll make it to Rome in five hours. Every now and then I had the driver turn on the lights so I could jot something down in my notebook, but then I told him to turn them off because I felt like a coffin, a votive chapel, or something indiscreet. I didn't open my mouth until Florence. My poor life, what a lot of talking I've done in it. After Pian del Voglio I was struck by the massive arches of reinforced concrete that will prevent the mountain from crumbling on to the road, and the thickets of signs—there isn't a yard without one, and each is placed there with a reason, so suddenly that silent and luminous landscape is transformed into a labyrinth of reasons more and more implacable, restrictive, and the white circles with a blue or pink diagonal, red with black arrows that break in two, or another rising then plunging down, make you feel a kind of anguish foreseeing that in the future they will multiply. All of a sudden printed on the asphalt the name of the city you can't see advances in big letters; the city's there, behind the blackness of the countryside with one letter lost among the trees, and we continue, no longer over the loose cobbles of the villages as in the past, but through an abstract place amid the pulsation of the tail-lights, the yellow islands of the Agip stations and the white ones of the Purfina, grazing infinite railings with their reflectors. I turned like Orpheus, and behind me was the night.

Passing Forlimpopoli at five in the afternoon I ate a *piadina* in the square, cooked before my very eyes by a huge woman who could have knocked me out with one blow, and instead she handled the *piadina* with the delicacy of the Mexican women making *tortillas*.
168

She takes it from the fire at just the right moment, judging with a painter's eye; you tell it's done from the color, which at that hour was the color of the air itself that came from the hills of Bertinoro (Or was it an impression? Because from my infancy, hearing Bertinoro mentioned, I've always visualized the name as a sparkling yellow, probably because of the *albana* grape).

At six in the morning I was already outside the gates of the cattle market in Lugo.* I had come to see if this is the right place for me to set a rather Boccaccio-like story. When the loudspeaker shouted the market was open, a hundred or two hundred or three hundred people flung themselves inside, almost running. The animals were already there in the stalls, but they lowed and shifted uneasily because this was the first time they were seeing people, since they were born they'd never left their stable except to go to the market. They're bought chiefly to cut beefsteaks *alla fiorentina* from them; in fact, from Lugo they're sent to Tuscany. They have broad backs, and I watched hands grope them rapidly on the withers, because that's where you test the solidity and the thickness of the meat. The bargaining begins with a lot of shouting in impenetrable dialect, during the deal, buyer and seller seize each other's hands firmly, the middleman sways these joined hands like a churchbell, trying to separate them, when they allow themselves to be separated, the bargain is sealed. The horns glistened in the sun because the owners grease them, and there were little clouds of talcum to make the animals' hides whiter, and I couldn't understand how these devices, these embellishments could still have any effect among people hardened to this trade. The veterinarian in a white smock moved around, keeping an eye out also to make sure the *paratori,* the herders, didn't give too much of a beating to the animals that were reluctant to be led to the scales. He pointed out one cow to me, her udder swollen full of milk like a football, and he said it wasn't natural, but a trick to make her seem more milk-producing than she was. One *paratore* had his throat cut by a horn three or four months ago, and was killed; another had his stomach ripped open like a torero: you have to see these *paratori* when they unload the cattle from the trucks, the trouble they have; and they are in danger every second, but they make good money; they're tall, sturdy, some with mustaches and bare to the waist, but when it comes to the picturesque nothing can beat the middlemen who

* Episode directed by De Sica in Boccaccio '70.

wear a kind of uniform, a dust-coat, the kind motorists wore fifty years ago, with an old bandana around their necks, a thin cane with a curved handle and often a toothpick in their mouths and their hats, soft felt, always crushed down in a strange way.

At dawn, in the square there were two or three people in all and the monument to Francesco Baracca, a hero I loved like Trento and Trieste. I'm told they no longer know how to teach children what the fatherland is. They gave me a theme to discuss in Venice: cinema of escape or cinema of reality for children? The answer is obvious, but we mustn't deceive ourselves nowadays that the cinema changes the world. Perhaps the cinema can do something for children, working organically. Let's dedicate a year to the fatherland, gentlemen, you who control the films made for children. But I have such little faith that we grownups really know today what the fatherland is. We don't even know what democracy is. I questioned some schoolteachers: they weren't capable of translating the concept of democracy into elementary terms. I suggest starting from the beginning, handing the movie camera over to the children. In the schools they haven't ever used the camera, because traditional pedagogical concepts have always kept technology distinct from humanism. Let's give the children some 8-millimeter cameras and tell them to produce the old themes, and they'll need a whole new interior apparatus, physical and psychological, and some contacts of a realistic nature. These children, even if they made only mediocre films, would become, unbeknownst to themselves, alert consumers of the product and discoverers of the specific possibilities of the cinema, because of their practice with the camera (I don't believe the problem of a little 8-millimeter camera in every class is insuperable. It's no doubt difficult to carry out, but you would also make the children even more independent of television), in the logical education of the children, cutting would have the same value as Latin, if not more.

A storm is about to burst and children on their bicycles zigzag wildly and rapidly as birds. In Luzzara they need rain, the earth is beginning to crack, with fissures so wide your leg slips into them, but the butcher told me this is good for him because the peasants sell their livestock at lower prices during a drought.

AUTUMN, October 2, 1961—I saw autumn arrive, I could tell you the moment: six-thirty yesterday afternoon. I was coming back to Luzzara from Revere, and in front of the car the first leaves ran off like tawny mice or played, allowing themselves to be flattened on the asphalt by the tires but, once we had passed, the lights of the next car illuminated their resurrected swirls. Instead of passing through Mantua, we took an unfamiliar route, the Moglia road, so from time to time we had to ask a cyclist if we were going in the right direction. It was pleasant to stick my head out of the window, emerge from my shell and hear, in the darkness, my own shrill question: "Is this the way to Gonzaga?"

We seemed from another planet compared to these people of the Po valley, with their shoulders huddled in the first cold on their shadowy bicycles that sprang out of the void with their red jewel and then the shiny handlebars. The voices answered, warm, fraternal, and this was like guaranteeing a patrimony on which we should have drawn, but we abandoned it, rolling up the windows again, absorbed by curious thoughts in the unknown space that the motor divided like a motorboat fending waves. After three quarters of an hour, we got out in the square at Luzzara—there were five of us—exchanging no look of complicity about what had happened within us during the rapid drive, because one's eyes had immediately fastened on a friend or another's ears had caught a familiar sound, even if, as we heard the sharp slam of the car doors behind us, the ground beneath our feet for a fraction of a moment was an abyss or a peak—something different in any case from its actual degree above sea level. During the journey, I had brooded over an old disappointment of mine, my sorrow at not being born handsome; I must have mentioned it before, it's one of my weaknesses. And there's nothing to be done about it now, even if we reach the galaxy. I would have liked to be handsome like a boy who, when I was young, stole a girl from me. He's dead now, but he was handsome. I even scribbled some verses once, envying that man who walked through the town while the women stuck their heads from the doorways to look at him when he had gone past. He's putrefying in his grave in vain; that back of his that was so admired is still in our midst, and that casual pat he gave his wavy black hair, which must have been two inches long. More than one wife recognized his footstep. He had bad taste. And I counted naively on the yellow shoes which he wore even with a blue suit. I counted on the girls of my village hating his brown satin ties with great white stripes; but I was mistaken because, of course, they always visualized him naked. He didn't have to make any effort, and his image has remained in the air where, every so often, a

171

woman's gaze moves away from us and runs as if to a secret rendez-vous.

Today I'm in a mood for confessions, perhaps it was the road toward Ostiglia, the *carabinieri* coming out of a tobacconist's with their report in hand, followed by a driver, hanging his head like a boy. We slowed down and the truck's shattered panes crunched under the wheels of our Taunus like ice (death must be a sudden sound of breaking glass and no more), but we didn't stop because you don't much feel like stopping: the point of arrival, however unimportant it may be, draws you on like a funnel. Yesterday, on the other hand, we were winding down the curves of Radicofani behind a car with a British plate and I said "Let's take it slowly." In the center of the rear window of the English car was the brown head of a woman who never turned around. After a mile or two I almost fell in love: that head which went from shadow to the sun-lightlight in the curves, swaying slightly, bent toward the North, became the head of a woman with whom I would have gone gladly —not knowing if she was beautiful—on those terraced fields, with the hesitant ants in our body hair, the wasp that passes from an ox's dunghill to the folds of her dress: you don't fear its sting, and everything has the color of the heavens that your eyes, half-shut in pleasure, see immediately upon you. At the San Quirino crossroads the English car vanished and I turned my gaze again to the oxen against the clay hills to forget the foreigner, but I could hear the rustle of *Time* that she will leaf through in her house with her beautiful hands dotted with freckles. Perhaps she will never read the half-column from Rome, where I am mentioned, I who a moment ago felt the blood rushing to my head because of her. "Macmillan, Macmillan," I repeated for no reason, then I vented my wrath on Bitter Campari, whose billboards along the journey often appear like a kind of bullying: they want me to drink. In Milan they've calculated that I will go by here, that the red on the billboard corresponds to my thirst and manages for a moment to collect all the heat of sex in my mouth, I'll stop at the first bar because in the drawing the red is frosted and cool with drops of moisture, and my epiglottis, because of Pavlov's reflexes, is already moving like a snail. It seems the owner of the Milanese aperitif company is an elderly lady of few words who has never seen her truckdrivers, one of whom we met at Torrenieri with the little bottles of the bitter concoction trilling in their cases at a curve. *Bitter,* my father used to say, with one *t.* Liquid is something like once when I was mak-
172

ing love with a girl in a ditch, little by little the water reached our lips; we were ready to die, to allow the supreme moment to coincide with the water's covering us, drowning us, but we finished in time to jump out like ducks, and laughing she spun around on her heels sprinkling drops of black water on the white dust.

SHEETS OF PAPER, September 20, 1962—Felice, the concierge, came to express his best wishes for my sixtieth birthday today (I'm older than my father and my grandfather: the former died at forty-eight and the latter at fifty-seven). The first concierge I found here was Saveri, who one day in 1953 said: *I'm fed up with this life* and went off with his wife and his two children. His place was taken by Mario and Irma, a Sicilian ex-*carabiniere* and his Veneto wife, my age. From time to time my maid stopped, broom in hand, to listen to the shouts that came from beneath our feet, because the concierge's apartment is at basement level. They quarreled in the midst of that humidity, preferably at dawn, he paused only to hunt for a new insult and she only for a new scream. Afterward they would bring up the mail with smiling faces as if they were two other people, they bowed in greeting and the woman seemed almost to do a little dance. They were very thin, so they seemed elegant despite their shabby clothes. Once I even put my ear to the floor to learn something about their past, but you could hear only the curses clearly, in whose acoustic range they expressed themselves with the most delicate nuances, as some animals must do. He suffered from asthma, and his apartment was a tomb for this disease. When I waited for a taxi, we would exchange a few words at the door of the building or some grunts about the political situation; to please me he always agreed with what I said, however far his heart was from mine. At his funeral there were seven or eight of the tenants, including an admiral and a general.

After the funeral Irma also fell ill and had to go to the hospital; of these two human beings nothing was left for two or three days but a chair in the entrance and the whimpering of their dog Bull, shut in the apartment, liberated by a deputation some time later. The concierge's wife soon ran away from the hospital, arrived with a fever, pretending not to have it; according to the regulations she was entitled to perform her husband's duties for two months after his decease. Irma attached great importance to this, convinced that she risked losing her pension through her absence; but the pension wouldn't go, they said, to a woman who wasn't the deceased man's

173

wife. She wasn't. She suffered an asthma attack, and they carried her to the terrace of my house, some of the tenants clustered around her, and she apologized for the trouble she was causing between one painful gasp and the next; the doctor poked at her and told us in a whisper that the woman wouldn't last more than a month or two.

Irma was persuaded by everybody to go back to the Municipal Hospital. Just before she died she had time to take a letter of recommendation to the Bureau of Labor for her pension, her mouth gaping, still in search of air.

Joined by the same clip I find two sheets of paper. On one is marked down the date of Irma's death, March 18, 1962, and the cost of her funeral—fifteen thousand lire—which I learned from a relative. Timidly making the rounds of the thirty-two tenants, asking them all to make an equal contribution, he kept saying *everything included*. On the other sheet of paper there's a note on an automobile accident: a little girl run over under my windows on the narrow Via Vasi; we heard a thud and, looking out, we saw the driver holding a girl of four or five in his arms, her face covered with blood. At every window they wanted to know whose child she was; she was unknown; from a cobbler's shop the mother came out cursing the father, tearing her hair (she said, rather than shouted, that it was the father's fault). They thrust her into the car as she was about to beat her head against a wall in desperation and she and the child were carried off, with a roar, to the first-aid station. In a few minutes we knew everything: they were Calabrians; the husband had come to Rome a year ago and had knocked up a woman in the Trionfale quarter. The wife, who had arrived from Calabria with two children an hour before the accident, had encountered her rival and her husband at the top of Via Vasi, and while they were arguing, the little girl roamed around with no one watching her. As soon as she came back from the argument, the woman had sat down dazed, by her brother's cobbler's bench, not even looking for her daughter. Hearing the thud, she had sprung to her feet: "My child!"

OVER ROME, October 19, 1962—At precisely noon today I was flying at a height of twelve hundred feet over the blond warmth of Rome in a little four-seater plane with Massimo Mida, the cameraman Piccone and the pilot. Thirty-six thousand lire: we hired it for an hour to examine the cardinal points of the capital. It's a re-
174

hearsal for what Mida and Piccone will do tomorrow with the helicopter, which allows hovering, sudden shifts and other maneuvers useful for the movie camera. I would have liked to stop for a moment like a lark directly over the city, and judge finally these stones, asphalt, bricks, rocks, marbles old and new, below me with their two million invisible people, but eyes leave thought behind and follow hues and shapes on their own, anti-historically. When Stendhal saw three quarters of Rome from the top of his house, he said no spectacle of the earth can be compared with this; but that distance was still to man's measure; it was sunset and he surely heard the everyday sounds of the Via Gregoriana.

We had barely taken off from the Urbe airport when Mida shouted: "A movie!" You could see horses and riders racing in an open field near the Via Salaria, some trucks among which the sound-truck and the silver flashes of the reflectors were very recognizable. A few miles farther on, we discovered with a second shout another movie troupe; it seemed something false was concealed down there in every thing and every movement. Piazza Navona looks uninhabited forever (like the streets in perspective on the stage of the Teatro Olimpico in Vicenza) and, with the millimetrical, designed exactness of the relations between the groups of statues, the square inspires a mixture of joy and dismay, since we love and hate perfection. What would I say of that thin, carved line amid the dark amphitheater of the houses, if I came from the moon? I would like to be that peasant Belli writes about somewhere: looking at the Colosseum, he asked whose palace it was. Piccone aims his Arriflex at the Victor Emanuel Monument, he is content because he can use the long focus, the lenses from 38 to 90, but the camera is without chassis, without film. Otherwise the authorities wouldn't have allowed us to take off. They forbade us to photograph, to head toward Ciampino, toward Fiumicino, the airports in other words (the sea is beyond the haze). Tomorrow our documents will be in order; you need complicated permissions. A white-haired production manager told me the story of his life, the struggles to obtain the necessary permission for this or that film; with bribes he often saved months. "I bribe them," he says, "I've bribed plenty of them." He also found honest employees, more among those with high salaries. I insist on his showing me the gesture, repeating the precise words. I want to see the formal moment of corrupting. He puts five thousand lire in my hand, takes my hand in his forcefully to prevent any reaction and says, lowering

175

his voice (he moves closer, I can smell his breath): "We're all one big family, we have to help each other out." I indicate a slight resistance and he says: "Nobody can live on air," giving me a shove to separate me from himself, to create the *fait accompli*. We pass over Monte Antenne and immediately the almost-finished Hilton Hotel comes forward with the crescendo of a monument; the plane circles it, dipping its wing, and the much-debated Hilton spins before me like a pivot, there is a chasm to one side which will be the swimming pool.

In the notes of Massimo and Giovanni Vento I find the system of speculation in the building trade has been the same for about eighty years. You build in an area, creating a housing nucleus, and thus you force the City to supply services. At this point, when the value has risen, you sell land. (Even Marcus Aurelius, for that matter, came from a family whose fortunes originated in real estate.) Massimo points out a spot to me, in the new development at Villa Gordiani, where the authorities have set up a column to immortalize the munificence of the Princes Lancellotti, donors of the acres necessary to the construction of the quarter, then he explains that the value of the two hundred acres they *didn't* give away increased immediately—thanks to the vicinity of that humble settlement—by thousands of lire per square foot. In a worker's budget his house accounts for between thirty and forty-five percent, but where are these workers they talk about? If we could move down about a hundred and fifty feet we might see a few, but we can't go below an altitude of twelve hundred and so only sheep and automobiles can be recognized. Rome is a garage, a foreigner said to me. On the Via Cassia (to reach it I had only to turn my head from left to right) there is the Olgiata, with its golf courses, and two or three miles farther on a reddish-orange bulldozer against the brown of some barely disemboweled earth. We saw four or five of these solitary bulldozers in the middle of inert terrains, apparently alien to human dealings; but at some notary's office contracts have been signed and one morning the sudden pounding of an engine spreads through the countryside. Around the railing of St. Peter's dome, before the gold ball, there are the red sweaters of tourists. One night last July Giuseppe Ferrara and I went to St. Peter's square at four A.M.; with the thought of watching the dawn break at St. Peter's we had raced across the city, breaking the traffic laws, afraid daylight would beat us by a few minutes. There was only a hack-driver sleeping in his carriage; what was he doing there at

176

that hour? It was absurd to hope for a customer. We stood there looking at the horse who had a bag of oats tied to his head, he ate so slowly the bag hardly moved. All of a sudden we heard the sound of another carriage, it arrived from Porta Cavalleggeri at a trot and drew up beside the first. Why so early? Because the first to arrive takes the first customer. This sleeping man always arrives first, four hours early (nobody takes a carriage before eight or nine). Ferrara and I were coming from Rebibbia, in the middle of the night we had followed the endless wall which yellowish bulbs make even longer. It is the Rome women's prison. The land around Rebibbia is deserted and rough; we proceeded dead slow in the car, waving a pocket flashlight at the distant windows of the inner building. A sleepy sentry told us to go away. On a tape I heard a conversation between Bernardo Bertolucci and a pimp, lasting two hours; the pimp said he went to Rebibbia to a place from which he could talk to the women in jail, and once he sent a friend to deliver a certain message and the friend became the woman's lover, even if only by words.

Now we are flying over the barracks in Viale Giulio Cesare, with their immense courtyards and their turn-of-the-century emptiness. The Ministry of the Treasury is among the most immense things, but not Via Veneto; it is gray and stubby. Regina Coeli Prison, elaborate, invented, has before it the shade of Via della Lungara where they are perhaps sweeping out the Cine Arte projection room in which tomorrow morning Di Gianmatteo will debate with the Russian film-makers Romm, Chukrai and Zharki on the theme of "Cinema and Society." Along the Via Tiburtina an industrial zone is springing up with workers' houses nearby, Nordic architecture. (The water of the Tiber, green and pale, doesn't seem water but something firm and compact; the river's embankments support the streets like hanging gardens.) We landed, grazing the roofs of the Squibb plant, the San Pellegrino, and the Lancia. The one o'clock siren was sounding. I recalled Pisa, the Pisa airport, where I took off for Rome two months ago. I was coming from Viareggio, (why don't they abolish the secret vote there? The Viareggio Literary Prize should publish transcripts of the judges' deliberations. Rejuvenating literary prizes means making the judges' responsibility more open, fuller). It was hot, a Chinese was waiting for the plane, looking at empty Coke bottles with the straws still in them; two American soldiers walked back and forth, guarding; another American in coveralls, with a yellow beret, very tall and rather bent, was

177

signaling to a plane that had just come down. These were military things. You could see planes, ferrous-colored, in frightening shapes, perhaps the planes that take our troops to the Congo. I went towards the steps of the DC7 suddenly afraid I might be something different from what I think I am, afraid I live in a fiction of peace, of freedom: we all pretend, the hostesses pretend, they distract us with lunch, with the pretty blue of their uniforms, and I deceive others with a laugh and a project for 1963.

IN SICILY, November 5, 1962—A man says: "Here the people are rather static, people move only to go visit members of their family who're in jail or sick" (I'm looking at the notes of my two-day trip to Sicily). Another man says: "When a fish stinks it starts stinking from the head." In other words, corruption is spreading in high places.

At Trappeto * we went into the house of a pregnant woman who was putting new underwear and sweaters in a suitcase, her husband was leaving for Germany. He would stay here in Sicily if he could earn two thousand lire a day, but more than a thousand the sea won't give, and they have a little boy with polio. He doesn't know what sort of work he'll do, a brother-in-law wrote him to come, and he's leaving. He'll make fifty thousand lire a month for about a year; after that it'll be more. On the shore in the little harbor there are ten, fifteen fishing boats ruined from disuse. There're no more fish. I remember a verse of my friend Orazio Napoli: "Don't damage the sea." In 1935 that verse was abstract. It's the Palermo men who come with their fleets and plunder everything, not even leaving the eggs on the bottom. But Danilo Dolci has already said everything in his famous books, and it's true in every place, especially through the shored-up alleyways of the Kalsa. It was like seeing illustrations of his denunciations, which out of cowardice you end by believing true only on paper. At the Cortile Cascino an array of swollen-bellied women, toothless, flies and scabs mingled on the children's faces, I felt like vomiting and I thought, as I had that time at the Cottolengo Asylum: "Let me not vomit, for the love of God, try to hold out, they wouldn't understand that I'm vomiting because of them, the smell of piss, the color of the soup a man was selling at twenty lire the ladleful, a drum of garbage filled to the brim with rejected spaghetti not even they could eat, the clump

* Where Danilo Dolci, writer and reformer, began his work in Sicily.

178

of girl friends delousing one another almost sensually with their naked children under their skirts and they adrift in God knows what evasions." I felt like a senator, when the people said to us as we went by: "Two years ago they promised five billion lire to rehabilitate this shitpile, now what?" I could only distribute smiles and a gelatinous inner movement that I think was half a desire to look, to know more, to accumulate indignation, and half a longing to run away, to evade an exact responsibility (There, in fact, the victims can be touched and, if you want, they also show you their identity card), and afterward go on living and waiting for another event so perfect in its grief and in its injustice that it would force us to the famous decisive action. What is imperfect in these events of the Cortile Cascino? No one has ever had the courage to come away saying: we won't make the revolution, the "sad and dirty" revolution, as the Syllabus of Pius IX calls it, or we will make it over a period of time that, in any case, has nothing to do with revolution. Sartre is a genius but he is beginning to accept—if I understand him rightly—a long-term goal for the effects of the intellectual's work on society, and from this it derives that the intellectual's trade must inevitably be carried out according to an order of its own which confirms this cultural and political duality. But only a new reality can generate a new reality.

We went back to the hotel among stands selling sugar crusaders and cheap ceramics all covered with gold. Leafing through the newspapers: in one there was Cuba on the front page with immense headlines which always ask miracles of others, and on the fourth page the trials and the shooting-bouts of the building trade Mafia. The big shots were wiser when I was going to school, they just gave advice, whereas now they go into the streets with machine guns. Has Italian life corrupted them? At Corleone we talked with the parents of a man killed and buried by his murderers in a ditch. The *carabinieri* found only some pieces. The mother, who had never spoken during our meeting, suddenly said, sighing, that she's sure her son's head is in Palermo. In a bar we realized with surprise we were talking in whispers. There are about a hundred *carabinieri* in that village of eighteen thousand souls, rumor says another young man vanished from his home two months ago and nothing has been heard from him, but this news doesn't travel beyond the Strait of Messina, and the United Press no longer buys photographs of assassinated Sicilians, they're tired of them.

A man in Palermo says: "Even in the next world the Sicilian dead

179

are divided into classes. They tell children it's the dead relatives who bring the traditional presents on the night of November 2, and when they have little or nothing to give the children, the living blame it on the dead grandmother, who was poor on the earth and, still poor in heaven, couldn't do any better."

Danilo Dolci was sleeping after a day's work that had begun at dawn, his words which in the morning, when we had just met him, seemed something in a book, became actual things before our eyes, took on flesh: there is the valley of the Iato, where the dam Danilo is fighting for will rise; there is the land which from above in autumn seems carefully cultivated, but if you look at it closely you see it's in the grip of a plundering agriculture, poor people trying to extract the maximum in haste, to live at least a year, another year, and from the land comes a product as temporary as their thinking.

Mingozzi and I, at midnight sharp in Partinico were talking with a young man while police cars drove by toward Alcamo because automobiles are being attacked along that road. He was wearing a jacket with vents, I learned he was a serious boy who works hard and doesn't even play the rustic roulette which is set up in the square near the fountain (for that matter, I saw nothing but flimsy ten-lire coins on the board), he didn't want an outsider to criticize Partinico (whose shopwindows glitter mostly with merchandise from the North, sweets and household appliances), "Dirty linen should be washed at home," he says. "As a rule, it doesn't get washed at all when you feel like that," I say. Sadly the boy says that in Sicily it's a great struggle to live. In Rome we met a woman who goes around playing pianolas, the agreement is that in bad weather she has to carry the handle to the owner of the pianola, as a proof that she won't use it that day, "But," she says, "I've had a fake handle made, and I go around even if it snows, so I make enough to keep from starving, me and my children."

VIGEVANO, November 20, 1962—Yesterday evening by chance I was talking with some friends about Vigevano, and this morning at eight-thirty there's a ring at the door just as the black rain was putting me in a bad humor, and in comes a man. "I'm from Vigevano," he says. He wanted to exchange a few ideas on the cinema with me. First of all I made sure that Vigevano really exists: it exists at an hour from Milan, on a plateau about forty meters above
180

sea level, all its thirty-five thousand inhabitants work and earn their living manufacturing shoes. The current year was marked by a dip of twenty-five percent, and a slight alarm was felt in the city. The fault lies with some designers of the town who went to seek quicker fortunes abroad, where they revealed all the secrets. Even the Germans, who make heavy shoes weighing pounds, are more refined today thanks to this contribution and, at the same time, they maintain the German sturdiness. Are there whores in this place conditioned by a single industry? "Not local ones," he says, except for an old woman of sixty, who used to be, after all, they respect her now. There's a season in the Ticino where you go in a boat (*barcé* in his dialect), among the daisies, with a hair-pin oar, and along the wooded banks men are fishing for the handsome grayling which lives in the rapids and has a brown back which becomes a delicate beige over the belly, and fins with orange glints. "At evening the town's deserted," he says, "People go to bed early"; a cinematic moment, he says, is about five in the afternoon when the long rows of buses with names on top of them like Garlasco, Mortara, Ottobiano, Gambolo are stormed by the workers eager to go home to their families. This tall, heavy man who is sitting in front of me, describes, lowering his voice, the sounds that come from the houses until late at night: it is the women, very delicately hammering leather on slabs of marble, to soften the uppers at the edges. The little hammers have flat heads. The story about the white death is true (the odors of the trade), there are acids that kill, and when a man becomes aware of the first symptoms it's already too late, but it doesn't happen so much in the big factories as in the little ones; because an artisan toils to build himself a little one-story, American-style villa, and in the basement he sets up his machines, but though the gases tend to rise from the chemical substances he uses, they are blocked by the low ceilings, no higher than a man. In winter, especially, you hear them shout "sera la porta" (shut the door) because of the cold—some men dig their own graves in this way. Another local sight is the trucks going by loaded with hides that have just been cut from the animals, with clouds of flies behind them, the fleshy lining of the fresh hide is used to make candies, did you know that? On Sunday in the square you can't tell the workers from the proprietors, in Vigevano they're all family men even if they travel around the world, they're proud of the cemetery, with tombs more monumental than necessary, and of their

181

minestrone, which they let grow cold until the spoon can stand up in the middle, erect. He stops: "It's as if I were noticing these things only this morning," he says.

CHRISTMAS, December 25, 1962—It's Christmas. What do I wish for the world in 1963? Perhaps a year of silence, and for one year I won't say we should hope, but that we should look for the means to begin to hope. It's half past five in the afternoon, and the bells of Sant'Agnese have the situation in hand. I caught a slight case of bronchitis the other night going to the flea market at Porta Portese after one in the morning, to the Neapolitans who put their wares on display after midnight, they were there gathered around a fire of cardboard and wastepaper which gave off a smell of sealing wax; some were stamping their feet with the cold in the midst of saints' heads and nineteenth-century mirrors, all of us bent over because of the cold, we buyers and they vendors, arguing about the price. For three thousand lire DiGianni carried off a damned soul, head first in red plaster flames, but then in the car we discovered it was a devil because of two little horns almost erased by time. We left people with their hands outstretched around the fire waiting for dawn and their customers. At the bar a tall, strong and drunk blond boy asked Mario Carbone for a match; Mario gave him a box and in return the boy ordered two grappas. "I'm from Trieste, I know all about grappa." He took a sip, lighted a match before his mouth and blew out his breath like a bellows, but the match didn't flame up, so he told the barmen the grappa was made with potatoes. Contemptuously, he drained the little glass in one gulp. He remained motionless for a few seconds with his eyes wide and his mouth which wouldn't shut. We looked at him, waiting for something; everything about him was begging for air and finally he shouted: "I'm on fire, I'm on fire!" and he ran out of the café to vomit on the marble pavement of the Gallery in Piazza Colonna.

NEW YEAR'S EVE, January 8, 1963—New Year's eve at a quarter past midnight I was wandering around, fairly dazed, in the neighborhood of Porta Maggiore, near the customs house, among murderous explosions whose source you can never ascertain, and broken crockery. I was coming from the Pentecostal church. It's a black zone, Milanese more than Roman; my shoes crunched the shards of bottles, plates, tureens, just thrown from the windows along with the lurid objects that the families rid themselves of on

182

this savage occasion. There was no merriment in the air, even if the remains of fireworks were still dripping along the facades. Not a soul to be seen, only cautious automobiles which drove half along the sidewalks to avoid punctures, and the rapid passage of empty trams and buses. I was looking in vain for a taxi, a taxi rank was deserted as if in some universal disaster. Every now and then another crash, more or less distant, of things falling from above, autonomous. I have little sense of direction: it seemed to me that, going under the huge gate, I would reach Verano, and from there I could start confidently for home. I began to encounter cars abandoned after their punctures, and finally some men, silent however, who were handling jacks. Convinced I was taking a short cut, I walked along certain streets, Via dei Ramni, Via Marruccini, and I found myself more distant than ever from the Nomentano district. There wasn't a bar open and I wanted to telephone my family, who had been waiting for me since eleven-thirty with one finger on the champagne cork, so that we would all enter 1963 together. They couldn't imagine that I was in the midst of a traffic island waiting for somebody to recognize me and stop (the vehicles were increasing every minute). Nobody stopped, and I thought: how unknown I am. I went down a slope that attracted me, I stepped over a bundle of greasy rags, tied with a string like a ham—what was inside?— and I saw a lovely luminous sign: Hotel. I walked faster. It's called Albergo Adua, it has a lobby with a capacity for no more than six but there were at least fifteen dancing and drinking egg-marsala manufactured by the firm of Beccaro, the air was impregnated with egg-marsala and outside with gunpowder. The man playing the accordion, so as not to stop for even a second, opened his mouth and they poured his drink into it like a funnel; he wore a *zampognaro's* stockings and trousers; in fact this hotel is frequented by *zampognari*, the Abruzzo bag-pipers who come to Rome for the holidays, but I immediately saw Elena, huddled by the telephone, talking in a low voice, delicately, and I knew at once to whom she was talking. She was wearing stockings, but no shoes, her last-summer's face pale but healthy had become waxen, especially the nose and the hollow eyes; her expression, however, wasn't in keeping with her physical appearance, indeed, she was smiling with the phone a millimeter from her mouth; you might say she was kissing her interlocutor. She was pregnant, and it was beginning to be visible. I had known her since that July night when DiGianni was filming a few yards from the Stazione Tiburtina, where the year

183

before, among the huge reels of cable, they had killed Pasqualina Rotta, a poor whore from God knows where. It was dark, with only the cinema's bursts of light, and we had collected at that spot a few whores of the zone to question them about the murder. Elena was the most taciturn and the most beautiful; as she hoisted herself up on a cable she inadvertently exposed her thighs; everybody murmured what thighs, except DiGianni, who kept asking insistently, not as a director any more but as a man, jealously: "What makes you stick with those pimps when they exploit you?" Then Elena said—destroying forever any hope of ours—she was in love with her pimp, the same man she was talking to, and now she broke off only to murmur to her girlfriend beside her that maybe he would be coming, so she was going up to her room to wait. I stayed there until three to see this beloved creature, but he didn't show up.

Before midnight I had been seated on the benches of the Pentecostals, half reverent and half irreverent. The faithful were kneeling, the women on one side wearing kerchiefs on their heads and the men on the other side. Out front, my taxi honked for me in vain, I didn't dare leave for fear of offending M., who is devout and also a dear friend. In place of the altar, a large chair looms with a microphone; a pastor, dressed like the rest of us, urges us to bear witness, each of us should stand up and testify publicly to the favors received from the Lord. They begin with prayers in a low voice, not like the Catholics who achieve a single tone, here you can grasp singular, confessional counterpoints ranging from the conversational almost to a shout. A woman of about fifty stood up and said she would thank the Lord forever since He had saved her from sin. The Lord had done wonderful things for her; I wanted facts, names, addresses, dates, but instead she remained generic. "The marvelous works fulfilled in me," they say. An old woman said that she wasn't speaking for herself but for her husband (she pointed him out among the men) because his legs shake if he stands up, he did all sorts of bad things as a young man, but now he's returned to the bosom of his family. One little woman had a few-months'-old baby in her arms, and she said that one day the baby had a fever of a hundred and four; and she prayed, and the thermometer went right down. The others without disturbing the speaker intervened with little vocalises in various cadences, which served to keep everything tense, like a vigil. They also sang a hymn taken from a new hymnal, entitled "Redeemed, Redeemed," which began: "I lived in
184

evil and error." They were absolutely like people you might meet on any street. From time to time there were tremendous explosions outside, war-like: what sentence could I say, what word, if there was war? I would have a mortal confusion inside me, I'd dissolve without finding a little hook of rationality to hang on to.

SHEEP, 1963—I saw a lamb being born in the long documentary on Sardinia which Florenzo Serra is shooting: it popped out like a soap bubble. Around its body the newly-born lamb had a glistening, transparent membrane which the mother promptly and rapidly started eating, as if she were cutting it with her tongue to free her offspring, which in a few seconds, barely out of the envelope, fell again and again on its legs, but started off at once toward the flock with its hesitant bounds, with his mother after him, licking; he managed to keep on his legs after thirty seconds and was beginning to mingle with the flock while the mother tried in vain to involve him with herself. Unfortunately at this point the sequence is stopped and we cut to another: hundreds of snowy sheep on a rolling meadow, perhaps no more than a week old, move all together abruptly from one point of the meadow to another, light-footed, as if there were air under their hoofs, suggesting the sudden shifts of birds' flight. They are almost still and calm, then they dart off as if to go a long distance, but after fifty feet or so they become calm again, you would think forever; instead there is a new gust of white, and you can never tell which sheep starts it.

SCALARINI, 1963—I've just finished reading Mario De Micheli's fine book on Scalarini, looking again and again at those precise, strong themes: peace, war, capitalism, imperialism. Some people considered him a Manichean who understood nothing about politics; politics, according to them, consists in avoiding these black-and-white contrasts. Coexistence is all right, but woe to those who renounce expressing their own ideologies at their most violent points. The more you agree to develop your private thoughts in a democratic environment, the more the cultural order must not follow the slow pace of the political order, the more it must seek its own pace in the attempt, inherent in every creative culture, to become politics. You notice a critical weakening toward established institutions; continuing with this slowed-down style, you would prelude war by pretending peace is possible without any necessity for

185

basic changes. The courage to be afraid, which has been much talked about, perhaps is no longer of use; let's seek a different courage—which we have always lacked—the courage to know things as they are, to run the risk of knowing. From this we reach the multiplication and the constant perfecting of the instruments of knowledge and that moral tension which never failed Giuseppe Scalarini. Dear Cecilia Mangini, dear Del Fra, I can't offer you a better wish for 1963: that you might make a film on the life of Scalarini, a film useful for the Italians like *All'armi siam fascisti* and with a man in its center, Scalarini: about forty years of our history, on one side the man with his wife and his daughters, a family closely-knit like few others, and on the other, his graphic explosions, the intuition that behind the shapeless news you must always sense the great. Scalarini's biography has a natural, popular power of synthesis, "an Italian without bombast," DeMicheli says. The Fascists broke down the door of his apartment with their shoulders and he was in the kitchen drawing, surrounded by his family, as Salgari wrote happily amid domestic noises with his children climbing over him. They bashed his face in, his health was ruined forever. When they were sending him to be confined at Ustica, he heard suddenly beyond the wall of the train the voices of his wife and daughters, who had managed to track him down in that Milanese dawn of his departure. He wasn't schematic as a man, he was steeped in the sweetest and bitterest sentiments. His grief at his daughter's death, his free marriage with a woman to whom he was devoted forever, the solitary walks after the war and his death in 1948. He said he was tired, very tired, and perhaps I understood those words clearly; the tiredness of one who in 1948 saw, in another form, the scuttling of what had seemed achieved in 1920; and he felt the desire to repeat certain words, certain messages, certain accusations, certain denouncements, recognizing them as true, necessary, and yet they were too toilsome to begin again, and there was even the danger of seeming ridiculous (at times the truth can be used only by ourselves and for ourselves). He had a capacity for immense grief, and he drew the reality of historic griefs, of the great repressions. I passed him no doubt sometimes in the street in Milan; we are accustomed, especially we Italians, to imagine a great man with something resounding about him. It's a quarter past seven and all of a sudden the Pope's voice arrives in my study. I reach the television just in time to see a tide of umbrellas in St.

186

Peter's Square, and the Pope (still a bit weak in his convalescence, he betrays his Bergamasque accent even more), who says at the conclusion of his speech from his window to the faithful: ". . . the law of forgiveness widely applied, triumph of perfect fraternity." I heard nothing else. I came back to my study with these words. When and how is the word made flesh?

NIGHT BIRDS, February 9, 1963—The pilot of the plane says suddenly that we will have to land at Trapani and not Palermo (today's newspaper carried the words of a cabinet minister: Trapani has one of the worst hospitals I've even seen). DiGianni and I looked at each other. We arrived at Palermo six hours later, with a slow bus. It was cold but in the trees along the boulevard outside the Alitalia office, hundreds, perhaps thousands of little birds were chirping in the middle of the night. At dawn Saturday I was leaving again for Rome on Flight 113, amid handkerchiefs and sobs. Three or four families were emigrating, seen off by little women dressed in black and a monk. Behind us the sea emerged from the shadows while all the light was absorbed by the runway which seemed another sea. The desperation of the farewells rose as from the void; they were there exchanging things, opening and shutting suitcases when, at the announcement from the loudspeaker: departure, they howled and flung themselves upon one another and you would have thought some of them would finally refuse to pass the gate beyond which the plane was waiting with its sacrificial steps. Instead, a few instants later, their cheeks still wet with tears, they were fastening their seat belts and the novelty of this means of transportation was absorbing them; there was no way, as there is with a ship, of looking back and prolonging the grief, but already the clouds (and some alarming jolts) were enclosing everything. From Trapani to Palermo DiGianni had slept, lucky him; he woke up near Trappeto and then we talked a little. I would go on to Partinico to talk with Mingozzi, who is there shooting a film tracing the ideas of Dolci. We agreed that the straightforward reportage-documentary is finished, even if we will go on seeing numerous examples on our screens for some time; it's finished inside us. Television will gnaw this dry bone, and there will be feature films based on scandals or popularization. Until now, the reporter has simply claimed certain rights and limited himself to the role of voyeur of injustices; and he believes he has fulfilled his obligations

187

when he illustrates certain things to us; but who are those reporters who are doing the denouncing? Their identity card is no longer enough. If they are making a film of investigation, they cannot consider themselves on the level of those authors, great or small, of the metaphysical film, who tell us of themselves in indirect ways, who define themselves through third parties: the responsibility of the author of the investigation film is different, it demands new forms of engagement, more integral: he must, among other things, know he is setting out on an exploration where behind himself he has another, ideal camera which films him as he is filming others, and the montage will come from the coupling, the cross-cutting of the product of both cameras. The author makes use of film in order to be involved in real life so completely that each picture he makes could be his last (either because they arrest him or because the tension of such a film is so great that it leaves no room for a sequel). I repeat that in the investigation film, a specific morality is revealed which may not presume to be the morality of cinema (at times one would be led to say it is), but is beyond doubt the morality of this *type* of cinema which requires the author to cross definitively the boundary of mere textual responsibility, if we want to call it that, and become involved, showing the degree and the stages of this involvement, with all the consequences his film may have even on the legal level. In this direction, any investigation film must inevitably be a total adventure, and when I mentioned autobiography in *Rinascita* I meant to indicate one probability of these public adventures of penetration of reality. But isn't the investigation film moving towards the metaphorical film and vice versa? The first, to reach certain absolute values of the second; the second, to reveal beyond its absoluteness responsibilities more current, more *ours*? The question remained inside me, I didn't even mention it to Di-Gianni, and I preferred to discuss with him a project I'd like to carry out with three directors. You take a man, an ordinary man. He's chosen by lot from a thousand or from a hundred thousand. He's an Italian, so you could say, chosen from fifty million Italians. He could also be a foreigner, obviously, but with an Italian we can develop our theme better. One director investigates him as a physical man. But he doesn't make an airtight compartment of him; the three directors work in agreement, they spend days and feet of film in contact, especially after we have studied our man elbow-to-elbow, the three directors and I, and we decide on the line. I even want to see his cells under the microscope—don't look away—his saliva
188

(we haven't any particular preference for the horrid, not at all).
The strongest reaction will be of wonder, but it mustn't blur the
precision of the data. The second director will question our sample
man for twenty-five hundred or three thousand feet of film. If he
lies, we'll tell his lies: he's a liar, why? The man must first accept
our conditions; we know the film might ruin him with the authorities, with his pastor or his boss, we'll guarantee him a sum that will
encourge his sincerity and will enable him if necessary to surmount
the events caused by the film. From our pitiless and affectionate
conversation, infinite themes will ramify like threads; this individual, this person, is bound to other persons near and far, to events
large and small, historic and otherwise, to localities, faces, memories
which are always something (nothing doesn't exist in this case),
and they tremble with a specific weight like bacilli and the atoms
we are full of; we'll even visit certain places with him, scenes will
be reconstructed (as if under a glass bell): some love affair of his
or some act whose reconstruction will better reveal his essence to
us—when he voted, for example. We'll try to clarify for him, for
ourselves, his relationship with his family, with the Church, with the
State, with trees, with work. And we'll arrange cameras to catch
him even unawares (Will a month be enough? We'll have to stick
with him at least a couple of months). There will be many special,
technical requirements, and, as I said on another occasion, instruments, which can seem coldly scientific, will give us warm, human
assistance. The second director then is the one who is closest to
him, physically. The third assists the second in his preparation,
makes notes on places to be filmed, people (we'll mix stock material with specially-shot film, long sequences alternating with sequences of just one frame, a snapshot) that also show the immensity
each of us has inside himself; the third director is concerned only
with the others, with how the others, those who have direct or futile
contacts with our hero, enmesh him in the texture of their lives.

DiGianni interrupts me; he says this film should be shot by just
one man and that man should be me. I was happy, I was becoming
enthusiastic, and with his words, DiGianni plunges me into an old
silence from which I am then extracted by that unexpected nocturnal chirping I described at the beginning.

OVER THE TELEPHONE, May 25, 1963—I telephone, impro-
vising this installment of the diary, from Luzzara in the narrow
booth of the telephone office, a café; outside it's as if it were snow-

ing with the sun shining, the air is full of the poplar flowers, of their down which is faster and thicker than drifts of snow, I see the Luzzaresi walking in its midst without amazement, which amazes me even more than the phenomenon itself. Coming out of my house on May 1, I found two old men, in Sunday clothes, in front of me, their faces glistening from the barber's rock-alum after-shave, with red carnations in their buttonholes, as in the old pre-fascist times. At that moment one of my fellow-townsmen gulps at the air to catch childishly one of the clumps I mentioned; the fish too in this season often stick their mouths out of the water of the Po because they are fond of these blossoms, and where the water isn't too swift there is a layer of the stuff, a dirty-white pap, a springtime manna for the chub. Groups of Luzzaresi that day were standing below the tower, at whose base there were the election charts and they were chatting calmly about the results. In Bologna a friend had said to me: "You people from the plain are extremists, you must be educated." I'm not sure what we are and still less what I am, but when I hear myself mixed with the people of the plain I fill with an immediate intoxication, as I do every time I'm removed from solitude. Among the trophies of heaped-up bicycles, it took me a second to reconstruct the faces of those old men, to make them coincide with faces I remembered, one had a nose that didn't fit, another's stature wasn't right, the flash gone from the eyes or the legs deformed now by rheumatism. But still I managed to rediscover that secret expression, of mutual understanding, that the heart had retained, outside the years' passage. When in my Roman life I have felt uncertainty, and I still feel it (the hesitations of the intellectual), I've managed to overcome it by recreating inside myself some of these Luzzaresi, the sounds of some nights between 1920 and 1924, like the rustle of Antonio the carpenter fleeing through my garden pursued by the blackshirts of Volta Mantovana, or the cries of Lusetti being clubbed. As the years pass everything becomes clearer than in books; there was the song of the crickets as now and yet with a difference, a special tone of that period of defeat, which at times I identify with melancholy itself.

SOFT DRINKS, July, 1963—We were talking about soft drinks during our sleepy wandering in search of a road we missed, with the calls of the guinea fowl and the turkeys behind us; the others were cursing the city administrations which don't keep the signs up to date, until, tired of speaking ill of others, we all became closed in

190

a cocoon from which in the silence I saw the chrysalis of melancholy emerge. I have always believed this originates in the Po, and elsewhere is only imitation; one evening Raffaele Carrieri, who is a poet, cried: "Who will take away our melancholy?" It wasn't a supplication but a challenge. Carrieri comes from Apulia, and his words made me suspect melancholy wasn't my personal privilege. I must say, however, that as soon as I come to my native region it's like crossing the frontier of grayness; I leave behind me trafficking, politics, blue, red, and I enter something imprecise, or rather the precision of the imprecise, and this isn't a play on words, I have seen many grays, but those of the Po are Gray, the other colors no longer exist, even the bright red of some women's sweaters or the white shirt of a bricklayer or the brown of the low roofs haven't the strength to assert themselves against the gray. To separate this sky from the earth, where generally only an almost imperceptibly different hue is enough, you can leave everything the same. And so it is with feelings; melancholy annuls all the others and even two lovers, who are saying as they sit on the bank that they are happy, yes, they are. I don't deny that, but with a melancholy happiness which becomes normal happiness as soon as they move, on their Vespa, toward the hinterland, toward the paved streets. I am obviously steeped in this mood and, as I roam around the world, I happen on places I define as melancholic because there is a hoe abandoned in a farmyard or a square with a few scattered people and a window half-shut, and I think: my God what a melancholy place, how melancholy, these poor people are. . . . I walk about, I ask questions, it turns out that they are jolly and the melancholy person is me.

Melancholy didn't keep me from interrogating like a member of parliament. When I went through areas marked by signs where you could read in clear, civil print: "Underdeveloped Zone," I was reminded of distant years dotted with signs on which a clumsy hand had written: "Epizootic Aphtha." Then I heard in the air nonexistent bells of lepers and lazarets and the lowing of those oxen swept away by the river in flood when you can see only their nostrils seeking air. How many billions would be needed to guarantee there would be no more floods? The billions exist. But not everyone in parliament agrees it's opportune to spend the money for this purpose. There is a reasonable man, with a family, who in good faith wants part of the budgeted sum to be shifted to another ministry. And so it goes. On the houses we could still see the marks where

191

the water had risen in 1951, and a girl was coming from a door, perhaps to go dancing, she was perhaps twenty yards from us, but you could catch the scent of her face powder very distinctly.

HOLLYWOOD, April 29, 1966—From the air Los Angeles is an ocean of electric lights. The evening of February 10th I stretched my neck in vain as much as the window permitted, trying to see the frontier of the darkness, but that plateau of lights goes on forever. Tired after the sleepless days spent in New York, I said: "I'm not going to eat supper, wake me tomorrow afternoon." In that hotel, the Beverly Hills, famous movie people have lived (perhaps Margaret Livingston, that beautiful cross-eyed girl in *Sunrise,* once slept in my bed).

I looked out and saw a black palm tree and a normal moon. The window thirty feet from mine framed a floor of polished wood and a golden slipper on a woman's swaying foot: the woman was probably reading. In the hope she would come into view I took a long time putting on my red pyjamas against which the white handkerchief blared. The curtains wouldn't close properly and this defect surprised me, up to that moment everything in America had breathed perfection and comfort (because of the circumstances I had been kept within the confines of official places), not one sign dented or with a letter broken; nothing was missing from what our European childhood had dreamed. I managed to block the slightest ray of light using some big paper clips I have carried with me for years along with other stationery items, causing my family to scold me for loading myself down with useless things, but now their moment had come.

Toward midnight I wakened abruptly, and there, like a still life, was a little table with two oranges, a glass, a bottle of whisky, a slender vase with a rose. I sat there spying for a quarter of an hour in vain until I fell asleep in the chair. There are roses also on the bosoms of old ladies between fifty and sixty who run the elevators in the hotels, they operate them seated on low stools with their purses in one corner, they have white or blue-white hair and the politeness of a friend, not an attendant. Handing my passport to the clerk, I had seen many more old ladies arriving for a gala dinner, dressed in yellow, blue, red silk, with an excessive number of teeth. There is a club for millionairesses over sixty, and I'm told if you cover their face with a pillow you can happily make love with them since the rest seems like a young girl; they've managed
192

to rescue their bodies even at death's door with treatments that cost each of them as much as the annual budget of the town of Luzzara. It seems sexual relations between young men and elderly women are frequent, and the women run the country as they once did in France, I've already told how in 1938 in Paris I was urged to believe only the white-haired bourgeois and the elderly Madame Verdurins were the bosses, while the following generations toiled in obscurity to accumulate years and achieve the same rights. On the plane I saw a film; the leading lady, Maureen O'Sullivan, who must be almost my age, played the part of a woman of fifty made pregnant by her seventyish husband, and for a third of the story the excellent actress carried around her protruding belly, very visible, with naturalness and joy. I had the suspicion that no one has ever died in Hollywood since it came into existence, you age, but only in the face. At a grand party I encountered venerated men, directors we loved like glory itself, carrying their photographs in an imaginary wallet, and I moved among their wrinkles with trepidation to rediscover that image, until there was a sign, a glint in the eye: there he is. But I was always left with a slight distrust. Apropos of age, in my bathroom I found lights so bright—brighter than in any other bathroom in the world—that in the mirror I noticed some white hairs my razor had missed for months, for years; I had never seen them because of the no doubt less powerful electricity at home. Somebody else might have noticed them, but who looks at you in Italy? The bright diffused light struck luxurious reflections even from the ice in the little silver bucket. I have to be sincere: in the morning I found that treasure transformed into a puddle of water.

The morning, however, was very beautiful; on the roof of a bungalow the American flag was flying. The sky was streaked by the silent chalk of some plane that must already have reached Great Salt Lake. Under the door I found a note, a printed form with words like "because," "door," signed by hand: "Lucie." Lucia? With my pocket dictionary I tracked down the meaning of the individual words, but not a shadow of their connection: I supposed that it was the custom in those grand hotels for costly Lucies to knock discreetly and come in, if the guest opens his door. The note surely announced the nocturnal event so that the guests—the majority of them subject to heart attacks—could be prepared without jolts for rejection or cohabitation. I learned later it was the engineer in charge of the hateful air conditioning, he wanted to instruct me

193

in the use of the device, but the "Do Not Disturb" sign had prevented him, so he was letting me know that he was mine to command when I woke up.

In a Ford they took me to admire the residential boulevards, golf-course lawns everywhere, not a foot of untended ground, flowers, leaves, foliage, and the famous little villas for people accustomed to birth control; in 1930 I had two ambitions, to live here and to write for the *Corriere della Sera*. On the asphalt of Sunset Boulevard a young man with long hair, tied behind with a ribbon of multicolored silk, raced us for a while, then he waved to us, defeated. Our driver, son of Calabrian immigrants, gave me data in his hybrid speech on the successive ownership of the estates. This one had belonged to a once-famous actor or actress, and so we proceeded as in my town we walk at night among the silent houses and my friends tell me, after an absence, who are the new owners of those apparently solid buildings.

With gestures I made my ex-compatriot stop at the Farmers' Market, to walk among people and touch them. They sell everything there, including pies where the cream overflows with the superabundance and greed of non-form. A few yards away, in a little cemetery with a hundred and fifty or two hundred graves, Marilyn Monroe lies, the only actress I loved. In the noise of the German and Irish families eating violently-colored foods: a sower with broad arms must have thrown red candied cherries about, you can see them everywhere, even on a few cheeks. Outside a Jewish pastry shop there is a line, in the window a rich variety of sweets of biblical ancestry. I was grazed by one of those pale Jews with braids at his ears and a penitential desire to make you uneasy. (In Jerusalem in the fanatical quarter I was frightened by one with cobwebs on his clothes and his hat pulled down over his eyes; he could see nothing but his own feet as they proceeded. A month before in Palestine the valley of Jehoshaphat had disappointed me, a short little plain with rusty cans and stray dogs, in other words, little places with big meanings: I appreciated man's imagination, more concerned with reality. In fact, a house hid Golgotha from me, to see it you actually have to go over into Jordan; your gaze is often censored by sudden, captious frontiers; on roofs or on terraces warlike sandbags still stick up and the barrels of new machine guns peer from walls, and we don't know if they are Israeli or Arab.)

In the Farmers' Market, to find my bearings, I first bought some crackers, made with perhaps the best flour in the world: a region

194

four times as big as Italy produces only flour, another region no smaller, only milk; this geography absolutely excludes the possibility of starving to death and—with all the drinking fountains— also of dying of thirst; and even if a drought arrived, there is always Coca-Cola. Alternating my attention between the city's ugly architecture and the fascinating perspectives created by the immense billboards, which at times the tornadoes spin in the air, I thought that peace will never be possible if we don't give up something we have. The noon hour caused even the extinguished lights to seem illuminated; at one stand a hundred color television sets were going all at once, perhaps you could take one home free. What could they manage to give up? A city, a river, a pair of shoes, fruit? I saw them complete, correlated from head to foot. Nothing they wore (and I don't mean the quality of the cloth, but its very cut and form) could now be relinquished. Still, it's deceiving people to promise them peace is near *rebus sic stantibus:* "Ladies and gentlemen, peace is impossible, we have to start talking from the other direction." What direction? I sought with my eye some interlocutor to talk with about peace (hypocritically I lack the courage now to write "about the next war"), but I found no one really convincing, because the tendency is to deny to the others that secret margin, that ineffable extra something we grant ourselves: each of us has his angel, agreed, but we deny him to others almost with anger. Little by little, I felt I was an invisible man on that soil. They moved, they smiled, pretending, like anyone else, to know what they didn't know; calmly they made their purchase, and I too purchased for my granddaughters some gigantic lollipops that would cross the Atlantic.

A young French film-maker who is working in Hollywood asked me if I knew that the Rand Corporation, one of the *"usines à penser"* supported by the Air Force and the Ford Foundation for pure scientific research, has completely *"mathematisée"* the third world war, and that Tempo, a subdivision of the U.S.A. space authority, has reduced the social forms of the future to equations? I would have knelt down at the foot of the aircraft companies' signs higher than my house to ask forgiveness for not knowing so many things. I am a man of the space era, and to remember this I have to pinch myself every now and then.

I found myself outside the Paramount lot, the side gate is called the "Cecil B. De Mille entrance," the director always came in there, and the newspapers of the whole world have mentioned it. I too

195

stared at De Mille's entrance, ashamed of it as I might be ashamed of the smiles distributed in a day, and those of the others are slippery and false, but we never find time to admit that ours are too and we won't find it, not even when we're dead, when we will have nothing but time. A *papier-mâché* mountain stuck up over the Paramount lot, and I took advantage of it to allow old rebellions to rise in me, for unfortunately the history of cinema is only the history of film, we must go back to the two original propositions: the camera and a man. Where did I say that before? Shifting about with rapid means of transport causes me at times to confuse places and ideas; it's hard to recognize Madrid on a Proustian awakening in a hotel if the day before I was in Paris. Last month in Barcelona, about ten of us film people went from one neighborhood to another looking for something to eat, and as we walked we illustrated encounters, projects. The Spaniards had many in their desk drawers: I have received a letter from those young people protesting against the censorship: ". . . We take the liberty of reminding you of the difficult obstacles that the cinema art faces in Spain, obstacles that restrict its freedom of expression. . . ." We came together and broke up, as we climbed in and out of the automobiles, at three in the morning it isn't easy to find a restaurant, and, during this search, at one point we felt hope and in another the opposite, not only for food but for quite another thing. A woman or the facade of a Gaudi house was enough to distract us from the struggle. What a film could be made from such a night! bits of forbidden stories, recalled by the group of eight of us in a car, along the street or around a table: one would suggest the beginning, another the end, a third a a speech, acting, shouting, murmuring, developing in a chorus. Five o'clock struck in the variations of mood I've mentioned, in certain moments the story no longer had a meaning, a tree outraged us with its indifference, and at other moments a sidewalk thrilled us like a truth. To do at once what you believe is right, to remove yourself from an indirect culture, to distrust those avant-gardes that leave behind what should be carried out as soon as it's understood. From whom can we expect the beginning of a movement in this period of apparent calm? From the old who have nothing more to learn, and can no longer take refuge in a proverb, if they want to save the modern soul. The young hate them because in them they see what they will become; a young man doesn't always know what he should do, an old man does.

In Hollywood, with gestures I told the driver I wanted to go to the center of the city, frequent arrows pointed Down Town, but you suspect you will never find it, the streets look like an eternal suburb, and in spontaneous germination they multiply beyond the necessary; the cars never stop, all is centrifugal toward vague meetings, the automobiles are more useful than false teeth, without a car, dyspnoea sets in and when you reach Pershing Square—which the authorities of Los Angeles labor in vain to populate—you can't stop, the traffic signs drive you on: out of the corner of my eye I saw three or four people in all, one was waving his arms. I learned later he was a religious speaker. According to the experts, Los Angeles will become more important than New York in about ten years (it's on the Pacific).

At one o'clock I arrived punctually at the banquet. De Sica was ten minutes late but was applauded nevertheless. A columnist asked me the traditional question: "To be able to work together for so many years, you and De Sica must have something in common. What is it?" I answered, amid the flashbulbs: "Presumption. Each of us believes, in his heart of hearts, that *he* is the decisive element in the success of our films." When the toasts came I said I began my career thirty-five years ago in Milan under the pseudonym of Jules Parme, writing invented reports from Hollywood. I had now come to check up, and I had discovered the remains of my youth and a brilliant hospitality. A little white-haired man slapped me on the shoulder: "I'm Polonsky." An interminable silence followed during which I fished up that name as if from a bottomless well. That kindly man used to send me, around 1934, for a weekly published by Rizzoli, careful packages of photographs of Mary Pickford, Fairbanks, Greta, Chaplin, and we used to quarrel by mail. We embraced three times. During the coffee we were all nicely flushed; one man congratulated me in French for a protest against Johnson's Vietnam policy, published in the *New York Times* not many days before, and signed also by me, then he disappeared. I sat thinking about my clumsy French, following the spirals of smoke from someone's cigar: *En substance il y a un procès d'intégration. Nous sommes presque integrés, le cinéma italien doucement* is being watered down, the processes of consumption have prevailed over our discourse and the law, *la loi.* Will the corporations that are growing, growing, growing, and the exceptions that will grow, grow, grow, succeed in blocking the aggression, the conditioning of what we must call foreign capital? Stop. It seems to me I didn't make these considerations then, are they older, or more recent? Last week,

197

yesterday, last night, a short time ago, when I was tying my shoe-laces and repeating with polyglot doubts: what is the precise responsibility of us authors *todos reunidos* and what is our duty one by one? *Les vieux* know.

LONG AND SHORT, January, 1967—Wars always begin because people think they will be short, and then they become long. We all agree that, in both the short and the long, we can repeat ourselves. But you were still born in that particular year, and the first film you made was that particular film and not another: I would like to stand up and shout at my interviewer: "I wasn't born." I would like not to die, this is a sudden decision, against the mainstream; life is neither long nor short: it is. I could accept death if we invented it ourselves. I will not die therefore, and I will not take refuge in belles-lettres; I want to act, the page is a coffin. I don't write. They say that on the very eve of death you collect your thoughts and you are summed up in a sentence, there are some wonderful ones— Petrarch's. No, it would be modern if one could say: "Before dying, he slapped Giulio," or else: "Supporting himself on his crutches he arrived in the Chamber of Deputies and shot X, who slumped to the ground in accordance with all medical rules." What does long cinema and short cinema have to do with this? Is there a connection between long periods and short periods in politics and in art? Make up your minds. Perhaps there is, in the sense that these measurements don't exist in us, we've created them as we've created New Year's Eve, and we end submitting to them. Just last New Year's Eve I was walking up the Via Veneto among hundreds of jammed cars. I met serious people with paper hats on their heads and their noses blue with cold, and I said: "I want to get art off my back. Do something important in the new year; *do*, not write." Long or short? We will be judged by what we have done, not written. I don't want to be an artist any more. I took no part in that pointlessly excited festivity; it seemed that at any moment we might witness rapes on the tables of Doney's, just to be doing something precise in a rather imprecise period; the Air France festoons were impeccable. And what about the armistice they keep talking about? Long or short? There is an effective song about Vietnam that makes use of reiteration. Young people were playing trumpets and, as if they were my children, I said: "Go on, go on, you'll be old even before you reach Piazza Barberini." Old or young? A time of dilemmas. How, in practice, can you shake off the fact of being an artist? My
198

flesh crawled as I sensed that perhaps nothing can be done; it's like being a humpback. Artists of the long or artists of the short: it involves a way of being rather than being, and we seek in vain to be. There is nothing left to do but inflate the *way*, which means trouble. The seraphic aspect of the debate between short and long lies in believing we are the ones who impose it, and here I laugh and attract the attention of some Trastevere boys who, on this night of San Silvestro, have ventured all the way to the hill of the Hotel Excelsior. I was laughing because it will still be a theater owner, still a banker, still a bureaucrat or a producer to decide: a bit longer or a bit shorter; or it will be machines, but not us, not us, not authors. Seated in front of a blackboard, I have been waiting since childhood for somebody to explain to me with creaking chalk the question of the long and the short. Is it that I don't understand? I'm so easily distracted. I came home, grazing the walls, convinced I didn't understand, walls mix you up. One stretch of wall reminded me of '34, another of '43, another of '60, another of remote, perhaps nonexistent years, you can't jell in one period before another is on top of you, when you understand something that worked in that period, now you have to bring yourself up to date and you're about to manage that when they snatch that period from under your behind like a chair. The long is surely what suits best a theater owner, a distributor, a banker. What's best for an author? You have to have patience, they say. The new science has demonstrated that parallels meet. And you, go on composing and everything is of use, honorable men like Antonio bear witness that under Fascism, the school of hermetical poets are of use for something. Let's try to join the parade, bearing a flag with no colors. The wind refuses to make it flap. The color of the short or of the long can only be a short or long color, adjectives unsuitable for color. We must look elsewhere. Can Socrates perhaps have ruined everything? If he hadn't taken that hemlock perhaps things would have gone better. Let's see.

P.S. Should a "diary" be short or long? It will have the size of understanding-in-order-to-do: an instrument, in other words, and not an end in itself. Its page-in-progress might always be the last, with the trepidation of a wing about to flap. I am not speaking of traditional diarism (still less of my own), which is a gentle mold of sentiments and thoughts, but of another kind whose dawn has barely come. It can usefully employ its portion of time from early childhood; I happen, my classmate happens, we happen together. As far as I'm concerned, I would gladly move away from paper to films with the frames all divided in two: at the same time you see me on one side eating, drinking, sleeping, and writing; and on the other side, the general situation. Can you hear the sound of the projector in the silence? Shall I wait until, through an optical illusion, I and the others pass the line of demarcation and enter into contact? Whatever happens I have found a language, say the experts (always consolatory). My dear man, do you want to be the prophet of the present?

II

going
back

Rome—December, 1963

I peer into the well of a thousand or more pages, written by hand from a quarter-century ago until today. Almost every day I've noted down expenses, income, and in a crude way, at times obscure even for me, a hash of names, events, thoughts: twenty notebooks of various format—from the early ones a furtive insect has just emerged: born where and how? All this evidence, accumulated with a view toward God knows what trial; I would be tempted to throw it out of the window on New Year's Eve the way the Romans throw away junk. Instead I leaf through it and dictate, on the spot, the things that strike me, putting my comments in italics and separating one theme from another with an asterisk. I began on January 14, 1941. I remember nothing of that inaugural rite, and yet my memory thought it was anchored there forever; among the interior and exterior objects of this present moment, which will be the first to vanish? Page 1: Would accepting one's place in the world as a man, emerging from the drama of solitude, be the artistic solution [*what would I have meant by this "artistic"*] toward which we all tend? *In the margin: I say no; rereading this on 6–12: I say yes; I conclude with a* hmm *curt, without exclamation point. Was it raining? These lines, half in pen and half in pencil, look like those clefts in the ground that suggest only absence. After the opening reflection, did I run out on the terrace to see the flares the Allied planes dropped to illuminate their objectives? No, the air raids began months later (and so a great quantity of time can be affirmed or annulled without consequences). February eleventh:* Speech in Genoa: I say that when capital's domination of cinema is abolished, the problems of cinema will be solved. Yesterday French ships

201

bombarded the city. In the square an unexploded bomb and vague incredulity. *The 28th:* A man was shouting "taxi" last night in Via Tritone, I was going home on foot, proud of myself. There's a war on, I thought: limit the taxis to just one cab which would continuously drive around the city, refusing its services to one and all. *The 20th:* Do we wish anyone harm? Our intention of confessing that wish one day seems to redeem us already.   ❇   I close the year by asking: how can you consider one thing marvelous and another not? *Then:* More than anyone else, the artist can smell the odor of the threadbare. *I wet my finger with my tongue to turn the pages more rapidly, losing on the way whole weeks and people like my mother, the furniture during our sad move from the plains to the mountains.*   ❇   We count on some merit of ours to throw in an enemy's face: hate me, enemy, but I sensed the polyvalence of actions; out of hatred M. killed Giulio and was sent to prison for life. Still, Giulio deserved his fate, having done plenty of wicked things, his daughter Gina on seeing her father in the little trickle of blood clotting on the floor finally feels sorrow, etcetera; an *oeconomicus* god who sets the stars in motions and also T.'s bicycle unable to concern himself with one thing at a time, but if this were the case we would all have set out equally; instead there must have been something off-center, two moments, because we can never find ourselves side by side, what a *diabolicus* god; or did he realize too late that the very idea of creation made everything dual, including himself? I can't find the key and, if I did, it would still be a compromise; I interrupt this nonsense which I don't want to correct   ❇   A man pretends his wife is dead while he is conversing with her, he becomes more and more immersed in his widower's role as the dialogue goes on and he lives in this future which helps him judge the present.   ❇   Thank you—I don't know whom to thank—but thank you, everything is so beautiful at this moment.   ❇   People in the street at evening whisper and with their shrouded flashlights play solitary games on the asphalt.   ❇   I am not good, I can feel this with my fingertips, perhaps I have a will toward goodness, perhaps goodness doesn't exist, perhaps only the will toward goodness exists, perhaps evil lies in supposing goodness.   ❇   The strength to seem what we really are always produces glory.   ❇   "Carlo II will come back because you haven't done sufficient penance," these old sayings have a lugubrious sound today but I have to laugh at them: ha ha ha ha! . . .   ❇   I pay for the evil I think more than for the evil I do . . .   #   A book entitled March: tarrum tum tum, all I have is a title and a rhythm.   #   I was brushing my teeth and I finally realized that life boils down to the man who is and the man who becomes: moments like these are the equivalent of a sexual orgasm, but a sterile one; the "understood" is already a norm, it's there, in fact it's inside, well-digested, it's as much a part of us as our nose is. A few hours go by, even less, and we are already violating it.   #   In a dream we see a man the way he would look if he were our son by a certain woman; as if the union between us and her had taken place, the resemblance is scientifically accurate, that curve of the ear which moves from the paternal to the maternal (by the way: I imagine a battle, in which the wounded have precise faces, certain autonomous movements so rapid I don't even have time to check them: how can this not have its weight?) August 4th: I meet A.B. (*a man who slanders me nowadays, I'd like to relive our meeting of that August 4th twenty-two years ago: we must have shaken hands, please have a seat? our voices raised in greeting in that bar, our temporary but whole-hearted agreement, almost amorous, in those minutes with the aroma of coffee, a point of fusion that allows no change, there is a compenetration even on transitory issues that becomes symbolic; to argue, in that happy mood, about the future time when we'll argue, like interrupting coitus to say to the beloved woman—and be told by her—we'll be unfaithful to each other, and then resume: this would avoid the miserable future*). Infinite truths within a circle that isn't true.   #   I'm aghast at the thought that a man I despise can feel as much pleasure with a woman as I do.   #   The possible has already happened.   #   Yesterday I saw a sailor with no arms. His voice was the same as when he had them.   #   War is more enormous when you're out of it.   #   Ants have invaded a wall of the kitchen. They move in a row in a manner that seems to indicate their certainty I won't find their nest, but I do find it and . . .   #   We always consider ourselves more intelligent than yesterday whereas merely seeing ourselves with yesterday's eyes would show us the truth.   #   Anguish (*every now and then I find this word, inserted like a classified ad.*)   #   Motionless, staring into the void, a pair of lovers on the 107 bus were making love with their hands interlaced until the fingers seemed to have an awareness and a lasciviousness all their own (*I remember that, having bought our ticket, we were calm, at least for the contracted journey, as if custom*

203

*were strong enough to guarantee us that if we stayed in the bus
we would emerge from the war unscathed*).　　❀　　The fear of
finding myself suddenly without money, facing a month that becomes like a person.　　❀　　It's possible or impossible during
wartime, it's possible or impossible during peacetime: talking like
this we don't overestimate the war, we underestimate the other
times.　　❀　　Cleverness is perfect when, in action, it is taken
for something other than itself.　　❀　　Even a lovely poem irri-
tates me these days if I think that the poet revised it.　　❀
Women writers: in my mind I immediately stretch out beside
them.　　❀　　A little parrot with a broken leg just died. My
mother kept it in her bosom to make it live. In that way she once
saved a canary.　　❀　　War is approaching me.　　❀　　I believe in free will at three in the morning of the 18th.　　❀　　My
stomach is polluted, my kidney too: all this happens in silence and
without dates.　　❀　　Mar., in a bad way, returning from Africa,
says that when you're in the war you forget for whom you're fighting it.　　❀　　Alternation of erection and limpness of intentions,
the eternal erection, but then comes the limpness, equally eternal.
❀　　I'm afraid they'll steal a story idea from me but I don't hesitate to tell it to the first passerby to enjoy the fleeting praise,
attempting afterward to blame the impulse on my supposed generosity (*the typist lives apart from the things I dictate, with long
smiles behind which she pursues her own affairs; I suspect work
is immoral when it is so indifferent to another person. My scruples
often make me interrupt the straight line, the fine rhythm of attack. I slow down, having trod on a caterpillar or having involuntarily jostled a pedestrian*).　　❀　　When the antiaircraft began
shooting the first night of the war, I said: so it's true.　　❀
You can live a whole life in error without any sign from nature to
warn you.　　❀　　This is the moment of overcoats, as if they
were war communiqués.　　❀　　P. is going North, he says he
will be cynical all his life.　　❀　　To pick flowers in a hurry
so they will retain that light.　　❀　　Idée fixe: to buy a house,
as the son of a family who haven't had a house for three or four
generations, café-owners don't have a home even when they own
one; they eat among their customers, coinhabitants; where did I
write that I have a complex about café owners? Always ready at
the call of others, even if you're thinking sacred thoughts, you
spring to your feet, smiling and available; my mother's breast, still
dripping, stuck hastily back in her dress as my sister's mouth still
204

seeks it.   #   Suggestion to a rich fellow-townsman of mine: to collect pictures to put in a great room he has, in the heart of the plain; below sea-level, a modern gallery rises.   #   I arrive at Boville where my family has taken refuge, as I speak of my happiness for this week of peace I discern a desire to go back to Rome.   #   I feel guilty seeing everything from the point of view of painting, everything becomes pictures.   #   Fall of Tripoli. Often it's as if I had dreamed other people, in the end the only real thing is my mood when I wake up.   #   I have a reserve of twenty bottles of liquor which I count on in case of sadness, foreseeing a long and general sadness which only a man with such reserve supplies will be able to overcome.   #   I quarrel with the conductor during the train journey, if they weigh us we'll each be a couple of pounds heavier than before since each has an iron bitterness inside him, and the less we looked at each other the more we spoke privately.   #   One day in Bologna (*I don't seem to have written that there was an air raid alarm, and yet I always recall this remote visit of mine to Morandi with people in raincoats looking up at the sky, fearing airplanes*).   #   In Florence I learn Milan bombed, meet Rosai, the curve of his Via San Leonardo now far removed from everything (*the following five days are filled to the margins as if with balloons, with* waste *written inside one and in another* the serpent—*what we fear too much happens; I sense the reptile's dragging on the pavement with a human quality; each page, I might say, contains the denunciation of myself as a waster of time, there can be nothing more infernal than this huge senseless serpent I will meet in France or that will come up from a garden at San Giovanni Persiceto*). How much have I not done! (the nondone of the past could become the material for the present).   #   The gambler complains for years of not having bet on a number that came out and he doesn't realize that his making the bet would have created other imperceptible mutations, a different glance from the croupier, giving his hand a slightly different impulse, and that number still wouldn't have come up.   #   *In a page left blank, some time later I wrote:* is it possible to fill an empty space of the past?   #   B. is trying obsessively to instill a fear of god in his wife to insure himself against her infidelity.   #   Signora S. telephones and says I have something Christ-like about me (a new gap in our reserve of food upsets me as much as the loss of a dear friend).   #   We ask of others what they can't give and our anguish derives from

205

this demand. ⁕ I'm in such a hurry to kill you in order to weep for you sincerely. ⁕ A mouse escaped the trap, I had seen him thoroughly caught in it, I feel a rational threat. ⁕ I admire Turgenev, but with that hint of uneasiness in the face of every novel's hypocrisy. ⁕ A woman killed her husband, a veteran, in Piazzale Annibaliano, and when people ran up she said: all we need is a camera and a director and we can make a film. ⁕ Br., ecstatic painter, in one of his bursts of rage ran into the barn to kill piglets and wallow in blood—he is tall and heavy with a priest's face—then he calmly came back to his friends to go on talking. ⁕ This morning, seeing the errors of the world clearly becomes a coat of arms, and everything ends there. ⁕ A woman acquaintance of ours writes anonymous letters denouncing those who have more (food) than she. ⁕ A married couple (ministerial bourgeoisie) blackmails the peasants: "If you sell your flour to others and not to us, we'll report you." ⁕ Alarm, antiaircraft, a friend comes to see me with his mistress, the unknown girl who three years ago called me up without telling me her name, speaking obscenely of cu . . and co . . , I learned who she was from M. who had been present at the call: I take a long look at her, this calm voice of hers as she says it's a pleasure to meet you has the value for me of Newton's apple. ⁕ Insomnia has covered me with mold, I go out to rid myself of it, twenty yards away the leaves on a little tree are trembling at a slight wind coming toward me, now the leaves are still because the breeze has passed me to enter a ground floor window, it swells the curtain, there is no one in that room to see it, I assume the responsibility. ⁕ Official news from Sicily is good. For whom? ⁕ I return from Boville on the roof of a bus. To make more room a soldier throws off a bundle of things belonging to somebody who found a place inside: I cross two different zones, one with a man in a field beneath the last sunlight rich in possibilities with his sun-lit thoughts; and a second zone, in shadow, with people returning from work, already with evening movements. ⁕ Bombing yesterday for three hours and a half. The planes fly over, then come back. Very distant explosions which make a chandelier sway. My mother and two guests put their heads in a clump like sheep. I go into the street, there isn't a soul. I could stay there and see what route the planes follow, avoid a useless fear if they're not flying over my house, but I run inside again to join in an irrational waiting. There was a great light:

the motors gleam. If I had the flier before me, I armed and he not, I'd make him blanch at my weapon. His features are so distorted he seems someone else; then I shoot, but I feel no pleasure in seeing him huddled, dead, dusty, it doesn't satisfy me. I would be satisfied if I could convince him he was wrong, or at least open a parenthesis of doubt in his serenity; the squadron is all with him, one scratches his hip, cigarette smoke comes from his nose. My mother was holding my three-year-old daughter. I took her in my arms, she wasn't frightened. I tried to underline this picture of myself holding my daughter in my arms without lapsing into the saccharine, and to face the pilot in this way, assuming the rights belonging to this image with the child in arms, the right to shoot after our conversation. I wanted one shot not to be enough, a second, and between first and second there should be time for him, already hit, aware of death, to be amazed at what he has done, but it wasn't possible for him to recognize the absurdity of his action, since even in that awkward silence he was opposing such a desire to live, with some preconceived ideas.   ※   Desperation of a man whose wife is faithful, he understands lucidly that faithfulness is unnatural, infidelity so-called is natural, if it hasn't already happened it will happen, in a crescendo of equating the possible with the actual he flings himself on his wife and beats her.   ※ Riding around Rome on my bicycle, I find not a sign of yesterday's raid, I contemplate one street for a long time, in vain.   ※   At San Lorenzo a priest with a black stole and an aspersorium skips like a deer over the rubble to bless some dying people; my desire to make a vow; I got out of it with this determination: to risk unpopularity and break down commonplaces, namely history.   ※ From the terrace: rockets fired by silent, invisible planes toward the hills, the sky is starry, the alarm ends, on the 23rd the leaders of the film world met to decide whether or not to continue: doing what?   ※   The city is only rumors.   ※   One P.M. Metz telephones that Badoglio is prime minister, Mussolini arrested, I listen, as if I hadn't had ears before, to the neighbors making noise, in Via Vasi a man is running and I translate him into joy, I go out, seated on a wall with Ba., I see Maresciallo De Bono arrive at his house in a little Fiat, the car's headlights illuminate the carabiniere on guard, it's two-thirty in the morning, my happiness vitiated by the fact that I can boast no connection with this event.   ※   Villa Torlonia at ten o'clock without a guard in front and without the doorman (*this may have been the time that I saw two little girls ring the bell and run off*). Freddi arrested, everybody pleased, all of them shook hands with him until a few hours ago, I go back to Boville, the sun is red, August 4th in Rome, at night from time to time a shot in Via Nomentana, lowing of oxen from some cattle-train that has had to stop.　✳　Letter from E. in Milan: a fight for jobs on the newspapers; in bed with a fever, my allergic face in the mirror, shiny, bigger, who am I? You have to keep well in such an important period, you make a rapid calculation: do you have any troubles that prevent you from enjoying the big news? Discovering them is like being in the theater when halfway through a performance it's spoiled by a suspect pain.　✳　Writers exult over freedom, few deserve it: to hold out my hand to those who extend theirs to me on this festive day fills me with a humility that I presume inimitable, to start an argument with that ostentatious happiness.　✳　A boy from Emilia I put up in the house steals two suitcases, books, I had always admired him seeing him arrange the books on their shelves with the delicacy of a hairdresser.　✳　A film that compares two hours, one from 1933 and one from now, to see how it was possible not to act having then inside us all ready our outcry of today as if we had acted.　✳　I have a hurt finger that gives off a smell like the smell yesterday at San Lorenzo.　✳　In a newspaper the headline: Sly behavior of Italian culture during the tyranny.　✳　Ideas don't anticipate, what happens is the ideas of tomorrow.　✳　Franci telephones me, crying, he has lost his library in Milan under the bombs.　✳　The heirarchy of actions doesn't exist.　✳　A friend from Torrice gravely ill, surrounded by his children, in the valley the planes go by, the children call them liberators and run to the window, my friend also gets out of bed painfully to participate a bit in the future like the children, shut the doors against the drafts, look for my slippers— he doesn't want me to realize the general indifference toward him.　✳　Everything happens in order to punish me.　✳　As a boy my imagination was struck by a man who said: ah, no pyjamas? have a pair of mine, and threw over some silk pyjamas taken indifferently from his suitcase.　✳　I am reading about polar explorations: what willpower, on the icepack without the support of the usual objects to establish a relationship through them, pure white, everything left to the mind.　✳　The nephew of CR, who has just died, rejoices because he is the heir, but one day he will pay for it when a peanut vendor will call him an old man: it will make him suffer and being already worn down by accumulated discontents on that afternoon, he will weep, his wife will see him, and he who previously had an illusion of domination or respect left, will now have to live his last years under his wife's all-knowing gaze.　❉　In the procession as the hot wax of the candle dripped on my acolyte's hand, the pastor told one boy to walk faster, interrupting his solemn chant; did my disbelief begin from that sudden commonplace tone?　❉　Landing in Calabria.　❉　Christ is at the gates.　❉　On some mornings the news in the paper is so far ahead that you feel inexorably outdistanced.　❉　I carried my father down the narrow steps to be put in his coffin in the vestibule, I held his head, Peppo his feet, the head had a special volume, neither heavy nor light, it gave off a bad odor, I was horrified because I couldn't bear it and had to turn my face away.　❉　At Colleferro we dived into a ditch because a plane flew low over us and we didn't know if it was theirs or ours.　❉　N. says that a German, when an Italian asked him something, threw a slipper at him in reply.　❉　All night along Via Nomentana the sound of tank's tracks to frighten us.　❉　A woman says some Romans are shooting at the Germans at San Paolo, two grenades explode nearby, one in Via Vasi, from the window I see my sister running home with her hand on her head in self-protection.　❉　From the Aniene come soldiers who have removed their insignia, one has three pairs of new shoes around his neck, the children in Via Vasi imitate the siren to scare the grownups.　❉　A grim, sunny Sunday, I am looking for a medicine in the empty city, shops are closed, from an abandoned freight train people are carrying away rice, grain, pianos, I have my blood tested and I calculate we can hold out for a few months if money isn't devalued, the men of the future will not be intellectuals but men. Bz. brings me a chicken, how can anyone today have so much compassion for the family?　❉　A little monk hit by a German car; it doesn't stop.　❉　A certain C., in 1917, during the last war, pink, tender, with dishes of food always covered, and he would uncover them slowly from beneath snowy napkins or overturned porcelain soup plates, he got up at dawn to pick salad with dew on it and never thought about women.　❉　Inside the door last night I listened to my children who for half an hour improvised a contest in making up meals.　❉　They discover a soldier disguised in women's clothes, now we'll kill you, in the courtyard of the barracks screaming he tries to scramble up the wall to escape, the Jews are forced to witness the scene; a carabiniere sergeant that the Germans are taking away with the others has to use a chair to climb into the truck by himself he is so fat.   ✱   My son Arturo looks at me while I work, then falls asleep full of faith.   ✱   The night of the looting at Vinadio, those who stole a little accused those who stole a lot, an officer's wife was dragging a sack of rice, furious at her lack of physical strength.   ✱   Olive trees burned with flame-throwers.   ✱   Cottafavi talks to me about the unconscious.   ✱   Orte, a sealed train loaded with Neapolitans, being carried off as hostages, hunger and thirst, they were pleading, a note thrown out said avenge us. We live as if we hadn't let them be taken off.   ✱   Rome, full of strange, new faces, as if I alone had been shifted fifty years into the future.   ✱   I jump out of bed mistaking an unfamiliar burst of noise for a bomb; in a fraction of a second I was on my feet, but with nothing.   ✱   Antiaircraft fire. In a flash we run to the window with our friends, the lapse between our conversation and this looking out is five seconds, even less, but we are absolutely not the same people.   ✱   All of us in the street look for a face that will reassure us for a day at least.   ✱   At the Centro Cattòlico the reading of the first half of a film, Gedda suddenly stands up with a rosary: Ave Maria, they all echo him. I hadn't had time to find a demeanor that would satisfy both me and the others, the Sign of the Cross would have been an imposture, I made it sketchily, blushing but in repentance grabbed my matches to convince everyone that the movement of my hand had been only the prelude to lighting a cigarette. I tried to pray a month or two ago, if there had been a prie-Dieu I would have used it, but I managed to feel my organs, I suppose real prayer is something so whole that you don't even feel pain, because it is in a part of you.   ✱   Like a preacher I cross the rooms of the house when a quarrel breaks out and I yell that everything that happens is to test us, the quarrel itself would be a pretext for tomorrow: a German order we'll find on the walls as we open the shutters.   ✱   If the Pope slept every night in a different place, here and there around Rome, they wouldn't drop any more bombs for fear of hitting him (*the night before this Pope's funeral in St. Peter's, the two embalmers climbed upon his high catafalque, there was nobody but them, a Swiss guard, and the hasty flashes of a young photographer who had slipped secretly into the church, the Romans were asleep, wait-*

210

ing to be moved by those pictures).   ✻   Germans in their cars with Christmas trees (*these are the last days of '43 and I have left out most of it, much has weakened with time and no matter how you handle it, it doesn't resound: like the face of a once-loved woman, you ask yourself how it must have been in those days*). In Piazza Montecitorio, Musso saw two bombs thrown at a German truck, I try to imagine the man who threw them, when he eats, when he shits, when he laughs: so there is somebody, of flesh and blood, who has more courage than I have, he exists!   ✻   To bed early, with the chickens, a wind such as I never heard in Rome before; shots at midnight, the revolution would consist of being able to hate oneself as a writer.   ✻   Near Guidonia streaks of smoke in the sky which, once the planes have disappeared, widen and become normal little clouds, nobody could tell the difference.   ✻   Tired of admiring men.   ✻   They have shot Pacifico's brother, his twin.   ✻   Certain neighbors of mine (bureaucrats) go and wait for people to get off the train with oil and cheese, they pretend they're police, take the people to their house and make them sell the stuff at half-price.   ✻   We love those who, we believe, love us more than we love them.   ✻   To enlist and to die, shouting: don't imitate me.   ✻   If I didn't exist, the situation would be less black.   ✻   My mother in tears because she has lost her ration cards; instead of consoling her, I scold her.   ✻   There is an hour in which nothing serious can happen.   ✻   Sincerity is the sense of before and after, it's historical.   ✻   I'm amazed when insistent application makes the painting I work on better, five minutes before it didn't seem susceptible of improvement. The next time, I don't recall this experience and set to work patiently; the need to resolve things extemporaneously always prevails. Like vegetables, if I eat them I enjoy them, still I always have to be coaxed, it must be a repulsion that exists beyond my palate, all in my eyes, from chipped dishes of the past; for painting, the cause lies perhaps in the fact that I find something funereal about the retreat of the immediate, sizzling moment as if everything that is steeped in the senses can be saved. It's curious that anti-death is sensed in what is most dead.   ✻   The photograph of an actress in a magazine, smiling, leaning against a tree; I saw her, having just got out of bed for that photograph, suffering from a painful abcess in her behind.   ✻   De Sica and I run to Via Bertoloni to get home before curfew, a shot in the distance makes us run

211

even faster.   ❋   Aren't these thoughts that torment me perhaps the consequence of my not wanting thoughts that torment me?   ❋   De Bono executed. His cook tells me he was a good old man and anybody could make him change his mind.   ❋
So many planes over Rome, bursts of smoke in the sky, noises that perhaps aren't there, we put a neighbor woman to bed in a faint, a train that goes by with its own smoke, space is bristling with sharp points and in an hour it will be thin, horizontal. Refugees from Cassino look at me as if I were the State, a woman wants to be taken back to Sora where she has five children and she shouts this at a random passerby, my sister arrives from Boville taking advantage of a German truck full of seriously wounded men wrapped in paper bandages, the officer was looking for shirts for the dead (*a drawing at the bottom of the page with little crosses that stand for planes, like fruitflies on the white of the paper, and a long tail, a very thin line, the wake of the exhaust*). De Sica, D'Angelo, Fabbri, Musso, Franci, and I wander from one room to another, while the bursts and rattle of the machine gun are heard, we invent sentences that will be indestructable because of their obviousness, the visual joy of the planes in the splendor of the day, impossible opinion with that beauty of lines, fear that collapses, a meeting of eyes in an agreement that wasn't there.   ❋
When we read history, we wonder how certain monstrous injustices were possible, I would have done something! But don't I now live in the midst of even more monstrous injustices? Between our concept of the just and the action that should derive from it there isn't a short or long distance; they are two different things.   ❋
B. says: the foreigners will bring new misfortunes. T. answers: I'll screw them, I'll die first.   ❋   I wake at five, I hear the allied planes, then a big explosion, I fall back asleep.   ❋   I never write the whole truth because I'm afraid I'll have to live it down.   ❋   Two hundred planes pass over Rome at noon, they don't drop bombs, but how slowly they cross the sky.   ❋
We were so well off, Dr. G. says, among his synoptic papers on syphilis: I had my patients, I was a commendatore.   ❋   I tried imagining: it's peacetime, here I am free, I can go wherever I like; but the sense of death weighs on me again at once.   ❋
Bombing at Porta Maggiore. At 12:45 a woman streaming blood, her legs stradling a bicycle supported by two men, one on either side.   ❋   Rome crammed with people, it grows every hour, there is a holiday appearance in the quantity of shoes on the side-
212

walk.　❋　I am looking at the refinement of Milly's nose as a plane buzzes over the neighborhood at nine in the evening. A bustle of cars with household goods.　❋　Fear depersonalizes like courage.　❋　My mother saw a well-dressed woman shouting: I'll go mad if you don't give me some green vegetables, my daughter will have TB.　❋　They say we'll come and find the food where it is.　❋　Things work out so there are dead and sacrifices for all. I tried pouring some oil and it seemed to spread out, however sinuously, toward a sole direction, those who find themselves in an inlet think they are out of everything, but the very force with which it headed toward one point, moving from the source, draws the residue toward another zone, where it arrives neither late or early: it arrives; it assumes the shapes of the amoeba, unpredictable even if its dynamics are finally circular, so every political idea has a secret perfection which eludes its adepts, a perfection probably of divine order (my God, I don't believe in you) and I never underline this, even if I witness its realization every day, so as to forget it.　❋　I meet a German in a lonely street, Via Belisario. Let's kill him. He comes forward, he doesn't even look at me, it's incredible he doesn't sense my intentions. If I struck him he would have time to notice me. I killed him, how easy and how unjust, no no, it's easy if, at that moment, I am only "collective"; otherwise it's difficult, impossible, you can do it screaming as if you were being struck instead of striking. It is suicidal, if anything.　❋　Even Jesus was violent (*the typist unexpectedly asks me in what sense was Jesus violent, perhaps because he considered his thought unique. I dictated this in the euphoria of my preceding conviction; I had felt it, even touched it and it was a garland of lights not of things, destination of flotillas but the question makes them sink; imperturbable, as if we had known how to answer, we continue to. . .*).
❋　In argument, the pros and the contras move away from the theme like two butterflies fighting over a flower, shifting from above to below, dispersing the conflict in other zones of the air.
❋　There is no hatred for those who dropped the bombs but joy at having avoided them.　❋　Project for a series of blasphemous prayers.　❋　Giving the ball a kick, powerful, precise, well-aimed, means being in things, realism; I wasn't a good football player, after feints and other exhausting tricks I arrived toward the goal without the strength for the final kick.　❋　We make millions of people die for an idea of which we aren't con-

213

vinced but we attribute this conviction to others.   ⁕   With
Latt. and Bar. we drive up the Magnanapoli grass in a carriage,
from a truck Germans fall to the ground with machine-guns covering Via Nazionale as if it were a room, we tell the driver in whispers
to turn off toward the Quirinale, nobody looks at us, as soon as
we're in Via XX Settembre we run off, each on his own (*I was
tempted to revise this: he made us get out, he kicked us in the ass.
Where does the real difference lie?*).   ⁕   I paint with joy
and with the usual question whether I have a right to it.   ⁕
You brood over a thought born in the head of another man a
thousand miles away.   ⁕   Children who wander around
other people's houses to see what they eat, sent by their parents.
⁕   Almost like a racial difference the aristocracy of non-suffer-
ing is formed in us, of the flight from suffering, which doesn't annul
pity but directs it toward something that you believe, without
saying so, inferior. Naturally one explosion brings us all into the
common area, indignant against whoever, in that unharmed moment, looks at us. This sense of singularity that grows in us the
more we suffer is like the passing of a funeral, our utter extraneous-
ness, and when we are a part of the cortège, the utter extrane-
ousness of those on the sidewalk which astounds us.   ⁕   For
some days there haven't been any raids and we become accustomed
again to the non-war.   ⁕   The round-ups continue and can
take place at the corner of our street, but the distance seems enormous; the geography of Rome changes constantly according to
moods and conscience.   ⁕   I believe Pep., Gia. and Al. are
maneuvering politically, I make an effort to feel superior seeing
the problems *ab aeterno*. But on the 6th I ask myself: am I, instead, somewhat inhuman and can you tell it from my prose?   ⁕
At the Hotel Imperiale the Duke of Montaltino seems to glide over
the carpets despite his senile step; terror of old age as the final
point of understanding man's wickedness from which you can defend yourself only with a hotel's atmosphere.   ⁕   A director
selects an evacuee from Formia who lost his father and brothers
in the bombing, in the film he has to cry, the director tells him to
think of his father and the boy cries and they can't stop him.   ⁕
The thought that I know how to do a thing better permits me to
do it less well.   ⁕   The laziness from my paternal side doesn't
amalgamate with the qualities from my maternal side, all hard
workers, whereby I am either one or the other.   ⁕   The
necessity for grand-scale medical operations on man. He refuses
214

to recognize that we are generally ill and are surprised by it gradually, as if by accident; but it is tragic to see that son swell up or have a deformed arm or throw himself into the river one day, and we open our eyes wide, but there is nothing mysterious. But how can Paolo be prevented from sleeping with Giulia, so sweet today, even if the teeth of their second child will be stumps and the veins varicose and he will suffer from it all his life? We hide a pimple from others like a crime or we conceal mental disturbances with desperate expedients to appear coherent, then all of a sudden we collapse; since we have covered up the traces of ourselves, no one knows who is collapsing.   ✳   De Sica telephones: "What do you hear over there?" "All quiet," I answer.   ✳   Title of my show to be directed by Fulchignoni: Variété (the m.c. myself in person), twenty very short acts, one act is a character doing something, a second character watches him, the third watches the second watching, the fourth the third, with not a moral connection, I keep using this word "moral," unthinking, it's there, ready, like the word "moon."   ✳   My wife telephones in sobs to say a bomb has fallen on the Troianis' house, five yards away, opposite ours. I arrive, from the window I see the collapsed house, my family is sitting in the room, no longer wanting to look out, no shouts or sounds. The Maggiorellis on the third storey are still suspended on the few feet of floor left and they are waiting for the firemen. The sun's shining and I don't see it. A fragment wounded Signora Troiani in the stomach and she had a baby yesterday, the infant covered with dust is in the arms of the crowd, in the interstices of emotion—the usual emotion, at unusual events—the cross section, precise, of the house is inserted. I notice that stone and mortar prevail, man's enormous creative effort to keep things together, the children of the old woman buried under the rubble arrive, they embrace one another desperately, they hope in desperation that something will change, (*the house was rebuilt with funds from the government, unknown people rented the front part; a short time after the catastrophe a door that gave on the void came open every now and then and somebody looked out*), the whole night through the broken panes the sound of picks, they found the old woman about eight, in the evening her soldier son arrived, two or three minutes of screams, then calm as a plane dropped a few random bombs. Ba. telephones me from a distant part of the city to say he's found glass for the windows, the Maggiorellis came to see us, invading the house with happiness.　❋　A German ties me up then possesses the woman I love, the woman cries out to me, summarizes in herself the tones and the absolutes of daughter, mother, bride, everything, but he crushes her like a boulder, her mouth eludes his with fragments of screams, he manages to take his place in the cavity and stays there so long that in the end she has a moment of physical pleasure; what can I do for the rest of my life?　❋　We eat a cake, I say; it wasn't born cake, it was flour, first earth, then something else, it has an appearance that seems made to calm us, to make us feel a banal act, eating a cake, might evade, especially in this moment, the law that all is either good or bad.　❋　Reflecting when I want to reflect is something that has never happened to me, if I set myself to do it, I can't remain still a moment, and yet I am constantly reflecting within my non-reflection, and even if much is lost something remains, you might say, under the palate, piling up on its own, and I'm proud of it. Perhaps maturity is the recognition that another, another and yet another has already created and then you want to turn toward the wall and sleep forever; this realization—isn't it a unity, something autonomous? Not even that. In fact, I spoke of maturity, and not of myself as mature. It's peculiar to that condition, and my having written it will count for nothing with someone who didn't write it. The illusion of a privileged defeat falls away, of a nothing that exists only in that I recognize it, and still beyond these words ("all," "nothing," "end," "beginning,") beyond their echoing and their answering one another and their pattern-making in the air like a swift firebrand that the eye believes existent until they fade, there is something toward which I prick up an ear; but I have to keep still, because every movement already has its words which are always macabre compared to this patient absence.　❋　Bombardment of the Castelli Romani, the women were screaming, and the children, even though they were at least eight miles from the planes, all with an identical tail of smoke, symmetrical; perhaps this terror rises from the repetition, which brutally cancels out any dialogue prompted the preceding time.　❋　I meet Lat. after twenty-five years; saying "twenty-five, my friend," he chomps that twenty-five with his chin as if to taste its temporal flavor, alternately it seems long and short.　❋　I wake up, I think it's a fine summer afternoon, this is confirmed by the children's cries and sounds that give a sense of solidity, instead it's people coming out of the shelters where they had been shut up since morning and they are

216

still digging at the ruins of the Troiani's house.   ✳   I pretend to be blind but I can't stand it for long. I still play games; I go out, saying: today I'm twenty; and it works for a few minutes, as I manage to force everything to my pace.   ✳   A worker who survived the bombing of the Tiburtina station says that if gasoline turned to water everything would be solved.   ✳   We move to Via Barnaba Oriani in the Parioli district, in the building where De Sica lives; he says it's as if we were abroad; according to the policeman who stamps our papers I'm making a mistake to move because a bomb never falls twice in the same place.   ✳   I'm tormented again, helplessly, as in insomnia, by the question of preferences: whom do I most want to be saved from the next bomb? Everyone, I answer, but the insistence on some classification persists, I try to walk faster and avoid it, nobody suspects an executioner is going by, and in turn I feel myself being killed by somebody.   ✳   I read the conversations of Goethe and I find everything so resolved that I begin to doubt I've been born.   ✳   Hordes of tattered, happy children with money made from begging invade the bars.   ✳   Paola M. says a peasant woman on her property obtained a reprieve for her communist husband at noon and they had shot him at six in the morning.   ✳   T. confides in me that he and his wife are at daggers drawn, but when they run to the shelter they help each other, with reciprocal reminders of the thermos, the flashlight, and other acts of politeness.   ✳   They bombed Portonaccio, I learned by telephone from Via Merici, I wish I had been there.   ✳   A fast bus along the Via Nomentana and a woman shouting from the windows to the driver to turn toward Viale Regina because they're rounding up hostages.   ✳   Campogalliani heard a woman saying to her crying child: cut that out, I'm hungry too.   ✳   A flurry of snow, Marco's amazement, the clumps looked like locusts falling on the fields.   ✳   Rome seen from Villa Glori: with all these houses, we shouldn't have so much fear.   ✳   Confused as we are, we still go on teaching our children.   ✳   Via Nomentana, all the trees are leafless, but the quantity, seeing them in a row, makes them fascinating.   ✳   A plane was hit, it turned on its back, then we saw two parachutes.   ✳   Ces. says often: I'm innocent, what harm have I ever done?   ✳   Naples: a woman decapitated by a bomb on the Rettifilio walked without a head for a few steps (what is the use of noting this down if I avoid drawing the conclusions?).   ✳   We never think in

vain, our thoughts are exhalations that congeal in deeds, even the incomplete becomes part of the complete.　※　Today I felt the objectivity of the beautiful, which can exist outside of me, I went past the Swiss Legation, which aroused no sort of envy in me, I simply recognized it was a beautiful house.　※　Citizens with wheelbarrows, wagons, carts, tricycles, baby-carriages load up water at the drinking fountains. A certain gaiety in doing something unusual.　※　Broth made with a powder by a lame friend of my mother's; doesn't have any taste, Arturo says, because she's lame.　※　The year 1944 is equal to 1494 to 1449 or to 9144.　※　A waiter without children whose wife had a miscarriage thirty years ago. Since then he lives as if that son had been born, he has brought him up to the present day, now he's a seacaptain; when Bern. met him the waiter was worried about this son who had set out from La Spezia on a mission, he said, and hadn't written for several days.　※　I met a friend in Via Bertoloni, ciao ciao. He interrupted me; I was counting the paces that separate my house from Piazza Verdi, probable target of airplanes. They miss by five hundred yards, no more, I thought: a thousand and one, a thousand and two, a thousand and three, as the number of paces increased my family became safe and therefore I was scattering dead bodies for a radius of three or four hundred yards.　※　A woman on a roof near my house was horrified and drew back seeing the bombs falling in the distance, I saw her and not the planes, but instinctively I also drew back.　※　Warm sun, smell of toilets in the air, there is no water to clean them, oranges and lemons appeared after such a long time in a shop window nearby, then immediately disappeared.　※　Love thy neighbor as thyself: impossible; either more or less.　※　The banner of a just idea goes by, the man carrying it isn't honest: what am I to shout? Vova or viva or just Vi?　※　Impossibility of surviving: in other words, we have to die because our imagination is unable to visualize us going on after the end of the war, conceiving a future *us* identical to the *us* of today; try this as an exercise and you'll see how our body seeks another outline in the air, in space, even for what seemed unchangeable. Only those who will be really different will survive: so one death or the other has to take place.　※　What can be got from a man who loves only the lovable?　※　De Sica tells me he saw a woman with a decapitated little girl in her arms. What is the difference between De Sica who saw her and me who didn't?
218

Between events known and events seen? Even the latter turn into things we have learned.   ✸   I saw ashen faces during the bombardment, Glori's eyes, the dark hollows under the others' eyes, how will we be able to live afterward with our friends of now?   ✸   Two parents, at the sound of the alarm, seemed to fly off with their little girl, each holding her by one hand.   ✸ Continuing horrible descriptions, I subtract time from action. ✸   A well-known person commissions me to sell a painting for twenty-five thousand lire, anything over that will be mine. The painting is a fake: the person answers calmly, "Of course it is, I wouldn't have sold it otherwise for that amount." He has just published a little article, and I praised it, except for the last two lines. We discussed it in detail. What is the value of his being for or against the present situation?   ✸   T. says he hopes to fall in love, despite everything; he wanders the streets with this intention.   ✸   A collection of pretences creates reality. ✸   Give us at least an error to defend.   ✸   I will never be able to read myself like somebody else, who would like to experience what the author experienced, whereas I would like to experience what he experiences.   ✸   Tanazescu is writing an essay on Tommaseo as poet, he says that he buried himself under an aesthetic system.   ✸   Rumors that they will deport three hundred intellectuals to the North; Ba. and his wife, frightened, come to sleep at my house.   ✸   Every morning my daughter covers my head with the sheet and tells her mother I'm not home, her mother uncovers me and pretends to be surprised and my daughter's pleasure at this surprise is regularly renewed. I would like to understand how and when she will stop feeling it (*I interrupt this because Maria smells something burning and I send her to go and look. It's the croutons in the oven, five minutes ago they were ready to be transferred into a pink bowl and now they're ashes, to be thrown out. The rapidity of certain combustions is astounding; matter flares up in a series of metamorphoses too fast for you to follow them with their various definitions*).   ✸ Walking with Boz. and Bam. a distinguished-looking man is gathering edible grass at the foot of a wall. We encounter Cres., the art critic; he has half a sack of flour in his arms, he says in Rome there's bread for two days. It seems the fighting is shifting toward Tuscany and Umbria, the mood of the French before Napoleon's *coup* was more or less like ours. The great variety of forms deceives the historian, there are no more than two or three themes to dis-

219

cuss; you have to simplify; despots simplify with an egoistic impulse. Twenty years without political ambitions, this has harmed no one's career, but rather the mind, which has organized itself to consider bearable what is unbearable. It has carried out a division apparently affecting only the civil part of the writer, but it was substantially an unconscious, total philosophy in action.
❈ Sunshine, oblivion of everything, we go to the theater. I whistle, shave, my relative Elisa tells that at Cisterna in the caves dead and living lie side by side. What is the strongest horror felt so far? The woman's arm that landed on the telegraph wires and hung outside the destroyed house of Gaifami the obstetrician, and he stood below it, who the day before, probing a womb had said: adnexitis. I swear I don't think of style; I'm bent on understanding without style: there is a dead man on the ground, there is nothing extraordinary about it except the fact that he is dead, by a bomb fragment. Why should the thoughts he causes in me, the positive and negative considerations, be different than if he were there chopped into a thousand pieces that his mother is trying desperately to put together again? Hasn't he made a deep enough impression to drive me to act? Let's go and choose a more perfect man for the purpose. Weren't there perfect dead men in the past? In my village, the Fascists murdered Ariè, a woodman, like a dog. He had everything to move me for a lifetime; his mother, a little old woman, followed one man she thought was the murderer, but he wasn't, and she cursed after him in a low voice along the road. There have been plenty of dead men then, apparently it takes more than that (*I am about to die in my turn, a year more, a year less; I often meet those who in '43 I thought would slip away on seeing us at a distance, and in leafing through these pages I come across one who had stolen in 1942 and I didn't remember, he's come since for coffee at my house, and that other one lied and I had written he lied, and now we embrace as if he had never told a lie. Greetings become exhausting, what are we greeting? Is an encounter still with something that has a stability, or is it like putting each other on trial briefly, when nothing terrible on either side can then be found? And if it isn't dung—as it is—what can we do? Not call it dung. Or perhaps call it dung but without indignation and study it as such. But morality isn't dung, they say. It is dung. No more but in the same way, is the impulse that drives you to say morality equals dung a moral necessity? I don't want to know. These streets full of greetings are like a street of*
220

bloody guts, with some shop windows trying in vain with the objects they display to restore history; we can't accept the fact that this moment is no different from '44, that we have come this far among daily crimes, or things believed crimes which perhaps in the end may not be real crimes though all the mechanism is there as if they were, words and institutions. Unless as we know or believe there is only a pact between us human beings and it isn't something from our guts; there is a kind of secret understanding to give no substantial importance to the crimes, to pretend—but for whom?).

✳ In Via Merici the bombed house might be taken for a house under construction. ✳ G. accepts Badoglio, the King, everything in order to defend himself from Bolshevism (he owns farms in Tuscany). ✳ Some people say bloody revolution or nothing; under Fascism did they perhaps perform one act against it, of the same weight that killing has? This serenity with which they say "bloody" seems something that fills them like their affection for their children. ✳ R. speaks ill of B., who arrives tomorrow and they will talk together as if he had spoken well of him; there are *in nuce* transformations of thought, nothing of what seemed true will be true, but the imperturbable R. will speak ill of B. who will go on living as if R. spoke well of him and M. will listen, imperturbable, though he feels a presentiment of such changes. ✳ I tell the children the life of Van Gogh. ✳ Among the three hundred and twenty hostages shot were Ramazzotti and Malatesta whom I knew: when we hear of a great event, it seems that if we had known the protagonists something different would have occurred. ✳ Caracciolo says a friend of his who boasted of his superb cellar died by accident drowned in the wine. ✳ I fear the pain I have felt in the coccyx for some time could be either a trifle or something fatal depending on the way I behave in the future (*I was another person, I think on re-reading this, but if my breath were suddenly to fail what seems firm as a judge in me today would fall apart flaccidly*). ✳ A bit of grain arrives along the Tiber on barges. ✳ From the cave they blew up on the Via Appia after shooting the hostages inside, the monks of the nearby catacombs heard moans all night long. ✳ Drizzle and sunshine and vice versa. I keep writing, as if hammering a nail home, that God cannot have created anything of which he has to expect the outcome (*but I feel this drilling notion of God is for me a logical act, a concept that now takes place in itself. I try in vain to give it flesh. Only my laziness*

221

agrees to pretend so at times). ✻ My children stride around the house with signs on which they have written We want bread. ✻ The cabinet minister Polvarelli was lost in thought, all of a sudden he realized the newsreel camera was filming him, with a start he began to gesticulate and move his mouth wildly to give the idea he was talking, but he wasn't talking. ✻ Ce. doesn't believe in palingenesis: there will be a revolution Italian-style (sic), things will be worked out calmly. ✻ The head of the bank tells me he would be honored to have me among his clients. One never has this sort of courage, but I would have liked to say to him: don't you know I'm immoral? Explain to him in detail the discrepancies between what I think and what I do; see his face. ✻ In '40 I met N., he said I'm waiting for a plane from Sicily that's bringing cocaine, we all put on our bathrobes—he named some famous people, men and women—come and watch, then afterward you can tell us what we did because we forget it, however you have to put on a bathrobe too. A bathrobe, really? We argued for some time, they had about twenty bathrobes all ready in the hall. In the end I gave up the idea. ✻ Some people are murmuring that a friend of ours is a spy, I meet him, we chat: if he were, wouldn't the long speech he makes about something I've written from a stylistic point of view be absolutely different? ✻ *(C., below, is written C., it isn't an abbreviation of the sort I make every now and then for obvious reasons, I just can't remember who he is or whom he was talking about)* C. tells of the X couple who screw in the presence of whores, a whore told him, they behave brutally, then very politely take their leave. ✻ You suffer for the fear you might be seized with the desire to steal a book, then you feel proudly that you will always win at the decisive moment, but in the intervals you are bent over, dressed in brown and yellow, before the book which reveals its value which is not the current pecuniary one. You don't feel the desire to steal twenty lire but a very special object. ✻ At Leonardi's, the oculist's, a blind boy is waiting in the outside room and says he's sleepy, he shifts in his chair until he finds the right position. ✻ At my house they bought a dead man's shoes, they're disinfecting them. ✻ Over the telephone Gigante introduces me to Anna Magnani, we have to talk about a review for her and Totò but she says she can't say much because she's afraid, the airplanes are overhead at that moment and in fact the panes vibrate. ✻ A relative dying in

222

the hospital asks me to bring him a bit of elixer of quinine tomorrow and he wants to know how we're fixed for sugar, but then he dies two hours later.   ✳   Bern. telephones, fruit is needed urgently for a child poisoned by sulphanamides, he can only eat fruit, I saw some fruit at Del Giudice's house when I went there with Ba. for some pictures, I look everywhere for Bardi and Graziadei so they can help me track down Del Giudice, I find Bardi toward evening, he tells me the fruit was fake.   ✳   For a spool of thread the peasants will trade two pounds of sugar.   ✳ Logical qualities are less and less useful, events break away from logic, one thinks now that logic is one of man's inferior qualities and one has to try to perceive differently.   ✳   They told my mother some people saw an old woman sitting at the edge of the road and she seemed distraught and said: come to see me in such and such a place; they went, there was the image of a Madonna identical to the face of the old woman; they say the Madonna said that on May 20th the war will end.   ✳   Ask boys of various social conditions to keep a diary for a month or two; commission the diary of a single random day of that year from ten writers, or from anyone, to be buried. Put out a weekly magazine without a political idea, discover the idea by making the magazine. ✳   Trotting races at Villa Glori, we celebrate Arturo's school promotion, an immense crowd, golden heat, but the silence is so great when the horses go past that you can hear their breath, there is a point of perspective where the horses can't be seen moving on their legs but they move as if on water transported by a single swift boat, after the curve you can see again the tangle of legs that increases, striking the finish line. Grim faces at the arrival of the horses, only afterward we hear the shouts from the nearby stadium and see on the stands the backs of people watching the Rome-Lazio game; at the exit the Germans are distributing handbills with a loudspeaker playing gay music, in the face of the crowd's festive indifference they do this almost timidly; the handbills say it's the Anglo-Americans with their bombing who are preventing the arrival of flour.   ✳   Display paintings in the streets, set them in the walls or on special stands, with the most perfect technical protection, in special kiosks, Via Nazionale nothing but pictures right and left.   ✳   C. insists about discriminations: they must pay. And he was in that crowd; you can kill or have people killed to give the impression you are sincere.   ✳ I learned with some uneasiness that I am not old, not even aging,

223

that I don't have the age I have, and it gives me a sense of unnaturalness, not of pleasure, as if there were some being lodged inside me, motionless, always young, but not me.   ❊   Guilt complex. I consider the world a habit to be changed, I feel an attraction toward more radical forms because of their apparent suitability today, I reject them, I don't want to join up with T. who flings himself into it, shamelessly, in front of me, and I know his past; he involves me in this abandon of his as if he were sure of my complicity and silence. T. expresses to me some exact concepts on the situation, it is an exactness however that could stand up in another person, in anyone. It's true, they say, but it isn't a truth created by you; I beg you, tell me you want to live, reduce things to the essential, don't hide behind the majesty of public reasons. Perhaps we would embrace if he said, I want to live at all costs and the rest comes afterward. If we exchanged every confidence instinctively, some new aspect would emerge, thought itself would be stimulated but instead we lie as if that dominating impulse were marginal and as if in the foreground, the only thing coexistent with us were reason which can follow its course not only ignoring the flesh but going against it.   ❊   Black Sunday. I write a little and appease myself, it is the unused things inside that poison us, not writing them one can even die of cancer, because self-expression is the normal proliferation of the cells.   ❊   At Camp Breda seven thousand evacuees in a huge room for five hundred people: sick, hungry, dead who remain there two or three days, weak people who, lacking the strength to get up, relieve themselves in there, women kicked in the stomach as they cling to their men being carried off for forced labor God knows where; they arrive from the South leaving dead members of their family along the way, one has seven little stars on his lapel which mean seven dead. Meanwhile we were talking about a newspaper to be started as soon as the Germans have left, and the creative warmth rose to my face, suggesting columns, layouts. Situations save us, not ourselves. The ease with which I forgot the evacuees at Camp Breda makes me insist on my "de-dramatizing first," because if recognizing as dramatic the things that happen doesn't generate actions, dramatic decisions, perhaps the truth—or at least one truth—is something else; to consider everything without charity, without lugubriousness, grief and death as comedy; enough of this writing absolutely and living relatively, abused emotions have only to be repeated to make them rot; a theatre in which repetition
224

deflates all secondhand emotion.　❋　I woke up to make water, then fell asleep again, but in those three or four minutes it became definitively clear to me that organized religion overpowers, it's amazing the clarity of half-waking moments like these, the play of logic becomes reassuring to the maximum degree, on going back to bed you feel you have made one more verity objective and visible, the spirit smiles like a child when his mother tucks in the blankets.　❋　The water had reached the brim of the tub and I was spellbound: one faucet was already shut and I didn't know which one, it would have taken no time to try first one and then the other, but an instinctive desire to decide without testing, through some absurd economy of time, restrained me, and the water poured in, and I was stunned as if I couldn't make up my mind. It's one of those moments when we feel our personality come unstuck, as if our present being were a transitional point, a pattern in the kaleidoscope, made anyhow with what is and with what isn't, temporary.　❋　Everyone says: the Italians; even N. unburdened himself in Piazza Colonna, holding my arm; he punctuated his talk with: I have a clear conscience, and we spoke of his wife and his son. Then I watched him walk off—I had decided to do this beforehand, I had listened to him becoming more and more unacceptable, only waiting to see him go away, to observe him— but he turned (as if he too wanted to observe me), we both hastily raised our arms in a deceptive goodbye and hastily strode away from each other, I was perhaps seen by him as I saw him, it happens that if two of us say the same thing, with the same words, for example . . . I can't find the example, but it's especially true that when two of us do a bad deed together we excuse ourselves with ineffable alibis which are in no way considered valid for the other.　❋　To give the sense of the length of a morning, crammed also with your absences, the beginning might be: I want to write down everything that happens inside me and outside me, it's seven in the morning, peace, calm, sunshine, I have just got up and I already have enough material for twenty pages, whatever happens or doesn't happen, I already am, the facts aren't yet, and I'll see them form like the people who one by one enter my morning, what power I have, what breath, what strength and what weakness, what poverty, 7 A.M. how fresh I am, nothing of the things that will entangle me has entangled me so far, and from this state, from this glistening, without even a line, nothing material, first one segment will emerge then another, as in didactic animated cartoons, and the others will be born and their passions—but it isn't true, on certain days despite the encounters and the hours that accumulate you feel as light as you did at the initial stage.　✻　The communiqué says general breakdown of the Gustav Line; the fighting is at Pontecorvo, the *Bovillesi* will be in trouble—Be. tells me that R. says nasty things about me, I see the duration of the action, that is the length of time, like a torture, the contradiction between the wrong of the person who is against you and the non-wrong of his family actions—his kissing his child and being loved by his parents—ends by powerfully backing up his calumny, which is not expressed by a mouth made in any special way or by a person whose mother has three eyes; his mother loves him, defends him, and you would like to go to her, as if to enter the heart of the situation and extirpate the hostile opinion, but your dismay keeps growing to infinity since you will never convince his mother her son is wrong, and this impossibility is like feeling prevented from being what you are or hope to be: that mother will always be the one who prevents you. It's a delirium: I enter a family home where all are seated at table in the warmth and confidence of their talk, a dish, the oil cruet, and I want to accuse one of them, their uprising would be so immediate that I would be alone in the street clinging to a passion or deformed forever, and at those doors I pass on my way home I could never knock again. I have a couple of people I hate, but their forebears and offspring give me a form of "the snail's disease," that disease of the member which, once erect, deflates at the moment of contact; in other words I can't hate the bitter end (*another swarm of names in these little notebooks of '44, each of which, even the faded ones, would provoke speeches longer than their cause; a buzz of slander that so amazed me I marked it down immediately, hearing its bitterness I imagined a similar bitterness in those who attacked me, you'd like to attempt a defense, go to one of them, but what about that other one then? Or that other one still? You feel ice forming again beneath the crust, it's done, we ourselves accept that truth, which isn't true, it would be such a superhuman job to crush it*).　✻　A very bad night, poisoned. I saw splendid colors, pictures I'd paint if I were a great painter, or I should say if my own qualities were reenforced. Who knows why some are paintings with flaws, but the very flaw is arranged with the same harmonic law of the non-flaw? Pictures are not still, but constantly moving forward and certain corrective operations have to be made

226

in haste before the picture passes or is deflated.   ✢   We
tend to make everything definitive, but since nothing stops, our
stopping is changed continually as it stops.   ✢   C. was put
into Regina Coeli suspected of antifascism, he tells me the thieves
envy the politicals, the guards try to make friends with them,
fearing reprisals after the approaching change they sense like
animals. A man from the Marches with five children said to his
inquisitors: I'm not only antifascist, I'm also anti-German, anti-
English, anti-Badoglio, Italy must be made with new people. The
police chief Caruso answered: Italy will be made by people like
you or like me.   ✢   The hole leading into a trap is small,
and beyond the hole there is bigness, which no longer seems a trap;
you don't stop to reflect, you keep going in past the hole straining
your eyes to evaluate what is beyond as if to create an alibi.   ✢
Afternoon with some friends like a garden, Guerrieri, De Concini,
Lodovici, thoughts come forth, a lovely tender green, to be grazed,
thoughts on food, politics, love.   ✢   Rumors: the Parioli district to be evacuated.   ✢   Repentance takes place a moment
before the shot and you could therefore restrain yourself, but you
can't, your cry begging forgiveness comes from the bosom when
your victim is still swaying before crashing to the ground.   ✢
Enough, I said aloud, I wanted to free myself of the word table,
my mother has been saying table for more than eighty years with
a woman's nonchalance; with slaps I'm forced to say table, and
there shall be no other table: even if a girl passes the table without
seeing it what she doesn't see is the table, the table's will be done,
how shameful.   ✢   Film about a sack of flour, I would say
story of bread which we discover in its necessity; the sack could
arrive from Perugia, where, since there is no starvation, it still has
its literary garb, it arrives at Cesano (that concentration camp is
directed by a woman with a whip), its transformation into loaves,
less than the required number, one man eats his loaf, another
doesn't, if he doesn't eat he dies, one dies, another doesn't: see it,
see it.   ✢   It would be the labor of Sisyphus to remove the
objects of envy which are infinite; we must remove envy.   ✢
Zanatta, from the Veneto, enormous, in the torture chamber to
frighten the man being questioned says: well, shall we begin?
Rolling up his sleeves. With one man, he took a running start in
order to beat him and the man said: go ahead, hit me, hit me, and
then he fainted, bleeding.   ✢   Royal Opera House with Bart.
who has tickets: Stravinsky hissed, above all for the mimic slowness

227

of the ballet; in one box German officers among whom I recognize
Haas. In uniform he's another person; he was meek and he listened
more than he spoke when he used to come to the editorial offices
as a photographer and in him you felt no nation and heard no
clamor.   ✳   At midnight the final deadline is up for the
turning in of deserters.   ✳   Desant. reproaches me for a
sentence: a cat run over by a tram is like a war. I can't make him
understand that I am invoking continuous tension and correlating
examination.   ✳   Guttuso. "The catholic prince" considers
him a pictorial ideography.   ✳   Barbaro doesn't agree on the
spirit of the paper I'd like to put out: the man in the street who
begins from a position of doubt and looks for a truth in the public
square, he sees it born or he doesn't, with all the consequences of
yes and no. Barbaro and the others are already sure.   ✳   My
daughter has a fever; I make a vow if she is cured at once; her
breathing was shallow, gasping. I wish it didn't, but the idea of
making vows comes to me all the time, also in circumstances of
little importance; I try to avoid it but in the end it prevails even
in the case of an extra morsel of bread.   ✳   Machine-
gunning in the outskirts; a bomb nearby; I try to fill myself with
good thoughts since it seems impossible to me that I and my family
could be hit when I am in such a spiritual state.   ✳   A man
of about fifty is studying voice, with regular lessons, in Via Vasi.
✳   A little girl came up to beg, running, laughing.   ✳
Hearing the planes overhead a little while ago I realized I am of
one age and they of another, the coexistence of such disparate
things generates history.   ✳   Some prefer to risk their skins
rather than investigate their own position in life more deeply.
✳   We look for the guilt of others creating new guilt as we do,
with the therefore greater urgency to find more guilty people.   ✳
There is nothing generic—despite ourselves—in any action of ours.
✳   The *Bovillesi* are still hiding in caves, rich and poor, elbow
to elbow. They will emerge with the notion of the necessity of
self-defense in life now enlarged, the exacerbation of a principle,
of an instinct that will be turned against the very people who are
now their companions in sorrow.   ✳   The child beggars hold
three or four ice cream cones in their hands at once, one offered
twelve hundred lire to some other children who were playing if
they would give up their football.   ✳   Everything tends toward a form, form means being, being means explicable, even the
most abominable tyranny takes on form. From whatever sector a
228

line begins, on its trajectory events occur which tend to become discourse; all "persistence" emanates reasons.　　❋　　T. says: the unfaithful woman insists in her infidelity stimulated by the fact that her husband is a cuckold.　　❋　　All clustering around a certain Battista, filthy rich, compromised with Fascism, who is preparing books and newspapers for after the English arrive. F. says, in the midst of those cultural plans, he was studying the face of the future publisher to see if in the end he could ask for an advance.　　❋　　Today I heard a person who detests me say things that are right, that I say too.　　❋　　The price of flour is going down because everyone supposes the English will arrive soon.　　❋　　In the tram I think of a manifesto inviting the Italians to remain disarmed forever, our originality could consist in an absolute propaganda for peace.　　❋　　V. is courting a famous Roman shoemaker to get from him the faulty shoes of princes and cardinals at a big discount because, he explains to me, I've married a princess.　　❋　　Frosinone is occupied; Boville is free, I will tell Galluzzi: at one in the morning on June second I learned the news and thought of you, how were you showing your happiness, the end of your suffering?　　❋　　Clanging, racket in Viale Parioli of the armored vehicles. I look through the shutters at the dark night.　　❋　　A great open truck goes by full of lambs, skinned, gutted, bloody; I'm told there's a black market even in human flesh and that many have eaten it unawares.　　❋　　At Cinecittà cannons fling open doors and windows.　　❋　　There is a confused atmosphere around. To what degree does physical pain have the right to eclipse responsibility? It's possible to make a chart.　　❋　　The prisoners who play women's roles in the little prison entertainments go on bustling about like women for a while afterward.　　❋　　At ten A.M. on the fourth a big detonation, there are American parachute troops two hundred yards away, in Viale Parioli German trucks sold flour at a hundred lire the sack, wool blankets, all night the Lazio hills were in flames. A trailer left by the Germans loaded with pipes for the water system. Worth eight hundred thousand lire, some distinguished gentlemen were saying, touching and milling around with the desire to steal; everyone has the desire to steal, in a side-street off Viale Liegi where a house the S.S. occupied was blown up, they were taking away wreckage, beds, wood, one pretty girl of eighteen had managed to grab only a crushed roll of toilet paper.　　❋　　B. saw a florist approach a humble hearse outside a church where the

229

funeral was going on, he wanted a little wreath back because the family hadn't paid for it. A German asked a woman if he might pat her little girl on the head, the little girl didn't want him to, the German patted her, bursting into tears.   ＊   I meet Piov. and la V. shouting freedom, la V. last night saw in the moonlight—it was beautiful, she says—the retreat of the German horses with the oxen; I'm happy, she says, for you men who've led such an awful life. I hasten to say that I haven't a shadow of merit. German vehicles go by and Germans on foot, toward the North, some are singing, they display confident faces, one is transporting his knapsack in a baby carriage, another in a street-cleaner's cart, they have necklaces of machine-guns, they set up a cannon at the end of Viale Liegi to cover the retreat, a tall pale officer with flashing eyes, drunk with this dissolution, a man shouts because the Germans have taken away his son to load him with knapsacks like a porter, the mother follows the Germans and makes them give the boy back, the concierge informs us the English are already in Via Nazionale, my brother says we are living through a great event, we must think about it; with Caud. under my window we discuss joy, but the joy of the English and the Americans, the English, the Americans are sparks of a fire and we don't know where it is, and I will watch them become extinguished from my balcony as the others shout louder and louder "English" and "Americans" giving these nouns an absolute value, wisdom; would I get on a chair in Piazza Quadrata and say this? Nobody risks unpopularity, but what is popular? Confession of uncertainty? Each fears the other isn't uncertain and pretends he isn't either and so casts his stone.   ＊   In the sky two or three "storks" explore the arterial roads where the Germans are retreating.   ＊   Piov. told me a bloodless machinery clicked into operation, they gave the Germans eighteen hours to clear out, bicycles are coming back into circulation, there is reason to be happy without reflecting, applause on the right tells us a truck is coming with Americans, I feel a kind of resistance against looking at them closely, meeting their eyes which would force me, I fear, to a smile, I feel occupied by them— no, not even that—they are playing a certain role in which geography is accidental. My rejection of them is also a need not to accept them historically, because—until a moment ago—I was riven by years and months of anti-history. Acceptance would mean recognizing that fears and weaknesses of the flesh were included in that vision, how hard it will be to make distinctions.   ＊   Last

230

night reading Mazzini's "On the Duties of Man" I was forced to admit that some things had been said many years ago which I thought I discovered; he had clearly programmed them (*this is exactly what I find written: clearly programmed*).   ❊   Marco comes home with two little envelopes of coffee and a kind of lemonade from the Americans, he saw the Americans at Acqua Acetosa, he says they wash their face with milk. He wanted to ask for a can of jam for me, they were giving it to anybody who asked, cans full of soups, cheeses, cake, he says, a plumcake.   ❊   That Italian soldier of the PAI yesterday, boldly circling Piazza Santiago on his motorcycle while a troop of Germans filed past leaving Rome. People were watching from both sides of the avenue, with a touch of pity. A German stopped the Italian, took his gun, his bullets, and his motorcycle, the Italian started up the hill on foot in silence, the Germans were going down toward Via Salaria. Perhaps that evening the Italian would talk with his girl, giving her French kisses as if this hadn't happened or as if it had happened differently.   ❊   Six P.M., St. Peter's Square, faint sun which seems dazzling, ices on sale, huge number of American vehicles, people walk, smoke, laugh, applaud, I can't find adjectives, laugh, applaud, walk. The Americans amuse themselves on the bicycles they borrow, soldiers ask boys with gestures where they can find a screw, a boy says fiki-fiki and gives them an address, three famous queers arm in arm were rejoicing like the others.   ❊   My son brings home the iron seat of a tank, a dead man goes by on a little mule-drawn cart and an American photographer-reporter stops them, asks the name of the dead man, snaps a picture and says he will send it to New York at once; there is only the provisional reparation of my eye which frames him though he refuses to be frame-able.   ❊   Wakened at four in the morning by some antiaircraft emplacements three hundred yards away, the war is still on but it has another tone.   ❊   I must be afraid of music, it excites me, it causes certain sparks that could make me set off for the war, any war, with a hard c———. Love is calm.   ❊   My friends V. and G. presented themselves at Cinecittá to take possession in the name of the King; the soldiers sent them away again.   ❊   Make each individual put a card outside his door with a brief summary of his life: this is the house of X who yesterday was a Fascist and today believes in this or that, in '35 he said, in '41 he did, he believes or doesn't believe in God, with details, his frank compromise in the face of the present situa-

231

tion. The crisis becomes concrete for me in an apologue or in a gag, I could say a sequence; on the one hand I suppose this proves the scarcity of a concrete impulse, and on the other if I translate it into art, I personally profit little but I put into circulation, at least so they say, something quantitatively more significant than if I were to become a perfect private citizen. Hmm.   ❊ Alternation of like and dislike for the Anglo-Americans.   ❊ Italy will be reduced to the state of a mulberry tree where the silkworm cocoons have been, St. says.   ❊   Young ladies absent for lack of water and electricity, says the sign outside the brothels, the doors unhinged.   ❊   At St. Peter's sick, filthy people selling liquor and wine to the Allies, bottles that have spent the night in dens warm with stinks, I hope it's like this also in Whitechapel or the Bronx. Simply by moving these soldiers humiliate, but even if I avoid contact with them, darting rapidly like a swallow, they humiliate me in the others. On my bicycle a few days ago I was a bit drunk from the speed I could work up in certain zones among the American vehicles; it's a good article to write, I was saying, on my bicycle from Via Barnaba Oriani to Piazza San Pietro, the air was cleansed of history, the winding traffic in which we were all equally trapped put us on a par, I didn't feel the sadness of anonymity, I didn't feel a desire to shout *stop,* or tie them all to me by beginning the page of a book.   ❊   The Sirocco-smell of canned meat. Not understanding how you should behave (me, today) is only a deficiency of love. We were given intelligence to understand that history is all repetition, but we are never to exploit the knowledge in the moment when we must act, otherwise we would be enjoying privileges (*the door opens and a monster appears, the typist and I become horrible in fear; war is not the monster but the fact that such a rapid passage is possible from nonhorror to horror*).   ❊   I imagine I know, but I don't know.   ❊   Hitler is responsible for the death of ten million people, he will answer for it, but each of the ten million is not necessarily absolved by Hitler's trial, by his dossier.   ❊   In the newspaper I see two adjectives that make me indignant: bumptious and dearthsome.   ❊   Again I long for an "Italian's reader" which could contain those truths which ripened until yesterday and which the parties, in the very moment when they come out from underground, can no longer proclaim.   ❊   I trust those I don't know.   ❊   How exciting it would be to develop my thoughts on peace, on not killing, to publish them, if I had risked my neck.
232

✻   The concierge in Via Baracco has come back; he had enlisted with the Americans in order to rejoin his wife more quickly, they promptly told him all the whoring around she did with the Germans and he wept in the midst of a group of people on the street. One sentence: she with her legs spread and on top of her a man who speaks another language.   ✻   The war is a hundred miles away but already it's as if it were in a foreign country.   ✻ At the Centro Cattolico Cinematografico Moravia talks about the eight months spent on the mountains in Ciociaria, rapacious things, a whole family who attack a man who had been left in charge of some walled-up food reserves but the Germans had already broken down the wall, the owners don't believe it, even the old people with no strength are on top of the man.   ✻   Judging another, a certain man, for example, he will write "he was a man lacking in . . ." etc. . . . we imagine the person who wrote that sentence is perfect; an idea of perfection exists which we consume in judging others, an imperfect man judges perfect: a chain that leads to the postponement of the only thing that would count: personal progress on our part.   ✻   There are people, including me, who express their convictions in too loud a voice, the sound immediately creates a kind of shell around the idea, congeals it. Then the objections to it, which are often announced at the very moment a thought is completed as the shadow arrives before the body—these objections are rejected by the hard crust.   ✻   There is no thing or idea which doesn't have an influence on another thing or idea.   ✻   The changeable is only camouflaged time; but, in camouflaging itself, it moves. Time needs time to exist: there, words perform a mechanism of their own whereby if I say time it's obvious I should also say nontime, like the pencil on the sheet of paper which, moving to the right, senses it could also go to the left, and if it presses down becomes heavy but senses that it could also be light: a swarm of contrapositions in other words, which—though they seem merely inevitable—have a consistency and therefore are never in vain. Àpropos of the pencil, it's beautiful to see how even in an artist's calculated madness with a pencil, but also with a brush, he always leaves room to others for further madnesses; and when he closes, the sound of the closed door lets someone know that there is space, an opening on this side of the door. If you look carefully at A.'s drawings, you already see what B.'s drawings will be, and C.'s, and D.'s, and E.'s, even if A. himself wouldn't know how to draw them. His prophecy has a limit, how-

ever, since in the drawings of B., C., D., etc. there is a "something" which is released only as they are drawn. Whatever idea you may have, there is a portion or a world which develops unaware of it, reality's untidiness must derive from this unitary deficiency, from the two tempos. I thought this on seeing some Italian children of about fifteen with the American soldiers, the children smoked with American poses; that action went on so autonomously, whatever they were talking about with their friends (and I tried to vary rapidly the dialectic), it could never coincide with my tempo; it was happening before my eyes, irresistibly, naturally, with attributes of its own, like the hawser unrolling when it's thrown to the man overboard, with laws of its own whoever the man in the water may be.   *   God is equal.   *   On the film about Nobel: show him in the moment when he invented and also show today, a screen divided in two. One part yesterday and one today, yesterday-today, yesterday-today, yesterday-today, even if the sounds are superimposed every now and then and the voices. Our spectator's eyes, constantly shifting as if following the fastest ball in a tennis match, will hurt; it will be useful.   *   A mediocre person, guilty in every respect, has recently been given a very important political position; in not making my contempt public, I experience various dismays: one, that we conceal documents endlessly; two, that the wrongness of that man is not an anecdotal error but a total one, it will have ceaseless repercussions, on me for example, deepening a weariness whose shadow my children see, or anyone who has relations with me, not in vain. The monstrous always seems to belong to the past, in antithesis to a present not monstrous only because it's mine; and instead a continuity involves me, and I am no less monstrous, witnessing the monstrous, than the monstrous itself. I succeeded in evaluating the monstrosity of non-intervention because I considered it a guilt of the past, but I must say it, enunciate it: I don't intervene even now (I have never seen with greater clarity) and I help legalize a whitewashing like this one of the above-mentioned guilty and mediocre person (*two years later I dined at his house, years of quiescence, having accumulated an enormous quantity of excuses in flavors, in asphalt, in buses, in faces*).   *   E. tells me that Ang. (in 1930) killed himself also to leave his savings intact to his beloved brother, he was a good soul, a true socialist, and he suffered in seeing Fascism spread even to Gualtieri where he directed the cooperative; in 1902, he had Mussolini in his house as a boarder, when he was
234

schoolmaster in the little hamlet of La Pieve; I read a letter from
Switzerland written by Mussolini to Ang.'s brother, four lined
pages, in a neat hand. In the year 1903 Mussolini says he doesn't
intend to deceive people in his propaganda with bombastic phrases
and he has almost entirely given up wine and liquor, also women,
perhaps I wore myself out at Gualtieri? he asks. Ang. was found
in bed naked with a hole in his temple. I had gone once to ask
this relative for a loan of money for my father and it was summer,
an empty season with me in the center, asking a loan for my father.
✱   The Monsignor who lives in my building said the English
weren't bombing Terni, the steel works, because the majority of
the stockholders are English, then they bombed it.   ✱
Debts: what wouldn't I do in order not to have any after the age
of fifty, they roar resoundingly like a bull under a vaulted ceiling,
always in August. To put it more simply debts are an obligation
to emerge from pretense, the anguish at having to be what we are.
✱   Steinberg was here, with his slit-eyes he looked at my paintings and said I'm sly and don't want to seem so, unlike most
Italians.   ✱   B. saw a Negro get out of a car and slap all
the people who had forced him to slow down.   ✱   The telephone is working again.   ✱   I tell my mother I'm going to
spend two days totally with her; she laughs with joy.   ✱
Thou shalt not kill: I am unworthy of this principle, the more extreme the principle the more it must cost. I have paid nothing and
continue paying nothing to support it, I have only sorrows which
pretend to have a historical extraction, instead they belong to my
character and egg it on.   ✱   At moments I plunge down on
a truth like a lark.   ✱   Today this situation of poverty
doesn't upset me in the least. On the contrary. In my imagination I
try walking through the streets and I graze past innocences, calms
of long duration, I feel the pleasure of my leg going forward and
then stopping just long enough for the other to pass it then wait
in turn, a dispassionate dialogue with anyone, neither of us opening his mouth, as if we were already dead, but without the idea
of death, black velvets and silver fringe, even the patches on my
behind wouldn't bother me if they don't reach the point of in-
decency (I break off this thought).   ✱   An important novelist told me he is a liberal, but in opposition; he feels sympathy
for the extreme left; I tell him actions have to live up to ideas, he
answers that we writers must content ourselves with ideas. I insist,
he says "after all these are things that don't matter in the least to

235

me." Again I have the suspicion I reproach others because I haven't any work in progress, only plans, and so I exalt my civic role. ❋ I take my daughter to my mother on my bicycle in the book-basket. ❋ I had certain fits of rebellion even under the regime but after rapid calculations I repressed them, feeling I couldn't bear the consequences. ❋ The fact that I don't kill counts for nothing if I don't change my other actions, not so blatant but equally criminal. This morning I performed an action which goes on reverberating, and it was only a cordial greeting to M. whom I don't respect. ❋ There will be no inflation because in the North they haven't enough presses to print bank-notes. ❋ For the first time parts of Emilia are mentioned in the partisans' war comminqués: San Rocco di Guastalla, Villa Minozzo. ❋ An old friend of mine curses because his mistress is pregnant, he blames the war. ❋ The shoemaker tells me that the road from Viterbo to Rome is lined with abandoned vehicles, everything from milktrucks to Tiger tanks, from time to time a peasant is blown up in the fields still full of mines. ❋ Buy salt to trade it in the Viterbo area for potatoes. ❋ Met G. in Via Tembien, trying vaguely to make me believe he was somewhat involved in the assassination of Via Rasella. ❋ By mistake, F. made one hand of a pretty little statuette with six fingers, the purchaser notices, F. says that's funny I always count them. ❋ An Englishman during dinner: "Those slobs, the Italians." "You're referring to the Fascists?", "To the Italians, and if you don't want to hear it don't sit here and eat our bread." ❋ Last night I laughed out loud, as if there were people present, at the story of the Conte de Lauzun hidden under la Montespan's bed while she was making love with Louis XIV and the next day he shouts at her: slut you said thus and so. ❋ I have no money, I'm in such a bad humor I'd steal, I always feel an annoyance as if something had obstructed the light. ❋ For 500 lire a Negro raped a little boy. ❋ I meet E., ugly, tired, coming home on foot, they suspect him (wrongly) of having intrigued with the Germans, his mind is on that, and finally he talks to me about it. ❋ The three inquisitors on white mules, for the burning of a woman, the woman with her hair in flames through the streets of Naples, first they put pitch on her head: reading Colletta's History of Naples I discover what is happening now. ❋ At the Trevi Fountain a naked boy pursued by a policeman takes refuge like a mouse on the head of a statue, somebody shouts
236

to the boy come down, come down, because the English frown upon us, seeing children swim inside a work of art.   ⁂   In 80% of my actions there is only apparent goodness, honesty, such as in my confessing it here, such as in my writing "in my confessing it here" and so on and on like barber's mirrors; go ahead, do it.   ⁂   Milly woke up at three, in a dream she gropes along the smooth wall for something she can't find, then falls asleep again.   ⁂   I talk too much.   ⁂   I propose two films: Via Tasso, a torture interrupted by the arrival of the Americans; a girl raped and made pregnant by the Nazis and an Ally who loves her understanding the drama of it.   ⁂   In tears Gianna Manzini tells of her kitten which fell from the eighth floor and died after days of suffering, I would like to telephone home because I'm late, she says the phone is out of order, perhaps it's not true, I also suffer if others use up the two daily calls we're allowed. On my bicycle I enter the darkness of Viale Giulio Cesare, I go fast as at Luzzara, my hat falls to the ground, there is my hat with my shape, my hair on the ground, it upsets me. Liquid pleasure of speeding down the slope of Via Merici: for a fraction of a second I have to look at Monte Cavo, a reference point, to rediscover who I am.   ⁂   Fecia di Cossato has killed himself.   ⁂   Guer. says that we are pre-Christians.   ⁂   Bern. (on the 20th) in Villa Borghese says I am a moralist, outside of history, while he talks in the shady part near the Porta Pinciana gate I feel winter already.   ⁂   The former cabinet minister Suvich along the Via Salaria on a bicycle, neat, lighthearted as a boy.   ⁂   Bia. puts the handkerchief over the keyhole so his wife and two children won't see him while he is eating something in secret.   ⁂   F.'s wife has bought a closed-down parachute factory to get silk underwear and raincoats from it; I've solved that problem, Signora T. says, I don't wear underthings.   ⁂   Storm. I'm held up for an hour in a doorway in Via dei Lucchesi. Puc. greets me a bit coldly, his brother warmly, Lizz. normally: the three of them are going to the publisher Al. What a lovely sound of rain, in the doorway the mixture of people who don't know one another grows, priests and soldiers; dialogue partly in English, partly Italian and partly a new language, hurrah the storm's over.   ⁂   Give me a cot in a confessional, I want to sleep in a confessional.   ⁂   T. died in June, and his wife confesses to my mother the pleasure she feels in being alone at the table, she says: "my own little apple."   ⁂   In the evacuees' barracks there isn't one blind that works, in one

237

window I see only heads, in another behinds, in another hands.
❋ Over my head the S.'s pace back and forth until dawn with their crying baby, this past winter I heard the bed creaking. ❋ A woman in Via Nomentana asks me if I'll take her on my handlebars to Ponte Milvio. ❋ Dress rehearsal of The Legend of Everyman, a ballerina's baby suddenly cries (he was in his carriage in a corner), Ruggeri breaks off, shouts: Damnit, and then amid the general dismay: by God I swear that if something like this happens tomorrow, I quit! ❋ In Palazzo Venezia an exhibition of masterpieces, I don't understand Giorgione, la Buc., Br. are present, shouts in the square, I look through the curtains where Mussolini used to look out and I see a little truck full of women with a poster of Stalin's face. ❋ Be. speaks of the death of his young friend Traldi Zimmerval, they were in a room with other friends including the woman he loved though she loved another man, all of a sudden as if dancing he entered the next room along the white ray of the moon talking of the moon, then shots, one friend followed him in time to see the arc of a cigarette through the window. ❋ La C. tells me in the truck-bus she is working as a prostitute to reclaim her mother's ring she pawned, I go on one of these improvised conveyances for the first time, you stick your back outside so your shirt swells with air like a balloon. ❋ Cardarelli says he only needs to find a place, please look and see if somebody wants to house a poet as a paying guest, he has some complete runs of La Ronda to sell for two or three thousand lire. ❋ La M. is a skeleton, yesterday her husband stopped her just in time on the windowsill, we give her three cans of condensed milk, we argue whether three or two. ❋ F. is hungry, you can tell from his voice, but the thought of his son is always uppermost, he shows me proudly his drawings in Cosmopolita. ❋ The Catholic communists will be called Christians of the left. ❋ Maria's little boy taken to the hospital on the 18th with his head badly battered, still hasn't been examined, shortage of gauze, sheets, doctors. ❋ We're decrepit, Moravia says to me. ❋ "As they grow old (Mario Monicelli) my father and mother speak more and more in the dialect of Ostiglia." ❋ The women are all exposed, they wet the air plash plash with their eyes they copulate constantly, fists flying in Piazza Fiume between Italians and Allies over the women at the exit of the Pichetti dance hall, some boys cut off the hair of two girls to punish them for dancing with the Allies,

238

one policeman, when they arrive in force on black trucks, stamps his feet as if driving away some cats, but some of them don't move, I watch.　＊　　Film about a crime whose perpetrator I discover following the trail of what I would have done.　＊　An old friend of mine talks of killing himself because of the baby about to be born: "I could have been happy, everything is finished because of the madness of a minute." Fa. says: the English are better than we are. I say they make pacts with the Moroccan troops giving them the right to loot; to remove a Moroccan from a woman he was mounting they had to shoot him, like dogs when you can't pull them apart. What is the difference between the destruction of the woman and the pen of the Englishman who signs? The divergences are many but fictitious.　＊　　They drop bombs because they say: I am dropping a bomb; nobody would drop it if he had the patience to say: I am dropping a bomb which will fall on that square yard of that town X and will hit the home of C. and of P., of T. . . . and blow three fingers off N.'s hand, shatter P.'s left breast, C.'s neck, the teeth of S. who was saying to M. that R. is etc. There is no patience.　＊　　The Fascists spitefully cut off half of a prisoner's moustache but he walked around the prison like that, with half a moustache, rather than give them the satisfaction of seeing him shave the rest off.　＊　　Peasants in Boville asked my brother if it's possible not to join a party.　＊ If progress takes place one by one, *ad hominem*, why is it so clear in a multitude even when you personally aren't moving forward? Can it exist if you don't think about it? Perhaps thought has managed to realize that a thing exists even when it, thought, isn't thinking of it; in other words, thought achieves even non-thought. ＊　　Allow yourself to be killed and you won't be killed, the murderer in you feels also the hostility of the others, the excess of defense in your being, in your outline, in the space you occupy, space of egoism, of the protection of memories, of hours, of taste, of touch, of smell, as if by a mediumistic communication this stone-weight bears down on him and he dies unless he seeks an opening with his knife.　＊　　Italian movie people summoned by Palos, the Americans' film man. They went in joyous and they came out crushed.　＊　　X's girl tells me he has exploited her, he seduced her at seventeen and he is a real artist: yesterday she wanted to come with me in a moment of dejection, but it so happened I had made a vow yesterday.　＊　　Prostitution is infiltrating the middle classes, Mor. says.　＊　　Nervi, the engineer, told
239

Gronchi the heat is concealing many ills that the autumn will begin to reveal. ✳ Ri. explains with chalk on a blackboard why she is disagreeable to people, she can't mix, while her husband, she says to my wife, always fits in. She envies me for what I deplore. ✳ A Frenchman occupies a house, and when he learns it belonged to a Fascist big shot, he gives it up, out of homage to Mussolini whom he admires. ✳ If we could be sure something is moving, even with the slowness of continents. ✳ Rome is deserted by the Romans and by us: friends try to repopulate it, trafficking with the Americans. ✳ M. says an American soldier came into her room and stripped before her, she was in her little bed, ugly and thin, he had a member such as she had never seen, but then somebody else arrived and she was saved, she says. ✳ We die because we fill ourselves with things that take up space, gradually displacing the air of childhood; old age is this process of filling with these scenes, these ideas and fixed objects. We pile them up and we block the porthole, until we close it completely with the idea of death. ✳ Yesterday evening I came home at 9 P.M. On the terrace there was an atmosphere I like, the tablecloth, the family all neat and clean, the marine happiness of Via Vasi and still I said at once inside myself: I must die after all, to spoil such gaiety and yet I ate with an appetite that was noticed, also because of a brighter light bulb that made everything precise, outlined, beyond renunciation. ✳ If I could throw overboard this torment of morality I would write better. ✳ I become less and less capable of isolating the good from the bad, as soon as I have examined individuals or situations a bit, I find them interwoven with others, a snakepit of values. ✳ Is Pascal also a compromise? Like no one else, he knew that any point can be developed to infinity, and is religion only one of those points? He would object: it is *the* point. Yes, since it is irrational; but the points of the rational are infinite, all arguable, hence the necessity for tolerance. In the rational there are no better or worse points of departure; the positive thing is the equivalent of wanting to arrive—and of having to, each of us—at his own extreme, whatever it is; but then, having arrived, I will no longer ask myself if that point of arrival is good or bad. I continue using the words moral, rational, religion, reality, with an honest foolhardiness. At times they coincide—and I realize it—with their proper meaning, at other times I distort them but it isn't only an ignorant violence, it's the desire almost to do without them, to establish a vacuum of
240

words filled with essences that boast—within who knows what margin of play—of not being words. In my case however if at times imprecation, because it *is* imprecation, creates unexpected and yet existent reverberations, in the majority of cases they are imperfect instruments which make us perform naive labors and it may seem, as in races, that you are ahead of the one coming after you when instead he has already circled the track and is a whole lap ahead. But still, even with these errors, I have the possibility of choosing; or does a great part of my uncertainty arise from an imperfect possession of these words? Can I perfect them with the dictionary? Study? Action? Until yesterday when I said religion it didn't contain the concept of what binds together, I learned that only a short while ago.   ✣   Via Angela Merici, seen from below, from the railroad track, instead of being seen from its higher part, is a rise that the bright red of the sky interrupts; but when you walk along the street it seems flat. American soldiers come down it with girls, going toward the bank of the Aniene; I saw a hideous girl with an American, she was less than three feet high, thin crooked legs.   ✣   I hear the strange (new) sound of the American locomotives, many go by, a city sound; today I also heard the whistle of some Italian locomotives again, a village whistle; nothing can be done about it; we're melancholics. ✣   I saw S. in a street nearby unembarrassed, carrying home demijohns of oil and cartons of pasta, he is the chief-of-staff of a cabinet minister and until a short while ago he was employed in the Fascist Corporations.   ✣   On the afternoon of the 18th, listless, I'm convinced I'll die the way I am. Also on the 18th I'm convinced by the Catholic communists of "Voce operaia"; I'll get rid of my mysticism.   ✣   Life is made up of what you keep quiet about.   ✣   The liberals are civilized, but they have mineral water added to their ideas.   ✣   Bits of documentaries on Cesano, Castel Gandolfo, Albano, we are to use them for the film which exalts the actions of the Pope in this mass of flesh, the evacuees, the dwellers in hovels. I see only eyes like ours in tortured, disgusting bodies. I said the result would be a film attacking the Pope for not having done more. And where is my own more?   ✣   Fright in reading Marcus Aurelius, introverted and timely, in us, weak, confused echoes; he on his horse, solid by now, bronze; as I walk along a street I feel not only my own carnality but that of the walls, the ground, and as if I were walking in the belly of an animal and I am made of sinews that

hang from the hooks of a butcher-shop; if I return toward Marcus'
time and I overtake him, in a day, in an hour—there—in minutes
he resembles me a bit more.   ※   At lunch So. says we should
be monarchists not for the Savoys but for the Marquesses of Sal-
uzzo from whom the Savoys usurped the throne, among the pre-
tenders there would be Otto of Bourbon, handsome, So. says, he
deserves to be king because he's handsome.   ※   Yesterday
evening toward the Castelli there were still a few rockets, a few
thuds, the Germans' resistance now has something homosexual
about it, before it was romantic, now it's homosexual(?).   ※
From Lattuada's butler, a boy from Reggio, I learn they razed
Castlenuovo Monti to the ground.   ※   I meet F. in a bookshop with a vague reproach in his eyes because in his misfortune,
which is being idle and in debt, I am an accomplice.   ※   I.
tells obscene stories about actresses everyone idolizes, a mother
in seeing one of these actresses go by in Villa Borghese stands
still, her hand on the breast she is giving her baby, and waves to
her.   ※   For my daughter I write the fable of Adalgisa
whose hands were so beautiful that a poet couldn't find an adjective
worthy of them and was driven out of the village amid the gibes
of the people.   ※   Two parents want to make love and can't
get the child to leave the bedroom, they start out sweetly, coax-
ingly, then begin to threaten; it would be a sequence of closeups:
they are in a state of erection, in half a minute, as the child steps
over the threshold, they change expression and now speak reason-
ably, politely, to the child who refuses to move.   ※   I see
the powerful R.G. in the garden of the convent of the Ursulines
opposite my house; on this side of the fence along the street the
children of Via Merici have made little gardens three feet square
where they grow grass to eat; R.G. is displeased at being seen here,
this is the mother house of the Ursulines. The nuns walk backward, it must be a vow (*those little gardens didn't last long, first
the children saw their parents encourage them, afraid of starvation, then the black market made it possible to eat and the children
were abandoned; in the beginning they praised the children for
getting up at dawn to water the plots, of which there were a dozen,
of real earth, from which with patience food would have grown,
but in the end it became road again for the feet of the passerby*).
※   B. has changed allegiance in two days (*of the turncoats, some
are dead, or sick, or poor; if they had known I was making notes,
they would have wished for me to die. What was the value of my*

notes if, with the course of time, I also forgot, and I hated or loved
them according to new events, no longer because of the past which
should have sufficed to establish a relationship with them for the
rest of our lives?) I follow an American officer, clumsy and absent-
minded, with a stupendous respectable girl as if I were the father,
he takes her to a hotel and my impersonation ends.　　✻　　To
deal a blow to communism it seems they are planning to build
houses for all.　　✻　　Two hundred thousand unemployed in
Rome.　　✻　　Instead of addenda I keep marking down only
the total sum: the most apparent things, which I presume interest
also others, surrendering myself in this way. I never talk about my
daily climb up the Via Nomentana on my bicycle, slow, sweating,
or of my infantile evasions to alleviate the toil, inventing encounters
for fifty yards farther on, women hidden, waiting behind the trees,
a revelation that will burst out (of what?), or pretending the whole
street is a Via Crucis with Porta Pia at the end, toward which I
pedal heavily, it's a calvary in reverse, there is a point where the
curve makes the ascent worse and it's a symbol by now, not even
festoons could enliven it, another point, too—all wall—dejects
me as if it were rejecting the whole city and behind it there lived
somebody so strong that he could exclude you and all events.
But I am not reasoning; each time, I tell myself I will set aside
this trip for the logical investigation of one of the subjects that
torment me, but I abandon myself to sensations, to pre-enjoyment
of the pleasure of the next descent, the stretch of shade, to won-
dering if here, just where there is a spot of sun and the wheel
of the bicycle is reflected in it, I will ever have occasion to stop.
If I survive, I will write a story about the bicycle, gears sensitive
as viscera; between the foot which is wholly us and the pedal a
symbiosis is established, the common pace cannot be found immediately, there are trials, until all becomes one matter which is
neither iron nor flesh; it gives power, youth, and flight in case of
danger. Meanwhile the American vehicles graze past me, often
mortally; if we were in those vehicles and they on the ground it
would be the same, now they have the right which is not theirs
through personal achievement, therefore it is false; the circumstances elate or depress more than ever; and the more the Americans ignore me, the more I feel they believe they are what I am not.
I feel for them—as I felt for the others—impulses of pity.　　✻
A man in Via Vasi is out walking with his wife whom he wanted to
get rid of, we greet each other and this greeting will have seemed to

the eyes and the minds of my children a sign of the normality of life.   *   A little while ago a woman was talking, she talked for a long time and I, like a snowplow, made piles of her words left and right, while I passed between them.   *   In Naples, Monicelli was in a shelter for seven days (at Cancello, not in Naples), the clouds of dust from a house that collapsed nearby entered the shelter, about eighty people were in there and they thought it was gas, one man killed himself and his family; five people survived and Monicelli thought half-a-day had gone by, not a week.   *   I meet Ga. Ma. who blames everything on women. There is an increasing sluttishness, he says.   *   I realize I don't know how to react according to some fixed principle, I am a raffinated plebian, influenceable, local and suddenly international, from almost racial resentment I pass to a vision where the justice of the suffering we undergo, however, never absolves our punisher.   *   An Englishman at a bookstall tries to strike up a conversation with me, but I don't know his language, then another who is holding "Hyperion" in his hand speaks some Italian, offers me a cigarette, I refuse, he senses something hostile, asks if it's because of my stomach; he says that the Allies are reaching Florence where the publisher of that book is located while the other soldier cuts the pages with his fingers.   *   T. tells me his wife has grown thin, weak, he realized it for the first time during the war because he saw her when she sat on the chamber-pot, lifting her nightgown; he never looks and he shuts his eyes when he makes love, but that time he had to look (*she died about six years ago*).   *   My neighbors secretly buy the soup of the poor at three lire the bowl, my wife tries to persuade me it's good, the day of the test I pretend not to be hungry, my fastidiousness is obsessive, the little jar with the broken glass stopper depresses me like an action—what can I praise myself for?   *   In scraping my pallets Marco says: why don't you make a painted diary? One windy day in Boville a sheet of paper I used for cleaning my brushes blew away from the terrace, the *Bovillesi* saw it spin for a long time in the air, from the walls they followed its course, more and more upset, until finally with various changes of route it volplaned toward the Cappelletta; half the town rushed desperately into the valley and when the paper was in their hands one shouted it was the face of the Madonna, another that the war was over, until finally Marco arrived and told them what it was.   *   The kitchens of the Hotel Excelsior

244

from the big windows of Via Sicilia: lots of pastry, excellent, hams, turkeys, mountains of fish, the cooks' hands working for the victors; during the 1914 war the cook of a Neapolitan nobleman who worked in the kitchens of the Bombrini Parodi Delfino gunpowder factory at Segni-Scalo, before my fifteen-year-old eyes, spat in hatred into the cauldron of soup.　＊　Tomorrow I'll go into a church, I say; but the following day I forget my proposal; I see myself seated in a pew reflecting, because I never reflect, only in talking I'm forced to reflect. In that cool church I propose not to pray but to ask myself what a church is, what the gospel is, many things; an hour would be enough for me, for three years I have been living on these words and on others as if they were beyond appeal, I've seen people listen to me, be moved, and I don't know what they mean, perhaps I'll know if I don't think.　＊　Marco and I play at what we can see in the wick of the oil lamp, he sees a lion lying down with sizzling eyes and I manage to see it too. ＊　The bubbles that rise from the ashes which in my village they set to boil with water in great kettles for doing the washing; each bubble is a generation, it rises, explodes, the whole surface is these births and deaths but it is also a surface. Bubbles and surface possess both independence and interdependence: generations appear and disappear, some after a single spasm, others break into smaller bubbles that reproduce the phenomena of the larger one; and the larger, in breaking, mixes its steam with the steam of another at random in the magma and from the distance it is the smoke of the whole, the wayfarer says, and how can I exempt myself from it? The steadiness of this moment doesn't exclude the final instability.　＊　A famous painter is reconciled with his brother, weeps, in Piazza Barberini: with his mistress he had prepared poison so they wouldn't be separated in the event of a round-up.　＊　In his hovel Arturo gives milk to two kittens, his mother and I watch him for a long time without his realizing it.　＊　When I've had a bit to drink I feel I'm my father, the brief gaiety he enjoyed after dinner, lighting his cigar.　＊ On my bicycle, euphoric because of the shawls of air I flung behind me, thinking of adulterous women with gratitude (men are all equal and a woman reveals this). I was coming from a friend's house where we had been talking, husband, wife and I: our sentences were interwoven with a fluidity in which each is the other, and at the same time a hexahedron, so how can you then say I go to bed with the segment A. and not with the segment B.? She

could have slept with me or her husband indifferently, and where there were encrusted differences, it would be enough to accelerate the conversation to be caught again in the theft of resemblances. ❊ Be. says the film based on not killing, which we are preparing for the Centro Cattolico, is unpolitical and harmful today; he says I'm a Utopian and I provoke hatreds rather than love; non-violence is outside of our life and, if anything, I would be better off concretizing it in works of art. ❊ General M.'s sister-in-law says the nun who is preparing her little girl for her first communion speaks to her only about corpses, yesterday the child said she had lost her missal: God gave it to you and God can find it, just as God can take your father and your mother from you. ❊ N. says she heard an actor say to his wife: you were asleep and you spoke his name (the name of the American she is unfaithful with) and I was looking at you and suffering. ❊ A family, friends of ours, is about to run out of money; they have silver, gold, paintings, but they're frightened as if they had nothing, because what they possess has become a part of them like a nose. They feel as much despair as a poor man who owns only his body. ❊ I knock at De Chirico's door in Via Gregoriana and he looks out of the window with a brush in his hand. ❊ Da. says that in the morgues they've noticed that the dead, whatever class they belong to, have dirty feet. ❊ In a corner of the Caffè Greco with Fa. and Gu. we talk about the camouflages of fear, now it seems less only because it is operating in a less grim atmosphere, or rather, a bright atmosphere where the posters on the walls have resumed their gay colors. ❊ Thinner, Cardarelli says: I'm waiting for evening. ❊ I come home in the dark, the cars blind me with their headlights, the various outlines of the American vehicles stand out against the void, if God made them, why did he need so many shapes to make them credible as transport and mechanics, when I feel that they serve for something else? An enormous truck, all closed, alarms me with its indefinability as I pedal along. ❊ In the diaries of the kids of Via Merici all make the same spelling mistake. ❊ Sudden desire to be faced with death to see how I'll behave (my father's dying, clouded eyes which brightened for a moment before he died, so distant from our light, from me). ❊ To. says: "I'm not for the King or for the Republic, but for whoever guarantees me a good water-closet"; he's a man toward whom I have reason to be grateful and he tries to draw me into his mercilessness, I hold
246

out but my gratitude attenuates the reaction I ought to have. ⁂
T. says after three years of marriage he realizes his wife doesn't
believe him when he talks of his ideas about life, he thought the
nobler his ideas were, the closer he would press her to him, but
adultery is regulated by other laws, he says. ⁂ On the 23rd
I draft a kind of manifesto for writers who would be called agnos-
tics, apolitical, but these words have been definitively blunted, so?
We would like to live in a certain way, not writing, or live to write
differently, we believe only in immediate action, we are not far-
sighted but myopic, the word is in the deed, all of us for the present,
chaos isn't born from ignorance but from inaction; the more we
know the good the harder it is to practice it, to be always alert
for others, etc., but I haven't found an action that corresponds to
these intentions (*but an occcasional suspicion here and there that
they were only intentions; all in all, my hundred and forty pounds
of those days rested on non-suspicion; my name on the door of
the house responded to a non-suspicion or else I should have shot
myself*). ⁂ We belong to our own time when we feel that
it is passing. ⁂ A familiar voice over Radio Bari, I can
see him with his vast, mellifluous eyes, together we greeted the
big Fascist; I'll meet him soon in that sunny stretch of sidewalk
outside the Caffè Aragno, I see his hands moving responsibly, the
gestures seem frozen in truth and honesty as in an old photograph.
⁂ Before the portrait of Paul III: handsome, I say, excluding
the possibility that the man next to me can be thinking this with
the same intensity as I. ⁂ A father has hidden his son to
keep him from the Germans, the son wants to come out of the cave
to screw, to keep him from coming out the father goes to find a
whore for him: observe this search stage by stage. ⁂ On
the bus an old man touches my jacket, says the cloth costs at least
thirty-five hundred lire a yard then he asks what an ice cream
costs now. He used to be a tailor. ⁂ Like an orphan I
seek a guide for my life. ⁂ P. says: I'm a worm, a failure,
but if I catch my wife with another man I'll kill her. ⁂ At
the end of a long speech of mine, while Mu. is saying he feels up-
lifted, privately I realize I will reason differently as soon as this
fear and discomfort have passed. ⁂ A woman asked her
husband for some money to buy grapes, the husband had no money,
she said she realized for the first time her husband really was
without money. ⁂ I've always worked in order not to work
the next day. ⁂ Reading the life of Baudelaire, I feel heavy

247

and manage to skip a meal.   #   Opening an American can of meat, U. says: how could they have lost? Look at this red (the color of the can).   #   My brother and my son come back from the Viterbo countryside with potatoes procured with my mother's black dress.   #   A man who had never experienced sorrow expects it now like a bailiff.   #   In Milan S. kissed the picture of Mussolini who had made him a member of the Italian Academy, he lost his dignity in order to receive a title of dignity (*Milan begins when I get on the train at the Rome station, I savor in advance the gesture I'll make in wrapping my cashmere scarf tighter around my neck at the tram stop which is still electrically lighted though it is morning*).   #   In the Modernissima bookshop a Negro said to U.: read this, and he gave him Das Kapital, you who have lost are lucky, you can remake everything from the beginning, we will suffer for our victory; he doesn't want the change from the clerk, give it to somebody, no, throw it away, and he rushed off.   #   Who did I meet yesterday at Porta Pia? I try to remember, it was somebody I like, somebody good, the atmosphere bore out this conviction of mine, and through various moral and atmospheric attempts, suddenly a moustache pops up: ah, it was Giulio.   #   Seeing the Viterbo countryside from the train window, my brother says he enjoyed himself as if he were eating a loaf of bread.   #   They arrested a boy of eleven dressed as a girl.   #   I meet Silvani, they arrested him in Via Rasella when the bomb exploded, they put everyone against the wall with their hands crossed over their heads and meanwhile they were loading into a truck legs and arms which had been blown off the bodies.   #   I talk too much about morality (*this is written in big letters with a red pencil, it must have been one of those moments when you understand that you don't understand, in any case you go on living as if you hadn't made the discovery, filling the voids with the secret substance of the ego which has, as only attribute, the ego itself*).   #   In Via Tritone a drunk American was spitting on the passersby.   #   As I dreamt, I was analyzing the dream; the initial object was a circus, which turned into a wheel of cheese because of the analogous rotundity, we move farther and farther from the initial meaning with a multiplication of analogies which even in the most miserable creatures follow strict rules, the golden proportions.   #   M. says P. has the evil eye, then we talked about other things, you always talk about other things afterward, you slip away as if greased; I went to a bar, M. got into a bus, but the words continue to exist, to materialize, a chemist would be able to find their traces in a crime or a laugh.   ❊   In the Bellarmino church a Jesuit preached political forgiveness, many of the faithful muttered against him; at the pastor's advice another priest went to the pulpit, one whose family was killed by the Germans, he said they should be punished. The order then sent pastor and both preachers away from Rome.   ❊   I discover with alarm how we talk to excess, it's like flying over an area without feeling the terrain under your feet and then believing you know it.   ❊   E. is marrying an American out of gratitude; she was suffering hunger.   ❊   More and more meetings to form associations, offices are distributed, false words and actions become a definitive part of the mechanism, convenience is truth, only I could stop this process if I said what I know.   ❊   I meet the laconic Matthews of *The New York Times;* I say Allied propaganda is strengthening the German stand by insisting the Germans must be destroyed; he answers: they have to be destroyed, then we talk of the lack of clarity in Badoglio's message of September 8th; he corrects me: the lack of clarity is in Badoglio's intelligence.   ❊   A man falls down at Porta Pia in a spell of dizzyness, first everyone gathers around him and then they abandon him like foreigners, there is no nexus between the two moments.   ❊   One of the many nights I wander about the house with a headache, arranging a book, looking at myself in the mirror, turning on a light, turning it off, the muffled pause at the doors to listen to the others' breathing, the hypothesis: suppose this ache were to last for years. It actually seems years even if it will pass without fail in two or three hours, moments of wretchedness with my shoulders hunched and one eye half-shut, moments of new wholeness reading the headline of a paper. The reading time is without pain, without nausea, with a cold, logical faculty of judgment that involves also the body, a few moments before vomiting you feel like saying aloud I can't stand it another minute; you do stand it and still each fraction of a second contains an acute condition which isn't lessened by the one before or the one after. It is a repetition of peaks of pain without any habituation, you realize we can have miles inflicted on us in which each inch is suffering; during the retching, in the intervals between one spasm and the next, a moan escapes which would and would not like to be overheard, a broom pushes toward the garbage pail, you are a bat which first fills a room with its wings and, when struck, frees the air and occupies the most wretched space. Think about writing it. ✳ I knock at No. 2 Via Margutta, I don't know whom I'll find. F. and L. said to me: come, it's important; two women talk about a theater with very short pieces to be staged in Via Stefano del Cacco; a man comes in with thick brows, he's the head of the house. Lon. says Mussolini hated the man so much he wanted to dominate Italy just to spite him, he embraces me, I don't know why; coming out, I learn that he is Pippo Naldi. ✳ In the bookshop in Piazza Barberini they sell wine, cans, there is a great commerce in the back room. ✳ L.B.: "I exalted Mussolini?" Question mark. I never wrote Mussolini was a great man, but does a greater man than Mussolini exist today? ✳ T. says: it's absurd for my wife not to be unfaithful to me; she's a woman with some moral judgment, and having seen me eat shit like so many others, she'll feel the need of a man who seems better to her; maybe he only has to be somebody else. ✳ A woman assembles her lovers and in confessing herself to them all she makes you feel that instead of advancing, as she exchanged one for another, she remained still, it was as if she acted with her hand covering her eyes: how sinister humiliating is and being humiliated. ✳ A man says: you should have to kill a German to be readmitted to society: aut, aut, expelled from a drawing room and from the future if you don't bring a corpse, time is pressing, the Allies are about to arrive, in the curfew darkness channels of light have already opened where friends have installed themselves with the motions of tomorrow. The others, the rear guard, will die on the snow; perhaps there is still a bit of hope. A German usually goes by at nine from Piazza Mignanelli—T. has thought about it, so has U., but the rule is one apiece—this would be the easiest opportunity, quickly, otherwise the danger increases. ✳ If I or one of my family were to die I wouldn't have the money for the funeral. ✳ Discussion of the manifesto of the writers of the left. You can't say: my written works are of the left; your daily life has to be of the left; the gap has to be closed, the manifesto isn't signed by books, but by people who have also written books. We are writers of the left but men of the right, I shout, let's have an examination of conscience; A. Tr., coldly: I don't need one (in fact, he risked his neck); I am aghast as I realize I am trying to involve in my vague Christianity people who have acted. ✳ A black marketeer showed Admiral F.'s wife a pack of thousand-lire notes and

asked her what they added up to. She counted them: a million. He
started shouting that he was a millionaire, a millionaire.   ❊
A delegation to Undersecretary Spataro; one of our group had
borrowed an overcoat until 2 P.M.   ❊   A certain La Rosa
tells me his ship was torpedoed, a German submarine rescued all
the survivors except the Captain, who kept yelling save me but
the Germans thought he was yelling to them not to save him, and
they lined up stiffly on the deck in a long salute.   ❊   A maid
says every night she hears horrible quarrels between her master
and his wife, barefoot she listens, then in the daytime they behave
so normally she thinks she dreamed it.   ❊   In silence I find
myself totally; in words, incompletely.   ❊   A nun, made
pregnant by an American, went to a man I know for an abortion,
a little house with flowers around it; I can't imagine her naked on
the cot, she always has something of her habit clinging to her,
her uniform.   ❊   B. says he jumped in his parachute, even
though he was afraid, to redeem himself, and now he can be an
anti-Fascist with a clear conscience and he feels he is good (he reads
me some poems).   ❊   To write, opened, stretched—ouch
—until your bones break.   ❊   I begin November talking of
the white slash in the roast chestnuts as if a slash of self-confidence
(*next to this there are household accounts*): sold a pair of gold
cufflinks for a thousand lire, a thousand lire earned for a gag in
a scene for a film of Latt.   ❊   My mother puts a sprig of
lemon verbena on my desk, her mother also used to grow it in
pots on the balcony and at night when she heard my voice in the
street she leaned out in her gown and threw me down a sprig. I
put it in my pocket where it dries and retains its perfume for a
long time, if my fingers just crumple a leaf and I pass them beneath my nose for a moment they free me, for that moment, from
every concern.   ❊   Barilli asks his nephew to lend him a
hand in writing down some things because he tires of putting in
commas and the other material obligations of syntax. He washes
all the time, I don't want to stink, he says.   ❊   Make a newspaper with items to which other papers dedicate six lines; six
pages on a minor theft.   ❊   Bec. says: I lost forty pounds
but I didn't sell the Morandi.   ❊   Rib.: they're giving Umberto II's son fake blond curls down to his shoulders to make the
Italians weep.   ❊   In the Basilica of San Paolo (the film
on Loreto), the extras relieved themselves in the church and in one
of the confessionals a policeman was found screwing (it's no less

251

amazing than the fact that I note it down and pass on). ⁂
The artist is still unconnected with the rest, he's an alibi for the
rest. ⁂ I look out of the window, a woman harshly slaps
my daughter, I shut the panes with an anguish no one will ever
know about. ⁂ On June 10, 1940, in Piazza Venezia
while the Duce was announcing the war, a certain G. interrupted
him shouting: it's not true. It was he who prevented the war. I
spoke to him at length, he is a man of average background, married in 1935 with a four-year-old son; they broke his nose and tore
out a handful of hair which has never grown back. At present he
is running a little soap factory at Iseo. ⁂ My daughter
says nuns don't make pee-pee. ⁂ "Il giuramentado" (a boy
in Via Vasi) has promised not to steal on Sunday. ⁂ My
daughter asks why other daddies have hair. ⁂ A man keeps
a secret diary all his life, doesn't know that his family reads it,
falls ill, his only worry is to burn the diary; after that he dies
peacefully. ⁂ He sets out to kill G. who at that hour is
alone in his house; G. brought about his financial ruin; he greets
people, exchanges a few words, arrives at the house: G. died of
a heart-attack during the night, he expresses his condolences to
the family. ⁂ That Lieutenant Atkinson who held out his
arms to protect Carretta, but the crowd tore Carretta from him,
scratching him, and when somebody asked the Lieutenant how he
got those scratches, he said: shaving. ⁂ The painter G.
asks me to help his girlfriend's father; G. breaks up with the girl,
wants me to have her father fired. ⁂ The Fascist Republi-
can Radio makes the parents of the children bombed in the Gorla
school speak; their sobs; you can come to desire enormous disasters in order to exploit them, it's the equivalent of murder. ⁂
At Gua.'s house, on one wall De Chirico's famous slice of cake;
he is a man greedy for power more than for money, in my mind
I have swept away the rich, but I save this one's skin because of
the way he offers me a cup of tea. ⁂ R. talks as if he
weren't mediocre: that gesture when he takes one picture from the
easel to put up another and calculates the proper light fills me
with a piercing desire for him to be great really, confused with
the desire for him to be atrociously disappointed. ⁂ How
many forgotten things form us? ⁂ I cover a hundred yards
on my bicycle forcing myself to think of nothing, to be a thing,
but out of the corner of my eye I see that passerby, looking at himself, attributes some meaning to me. ⁂ At De Chirico's in
252

Via Gregoriana, his self-portrait, naked on a chair. Dürer painted himself, he says, with one hand pointing to his ailing liver; I'm not modern, he says, because I paint like the masters, I perfect myself, I don't progress.　　✳　　Anton. thinks he is persecuted by fate.　　✳　　A performance of Gorky's Bulishov, bad atheist propaganda with some good hysterical flashes, the new bourgeoisie (which is, in part, the old) in the hall; they would let themselves be buggered to maintain this privilege of going to the theater.　　✳

A cart loaded with little barrels of wine; the brake gives way at the top of the steep Via Vasi, the horse is pushed down the slope faster and faster, he bashes his head into a wall and slumps to the ground, the master pulls his head up by the bit, lets it drop again. From the balcony I glimpse the horse's staring right eye; I've never seen the passage from life to death so rapid (unacceptable).　　✳

I talk with a young man whose brother has just been shot, a spy for the Germans from whom his mother collected ten thousand lire a month, her son told her the money came from the Vatican to set her mind at rest, the sister is suffering, what echoes does the word spy have for her? The firing squad shooting, going off, right face, the mother throwing herself on the son's body, the squad which is called a squad but is really six distinct men with temporary ideas, different ideas about their assignment, or without any ideas.　　✳　　They inform us we have eaten the meat of a tubercular cow sold illegally.　　✳　　They came to suggest the purchase of some pounds of horsemeat; the horse died yesterday.　　✳　　There is talk of a hunger march.　　✳　　N. takes B. to the home of Marchesa S., the house is full of paintings, he warns B. not to offer to buy any, this would offend her; B. sees a painting he likes, N. gives him a look to remind him not to talk to the noblewoman about buying. Afterward, in the street, N.: that little painting is really precious, he says. The next day he announces he could persuade the Marchesa to sell it, but at a high price. B. later learns the painting belonged to N., who with this device sold the painting at a profit, giving a percentage to the Marchesa.　　✳　　Ecstasy when I realize that in an argument I am defending heatedly I can instead be wrong; error as delight, as youth.　　✳　　A certain Cruder, before they shoot him, tells a woman in prison there's a bargain in Via dei Serpenti, an actress is selling her fur coat for very little, when the woman is set free she goes to the actress.　　✳　　"Many monuments to the war dead in Italy are me," says la T.; she was the model for their

253

sculptor.   *   I ask Guttuso to speak on "color and cinema,"
he has stomatitis, we talk about color as motor of actions, intuition
of a film conceived from the root and not as attribute of the plot.
*   Some young people go off to Teano as volunteers; they consider the literary world false and static, no word has convinced
us, they say, but the fact that other young men have gone, the
purity of the sky and this meeting convince me to join the most
extreme party immediately, or tomorrow. Tomorrow.   *   A
letter written in March arrives at this moment from Luzzara, nine
months later, and the emotion is all today's.   *   Radio
Monteceneri announces that my friend Buzzichini is dead, a year
ago they said he was dead, I wept for him, then the news turned
out to be false; today I didn't weep, having consumed last year the
quantity of grief at my disposal for him. He died of a fall from
a horse, which reared up on a quiet road, it was going at a walk,
and then it was as if a ghost went by. In a book of his there was
this story.   *   My mother is limping about the house with
rheumatic aches and pains; she'll go to a doctor who gives injec-
tions refusing to tell anyone what's in them, he glances around
like a thief before he gives them. At Montecatini there was a man
who worked miraculous cures, even more cautious; they killed
him.   *   I am three quarters my mother, one quarter my
father, with fluctuations, shifts that send a bit of the three quarters
into the quarter and vice versa; I can feel when I'm approaching
my grandfather Antonio or the other grandfather, certain instants
are theirs; perhaps I consist in saying this; at times you have the
sensation that ancient events are holding you together and it can
also happen—as when a thousand-year-old tomb is opened—that
you crumble to pieces.   *   I think of a newspaper that would
record our present acts, today I gave a thousand lire to, I quarreled with, but as if we were never to write again.   *   B.
wants to snip the hairs that stick out of my nose, he is a trichotil-
lomane (I believe I'm one of the three or four people who know
what this means, I read the word as a boy and it made a lasting
impression).   *   I think again of the boys setting off for the
war, I was excited, they were excited, perhaps a common error,
new impulses which lead to old actions; we're in a hurry to pay
a debt no matter in what coin.   *   I know a short painter
and a friend of his, also short, who has so much tartar on his teeth
that you can't see the cracks, they are both retouchers but they
also paint on their own, they slip along the walls talking privately
254

A PORTFOLIO OF ARTWORK
by

CESARE ZAVATTINI

DAL 9 NOVEMBRE AL 5 DICEMBRE 1968

The Artist

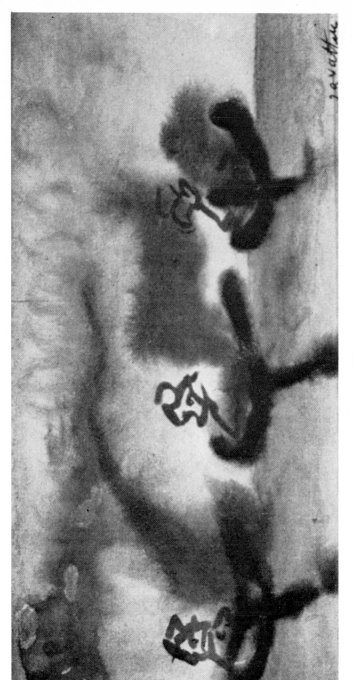

Flotilla

Funeral

Crucifixion

Priest

Authority

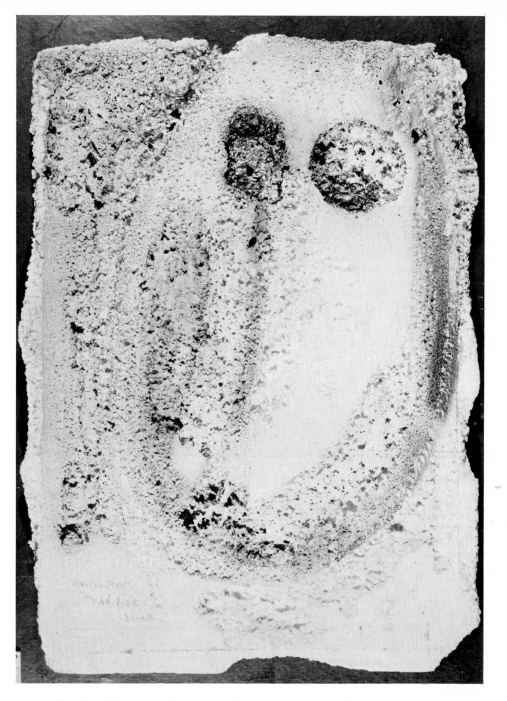

A "collage" of various colors sprayed on a relief melted into plastic styrofoam.

In the Street

as if they were going along a corridor, never entering the rooms where the other people are.　⁑　As she is giving me an injection, the nurse is in tears because her husband has a mistress, I console her with the usual words.　⁑　Abyss between the amount of time we give a living man and the Ah of condolence at his death.　⁑　The grandson of a Fascist bigshot has changed his name, but he resembles his race bodily even if his ideas diverge: his vocal cords have the timbre of his relative but they say things in opposition to his relative.　⁑　After an abortion S.'s girlfriend was at death's door, she's an ordinary little woman to whom he is bound sexually because, he says, she is the right size; he said noble things *in extremis* about their future, but if the operation had enlarged the receptacle a bit too much their relationship would have ended.　⁑　In Via Nomentana I saw E. who embezzled twenty-five thousand lire from the Assoc. Cin., he was strolling arm in arm with his wife, they were eating something, certainly with their diction somewhat muddled by their full mouths, their reasoning followed lines independent of his honesty, the subject was, for example, whether or not to buy a flannel shirt, but his honesty must in some way have affected the subject, everything can't be in water-tight compartments (why not?).　⁑　They want a comic story involving the Barber of Seville; I think of a dictator who forces his subjects, under pain of death, to express themselves only by singing; the difference between this and the real impositions of dictatorship is only tonal.　⁑　Ces. said: did you see that wolf Zavattini? Wolf? He says this isn't an insult, everybody looks like an animal, N. like a seal and he himself like a horse; in any case I enjoy this opinion which removes me from the undefined, where I graze like one of the flock.　⁑　A dream: two naked girls on the beach, as if left there by a wave, the air teeming with little wisps of shade, shining twigs, circles that dilate beyond the pupil, a great tongue emerges from the curly waves, slithers toward the girls then sways, its tip between the blonde and the brunette, the younger leaps to her feet screaming, the tongue, made heavy by the sand, painfully glides back into the water where it disappears with a glug.　⁑　A man says in a month or two the Germans could be in Rome again, the news is ambivalent: it frightens me and makes me smile; if it were true, I think, it wouldn't be a war development but a pretext to fall suddenly on those who in the meantime have already begun a process of sedimentation like coral. The Germans arrive stupidly

with their goose-step, convinced they are creating when they are only a tool. ✳ In the theater they threw down handbills protesting against the high salaries of the actors. ✳ A goat killed itself only a few moments before they were going to slaughter it. ✳ I saw R. in an automobile, seraphic; at this moment in the North, G.B. is rolling in the dust, shot, he joined the Republicans, convinced by R.'s newspaper. ✳ V. is selling a new fountain pen, he says, to hold out, he is waiting for the moment when he can direct a film; stronger than pity, the desire for the truth rises in me, to tell him he has no talent. I don't want to disappoint him out of nastiness, but because of an irresistible need for the truth, as when the insulted starts firing on the insulter, and he empties his revolver, not to erase a man but a symbol, an apparent ferocity which is instead a desperate rebellion against imperfection, against the primordial error of the creator himself. ✳ Ra. was talking about what the Mediterranean will mean in future politics, it was all logical, but he could have said this also five years ago, and so I see him dead, stretched out, useless. I let myself be drawn into the talk to avoid the odor of decomposition, I decompose too—the problem of the straits!— and the two odors mingle. ✳ In these days a great flurry of adoptions, for three hundred lire a month you can adopt a baby. ✳ I'm paralyzed, my left side, for the rest of my life. At five past ten I was whistling and painting, at ten-thirty I'm here with saliva drooling helplessly from my lip twisted to the right, and my family is around me to help me into the next room. I drag one foot and I can hear this noise distinctly, they keep saying it's nothing in terrified voices, with extraordinary rapidity I make a list of the things I won't be able to do any more, it's unbearable and I will bear it (the fact that this is all imaginary doesn't change anything). ✳ L. says that Bt. is a thief, blackmailer, liar, paranoiac, but an artist. ✳ With L.E., I argue about not killing; Ge. is for killing but without hatred. ✳ The sister of the spy shot recently makes me read a short story of her brother's, I force myself to see him at the moment he is thinking how to change a verb, there he was incorruptible. ✳ 1945 begins with bitter cold; I provide food for my children every day with work in which they have no part and yet it is chalked up in my favor. ✳ I try writing the letter of a wife who calmly explains to her husband that she was unfaithful to him because of the inadequate thickness of his member, calmly demon-
256

strating that she couldn't have acted otherwise, it's a scientific explanation on the one hand and on the other there is also feeling, she tries to block the irrationality, the passion of her husband, she doesn't want him to suffer, she thinks it's possible, any other available explanatory solution seems unacceptable to her, he can find women made in a way suited to him and he will be happy; you may kill me, she says, but that would be stupid, she describes what she derives from a perfect copulation, she even got rid of an allergy.   ❋   It's hard to express, but today as never before I felt that I am alive, or rather that they have left me alive; a localization, a perfect fit in the air, a neatness of my person, something more than the usual feeling of being alive; why did they leave me alive particularly and that man going by over there? I catch his gaze which should be one of complicity or understanding, in view of the enormity of this situation.   ❋   I am going to work on that hateful newspaper, M.C. says, because I'm tired of having to sell some object from the house every day.   ❋ Sleepless night: in '38 I wrote an open letter to the Chief of Police of Milan telling him to send his men to play mandolins under my window, lullabies to make me sleep, insomnia over a prolonged period arouses thoughts which can lead to criminal actions and it's his job to prevent crime. He had a pink face and snowy hair, pointing his finger at me, flushed, he said that if what I had written concealed some criticism of his men, sooner or later he'd make me pay for it. A year after that he shot himself.   ❋   God is confutable, how I like that word confutable, which lifts arguable to a tense level; it seems born for this subject and this moment, it becomes organic the instant you utter it.   ❋   Ferociously he was given enough intelligence to realize he has little, but this doesn't mar his ambition, we are ambitious for what we could be and not for what we are.   ❋   Loved, even without virtues, what has he done to enjoy that girl's hand which in embracing him pauses at his nape with the tact of a dove at that spot where his hair ends and his baldness begins.   ❋   To keep from going into the army I pretended to be an agoraphobe, G. says to me, he lived for four months in a mental ward, now he is directing a film and I have to believe him.   ❋   We're putting the Chamber into good order, G.M. says to me paternally, making me take a look into the hall of Montecitorio, when we inaugurate it the Deputies will find everything in place; but aren't those wooden panels, those rugs already too close to a certain way of

257

thinking?   ❉   At Ca.'s funeral, Bl. says: ah, if we loved one another a bit more; in a whisper he recites to F., holding his arm, a sonnet in Roman dialect, as we pass a little cart with two wreaths that are arriving late.   ❉   At the bedside of my daughter, who has to undergo an operation, I admit with amazement I have a hearty appetite.   ❉   He's a big snail, U. says about Q., who sticks out his head only to paint and make money.   ❉   A blonde lady, sweet, speaks of the voice, which can be corrected, changed; we accept everything, she says, and yet how many things can be altered; she is going around Rome at a time like this to seek supporters for a foundation concerned with the voice.   ❉   A series of revulsions: one against the body which I suddenly feel like something hanging, extraneous, another against the apprehension I feel for my sick daughter and none for the others. After the operation she was inventing words, "at oncely."   ❉   I defend the Negroes, Mt. says, but I would never give them my daughter.   ❉   The night of the Epiphany at Ar.'s house: M. wore a green wig, la F. a huge 19th-century corset that swelled her breasts, Er. was dressed as an old woman, P. in an English bowler, a group of friends arrived who called Ar. a queen; he answered that he's proud of it, and the other answered: I say queen as an insult, and all present are shits; a man with an ambassador's hat looked around from a curtain, do you mean me too? F. said, yes. A painter said: I'm here to watch the fire in the fireplace, the glasses. Yes, you too, you too. The host said the world is in real trouble and we're here arguing over a trifle, outside it's snowing; the group went away, T. will send a round-robin letter in which he demands to know openly who is his friend and who is his enemy.   ❉   On January 29th I saw C.E.G. who was asking directions of the painter De San., I am about to call to him, but I miss the right moment. I tell De San. he has given directions to one of the most worthwhile Italians, he was a bit bedraggled and perhaps it's just as well he didn't see me with my brand new wool scarf.   ❉   A film maker gives a newspaper to the carabiniere who is guarding the entrance to a restaurant for the Allies in Via del Gambero, the carabiniere brings it back with some bread inside; the proprietor gives it to the man every day in memory of the times when he was a wealthy customer.   ❉   "Kiss him—I say in the bus—see if you can kiss that one too"; I managed mentally to kiss all the other passengers, with an effort, all but him; impassive outwardly, I am upset inside, my guts bounce up and down in waves taller

258

than my height, but I see the course of the seventy-year-old's food as in an anatomical chart, the bus jolts us, he clings with his gloved hand to an iron bar and wants to be jolted less than the others, he stretches his anteater's neck toward the darkness to discover what street we are on, he asks where we are in an over-self-confident voice, I imagine him as a baby in his mother's arms, no use, it's beyond my strength to touch my lips to that presumption; even the place where he has to get off becomes hateful, it will remain behind us, all for him, a street with huge buildings, shops, talk. God, if you exist, would you really have kissed them all? There wasn't this smell of diesel oil then, it must have been easier in your day, with the palm trees; leave me at least one that I don't have to love.   *   To know myself I would need a point that is me and is outside me, I try at times to draw back as far as I can but I need just one millimeter more, and then I would fall into the void.   *   The more I perfect means for deceiving my neighbor, the more I realize it doesn't matter. Everything is soft today, written in pencil; a weariness that says to itself I'm going; you walk along the same street that the funeral procession would take, explaining to friends and relatives that you can't think straight any more, you can't judge, and they explain you're exaggerating and they would like to stop in a bar and have something to distract me. Everything is crumbling, but they say no, they cite examples, one even names heroes. I see in a flash the handkerchief of a friend who is weeping, at the gate of the cemetery the insistence gets out of control, but by now everything they say has nothing full or warm about it, I feel a bit of nostalgia for a truck that becomes intense as a face. I really must go, I step back with a polite smile, I disappear with my name they are repeating, Cesare, how often in conversation I have sensed the passing from last name to first name as a kind of blackmail, I have exploited it too—Paolo, Giulio, Antonio—wanting to make the name throb with remote pacts. I don't fall into the trap any more.   *   Yesterday the sixteenth during a concert, the conductor let out a cry—it isn't the first time—and fell back in an attack of a disease, it isn't right!   *   La E. was weeping copiously, I've realized, she says, that P. loves only my a— I explained that there is always a nexus between body and soul, love needs a carnal point of support, she still sobs and says that on a photo of her he drew a red circle around her a— there, she said, the rest of me doesn't exist. I was disturbed by that circumscribed space for which P.,

259

who writes also for a magazine in the Veneto, behaves so foolishly, though he has a family. ❋ To write a poem, to sit calmly at the desk, see a thing, however small, that the others haven't seen, a dozen lines. You want simple themes: home, woman, wind. In forty-three years there must be something that is really mine, I have only to break it off like a stalactite, I have only to confess as if the priests were already chanting psalms, say I loved if I loved or the opposite, without circumlocutions. There is the embankment toward the Cir. Nom. with two men working, they are working on the embankment, this is a verse, twelve verses are about a hundred words, the two have already made a bit of road, the first disappears toward the bottom, his head is out of sight, and the other walks more slowly, he is at a point where he seems tall, which he has never been, and before I have finished the line he will have also gone down gradually and then he can sit and eat or he will attack the other man treacherously and I won't be informed about it. ❋ Going up the Via del Muro Torto on my bicycle, I feel I will never get out of a damp, cemeterial Rome connected with my dismay at difficult Latin and at the Americans I will see at Porta Pinciana in their serene clothes as if they were right. ❋ La. says that months ago he wept for a long time, suddenly feeling all the weight of the war on his shoulders, and even Mt., a few days ago when he was in bed with a fever, felt like weeping; he wept and the fever vanished. ❋ In the windows of the evacuees' house, opposite mine, there are always heads bent over newspapers, from time to time they are raised, they look around, then like fish which for a moment have stuck their mouths out of the water, they dive again into those deceitful lines which are believed to be the real life of which they would be only a reflection; if they aren't reading they quarrel, they sway in the cautious shoves they give one another to test their adversary's strength, they decide to shout and scratch each other because they think that during the fight some change will take place, and instead they find my face which draws away slowly from the window like a moon. ❋ A father and a mother in Via Melaina run off with their respective lovers also taking away the gift packages distributed by certain trucks, leaving their seven children with an aunt. ❋ A subscription of sugar is opened for the children collected at Cinecittà. ❋ You should write as if you were in prison. ❋ With P. and his wife we meet frequently on Via Nomentana people begging, to one P. says, "we're worse off than you, don't go by appearances."   ✳   He is so totally everything, he so occupies everything that he has no space left for reflection, and then he doesn't exist.   ✳   Ga. in '38 was forced to follow a Fascist parade and he kept changing step like soldiers in old comic films.   ✳   Fighting at Gonzaga between partisans and black shirts (*I had a vague knowledge of the partisans before the people of my home town joined them: boys at night went secretly to the Po, they signalled each other with bird-calls and they drove holes into the enemy's boats, ten lost their lives. Stop. I have come only to the beginning of 1945. I still have about twenty years to leaf through. This isn't a literary device: they are there, mysterious as the future. I'll continue in a few months and publish them with the title: 1945–1963*).

III

*little
journey
along
the po*

Cerreto Alpi, October 7, 1963

The Cerreto is swollen with snow, the glare creates a fictitious feeling of warmth, the little gate's iron bars allow me to recognize the cemetery on the slope, with the grave of my brother, who has been dead for forty years. In those days my family lived there in the mountains and I lived in Parma; at Castelnuovo I missed the bus on purpose so as not to arrive in time for his funeral; I was afraid of grief, not only of feeling it but also of seeing it. I arrived late in the evening when there wasn't a tear left in the house, and I said: "I missed the bus"; I can't forget that tone of my voice.

Along the road a little while ago I held out my hand to watch the flakes dissolve on my palm, they call it *"neve volona,"* snow that flies, because it's dry, and the North wind rapidly piles it up against the walls. Soon the clear sky will freeze it, we will hear the creaking of glass before the thaw, which extends the humiliating season of mud until after March.

Cerreto is a little heap of old women dressed in black with large gums and men's shoes, plus a few men who come home from work on Vespas hiding behind the windshield; but little by little, the crude impression becomes articulated: those who seem decapitated under loads of wood exchange signs with the others, I see conspiracies and hopes, as in every part of the earth. Here they are all related, and they were all relatives too of the poor man found in '45 in a grave with his hair still standing on end because they had buried him alive in the days of the partisan fighting.

I go out for a little walk before supper, and I stroll with clouds at my feet. Imagine my cane's rapping on the rocks and a nanny goat, late, climbing a narrow street; yesterday evening a boy with a pale, delicate face, illiterate, cried *topa* (mouse) to an old woman
262

who lives with an old man in a hovel. Their dog defends them as if they were angels, and the old man deflowered his own daughter; the old woman didn't like that word *topa*—it is what they call a woman's thing because of its long softness—and she and the boy started fighting. I shouted "Stop, stop," even at the villagers who were indifferently loading sacks of chestnuts.

The room where I work, nine feet square, suits me, and I should finally remain seated at my table eight hours a day instead of doing nothing, imagining the joy I would feel in doing something. I am kept company by the little wheel set in the windowpane, it spins to change the air, and is powered by a mountain stream. As soon as I arrived I said to my sister: "I won't be able to stand this noise"; but by the end of the sentence I was already used to it. The stream soon joins the Secchia, and the Secchia after a night's descent with its trout and its narrow, nervous water, flows into the broad, calm Po, which passes Luzzara, where I was born.

I want to go and see the source, those few quarts of water on Moviso which become the Po (I said this last July, because I'm one of those who always have to see the exact spot where the girl threw herself into the lake).

On the ninth, in a Renault, we arrived at Pian del Re. A man said: "It's there, the spring." Some freshets streaked the mountain, apparently still, but the insistent eye managed, despite the distance, to catch some vibration; in its morning transparence the moon was more a sound than anything else. You could see people, not many, in brightly colored clothes and some automobiles put out to graze beyond the narrow passages of the parking lots. Some people wore collars and ties; a gust of wind had borne them up there from the Sunday of their village. A little cloud formed before my eyes, and, with the same magic of its formation, I saw it dissolve, leaving the landscape more limpid than before. This is where King Vittorio Emanuele used to come on holidays with noblemen, generals, sentries, and the flag over his tent. At Crissolo, which you come to before reaching Pian del Re, in a room of the oldest hotel there's a photograph of the Prince of Naples at twenty, very handsome, and for such false beauty the people of the valley would give their lives.

I went toward the spring, determined to become elated, tramping on ranunculi and gentians: in a film they would have put a little march-tune under it. "Here we are," I shouted. Huge stones, bigger than I am, enclosed a space the size of a bathtub with some turgid water which presses, with eddies and gurgles, seeking an outlet until finally it finds it and vanishes, to reappear fifty yards farther down in the form of a trickle. I would have stretched out and drunk with my tongue if Signor Rossi hadn't offered me a glass; the water was thick as milk. Realizing I was sitting on the slab like a man of sixty, with a thrust of my back I was again simulating youth. I found some snow in a hole—it was the fabled snow —and I crumbled it in my fingers to feel its non-fabulous composition, but the fables multiplied.

Suddenly my heart raced, and I murmured Mendes; for less than an instant I thought I saw my friend Mendes, who died in '60, go off on a bus with his party. In this or that place, you seem to see a dead person and you would call out to him if his eye, meeting yours, didn't look past you. That very perfection rekindles the suspicion that deaths are only changes of address to be kept secret at all costs; I could meet my father in Bressanone, he with his forty-eight years and black hair, I with my sixteen years more and my old awe; perhaps we would go away again without saying anything to each other? Where could we begin?

We set off toward the plain as the shifting wind brought the smell of fried onions from a trailer.

For its first miles the Po moved negligibly among the hoofs of spotted cows; a little wall could have blocked and scattered it. I kept turning to see its metamorphoses with losses and recoveries of water, a steep descent created a little cascade, promptly channeled, and the road continued to be no more than four or five times the breadth of the river.

At Pian della Regina I read in the paper that yesterday, right at Luzzara, two boys drowned in a canal of the Po. My fixed idea was to reach Luzzara, for the first time in my life, by water, taking a boat: at Piacenza? At Cremona? Viadana? And meanwhile they were preparing the funeral for two of my town, one died trying to save the other, slipping along the bank: the shops close as the bier goes past, there is a moment when all are equal, the dead man's family and the others, when the coffin, carried on the men's shoulders, comes through the door of the church and is put on the hearse, but then after a few steps each retains only the portion of this sorrow that is his due. Huddled in the car, I reconstruct the tragedy while Zanca prepares the tape recorder in case I want to talk among these beautiful mountains.

At Ponte di Villafranca we encountered the first iron arrow with the word Po, white letters on a blue ground, and a fisherman whose

264

pole was invisible because of the distance but it could be sensed like a vowel missing in a sign. And his presence guaranteed that now there was a certain volume of water accumulated by the trickling of a few tributary streams. I fell asleep to wake up as we were crossing expanses of blue herbs (they use them for vermouth and incense), and the cries of the guinea hens were recorded on the tape with the same care as my words.

About five we reached Turin, I was anxious to get away from it; I prefer empty spaces to agglomerations. At the Valentino park under a well-distributed sun some whores were sitting; a man less sensual than I wouldn't have noticed them among the tricycles and the trajectories of the rubber balls. It was the hour when you would say that nothing abnormal exists, and perhaps at the Cottolengo Asylum the stink of the poor monsters may be for a moment overcome by the saffron color that spreads from the great windows. In the midst of the park a urinal near a wall of moss has a thermal innocence; evening will come and a man, subordinate or chief, will wander around the area, then remote, in search of another man to touch and to love, they will kiss, and perhaps they both have moustaches; I have seen some look at each other from a distance, in the half-darkness shadows rather than a Giulio or a Paolo, but they sense each other, like a species, until one of the two makes the first move. Disabled veterans with aluminum crutches created a hanging-garden atmosphere of convalescence along the paths, a woman, fiftyish, supported by two attendants, came toward us rapidly, tilted forward, as if anxious to reach a vital goal, an ancient limousine followed her slowly.

We stopped on the San Mauro bridge in the twilight to contemplate the Mole Antonelliana, veiled by the dust of the cars coming home. In the city the river was not Po-like, my Po cannot stand manufacturers, it annuls them with its immensity. Eluding trucks and fleeing Vespas with their headlights already on, a woman asked me if I knew Vimercate; she's from Milan, she said, she saw the license plate. In Vimercate there should be a son of hers from whom she has heard nothing, he isn't really her son; she took him in when he was a few years old, in '51, they all fled to Turin from the Polesine because of the flood at Occhiobello, and the ingrate ran off one day with a girl; the woman keeps saying he's good and kind: "Don't you and your friends ever go to Vimercate?" (Zanca was photographing the sunset, he had been waiting for it like an aviator; he says it amplifies the sky.)

Under a roof of fog we reached Casale Monferrato where my interest was aroused only by a remark of the parking-lot attendant: the bar in the center of town changes hands often, they all fail; the movement of the clientele and the profile of the woman at the cash register, the noise of the spoons handled by the bartender and a good odor of coffee—one would have thought these positive in whatever situation, and yet every now and then they fail.

We went on to Valenza and I was daydreaming about supper, allowing miles and miles to go by as if they had no souls; we imagine we are entering a dazzling hall, our shoulders still hunched from the cold of the street; those who arrived earlier regard you, an outsider, with veiled hostility, but once you too sit at the table and have munched a bread-stick you become one of them, united against the last to arrive.

Reluctantly we gave up a side-trip to the Langhe; I had been there a quarter-century ago, to the house of an Academician who had said shamelessly, "Well, now I am a member of the Academy"; and he meant he was on a life raft which had few places in this shipwrecked country. Then I didn't know Pavese existed, he existed and was already thinking of killing himself.

Lonely as a god, a motorcyclist preceded us in the night of laughter, and the headlights illuminated his proud back; with a jab at the accelerator we passed him two or three times to humiliate him, and he again attempted a spurt; suddenly he stopped, a moment's glow, and then he disappeared forever; it was at a stand selling watermelons. From a mystic tension, at an application of his brakes, he was transferred into that cheap semi-darkness with the chorus of frogs.

At Morone Po we got out to make water, the Po was flowing a few paces away, we moved toward it with our flashlights, against the screen of the woods our shadows loomed at us in clouds of mosquitoes and cobwebs first impalpable than sticky, imprisoning ears and noses for long seconds. Can silence be recorded? Unfortunately we left the tape recorder in the car. From the shore you could see only a little light downstream, and, whatever else there might have been, it too would have increased the heritage of my traditional melancholy. We left again at top speed to shake it off and, striking trees and milestones with our lights, we gave a daytime concreteness; the cars that went by on the overpasses, preceded by the radius of their headlights, seemed to come from another world which lives

266

alongside ours but can manifest its presence only through these fugitive signals.

A shot in the distance made my ears pop up like a hare's, for an unmeasured amount of time I remained in a vacuum waiting for more, was it the revolution? It was surely only some petty thievery.

After the night at Valenza, day came and I was dozing beside the driver. A shout from him wakened me near Lomellina: a skunk. Somewhere else we had glimpsed a squirrel on a beech with a halo of embroidered leaves. Waiting for the tires to be pumped up, earlier, I touched a caterpillar with the tip of my shoe; in self-defense he rolled up in an instant. I waited then for that hairy ball to unwind, but it didn't, and I left it a prey to other feet. How great and of what nature was the time lag between the rolling and the unrolling? Only membrane-time, a membrane which withdraws at contact and needs a preestablished number of minutes to relax again? This must belong to that branch of forbidden knowledge in which, if we could grasp only one secret, we would know them all. Suddenly a bird plunged in front of the car; had we killed it? We should have heard a little thud against the radiator, but the dust cloud prevented us from looking back.

I cursed a truck driver who spitefully wouldn't let us pass him. Frustrated men, they are not in harmony with their sturdy trucks, they change locality too often; nothing is secure; at the places where they unload, a few minutes between one crate and the next are all they need to screw . . . whom? They don't even know if it's the maid or the mistress.

At Pavia, it was one o'clock. I happily soiled my suit climbing up to see the figures on the facade of the church of San Michele which the air was dusting; the resistance of the human outline is great; we can trace one of our kind even in the remaining inch of a relief. We traveled over Longobard cobblestones, along ochre colors and Visconti escutcheons half-covered with ivy. In '50 L. began to avoid me, and in that little square with its triangle of trees, a stone's throw from the prison of the innocent Boethius, I would have given an arm to know why. For a slander spoken in the same tone that one uses to say to a child: "Put on a sweater, dear," or out of real dislike? Which can be inspired simply by a vein on your nose or by the very conviction that nobody can dislike you.

We were still on the outskirts of the city when Signor Rossi surprised me by starting to play the first reel, so I could listen to it.

267

My voice had the senile resonance of grandfathers when they jokingly frighten their grandchildren, and sounded older than the armature I have inside me: I was trying to make lyrical everything that passed before my eyes, failing to extract the social component that everything has. I said that the mountains, in the funereal twilight with the silvery flashes of the milk cans being taken to the collection center, became more and more the end of the world, and the peaks were the profiles of friends and acquaintances. They had a grandiose quality that had escaped me before, but as the car changed perspectives it brutally annihilated first one then the other, no matter how hard I tried to preserve the recognition.

We had lunch at La Becca in a summerhouse surrounded by poplars. *What does the hydrometer at Becca read?* When there are floods, this sentence appears often in the papers. Some children came, who stripped and disappeared while their bicycles, flung on the grass, were still spinning their wheels.

We climbed into a motorboat; as we started, the boat reared up and I fell backward. Still I urged them to go fast. The signs lined up along the bank guide navigation: white means the way is free, red means danger. You are willing to die, the pleasure of speed is exhilarating no less than the pleasure with a woman even if it's impalpable, we become a sculpture of air. If the motor explodes there's no escape, perhaps Zanca, who is thirty, will manage to carry me to shore in time for artificial respiration, provided I don't cling to him and drag him down. I couldn't see another boat, or any sign of civilization; I would have liked this tropical zone to continue forever, but already the roof of a house is rising from behind a dike; then the whole house, a man at the window, a cart, and your debts, even if you don't have any more. From the little beach of Arena Po a man shoveling sand waves at us and he thinks: *my stretch of water,* but the water never stops. In the tavern of San Zenone the heat made the ceiling lower, the natives were following the world bicycle championship race, their profiles glistening in the reflected light of the video, with the certainty that this competition was being held solely for them; sweat and years of bleach had changed the color of their jerseys from vulgar to precious. We too had the presumption that we were the only travelers, the only ones coordinating space in a project, and therefore the other cars seemed ephemeral.

At Piacenza a young man was wandering naked around the

268

showers of the yacht club, a toothpick in his mouth. I couldn't find a boat for the trip to Luzzara, and in my heart I had conditioned myself to arrive there that night. I had stopped in Piacenza a month before for other reasons, waiting for the sad hour of bedtime, pausing outside the window of a record shop in a deserted street; from an open-air movie theater the confused dialogue of a film could be heard (I might have written it); a couple on the sidewalk brushed past me, walking hastily, heading for the provincial double bed which I imagined wider than the city version. You could sense that, before me—single—they were boasting that they were two. At ten P.M. there wasn't anyone left, like the lower part of Via Cavour in Rome, still intimidated by the Pope.

In Cremona the Cremonesi were having supper, the city seemed inhabited only by a dozen people none of whom, crossing the square, looked at the famous cathedral illuminated by fake moons. The warmth the walls gave off assured me we had returned to the happy times when the seasons arrive on a precise day with the click of some lofty switch. Near Isola Serafini first we lost the paved road, then found it, asphalt is the equivalent of the little light in the forest of the past. We asked an old woman when the sun set, and she answered "At 7:59."

After villages of one-story houses and posters for circuses that perhaps never existed (sad places: we stopped to buy matches and the tobacconist was very jolly), we reached Boretto, on the bridge of barges where automobiles and trucks cross dead slow; a plaintive creaking and an adventurous wooden roadbed. The planks seem always about to crack under the wheels of the trailers; they support up to two tons; if I put a sheet of paper on a two-ton truck, will the truck plunge through? A single ounce can't make the difference. I put the sheet of paper on the truck and I wait a moment (it's a trick: putting them one after the other in haste, you have the impression they have more volume) then I add another sheet of paper, a butterfly; the moment of collapse will come—but if I had waited a bit longer, if between the next-to-last sheet and the last I had left the country?

I asked if somebody would take us to Luzzara with a boat. "It's too dark," they answered. They were dancing under the trees, they come to that dance floor also from the Mantua shore, from many miles around, it's so beautiful! "It's beautiful," I repeated, beautiful too was the dampness on the roofs of the cars. On one of them

269

I traced an O with my finger, but Signor Rossi said my finding everything beautiful prevented me from drawing useful considerations from reality. I loathed him until the next day.

At half-past eleven I set sail for Luzzara on a ship: the mayor arranged it. Amid trumpet blasts the ship moved from the shore, with its hundred horsepower, it could carry several dozen people; a month later it was to make its first official voyage. They turned on a spotlight. Its ray, moving from one bank to the other, bared high-water beds of sleep beyond the willows. One of the two helmsmen had been torn from his card game, the other from his bride's bed; standing where I was, I could see only their bare feet planted on the deck of the bridge, pointed as they stood on tiptoe to see more clearly ahead. In less than an hour we would arrive. Too soon. The foam of our wake was wealth and the sudden cold, which saps my lungs, made me happy, a danger that made me worthier of the approaching goal. Emerging from the clouds for us, the moon ran among the poplars faster than the ship, but towards Gualtieri it took to the woods and left only the sky. What I had dreamed of was happening; what precisely was happening? For years in my heart, the Po began half a mile before Luzzara and ended half a mile afterward, on either side, beyond that point, there was Scythia and frost. Zanca placed the microphone in my hand and went off discreetly, he supposed the moment had come, in that corner of the prow, for me to say everything. I was about to sight the blue clock of my hometown, where I will be buried. You think of all this as of a secret hoard that will be decisive for what? You touch yourself with your hand, which grows vaguer every year, to know if you still have this treasure inside. Snatches of my friends' talk reached me: river transport would never develop because there are family interests behind it. I was empty as a student at exam-time, with the suspicion of showing off. The spotlight's ray hindered by the fog became a white globe suspended over the river; in the blackness of the Lombardy shore there was Dosolo, the town of my forebears, and Pomponesco, where I like to go for supper at Cagnolati's, encountering along the uneven roads only petty thieves and those who cut the stooks ("because it's better at night than in the daytime"); on the opposite side, in Emilia, Gualtieri, with the houses that still bear the dark line of the last flood; Ligabue is in the hospital rubbing his hand over his bald head, incredulous at the paralysis of his other arm, he wants his visitors to assure him it isn't true; he understands they're lying, begins to curse in front of

270

the nuns, and tries, weeping, to procure a miracle. Down in the courtyard his two old automobiles are waiting for him, covered with a tarpaulin, the owners of his paintings look distrustfully at those who go to ask if there is a lion or a tiger of Toni's for sale, they don't sell, waiting for his death to raise the prices.

At Guastalla as they detached four barges from the bridge to allow us to pass, the question of what sort of man I'm taking to Luzzara appeared and disappeared. To evaluate it I pretended I was a native of some place much farther ahead, I transformed my hometown from the terminal to an intermediary stop. It wasn't the first time I had spoiled happy moments with demands of this sort, they are stenograms my conscience specializes in; it couldn't do so much work if it obeyed all the rules of a language like ours. Meanwhile, as our progress was resumed, I recognized the bank where I once painted (while my son was fishing next to me, I dipped my brush in the current). There was an automobile on the shore with its headlights burning, it seemed one, then it became two: I was expected. The trumpet blared, and no doubt its echo reached the square where the cafés were closing wearily. As the engines stopped, all sound ended abruptly. The ship proceeded with equal speed, or even greater, but in silence. After a few seconds, the engines started up again, now at a different pace which, though we were advancing, gave us the sensation we were moving backward.

Prepared in my chest, the cry to greet my friends whose white shirts I could glimpse, suddenly seemed already useless; setting foot on the ground I said *"Ciao"* with modesty that reduced my arrival to customary proportions. A cigarette lighter revealed Soliani's face, the introductions between Borettesi and Luzzaresi took place blindly and in whispers as if the others had sensed my state of mind.

We left the water behind us to continue its course toward the sea, and barely a mile further on, our Italian *e*'s were changed into the *i*'s of the local dialect. Piled into the car with five or six others I tried hard to persuade myself I was better than I supposed—wasn't my very self-doubt proof? So allow me to enjoy in peace (whom was I beseeching?) this kind-hearted, sincere homecoming. Was it exactly that? I made an effort to be interested in the others' talk, to struggle out of the funnel, but if you try to hurry you end up being driven more toward the narrow part at the bottom: an opening yawns and when you drop into it, it's a trap. So on entering the tavern, welcomed by the white of the tablecloth as if by a person,

271

though sharing in the general laughter at Celso's recurrent expression: *how beautiful life is,* which brings any ambiguous situation to its absolving climax, I was a hair's breadth from bursting into tears as if I were coming from a crime. I restrained myself from saying: "My face was an asshole that time when money drove me to shake hands with the detested N." Silvio was slapping me on the shoulder to arouse my trust or to attest his in me, a thousand miles from supposing what I was suspecting inside: that I came back to Luzzara gladly because I had now bought houses there and could talk in front of them about drainpipes to be replaced, moving my head and my hand as I had seen rich men do in my infancy, with the enchantment then and the tyranny of the unattainable. And at the same time I was feeling pleasure in the glistening of the glasses (why does glistening produce pleasure?) and the thin knees of the landlord's daughter, as she squatted on her heels to pet the cat; every now and then a hand was raised from some point of the table to wave and greet me, or was it to comfort me? Afraid they might read my thoughts, I immediately looked away from those who looked over at me, and the more I felt they were prepared to exalt me, the more I denigrated myself, not without noticing the flavor of the ham, which is aged perfectly at Langhirano. I sought a guilt sufficient to remove me abruptly from the horizon like a house that collapses. I insinuated that through one assonance less in a page of mine I'd be willing to falsify history and for the sake of temporary truths I establish permanent subjections, and I desire to be alone, to crawl into my lair, but once in it I'm frightened and I call out. I'm cowardly, I concluded, from which the landlord's daughters tried to save me by singing *"Quando quando tu verrai."* The girl bent over her accordion as if she were copulating, opening it like a fan; I found myself in the chorus at the moment when the notes plunge, after the suspended *quando quando,* and excite group applause and impulses. As soon as the song ended, there was a silence like an imaginary darkness where you could see only the eyes of those present, questioning one another with the uneasiness of an imminent catastrophe, and to arouse pity I fled to a village in the Gargano (Peschici?) to grow old, sustained secretly by the boast of my confession. I wrote in my notebook in big letters: "Suicide at Table." It was the title of a short story, but it could really happen. I could kill myself while eating, more slices of salami, more, and the skins pile up on the plate or are thrown under the table where the cat glides among our legs with its hard tail

272

which arouses, and the others laugh and I am killing myself. I chew so calmly that no suspicion of my plan is possible among my tablemates, I foresee that at about four in the morning, when they come to whistle under the baker's windows, I will begin to die unless I'm saved by a purge. I considered the behavior of the others at the table nauseating in its banality, even if my own, to all appearances, wasn't any different. Would we have been distinct from one another if the bomb were to fall? Turning a dial I focused the mushroom cloud rising from the Carrobbio, slow, stirring in coils not without an objective beauty, it turned into Via Dalai, with anthropomorphic precision it followed the fleeing townspeople, very tiny, those who, as the homemade cake now appeared on the table, were full of gaiety. I laughed too at the Luzzarese rapist who defended himself to the judge, saying *agom stu bagai chè, sciur* ("We have this thing here, sir"), humbly pointing to his member. Meanwhile all were honking their horns, a roar burst like the sound oxen make during the flood, the noise was multiplied as when, some nights from my Roman bedroom, I hear the horns' insistence at the corner of Via Nomentana, it comes within my walls from a clogged world, and in what world am I? When I least expected it, I learned that by inserting the theme of the bomb with real names in a composition I was working on, I could achieve effects that had been unimaginable until a few seconds before; then I put the notebook in my pocket after having written: "bomb with real names." I had a prize in my game bag and for the rest of the supper I could devote myself to the food like my friends. Meanwhile, despite myself, I was shouting to somebody: *"The bomb's come. It's come. You see? It's come!"* All that massacre was worth it to be able to shout in a prophet's voice to an unidentified interlocutor: *"It's come, it's come, I knew it."* My accusations and his excuses came from our mouths in such a rush that instead of being enunciated they were an identical howl, in the background, flames that had been persons rushed by, obeying new laws; in the air you could hear broken words like those of a man about to be shot by rebels when his condition, which is historical, seems extraneous to him and irrational since it can't be resolved with well-argued protests. My eyes were forced in another direction where my daughter, no matter how much I love her, is becoming ash which a fleeing truck, avoiding her, blows away slightly. A., who is offering me a slice of cake, was there with the others discharging stuff from every orifice (in Rome? Luzzara?);

273

in the square there was already more than a yard of this grim ooze
where the six o'clock sun cast the same reflection as it had the
(innocent) day before, along the sidewalk and on the desperate
hills people try to stretch to raise their mouths above the rising
slime (my imagination instinctively borrowed something from
Doré's Stygian swamp) which was stifling their invocation: what
did they hope for from me? I couldn't set myself in the event in a
definitive perspective, I was co-responsible, avenger, witness, victim, and in these metamorphoses I was also conjecturing means of
salvation. Somebody shouted: "When will your book come out?"
I answered with an evasive gesture while I snickered, belched,
stoned San Bernardino, and this lasted less than the foam in the
glass of wine that Mora was pouring me, and I can't dismiss the
thought that beneath my revolt there was envy of a perfection
achieved by others, even if that perfection appeared the final insult
in such an imperfect world.

I went to bed at four as soon as the Borettesi left, I had accompanied them, to see them from the bank as my fellow-villagers had
seen me a few hours earlier, in the midst of the river with the spotlight that accentuated the independence of the landscape. I was
tired and everything was thinning, I was no longer assailed by too
many things at the same time, it seemed there were really few and
with those I could restore my fluent intimacy, dawn was dawn and
nothing else.

I live in a house where I usually arrive from various parts of the
world, tired of accusing, and I fall on a double bed like an ox and
snore. When I wake, before opening my eyes, I touch the grain of
the silence to guess the hour. It becomes precise against my palate
as the date of wine does to the taster: a little hole in the blind
gleamed with the diamond rays of eleven o'clock, and an hour later
we set off, leaving behind us my friends, most of them on bicycles,
unaware that they had been killed in the night.

Around noon we were on the Borgoforte bridge, and we met
Battaglia's son, whom the Germans had been about to shoot. He
saved himself by escaping suddenly (to be him when, as the pursuers' shots died away, he found himself alone in our countryside!),
and now he was driving his motorcycle with a normal expression.

The sign pointing to Volta Mantovana carried me back to 1923:
"The Fascists from Volta Mantovana are coming." The houses were
the same as now, one has been painted a different color; I could
see it from the half-open window. Tognetti the woodman drinks a

274

glass of castor oil and around him four or five menacing black-shirts. Tognetti rubbed his hand over his lips to remove the stink, one Fascist's new belt looked so good on him he couldn't be wrong, and I could read the hearts of the women who watched from the shadow of the arcades, they would go to bed with those self-confident strangers and no longer with Tognetti (in a confused way I too felt a widower and deficient as far as being suited to real life was concerned); with a slap they knock his hat to the ground. There were cobbles then, and when those stones, the *giaron,* were removed they left a shiny, important hive in the dirt. I was almost twenty, I was in love too, and I could have been a hero. I recall that event, availing myself of figurative experiences that ripened later: a close up of the nape of my neck occupies a third of the frame and, in a long shot, Tognetti, with a grayness that sums up everything that has happened in life before my eyes but without me and against me, righteous but inactive, though that time was furnished with a space that, like today's, allowed every choice.

It was a burning one P.M. of a Sunday when we reached Mantua, in the swamp below the city walls the children were resting on the enormous lotus flowers after their swim. There are little flat boats; a man standing on one seems to be walking on the water.

We climbed into a lighter that would take us to Castelmassa sul Po, its speed was kept under four miles per hour so as not to cause harmful vibrations against the embankments, the mildness of the voyage is functional. An engineer with a love of geometry explained to us that they are working to identify more accurately the always indecisive bed of the Po, and the first aspect of navigability is that the current must always have the critical velocity, in other words, it mustn't be too slow and deposit sand, or too fast and erode the dikes. This year on the mountains there are reserves of snow that allow continuous navigation, floods are produced by the passage of a too-high wave of the full flood that cannot be contained by the embankments, it is simply a maximum that doesn't pass, it could be avoided by draining the hydroelectric basins when the danger is announced, but the owners would lose millions of kilowatt-hours, private property has invaded the high-water beds along the river, they should be kept clear: the struggle is between navigation and agriculture. They fight over the use of the water; a sandy coffin, the bed in dry weather, the Po branches out, the embankments crumble, the embankments become fragile: only love and knowledge can inspire such a vocabulary.

275

Beneath our feet, for the length of the upper deck, painted red, there were tanks of liquids. The captain put on a mask to show us when, after the draining of the crude oil, they go down into the bowels of the ship, still saturated with gas, to clean the tanks. You couldn't hear the noise of the engine, not even an echo, as if the *Concordia* were made of wax. Its thousand tons don't make a rustle, a ripple, and since the bitt I'm seated on is at the farthest point of the prow, I dolly in the air, already a bit damp, even the people I see on the shore are harmonized with the silence, we cleave flowers of foam made of sand refined by the cascades, lighter than water. When the craft slowed down as the moment approached of the meeting with the *Entella*, another tanker, somebody explained they needed broad lands where the impulses of the current would lose their strength, the methane gas deposits offer a natural support to the embankment, by removing the gas they have made them fragile. We knew we would meet the *Entella* before Governolo. Every now and then our helmsman rang the regulatory two bells. At a curve all overflown by swallows, with willows half-sunk in the water, the *Entella* appeared, huddled against the bank to leave us more room. "She's empty," a sailor said. "How do you know?" He answered that if she had a cargo, she would sit lower. Fifteen minutes later we were entering the Governolo basin, immediately behind us dropped the partition they call the Vincian Gate, Leonardo invented the basins that allow navigation even with differences in water level: you remain shut for a few minutes in a brief canal as in a room while the water drops and the boat also sinks, leaving a wet mark on the wall and some little fish struggling in the muck, then the partition opposite opens like a curtain rising and there is the Po, the sun makes it glisten and transforms its extinction into festivity. Still slow and noiseless we pass under the bridge, and the Governolo spire, prominent a few seconds before, now vanishes as if through a trap door, and with a slight headache I am in the midst of an intersection of planes, the sky for example, and the iron beams of the bridge which pretend to shift from right to left, and an arch, indifferent a yard earlier, bears down, then becomes indifferent again a yard afterward. The engine resumes at half-speed because this is a zone of fragile banks, in less than a mile I saw three or four slices of earth crumble into the water, not hearing the sound because of the distance, the sound is never loud but has a soft sadness of its own, these disappearances make us regret a patch of ground where we will no longer be able to leave our print.

276

In about fifteen miles we met perhaps two boats; this was a feared and uninhabited stretch. When the churchbells signaled furiously, in my village they hastily threw out household goods to raise the embankments, but when the water comes raging down into the plain it doesn't so much rise as it penetrates, the man with eyes tired from his vigil has barely unloaded the last sandbags on the embankment when he can see a frightful jet come out beneath his feet, a leak.

We ate supper, and when we came back on deck we were gliding past an island. It was night, I went off in a corner with the tape recorder, the modest wine of the ship had made me euphoric and I spoke for a few minutes almost at random, I said I had a great desire to buy a ceramic flower vase, with lots of gilt, you see similar ones on the tables in poor houses, and in grim moments the family attributes a fantastic value to them, and there is nothing more beautiful than to see a woman become pink in the face as soon as you enter her and instead of continuing you would stop to contemplate the color that the blood you have stirred produces, and I asked, are deeds made of crystal? And can you write a poem against poetry, which has reduced us to being the image in the mirror? Zanca, without warning, had the beam of the spotlight turned on me so he could photograph me, I would have started singing if the beam hadn't moved away, orphaning me; where are you, Angilen? I went to visit him three years ago, in a darkened room, because he refused to be seen the way the disease had left him, we embraced and he said: "All my life I've been afraid of this, let it come where it wants, but not in that place, and it's come, and in that place"; his eyes roamed around as if he had been caught in some flagrant act; he had to remain standing all the time for a few days before his death.

We spent the night in Ferrara, the tanker went on imperturbably for Venice without us. In the morning we hired a car which in a little over an hour would take us to the delta, and our eagerness made the country we drove through insipid. The car was badly sprung and its jouncing made me hard, this happens above all when you're tired: the member acquires a persistent and independent hardness of its own: We nearly ran over a little boy playing with a football, he kicked it into a primitive goal; I too instinctively moved toward it, every thing of every kind has a quality of copulation in the happy conclusive instant. In Storchi's garden I saw a rabbit mounting, his piston speed would make you laugh if after

277

his ejaculation he didn't fall back with the same mindless abandon as a man.

We had a soft drink, a boy was watching a girl hanging out laundry, he was of the age when you believe you'll be the preferred one if you reveal to your beloved that your rival can't spell. Signor Rossi's voice asked: "Porto Tolle?" And I glanced at the papers, breaking the silence as I unfolded them and the paper rustled: we would like to dive into the midst of the teeming news perhaps even with a crime; the right-wing papers inform us of a solidly-laid-out world to which we return like prodigal sons trying not to be seen by the neighbors; how long will it take me to recover the convictions that the turning of a page upsets?

We encounter some gypsies whom I despise for the freedom they know how to enjoy. There was a sudden clouding over and I was running up imaginary stairs to shut with fear and joy the windows slammed by the first gust of wind. In one of the canals that were beginning to intersect our way, a fish appeared and disappeared with a silver somersault.

A little later I was in the midst of the river on a barge, in the midst of the disastrous midsts of the Po, pregnant with understated waves. The crossing lasts four minutes and the white gulls, through a trick of the light, are black.

We ate lunch at Codigoro; the vanilla ice cream was mediocre. "Poets walk on the water," Signor G. said to me, "and I stumble everywhere like a pedant."

We crossed roads below sea level ventilated only by thoughts, we were in the area where the land begins to turn white; it is the salt of the nearby sea which mixes with the river. There are houses abandoned since '50; I stuck my head into one and though it was all in ruins, a chicken pecking at some weeds in a crack guaranteed the presence of my fellow-man. An old man pointed to a wood where three hundred head of cattle were saved: Pigs, dogs, oxen are able to swim at birth, but not humans. "I won't move away," the old man says, "How can you change your soul?" He had survived on one of those rooftops you see on the television news with motionless people who daren't even shout for help for fear of sinking and they seem to pass very swiftly before our eyes, whereas they're still. On the line of the horizon appeared sparse, cubic, primordial houses, and also the tombs of a cemetery were cubical, but of a childish smallness. Women seated outside doorways looked up as we went by: the exchanged glances with the driver are a

278

coitus the roar of the motor sanctions. What a need we feel to be beautiful, the more the landscape becomes sad, as if to say: "Become also hostile and lugubrious, landscape, but the only woman who inhabits you won't reject me. I was beautiful; as a child I fell into a brazier. I became ugly; beloved, if I were handsome you would love me, you would kiss me for the rest of your life also in the dark, so trust what I say: I am beautiful."

We came to a village of fishermen who, for three thousand lire, would have taken us in a little boat to the sea, about a mile away. In the cane brakes there wasn't a vibration, and if you threw a stone, a cloud of birds would fly up. In this area every year the Po rises and the earth sinks; it's been going on since the time of the Venetian Republic, the Council of Ten said: we need a *sboratore* (a squeezer): in Luzzarese dialect, *sbora* is sperm, and the word in fact means a sudden, impetuous bursting—as must have come from that apparatus which thrust the water toward the sea and freed lands where in three years, rather than the usual nine, the good mire made thousands of poplars spring up. How I would like to see the Po of those times, live there a day. I would believe in the soul if I could move about in time, insert myself into certain days of 1943 and 1944: it was clear what had to be done—even a cart, so to speak, a traffic light, helped you understand—but now everything becomes dilatory. The boat left behind it a broader and broader path of light, the boatman said the ship that inspected the lighthouse would come the next day from La Spezia. Or from Piraeus? On one side we could see the Pila lighthouse which seems a minaret or a silo; on the other, the swamp with a burned house— a fire in the midst of all this water. In this setting the Po is about to die, toward six P.M. "The Po on either side and the sea facing us," a line from a sonnet by Tasso, elder or younger, I remember nothing else. Instead of looking at that infinity which I wasn't ignorant of, feeling somehow as if I were photographed from above, I consulted the notes of my little journey: *At Ostiglia, I realize that individual means not divisible—In the bar at Spina, bang, a bullet hits me in the forehead at the moment I become aware of my error in hurling myself against the enemy trench—The ferry costs two hundred lire, it's a concealed tax—The desolate branch of Gnocca—We can bear any discomfort provided we remain capable of making love, it doesn't even matter if we do it, provided we remain capable of it—Why don't they give us an overcoat that comes down to the knees to cover ourselves better!* This last is a sentence

279

of afterward, when on the lighthouse, fifteen hundred feet high, the custodian was complaining about his treatment. There are hours that agree with you and hours that contradict you; in climbing the circular stairs of the lighthouse which moves in the wind—all of it, including the brass fittings of the lantern—I was walking bent over to keep below the railing in the fear that a sudden gust of wind would blow me over. Everything confirmed my belief there is nothing better than closing my life in a lighthouse, I fulfill my duties and read the books that have been accumulated for my old age which begins—when? But what will I do with what I learn? *Water and land, land and water,* where does the world end? They point in one direction and I set off, walking on and on, in that direction for days, months, on and on, for years, and all of a sudden I hear laughter: *it's a joke, you should have gone in the opposite direction.* "F—— you," I'm about to shout, then I shrug and turn back after all, considering the unimportance of what I have to do.

I say to my companions, to react to the apologue: "We have done what we set out to do." From below comes a cry: "The boat!" Our boat is drifting off indifferently toward the Adriatic, these expert people tied it up carelessly, if they don't overtake it with the motorboat we'll have to spend an uncomfortable night here, they won't have enough blankets, first I'm irritated, then I rejoice.

IV

letter
from cuba
to an
unfaithful
woman

—Maria,

I'm happy, I'll write you every day, you must know what I know, we'll coincide like the black and white of an eclipse. Here the weather is mild, on certain days you can see the Jamaica mountains, there's an abundance of rivers, waterfalls and lakes where you only have to dip in your hand to catch trout, and those minerals called strategic which the foreigners carried off left only a hole in the ground but after the revolution they have to pay twenty-five percent. In the big estates which are breaking up, many herds graze, near each animal a white bird with kindly pecks frees him from flies, they have a lot of fruit—the mamey, the anona, the piña, the papaya, repeat papaya with me and I am inside your mouth. With the rum I drink also the handsome italic label Bacardi. This refers to a dynasty that has fled to the USA and supplies funds to the little planes that come from Florida to burn the cañaverales, tonight I have drunk a lot and I will drink more, why? From the window I see the Marianao beacon, you are in it with your name, Mariatta, Marionta, the more I distort it the more substantial you are; the variations drip down my chin like watermelon juice as the face disappears into the slice. In the army there are boys of twelve, you know that? And one day Castro, who is like me, said they had to change from the root, do you think it was a day that was special in its light or in its gestures? It seemed eternal, in fact. I went to see a cockfight, "Hurry," I said to the

281

taxi-driver and, the moon began to trill as it grazed the tops of the trees. On the Malecon promenade I saw the waves of the Atlantic wash over the parapet and hit a car where couples were embracing and laughing amid that foaming din. What meaning would all this have if you didn't exist? The conservative press publishes photographs of the Batista men shot against the paredon, a scalp flies off with the effervescence of a cork but horror never begins with the horrible. What are you doing at this moment? Women will leave their buckets at the wells to listen to the story of our love, my dear. I also owe you this wonderful sunny afternoon, from Rome you prolonged it, mariapotens, what can keep me in this island, this history, if you are waiting for me among our impatient objects and I can arrive on top of you in twenty hours? I'll stop in the hall: are you in? I hear the creak of the bed, you're there, you're there, what a yell. Ah yes, the cockfight, along the way I betrayed you with a black woman who wore a yellow blouse, but at the curve you were again queen, black women have thick ankles, not for stockings, but they compensate in the rest. Will a day come when we will separate? How easy it is to say a day will come when we will separate. At the airport you secretly pressed my palm with one finger, would your finger draw such insistent lines if it didn't love me? It was a constant marrying. When I met you the first time in Via Nemorense I was struck by the hollow your skirt made in front, the cloth looked like flesh. I would have been content forever just to kiss you outside and let mold grow on your tingling body hair, mad with gratitude that you exist; as I followed you to Piazza Crati my shadow shortened and lengthened on the sidewalk enfolding you and you saw me behind you with your gazelle eye.

What are you thinking about? The clock says eleven, less where you are, the sea makes funereal thuds against the shore, in another half minute the night is long, can the thuds that will come be forgotten? If I can't sleep I'll make love with you transformed into a pillow, it's incredible that you don't constantly boast of that well, that warmth, those hips you have.

Well, I got there and they were all cursing, bent over the arena, and I wanted to see too, running along a wall of backs with an eagerness that the noise exacerbated, I suddenly became aware of my limitations. I was going too far, becoming what I wanted to see; somebody left an involuntary peephole and a feather floated down, but I was pushed away by a knee whose meaning was: we

282

don't care whether or not you love Maria. Two cocks were facing each other, the eye hooded by the already-extinguished membrane, with a short leap the red one pecked the neck of the other, which pulled in its feathers like the sea-anemone and began to die. Am I boring you? The barbutos marched towards the North with their feet covered with sores; their feet wouldn't fit into their shoes any more. What is better than talking of others when you're in love? and in giving details when with every detail you confirm that the world exists and she loves me, you give more details: they drank horses' blood they were so thirsty, and if she doesn't love me? You don't love me, and for three pages I've been pretending you love me, you whore. I was spinning along in the vacuum, then a voice warns me of the absurdity and I fall; who's a whore? You whoooore, I saw the two of you in the mirror at Ciampino, and while the hostess was saying "Fasten your seat belts," you were already on the Via Appia with your tongue in his mouth forever; you castrated me, you whore, the insult is deserved and it doesn't do any good. I've smashed the glass against the wall; now calm is restored and your name is as indifferent as a dictionary. I no longer invent it constantly, the vowels and consonants rubbing together with the accents of your mother, my own, and a call from the stairs, making a sound greater than the cause. What were you looking at tenderly in me as I walked against the wind of the propellers with my hand defending my poor hat despite everything? I was going because I always believe I'll find, a step farther on, something that makes impossible what has happened, and I said "slut" over the serene houses of the Prenestino seen as the wing tilted. I'll come back, I'm coming back, and on the point of reaching a climax of pleasure, even if I'm worthless, in an instant you will feel pleasure; I'll draw back with a leap and dress again in silence against the background of your fright at the interrupted coitus. Once it was sublime when, as I dressed, my foot rustled against the satin garters, and then the metallic tone of the belt, and then the sudden tramping of my shoes on the parquet which marked the passage to community life; I had pressed you on the sheet, and you would remain there waiting while I went to the war, then you would open like a magnolia under the returning veteran. We fitted into each other; find us tomorrow worn out on the rug: whose thumb is this, whose ear? The boy who from the other bank of the Aniene had seen my back rise in the grass, and a stone was also thrown; we took shelter in a cave, the blanket was mud-

283

stained, we wanted to go still further in—perhaps that darting was a rat—and grow old there, despised, with the stars and the crickets. The intellect becomes glans and the glans becomes intellect, you could even grow decrepit and my mouth would always find among your wrinkles a tender spot; you woke up suddenly alarmed by your snoring and asked forgiveness, swearing to me that an infidelity of yours would never take place without a great clang being heard first; I kept my eyes shut, I bumbled on your navel when I thought you were far away; I couldn't find the end of your back any more, and concave becomes convex. If I opened an eye I wouldn't recognize the bureau; it had changed its place. In the Pensione Sereni I forgot to lock the door; unaware and good, you were ubiquating yourself amid proparoxytones which became amphibrachs and I went on without passing the beforehand; there were those sudden pauses where a lost word seeks its root, suddenly solid and hostile the daylight burst in, "Oops, sorry" and your "Nooo" shrilled to horror, who had been caught, us or the intruder? I should never have believed you after that, your voice was so prompt in shifting from fear to a normal register, lascivious again in two or three seconds. Your son's death kept us apart for days, it was raining; the horses on the Palace of Justice gleamed, which of us would be the first to say "Shall we meet this afternoon?" We met there, and you opened your coat with almost ill fingers, and in a moment biting we unmasked, I disappeared under your clothes and emerged only for breath, I wanted to leave nothing to anyone else and instead I increased you for all. How sweet you are, how silly, generic, specific; if you were this very moment before me I would succeed in making what happened untrue, don't be born, Maria, I'm not suited to this suffering, and even if I were another I'd love you. I watched you cloud with your breath the grille at Sant'Agnese, and in going towards the altar you were enlarged on the pavement of rhombs framed from below, you can't imagine how gently you bowed your head over the little gold platen of the host, and I said, "Keep your god of rustlings then," I may be wrong, and the vestments and the oval flames may be right; standing in the nave I felt good in my attitude of harmony with my neighbor, you made the sign of the cross like a gasp as you stepped back to the leather curtain at the door, and I am writing because if I don't stop there is still hope. Did your weariness of me have some presentiment like the air when it's about to snow? The evening at the stadium when I introduced you to

284

your present ram (don't expect me to mention his name), you and he raised your hands to drive away an insect, and they sketched a pattern together against the light, even if then you were wearing a dress that loved me to rumple it and remember how, to have you again in my context, I said hastily, "I prefer night games," because with the gaiety reinforced by the field's false green without facing the usual twilight, you rush to the parking lot to avoid the crowd, and afterwards there's the Via Olimpica and bed? He insinuated himself into the conversation, and it was as if he were feeling you. Then I cheered Sivori Sivori to deflect him, but I wasn't sure I had made you lose his trail until the bedroom where your moans seemed so irreversible that I put them away as a secret hoard to comfort me when doubt cropped up. Will I have peace of mind again? There is no moment when you are thinkable alone, even during dinner between courses you can slip away for five furtive minutes to have yourself stuffed behind a door, and reappear calmly to insist your husband should eat some more chicken. I'm not in a precise place on the earth but in a narrow mire with my heavier weight of years, and the footsteps of your fancyman in Largo Goldoni inform me his life is beginning and mine is finished, I listen to the tape on a recording machine running backwards, of those evidenced voices a screeching remains, whore, non-whore; in the course of a single hour the moods of the sky beautify or uglify a roof, "whore" has resonances that are neither good nor evil, and if god who doesn't exist sees, can you imagine a grimace of his, covering his eyes when (to derive greater pleasure) I murmur to you to shift more to the right? He is irrational and irrationable, he has no stomach or teeth, gods pass things without digesting them, and here I am bumping against corners, the unloved person lacks even what he has; I feel like dirtying everything, raping a hero's wife; by now you see me with marble adjectives and even if Cristina (she hates you) resuscitates me, I will always taste of death. Passing your husband you touched his shoulder just enough not to displease me, how many times have we said clear away, the government should clear away? Questions and answers corresponded politely, we judged, some of the guests stood out in their calculated relationships between shoes and suit, and as you asked "Who wants some whiskey?" in the midst of opinions on the Common Market, with a flash of our eyes we recalled position number four, such was the difference between outside and inside that our skin should have sagged and filled with

bumps frightening a child as when he discovers his father in front
of his mother with his pants off and running. On foot I went to
Piazza Crati, where my wife when she wants to make love invents
an excuse to laugh, and if I laugh too she prepares herself in the
bathroom with the ritual water, and the bottle always tinkles
against the shelf, she lies waiting reading a book and doesn't know
it's the thought of you that arouses me, but she takes advantage
of it, and then we turn our backs to each other. My house is just
far enough from yours so that as soon as your door opens I am
already recharged with desire, I would run back, but the outline
of my windows draws me into a certain mechanism; once I wanted
to find her dead, you would have come also to the funeral, I
would have worn sunglasses and made efforts to cry, I cried at
not being able to cry with my handkerchief clutched in my hands
between a sister-in-law and a daughter-in-law, I could distinguish
your footstep without turning around, at a sob from somebody we
broke off our relationship to reestablish it a few yards farther on.
What is it in me that you don't like? I warn you I can't be taken
to pieces, you went with only a part of me because you're anti-
historical (said by a cuckold, this is funny), can you leave me,
knowing the crimes I might commit? He who doesn't love sees, so
my wife's fat is fat, yours isn't, woe to you if you lose weight, all
of you is necessary as in a painting, and your urinating at Sutri
didn't arouse crude thoughts and you said "Let's sleep" in an accent different from mine which excited me at the existent differences that flowed together harmoniously on my chest with your
hair. A cybernetic promptness drained our meetings of any other-
ness, whole cities vanished as the housewife blew on the ladle,
and we hibernated families which only after our final "ah" began
living again. Perhaps I didn't love you, even if because of you I
will fill these hours with actions serious in their consequences, how
much trouble I took to see if you loved me, and never if I loved
you! You appeal to him because you are loved by me, I don't
love you, so what does he possess? He sums us together, thinking
"What a hegemony," but I don't want to be slammed between
your pelvis and his, and I can only say it or get drunk; does getting
drunk mean that from one thing something else can come that has
no relationship to the first? I am ambiguous and triguous, it was,
however, my invariant that saw you walking along the arcades,
the columns intervaled your vision, you vanished for a moment
and I was afraid of losing you, but you appeared with something

286

extra, and when you stepped into the square you became fullness itself. To whom am I talking? I would have loved you better if I had known how to describe you, at the first meeting I summarized you in an impression, and I went ahead with that. Will there be a man who doesn't notice you and saves me? I would know how to find you in the midst of thousands if I love you, if I don't love, it's a soft boredom. Vulgar as I am, I suffer like a saint, farewell to the time when I jumped on a bus and gripping the pole thought: *Dead people, fend for yourselves.* What beautiful days of cold like the surge of the water which seems wealth as we wash, and from our face that dries as we go from room to room, something of ours evaporates and enters reality; I was happy not because of what was happening but because of its promise of repetition, in Venice in the fog, you said, "Let's try being chaste until tomorrow," and in the room with all the lights burning my breath warmed this future, not your feet. I should interrupt all these moans considering the phenomenon of your presence-absence (you are unaware of me and you cause me), I have drained the bottle whose shape is so cleverly worked out that it seems made *ad personam* and meanwhile the pen on the table was waiting, ready for anything, the page is stained, and you go on reading without a break, you haven't even realized that after *this future not your feet,* I went to shut the window, and I could have jumped out, what sutures we are capable of! I would never have used the words *ad personam* if you hadn't left me, I found them ready-made, and I follow words which I think I am preceding, sometimes I watch their autonomous games like the birds in Villa Borghese and even silence is a word; ignoble, you inspire noble laments, in my slippers I look on to the balcony, and the wake of your ship which has just sailed almost makes me faint and the handmaidens carry me back to my vain bed. I haven't even the strength to do harm, you have defused me, this morning I saw people moving with a sound of already-sucked mussels and the olive drab uniform of a soldier leaning against a wall in Calle Martí, which could also be Fano, seemed no longer intrinsic to events but submitted by a costume-designer, and the passersby interested me only so I could imagine who was more unhappy than I, I can't restore the time when cablegrams from Cuba inflated me with clarity, in undressing I talked to you about it, and I exalted the *rexestensa* you are, to burn you like tissue paper! and the last fragment disappears with the speed of the soul, at the movieola I linger on the frame of the trees that precedes your kiss, I would like to turn you to stone, but a tiny movement of the crank reveals your blissful eye, I move back with fright; I try again more slowly, before-after, before-af. . . . time comes forward with your skin that flutters toward the end of the film. I'll go to Santo Domingo with a new passport, it takes half an hour, what a liberation! the knees of a Santo Domingo woman are pressing against my hips, I gallop until she says, "Let me get off a moment, Antonio," she sinks back on the grass, and I hide my gasping behind a palmtree. If you were that woman!

Is there really no grandeur about my being there on the cliff over the Ionian sea? I won't have hair streaming in the wind, old baldy that I am. What a bellywhopper into the metal water. I would like to know if I'll shout the moment the void opens below me. Falling, who can see the blue? And yet the eyes are the same. Perhaps a fish makes itself noticed before the impact. Along the trajectory which served for the law of weighted objects, will I think? From the distance I might look like a diver. Let's try gas: the same jet for two fried eggs. Are the windows all shut tight? Every now and then in the newspapers they say an innocent by-stander is killed. To be *commiserered* (sic) by some pain-in-the-ass whose new shoes squeak at my funeral. Trotting like Aniene Secondo, I came forward majestical like everything in our rela-tionship and suddenly I broke out; the others are already, con-stantly far away, while I, with a diminishing pounding of hoofs at the curve of the track, orphaned of onlookers, start through the exit. I can only allow myself to be deceived by the leaders through a clump of microphones. No, listen to how I regain importance en-tering a dark room with my heart beating, provided a woman is there, I know no more about her, the agreement is that we will touch, and I search her, trailing her breath which is coming shorter and shorter, "Give it to me," the nameless woman says, you and the world plot together in vain to devaluate me; she exalts me with a primaeval voice. To hell with it, it's not true, a mortal god has ruined this way, Italy, I don't love you, within your borders there is Maria and public opinion. Where are you? As if changing apart-ments, I keep entering the empty rooms to see what's left while the hearse hasn't yet moved off with its decisive sound. There are many things I mustn't love any more because L. loves them, we want to occupy the same space, and we can't because we are equal; imperturbably you will hold your lips out to the lipstick and they will stretch, deceasing you, and I discover your teeth are bones.

288

I will arrive on the twentieth, I'll go home the twenty-first, we'll spend a whole day in bed, you see my flabbiness, you see I can't give up, yet, the plan to spit in your face at the end will allow me to profit by your knowing jerks, to save myself I'll have to run away buttoning my pants on the steps. In Via Basento I took you standing in the doorway, and that doorway to be crossed, a step, is the patience I will never be and which you make me atone for, I can't wait for faces to become faces, and a girl swimming appealed to me because of her spreading under the water without identity, she said straightforwardly, "My name is (Ester?)"; how can a man on certain wordless afternoons reject a woman, irritating at other moments, who with a single glance of understanding becomes an archetype? Both gazes are reflected in a shopwindow between a blender and a hair-dryer where the space of the street is condensed into a cabin. I never got to the bottom of it. I pay attention to the rules, even if in a little while I'm going to die. "Who would ever have thought it?" my friends will say. I'll kill myself outraged by the obtuseness of this "Who would ever have thought it," one man raises my head with two fingers and I let it fall back heavily, he says "He looks like a foreigner, *estranjero,*" with the *j* that catches sexually in the throat. Does your right breast still hurt you a little? It hurts, you said, if I kissed it, don't say that to him, do something with him I can't think of; help me suffer less, once you helped me only by existing and now you unhelp me, I am no more than the sound of an event that has occurred, and you exploit it to have yourself mounted and saying this in our local slang makes me feel the insult more deeply. Do I love you or do I olve you? You see, I could break the spell (I'm lying and draw in only empty nets). At eight I'll visit the *bohíos,* the huts of the *guajiros* which means peasants, only more affectionately. I'll utter sentences from which something good might even follow and nobody will suspect this letter, and that having arrived *lunes* at eight P.M., at noon on *martes* a black woman, *prieta prieta prieta* (black black black), threw my handkerchief in the air, moving with her snub nose towards its perfume of lavender, in comparison, your flesh was boiled, then I'll tend towards the mulatto women's paler color, I'll blanch it with lilies by the handful to rejoin the race, mulatto women can be had in various combinations, even Sino-African. You get the male that suits you in thickness and flavor; by the nose you can tell, and though gracefully you have squared the account, meeting me the first time, and for years the sum worked out, meanwhile who knows where they were manufacturing the suffering that suits me, or is suffering a byproduct of what we are? My dear, I'd give my life if you had toiled for me on the stones of a stream, with your hips that become thin as you stand and broaden as you bend over, love is a woman who washes her husband's clothes, monogamous she immerges the jacket in the water which gurgles below her; I see you, Maria, in vain you pull down the noisy blinds, if I have to go mad I won't let a second pass without seeing you and I'm spoiling you, I'll prevent the acme which would remain still in the air even if in a year you and he break up, or if I can't hold out, at the cost of the hand that strikes me on the neck, it's a humiliating blow in wrestling, stay there, look at Lorenzo who undoes the double knot of his tie, look at Maria who, on the point of lying down, mechanically adjusts the pillow which will soon be crushed, stay there, describe it with the exactness of a caption which alternates between being enveloped and thing enveloped, erasing gesture by gesture what I constructed—you grow before my eyes until your panting reechoes and you break and mingle like water. Will I be able to bear it if you suck his finger? (afterwards with me you laughed), I would have the strength to see even my mother in the arms of a pimp in order to understand more, I understand three and I act four and perhaps really understanding, my rage would be appeased in a cultivated light where lines are traced by your prehensile legs since your arms aren't enough to contain the excitement that flares up, I no longer find those lines obscene, and your action is no longer wallowing, it's moving—the jugglers' harmony towards the hypostasis—and each draining has the radiance of the drop on the hedgerow after rain. At this hour your arm comes from the window of the car in the thicket of Castelfusano, you are one of the many couples, don't fool yourself, in fact the little cloud of fruit-flies passes from your headlights the moment you turn them off to the headlights of those who are arriving. You have never seen me make purplish grimaces like this, I can carry liquor less well than my father, for him too, the moment came when the serum flowed into the noisy bucket from the tube stuck in his belly, and when he drank with his mouth on the glass like an infant, he believed that the appointment with the tube was very distant, and instead it was right behind him, for me too, less than a minute has gone by since the first spreading of your legs so absolute that after it there could be nothing but retaliation, you don't know what this is, and your ignorance makes you beautiful. With one hand I'm writing and with the other I shield my eye from the bothersome light bulb, a little while ago an access of bile was about to slam it into the sink, and in the room I looked with a sheep's gaze for a patch of analgesic wall. I flung myself on the armchair without pushing aside the open book in the illusion that sacrificially damaging it would hasten the cure, even the pink of the ceiling chokes me, even a phrase of the book that with the liquidness of gall surfaces against the palate of my recent reading. Usually my wife takes charge of my attacks; this is her regal moment, I am not embarrassed with her, let her hear my womanish moan, "It'll pass," she says, wiping the sweat from my brow, and it will, but knowing that doesn't help me, in an hour approximately it will pass, and dozing off I will observe that I don't feel pleasure at not suffering any longer, I enter immediately into a rightful condition. Seeing me you would run away, trying to tear off our memories, thinking, "I don't want to have been with this man who stinks." You were with him. If the migraine lasts long I would beg to die, and my naturalness is my not dying, what is the infinite to the mouth of an asthmatic? A retch of vomit suffocates, and who then will call the priest, who arrives, gliding along the walls? Not dying wouldn't be a mere prolongation; you, for example, wouldn't have the quality to bear it, I could list for you the hypotheses that fatally involve me in the range of accepted death: to kill you, to kill myself, to feel sorry for myself, to weep, to poetize, or with a long-distance call shout "pig" at you in the dead of night, dumbfounded you shut doors and open them, and your husband, burdened with laws, alarmed, asks in his pyjamas "Who is it, who is it?" or else arriving tomorrow with Flight 815, gather together the scattered silences of complicity and make the usual day of them and I would go first to the paper to put together a little article on underdeveloped peoples to be commented on in a group, if I had been capable of giving you up, would a different article have come from it? For what I caught of myself a moment ago in the mirror—the firmness of my intentions is dubious—it would take more Marias to make me undamaged by the priest. As a young man I was confident as a swallow that I would always have taken over from myself in the relay-race, don't argue that I would have tired, you consider not-dying with the mind of dying, to which I owe my having been walled between your thighs and repeating under swarms of shrouds familiar sufferings. Will I go to Varadero? I scrawled some cubes on an envelope and think of the palpitat-

291

ing of a larva/to get out/I, instead, long to go back in/goodbye, things! These verses should be a part of the findings of the police along with the heavy revolver, they are not of a different material compared to the rest of Antonio and everything. Should the "instead" be removed? We seek a closed form like jaws, it is skulllike; I face the page in the ideal position, testamentary and with one eye on the suitcases taken out of the closet, uncertain in a certain corner, I started a paragraph four times, I should have essayed a line that went beyond the page, is content only change of rhythm, and are epochs only different lengths of breath? *Virgo sancta virgo munda tibi nostra sit iucunda* and suddenly *vocis modulatio* that cracks and whacks. Lubricious fiddlings where you are absent, forgotten, and you gave the starting signal, I would like to be serious enough to express myself without manner. Can a poem be written against poetry? We are reduced to this labyrinth. Day comes and I don't want to see it, however, if the electric light goes off—that happens here every so often—I would have to reopen the shutters and reenter the humiliating day of Maria, I have been there already since a cry of adolescence, bathed in sweat in the role of halfback. I could swear I recognized you too, whom my companions (dribble, pass) overwhelmed along with the referee's whistle. To whom did you prefer me? You don't know how despicable a man despised by men is, and yet a woman can love him, your fancyman's lips are the very thing in him that should repel you, since they say servile words, those unkissable lips that you kiss, and you will weep also softly if he is taller and better proportioned, at seeing us go by naked, she points: "That one," and they go off hand in hand to mate, and I remain with my thoughts on the slopes of my body that was born earlier. Will I go to Varadero? Tomorrow two thousand are leaving for Varadero, but I don't even feel like lacing my shoes, I'm a metastasis, Antonio Natoion Noianto, and *a prioris* weigh on me like the earth on a miner after the cave-in and if he moves, more falls. To leave with a Garand on my shoulder one blond morning that a bullet in the forehead doesn't even bloody and they take me for any Guatamalan on that shore. How many times I tried to break with you! on election Sunday you were waiting for me, perhaps with your hand opened inside a stocking looking for the run. I slowed my steps against your assumption that infallibly I was about to arrive, a block separated us, was it a short space or a long one? I felt the prints of my soles outlined on the pavement as in criminal investigations. Having just emerged newborn and civic from the voting booth was I to slobber without respect my saliva on your thighs? It seemed to me that a warmth, an inspiration suddenly placed me on a throne. I could see, and it isn't that you see a particular thing. I stopped, in tenderness toward myself, and I sought the person to whom I could communicate my renunciation, one passerby proved intraneous and another too extraneous and as soon as I imagined him worthy, imagining him on the can, he became unworthy at the same time that the swirl of a bus made me consider I could never involve those fugitive passersby without throwing myself under the bus's wheels. Solitude increases gradually as we ask more than we give, and since the perfume of your talcum powder was advancing with the evening—a perfume often determinant even if anyone can buy it for a few lire—your thighs which had just become limp now began to take on flesh and I, Laocoön of the suburbs, took refuge in a movie theater to free myself of the molasses of contradictions which wells up in the traffic signs of the neighborhood. My shoulder was grazed by the projector's beam, and I occupied the same space whether I had won or not. A few minutes later you were letting the ice cream I had brought you melt on your navel, and I was making an effort to give you a value you don't have so I would have an extenuating circumstance to offer whom? I'm chipped, nibbled away, everything already thought, with the magician's wand I move around my own form to show I am free of strings, but as in dreams I slip and vanish in the crowd on the Ganges.

Did you hear the sirens? Is it a factory or war? Could war alter this suffering of mine? The reason cannot answer, not even with unreasoning as it deftly does sometimes to open a passage in the unthinkable. When they drop them I'll remain silent, and with me the philologists, the mothers, by chance left outside the lethal coordinates that were on a blackboard, leaning over a balcony to call their children playing in a field, they see them turn to ash with a rapidity that lacks the space in which to articulate even a cry, and therefore they will resume shelling peas only with a shadow of doubt in their eyes and the two girls on the terrace of the Janiculum are now will-o'-the-wisps with some glints fascinating in themselves, and what of you whose innocence is revealed to me as you end up a trickle in a manhole whose cover is not affected by the gas because of the quality of the cast iron? (this experience will be of use to posterity). Sparrows fall, hit by invisible hunters;

293

who is running toward me with flaming arms? He resembles my brother-in-law; what does this mean? He gives me a look that has still something of the past in it, idiot, what do you want? Bring your gestures up to date. I won't answer you, my pitilessness is my only hope, a zealous character has captured on tape somebody's stifled moan, in '70, will this enter a *Weltanschauungungung* of the survivors? This epistle is spattered with question marks like a council of bishop's crooks, and my intelligence rises no higher than the night revealed by fireworks, so do you want to stone me? And if I feel torn by the claw of a lion escaped from a circus, and his roar makes the gaping jaw even more real, what do I have time to express if not a curse? Still a day will come when an eschatological member with Neapolitan flashes will furrow the sky *zzzz* between Rovigo and Trapani, put out the lights of the cemeteries in the second strip London-Teheran, the dawn-colored tail which it leaves passes the doors, goes up the legs of the housewives: close-up of authorities in amazement of cream cheese and processions, the wax that corrupts drips on the novice's hand, and an eye through the rays of the Most Holy Sacrament held high with the huge hands examines the citizens with Scotland Yard suspicion, *Zzzz* it's under the dress of the queen, who amid the smoke of the Bengal lights gives in yelping and the subject turns his head away to mourn the end of a beloved era, bang! and what will happen to Lorenzo and me if you, waiting with your skirt raised on the battlements among your girlfriends, prove to be the Chosen One? We will snicker, the mass media are covered with oilcloth, and Giulio, Mauro, Pietro, Calisto look up from the newspaper where for years they have searched every morning for an event radiant with grief and synthesis to drive them finally out of the house with bread crumbs on their lapel and a hunting rifle, hurrah, they won't bat an eye when the bullet-ridden adversary hurtles from the balcony, and at St. Peter's the Pope in his chair passes by blessing; he can't be distracted for a moment, and one woman is converted seeing him at the very moment he is distracted, *Zzzzt,* a sudden rattle of shots towards Castel Sant'Angelo, the choir stops, the bearers run off, the fallen Pope stands up on his little human legs, at Varadero the fish cram together in the blue stretch where the oil of a sunken ship doesn't reach, and I shell myself over the proofs of an article that I would have liked to punctuate with scrotum, with vulva and I will be taken from it only by the call to our procuress, called by her you arrive in the little corridor,

294

grab the phone and a dispersed lament is heard, on the same cable Reuters is saying that the anti-Castroites are within rifle range of the shore, I hear the din of the sea which is perhaps a newspaper being rustled by the telephone operator in Shannon, in fear that your voice which is more and more faint and intermittent may disappear, I invoke you like a pilgrim at Lourdes. If I were to land at Sapri with ninety companions? There were no more than that on the *Granma,* a motor launch of the coast guards would be enough to destroy us with their tricolor flag flapping scholastically, it'll be better overland, they've sent me ahead, towns which the pencil joins rapidly on the map take yards of concrete to reach and big cars with Corps Diplomatique licenses going to the Quirinal Palace like altars, it takes years just to convince the people of Sarsina and I won't live long and even if I did, at the appointed hour many would no longer exist, and the Lucanian grandchildren in Lucania and those Polesani ones in the Polesine ask "What is this signal?" We often act for witnesses who have vanished. To be able to shoot with the calm of a theorem! From this the idea is so exact that you could run over it hopping on one foot, but once out of the Caravelle as I go into the everyday city I am no longer so sure as I was at a distance, truth ages fast, I held it too tight in my hand like a treasure for winter, to check us from some dark doorway there always come echoes of proverbs, but with a single glance around a boy finds his reasons, leave the command to him, away with all hesitation, along with a squad I pop out in flesh and blood in Piazza del Popolo, from the end of Via del Babuino come brand-new army trucks which in the ease of their maneuvering threaten to recapture me, hurry; a flight of doves can make a subject be changed in a moment into object and vice versa, it isn't easy to hit one of the armed men who come toward us oscillating between resemblances and distortions, right there where they are in a more lasting antithesis to us, if I don't press the trigger promptly, I will be the one to change and it'll be all to do over again, a policeman runs to take shelter behind the fountain, I didn't even have time to grab my musket, I was quicker when on the meadows near Viterbo I cut short the flight of the lark, it's a bad sign that I notice the weight of the cartridges in my bag, and there is a hint of a tendency to recognize myself as abnormal and the others as normal, lifted between my feet by the Southerly breeze, a newspaper page cooperates in this, dense with obituaries and condoling relatives and friends, what strength the others can draw on

295

without moving from places, and all we have left is satellite wonder
and lining up after the biers to be believed at least freedmen, from
behind the shutters someone on seeing me in the general picture
considers me certain and ineluctable as a telephoto, but that is
Oreste with whom I dined in '60, I turn the barrel elsewhere, to
Ciriani, who translated Gongora, I would like to explain to him
before I kill him that until a little while ago everything was only
to be read or to be written, Anselmi runs past me with a Colt, I'm
happy we're both on the same side, but we didn't return each
other's gaze, I was counting on finding conviction in his, I am
waiting for a loudspeaker with enviable timbre and syntax to give
the news that the revolution is such that the hilly Esquiline has
been added to the flat Trionfale, and wrap up the Coca-cola and
the kiosks that resist the event, even the tables at Rosati's overturned by the fleeing customers are there waiting for a new start,
which their pattern suggests will not be too different from before
(and the great date will have been barely a jolt of M.G. in the
midst of a vague collapse of cocktails), near the obelisk a three-
colored mortar explodes with lines of fire that we will see in an
illustrated weekly, from the roofs they throw stones on the armed
forces, and even if I can't make out their features, those beings
who stand out like a neon sign are infallible, I also move in their
tracks shooting a bit here and there with a remote dismay, a presentiment that the TV announcers will pluralize me in a little while,
at six P.M. they already tried, from the Pincio the capital has the
immobility of an engraved battle which even the disemboweled
trumpeter decorates, I hasten to say I have nothing to do with the
fact that an aunt was waiting dinner for three victims of the shooting. They twist my finger to make me talk, the mopping up is
continuing, I was disgusting in my confidence I would never be
kicked in a Lager, and with my arcane specific weight I would
render vain the attacks on me even in this police station through
whose window comes the creaking of the tram which certifies a
continuum, O fabulous kings, and for the future my ambition is
to be a part again as a concomitant cause, such as I considered
myself before my arrest, I can't bear to be excluded, and I will start
talking again in a low voice about the situation on the steps of San
Luigi dei Francesi with At. waiting for what has already happened. In Milan order has been reestablished, Caputo says, afterwards he says it's probable that . . . I don't grasp the rest but the
more modest the subject, the more I feel homesick for it, was it

296

about beer? In the next room I glimpsed the barman's jacket which I use only to call up domestic images, then I erase him. "But what do you want to change?" Caputo asks, squeezing my testicle, Ouch. I will wait patiently for years to kill him, no, I'll kill him at once, and the room fills with Southern moans. I would betray my father if they rip out a fingernail and throw sand over it; Caputo asks the guard for a match, it isn't their wickedness that tears me apart, it's their indifference, in vain I call them murderers, before I had to, before I knew them, there is nothing really new in this scene that I am shouting, then they throw me out, and on the Corso my shoes become dusty little by little as I go home on foot, did I tell the names? My granddaughter's hand plays with my two-day beard extraneous to yes or no, it's seven, Maria, they're cleaning the swimming pool that the sea invaded yesterday, it left sand there and other things, the chambermaid interrupted the sentence with my coffee, I didn't tell the names, I would like to see this joy of not having told the names blossom in slow motion, would I perhaps have told the names if Caputo had squeezed harder?